D1536469

THE GIROUX READER

Cultural Politics & the Promise of Democracy
A Series from Paradigm Publishers
Edited by Henry A. Giroux

Empire and Inequality: America and the World Since 9/11
by Paul Street

The Terror of Neoliberalism
by Henry A. Giroux

Caught in the Crossfire: Kids, Politics, and America's Future
by Lawrence Grossberg

Reading and Writing for Civic Literacy: The Critical Citizen's Guide to Argumentative Rhetoric
by Donald Lazere

Schooling and the Struggle for Public Life, Updated Edition
by Henry A. Giroux

Listening Beyond the Echoes: Agency and Ethics in a Mediated World
by Nick Couldry

Michel Foucault: Materialism and Education, Updated Edition
by Mark Olssen

The Giroux Reader
by Henry A. Giroux; edited and introduced by Christopher G. Robbins

Forthcoming
Reading French Feminism
by Michael Payne

THE GIROUX READER

by

HENRY A. GIROUX

edited and introduced by

CHRISTOPHER G. ROBBINS

Paradigm Publishers
Boulder • London

All rights reserved. No part of this publication may be transmitted or reproduced in any media or form, including electronic, mechanical, photocopy, recording, or informational storage and retrieval systems, without the express written consent of the publisher.

Copyright © 2006 by Paradigm Publishers

Published in the United States by Paradigm Publishers, 3360 Mitchell Lane Suite E, Boulder, Colorado 80301 USA.

Paradigm Publishers is the trade name of Birkenkamp & Company, LLC, Dean Birkenkamp, President and Publisher.

Library of Congress Cataloging-in-Publication Data

Giroux, Henry A.
    The Giroux reader / Henry A. Giroux; edited and introduced by Christopher G. Robbins.
        p. cm. — (Cultural politics & the promise of democracy)
    Includes bibliographical references and index.
    ISBN-13: 978-1-59451-229-2 (hc)
    ISBN-10: 1-59451-229-9 (hc)
    ISBN-13: 978-1-59451-230-8 (pbk)
    ISBN-10: 1-59451-230-2 (pbk)
    1. Education—United States. 2. Critical pedagogy—United States.
3. Youth—United States—Social conditions. 4. Education—Political aspects—United States. 5. Postmodernism—United States.
6. Social justice—United States. I. Robbins, Christopher G.
II. Title. III. Series.

LC191.4.G57 2006
370.11'5—dc22

2006002702

Printed and bound in the United States of America on acid-free paper that meets the standards of the American National Standard for Permanence of Paper for Printed Library Materials.

Designed and Typeset by Straight Creek Bookmakers.

09   08   07   06
1   2   3   4   5

Contents

⟜⟐

Introduction: Reading Henry Giroux   *vii*

PART I: Sociology of Education   **1**

1 Theories of Reproduction and Resistance in the   3
   New Sociology of Education: Toward a Critical Theory of
   Schooling and Pedagogy for the Opposition
2 Border Pedagogy in the Age of Postmodernism   47

PART II: Cultural Studies and Cultural Politics   **67**

3 Consuming Social Change: The "United Colors of Benetton"   69
4 Doing Cultural Studies: Youth and the Challenge of Pedagogy   89

PART III: The War against Youth   **123**

5 Nymphet Fantasies: Child Beauty Pageants and the Politics of   125
   Innocence
6 Disposable Youth and the Politics of Domestic Militarization: 147
   Mis/Education in the Age of Zero Tolerance

PART IV: From Critical Pedagogy to Public Pedagogy   **179**

7 Is There a Role for Critical Pedagogy in Language/Cultural   181
   Studies? An Interview with Henry A. Giroux, *Manuela Guilherme*
8 Cultural Studies, Critical Pedagogy, and the Responsibility of   195
   Intellectuals
9 Mouse Power: Public Pedagogy, Cultural Studies, and the   219
   Challenge of Disney

PART V: The Politics of Higher Education   **231**

10 Racial Politics, Pedagogy, and the Crisis of Representation in   233
   Academic Multiculturalism

Contents

11 Youth, Higher Education, and the Crisis of Public Time: 253
    Educated Hope and the Possibility of a Democratic Future

PART VI: Public Intellectuals and Their Work   **283**

12 Paulo Freire and the Politics of Postcolonialism   285
13 The Promise of Democracy and Edward Said's Politics of   297
    Worldliness: Implications for Academics as Public Intellectuals

Index   *313*

Credits   *333*

About the Author and Editor   *335*

INTRODUCTION
Reading Henry Giroux
Critique, Possibility, and the Promise of Democracy

CHRISTOPHER G. ROBBINS

⊸

In an age where irrelevance is fashionable and low expectations dominate public discourse, Henry A. Giroux's work is an anomaly. It refuses to be inconsequential or strive for mediocrity. Giroux's wide-ranging studies of education, politics, culture and society are not only engaging and challenging—sometimes even disturbing—they are, more fundamentally, crucial resources for educators, parents, young people, and other citizens concerned with reclaiming and revitalizing democratic public life and its supporting institutions, practices and languages. At a time of momentous political retreat, this means that Giroux's body of work is *necessary*. It demands to be read carefully, reread closely, interrogated critically, appropriated wisely, and inserted widely into public conversations in order to gain a sense of the despairing civic atrophy currently undermining democratic public life in the U.S. Giroux's work is instructive for citizens concerned with the question of how and where to begin building a political culture, and educating its agents, in ways that can offset a fundamentally reordered, mass-mediated, market-driven, and globalized world in the interests of a social order that is more humane, less exclusionary—more democratic in form, content, function, and effects. Hopefully, this carefully selected sampling of Giroux's many writings will help, in some modest way, in such a process.

Evolving over the course of nearly 40 years, 40 authored, coauthored, edited, and coedited volumes, 280 scholarly popular press articles, and 154 contributions to edited collections, in addition to a highly regarded teaching career and frequent public speaking engagements, Giroux's lifework is not merely impressive. It stands as a testament to this engaged oppositional public intellectual's commitment to the project of a radical, inclusive democratic social order. To society's benefit, Giroux's intellectual and civic contributions have always been immunized to the plague of rapid-fire thought and politics of premature conclusions that pervade the political discourses of the public relations talking heads in the corporatized media—with and of whom the U.S. has, unfortunately, become all-too-easily comfortable and accepting. Given the range, complexity, and diversity of his popular and scholarly work, Giroux's overall contribution is sometimes difficult and always difficult to define, at least definitively. I will thusly refrain from feigning such an effort. Rather, after making a somewhat unorthodox way into Giroux's work by providing a snapshot of how I have seen him fulfill his role as mentor, researcher, and teacher, I will sketch some rough outlines and highlight a few key facets of his work as I address the organization of the selections that are compiled and edited herein.

I will share these observations, of course, not to "make a case" for Giroux—this is something he has quite obviously accomplished—or to privatize the profoundly political essence of Giroux's work, but merely to provide insights to the person behind the work and how he approaches the practical and everyday aspects of doing it. This entrance to Giroux's work is important, I believe, because understanding how a scholar such as Giroux actually *does* the labor he so often researches and *theorizes* can possibly assist in understanding the studies he has published. What's more, these lessons, while basic and, perhaps, unintentionally provided by Giroux, are important for any mentor/teacher to teach his/her students: One needs to witness and participate in intellectual struggle of Giroux's sort, in order to learn that the public intellectual's and citizen's role is to be defined not by atomization, insularity, and competition, but solidarity, engagement, humility and cooperation.

Learning Giroux

The Person and Mentor

Solidarity, engagement, humility, and cooperation are some of the ways by which I have witnessed Giroux approach both his practice and theory. I met Henry A. Giroux some years ago when I visited his office unannounced. I was just a curious undergraduate student who had been exposed to—and appreciated deeply—Giroux's early studies in sociology of education and some of his early cultural studies work. His resistance theories actually inspired me to pursue studies in education. Though I completed my studies at the school at which Giroux taught but not, ironically, where I had been introduced to his work, I had been unable to take any courses with him, and I simply wanted to meet and thank the person behind the work that I was just beginning to learn and that had so profoundly impacted me.

Giroux is as, or more, intense in person as he is in writing. Giroux has a candid demeanor and disciplined thought, which are tempered by a playful sense of humor and informed as much by his experiences in the world as by his experiences in the academic institution. From a working class upbringing in Providence, Rhode Island, in which Giroux made his adolescent rounds shining shoes, "breaking in to movies," and scrapping on inner-city basketball courts, Giroux made his way to the center of a university president's political firestorm as a young professor at Boston University; has taught around the world as a visiting professor and directed departments, institutes and scholarly forums; has held distinguished or endowed chairs in different disciplines—quite a feat, indeed; and, recently, was awarded an honorary doctorate from Memorial University in Newfoundland in recognition of his contributions to society.[1]

This tempering of Giroux was clear during my introductory visit. Giroux was careful, deliberate, and critical, but by no means stuffy or guarded like many professionals, especially "scholars." In a way that could only be engaging, Giroux dissected my responses to him and, with generosity, concern and humility, helped me rethink and reformulate my nascent understanding of his and others' work—all this despite his initial telling me that he could spare only 5 minutes. Giroux, however, seldom slips like this. He has an acute awareness of time as a deprivation and not a luxury; despite his established position in academia and his entering the "middle" class, his working class youth and its etchings on his body and psyche often remind him of the temporal asymmetries that exist in a world of gross material and symbolic inequality. One thing was quite apparent and startling for me, and others have highlighted it: Giroux accordingly had little time or energy for small talk.[2] He wanted to know what I thought about the commercialization of public schools, the commodification and sexualization of children and youth, the representation of youth of color in the media, what it meant to have a project, and what I thought all of these things suggested about the state of democratic public life and the future. The fateful talk ended with Henry giving me his card and telling me he thought I should pursue doctoral studies. He followed this, in his generous way, with an offer to study with him, once his next student's assistantship was complete. I was shocked, for sure. Considering my background, merely attending college itself, let alone pursuing doctoral work, were remote dreams, but dreams all the same. To this thought, Giroux responded, "Bullshit. I come from a working class background. This is a once-in-a-lifetime offer. You either want it, or don't. Stay in touch with me if it's the former." As readers familiar with Giroux know and new readers will soon observe, rarely are things so simplistic for him, but he is, predictably, as straightforward. Giroux doesn't pull punches, and he takes great care to land them when and where they matter.

So began a continuing, challenging, and rewarding mentorship with Henry. Over the next few years, Henry sent me his new writings not only to merely share them with me but also, I assume, to learn what and how I was thinking about them. While the proposition to study with him was appealing,

I was unsure whether it was going to pan out, since I received his writings but no mention of the mentorship for quite some time. Many teachers mean well, but sometimes they have a tendency to blow smoke … because quite often they have been trained to be afraid of taking positions or being straight up for fear of transgressing professional codes of politeness or shattering a "nurturing" aura. I would soon learn, and have repeatedly witnessed since, that Giroux is unpretentious, and he rightfully harbors no such inferiority complexes about the work he does—in print or in the classroom. As I was preparing to go out one winter Saturday afternoon, a letter from Henry arrived on my Michigan doorstep, asking if I would accept the offer to study with him the following fall and to call him as soon as possible. So continued the mentorship with Henry.

These acts of generosity, while far from flippant, pervade Henry's actions. They provide the basis for the kinds of mutual give-and-take of everyday (and scholarly) solidarity and cooperation that is crucial to the work Giroux does and the radical democratic project to which such work is directed. Giroux is not only a generous mentor; he is also a supportive colleague. He openly allows professors, for example, to dip into his forty-year deep files of research, cutting some of their theoretical work, to a large degree, to the time it takes them to read his files. Henry also devotes his time and resources to study sessions with individual students and groups outside of his required course load. In the study group in which I participated, Henry reworked the traditional power dynamics of many classrooms by positioning himself as a student with us, knowledgeable about the background history and theory of the works, but new to the works themselves and thus the questions they provoked, providing a pedagogical context that was both supportive and intensive. (He bought the book for each of us and supplied the copies of the extra readings, to boot.) Behind Giroux's intensity and generosity is a profound sense of humility, which—through his demonstrating a critical self-reflexivity about his own limitations—underpins not only his understanding of solidarity but also the grounds of mutual respect that define his pedagogical encounters.

The Researcher

Giroux is a methodical researcher. He reads voraciously, widely and carefully, putting himself (and his research assistants) through a rigorous reading, rereading, questioning, cutting, pasting, summarizing, and outlining of texts until they are reduced to their most pointed forms. He also observes and listens assiduously to the everyday conversations occurring around him, the institutional practices in which he is enmeshed (and often trying to untie), and the wider social, political, cultural, and economic relationships informing those practices and conditions. To borrow from and rework the title of one of his provocative studies, rather than "channel surf," Giroux tunes into multiple channels, somehow surveying, apprehending, and analyzing a dizzying number of shifting and, sometimes, only seemingly incongruous social, political, economic, and cultural inputs at once. This process produces pragmatic and theoretical benefits for Giroux. In the former case, it allows Giroux to compile, and gain a second nature familiarity with, vast amounts of information pertinent to a set of specific questions he is pursuing. In the latter case, it permits Giroux, in the relentlessly probing style that has always shaped and marked his work, to hold these resources, their conditions of possibility, and the specific and broader contexts in which he does his work in conversation and dialectical tension, encouraging a synthesis and analysis that is at once sweeping, exacting, innovative, and often troubling. Simply, this approach underpins Giroux's uncanny ability to underscore the odious contradictions between how the social world is *represented* and how it is actually ordered and *experienced*. He keeps one eye on the symbolic, the other on the material, resulting in stinging insights on the ineluctable interrelationships between economic and symbolic power and, importantly, the *actual relationships of domination* and the *possible conditions for resistance and transformation*.

Moreover, this "method," to use a word that the technocratic heaviness of which will make Giroux bristle, backgrounds his talent for appropriating the tools of a range of disciplines and subdisciplines ranging from educational theory, sociology, political economy, philosophy and literary theory and criticism to art history, criticism, and theory, social and cultural theory, and cultural studies in ways that are conducive to investigating the most pressing issues of everyday life and the forces undermining democratic public life, which, nonetheless, refuse easy cordoning within arbitrary and preexisting academic boxes and the narrow methodological paradigms they shelter. (If it is not already clear to one that s/he does not live this moment in the economic, the next in the political, and another in the social and cultural, but that one experiences them all in different ways and at different times within a complex whole, as Raymond Williams would have put it, then Giroux is an indispensable guide for sorting this out.) Further, this "method," or process of reading the material world and the discursive systems constructed to represent it, enables him to not only bring new understandings to bear on how the power/knowledge nexus orders a range of oppressive and contradictory relationships and experiences in society and culture, but also reconstruct the academic disciplinary lines of power and hierarchy, which are themselves, in part, responsible for and related to the ordering of wider social, political, economic, and cultural hierarchies. Consequently, Giroux's various approaches to the study of social things both identify and use the mechanisms of power, while critiquing and rewriting their conditions of possibility in the interests of a more humane, radical democratic social order. As a result, Giroux's studies themselves and the processes by which he conducts them defy easy categorization, if any at all, and provide theoretical and practical resources that are far reaching. Test this conclusion, for instance, by Googling "'syllabus'+'Henry Giroux'." One will find that his work is taught in fields and subfields ranging from cultural anthropology, the sociology of advertising, government, and political theory to art education, educational leadership, social and philosophical foundations of education, sociology of education, literary theory, English, rhetoric and composition studies, cultural studies, and media studies. In my research, I have seen his work appropriated in the development of theory in fields as diverse as criminology, music education and public health, not to mention African American studies, whiteness studies, rhetoric and composition studies, critical sociology, and any number of subfields in education.[3]

Despite the broad, critical influence of Giroux's research, it is not free from sometimes rightful, other times misleading, criticism, and his work has not always been so widely disseminated, especially when he first started writing in the late 1970s. Consider the misleading side first. Giroux is a complex thinker who also publishes prolifically. Therein is part of the reason for what is often highly superficial and misleading criticism that is characteristic of what is now a destructively competitive academic market, which increasingly models its practices on the survival of the slickest politics of the wider market society. Rarely is his work taken up as a whole—to do this would, most likely, undermine the economies of efficiency that shape much of the conditions in which many academics must currently labor—and the result is that some of the criticism made of his work reveals an outdated position, because it has been superceded, or the critiques simply do not make sense, because he already addressed or preempted the criticisms in earlier work that, possibly, shares theoretical, analytical, and political continuity with the work being critiqued. For instance, it is nearly impossible to understand his work on critical pedagogy and what it might mean in the current era, unless one reads his later work on neoliberalism and public pedagogy, or vice versa; yet many reviews and some appropriations of his work begin and end with *Theory and Resistance in Education: Towards a Pedagogy for the Opposition* (1983), a book he wrote over 20 years ago! As he publishes more and in different areas, he is also an open target for scholars who are forced to publish for tenure, a glimmer of recognition, or for the purportedly "objective" rants promoting neoconservative think-tank faith, as opposed to publishing for the public good and social relevance, and he is thus subject to hit-and-run misrepresentations of his work.[4]

Now consider the (somewhat) rightful side. In more serious efforts at critiquing and extending Giroux's research, scholars who are wedded to particular theoretical paradigms have a difficult time pigeonholing his work, which cuts across multiple theoretical and disciplinary lines at once. As Eric Weiner has pointed out, modernist and postmodernist fundamentalists alike struggle to domesticate Giroux's work; for the former, his studies are too fluid and draw sometimes relatively indeterminate conclusions, and, for the latter, his conclusions are "overdetermined," not slippery enough and having few too little playful references made to "différance" or other once-critical analytical devices that the more apolitical approaches to postmodernist theory have fetishized.[5] In other instances, especially in his studies of youth, he is criticized not for advocating for youth, but for not allowing them to speak in his work.[6] This type of criticism is somewhat appropriate, but somewhat misleading. Surely, Giroux's studies of youth *might* benefit from the integration of youth voices. However, they might then be something altogether different since Giroux never makes a claim to "speak for" youth. Rather, he attempts, in part, to theorize, as a moral and ethical intervention, the total social condition in which youth can or can't speak in the first place and suggest, in turn, what this condition means for democratic public life and the future (See Chapters 5 and 6, this volume). Yet, in other instances, while being serious and fair in engaging Giroux's research, disciplinary piety can be seen to prevail over theoretical significance, and Giroux is inappropriately tagged a "postmodern" "critical theorist" who has important ideas but lacks "sociological" grounding.[7] This, I assume, is ultimately fine for Giroux, and the criticisms are somewhat correct, because the work he produces is neither this nor that "type" of work. Nor is he concerned with it being "this" or "that" kind of work as much as he is concerned with the ways in which his work uses the best tools offered by multiple intellectual traditions in order to shed light on animating issues of the day and determine, however provisionally and always partially, what that critical light might suggest about the tendencies of force at work in society and culture.[8]

Regarding the politics surrounding the dissemination of his early research, not until the late 1980s did Giroux get published by the heavy hitters controlling the education studies publishing industry. For instance, Giroux's first study, *Ideology, Culture, and the Process of Schooling* (1981), considered a significant appropriation and reworking of critical theory as it applied to schooling, was first published by Falmer Press in England and later by Temple University Press (in the United States), hardly a minor press, but hardly a central distributor of educational studies at that time. Giroux's second study, *Theory and Resistance in Education* (1983)—which immediately unsettled prevailing educational wisdom, influenced innumerous studies of schooling thereafter and is now considered to be a classic—was published graciously by Bergin & Garvey, a courageous, independent publishing house, but not one that nearly carried the distributional or disciplinary clout of industry players such as Routledge and Kegan Paul or Falmer.[9] Clearly, a politics of self-interest pervades the publishing industry on both sides of the equation: As some academics occasionally try to build publishing records vis-à-vis the acritical engagement of Giroux's and others' work, publishers, too, can be seen to act in "rational self-interest" when it comes to publishing work that is controversial, nontraditional, or which simply rejects the types of easy categorization that are conducive to targeting niche markets and puffing up profit margins. Readers, I hope, will consider these issues and others, after studying the sampling of Giroux's research compiled in this volume. But Giroux is not only a researcher; he is also, by art and vocation, a teacher.

The Teacher

Giroux is stupendous and difficult in the classroom. I would go so far as to say that the pace and rigor of his research and writing is not matched, but actually surpassed by his practice of teaching. *This* is a feat. It is, nonetheless, unsurprising when one considers that Giroux's work is, in part, a gutsy effort to rethink—and enact—what it means to "use pedagogy as a referent for analyzing how knowledge, values, desire, and social relations are constructed, taken up, and implicated in relations of power in the interaction among cultural texts, institutional forms, authorities, and audiences."[10] For Giroux, however, the critical pedagogical encounter does not halt here, but it is connected to the identification and transformation of the very conditions in which civic agency can be taken up and the demands of democratic public life addressed. This is to say that Giroux takes the practice of teaching to new levels. He plugs it in. Each of his classes, to appropriate a seasoned professor's analogy, is comparable to Bob Dylan's first electric outing at the Newport Folk Festival, where Dylan not only provoked the traditionalists and reformists alike by going electric, but also *disturbed* them.[11] He forced them to take positions by blasting them out of their common sensibilities concerning the given meanings of "music" or "folk singing/songwriting." Giroux's seminars and public talks have similar *effects* for which he, nevertheless, is more than willing to take *responsibility*. Giroux's seminars, to continue the metaphor, don't just rock; they also roll, they move. And like Dylan's first electric outing, they persistently provoke and prod, disturbing the heavy sedimentation of commonsense, habits of quick thinking and easy conclusions that often weigh on students' minds—and, occasionally, his own. Giroux's seminars, similarly, encourage students and cultural workers to rethink what it means "to teach," "to be responsible," and "to know something" and what one might do, under what conditions, and in whose interests, as a result of that knowledge. This pedagogy needles most students; one cannot avoid being engaged by Giroux, as the late Paulo Freire pointed out.

There is no question about it: Giroux's theory and practice are left-oriented, but he is not unreflectively or unreflexively left—in theory or practice. He doesn't pull punches, but he doesn't stand still. This is a reasonable strategy: The conditions in which he researches and teaches don't stand still, and neither do the questions and challenges they present. For Giroux's pedagogy to move, he must move and be moved, too. For example, I have seen him modify a position he took in one of his classic essays—because, in a graduate seminar, an undergraduate correctly called him out, not nearly the type of thing most teachers appreciate doing nor, really, the kind of thing most students would have a context and set of class relationships to feel comfortable and confident in doing. Giroux has been around, remember, and he understands that he, too, stands to learn something from the pedagogical encounter. Giroux has sat with and asked other students and me: What worked? What didn't fly so well? How could I have more effectively set up the segment on ideology? Did I provide enough practical evidence about the many ways the new racism works? Did that film resonate sharply enough with the arguments we read for the class? How could the relationships between intellectuals, academic work, and public responsibility have been explored more effectively? How can I make a context in which a conversation could be had with that student who is hard right [but hardly reflexive]?

On this point, a politico-pedagogical problem, for Giroux, is not whether students, or academics, are right or left, but whether they are responsible or unreflexive and acritical—about themselves, the conditions in which they learn and work, and the broader world—and, thus, whether or not they make it difficult to extend the conversation and perturb the basic conditions of arrogance and myopia that underpin dead-end polemics and a politics of annihilation. To put it differently, Giroux cares little about changing personalities, legitimating particular student identities, or involving himself in privatized vendettas over being "right" or "wrong," but about the making of appropriate contexts and the tapping of critical, civic skills in which questions about responsibility, judgment, ethics, and the broader public good can be raised—or why they are, perhaps, censored—in the first place. Here, in other words, are the practical trappings of Giroux's conceptualization of "political education," which is not to be confused with a "politicizing education" (see Chapters 4 and 7, this volume). Effective, which implies responsible, communication is a two-way street, with others and oneself, and it is the basis for any politico-pedagogical engagement that avoids smacking of elitism, vanguardism, or pretensions to a politics with guarantees.[12] One cannot avoid, and has to take responsibility for, this social predicament in Giroux's class and company—he's checked me a time or two. And it goes without saying: In the age of lowered expectations and civic atrophy where social responsibility even on the most basic levels is marketed as too burdensome or even treasonous, being held to this kind of accountability is disconcerting for some—and "too" political for the escapist and negligent, as if the acts of constructing, orchestrating and disseminating knowledge, organizing bodies within institutional spaces and time grids, using public resources, mobilizing desires, and reinforcing or casting visions of social relationships were not already political.

What can be seen here is a *performative* facet in Giroux's pedagogy, which has at least two related and intended consequences. One, quite like John

Dewey would have had it, Giroux founds his pedagogy in a belief that democracy is only a form, emptied of any potentially just substance and capable of being filled with the rudiments of any political form such as the variants of authoritarianism, if the primary conditions for the practice and experience of civic skills and democratic social relationships are denied.[13] Two, the intellectual for Giroux, in theory and as close as s/he can come in practice, must not only practice social critique, but also *perform self-critique,* and this will be observable in the selections of this volume where, through the trajectory of Giroux's work, the reader will see that he has read against, reworked, and rearticulated his own positions over time and in relation to changing social and cultural relationships and political and economic demands. More: As Giroux has insisted many times in practice as a teacher and in the broader world as an engaged public intellectual, the intellectual has an obligation to link critique with a discourse of hope, a sense that individuals and groups can both make history—though not without struggle—and, under certain circumstances, make it for the better. Critique in this instance is inextricably linked to and enabled by a sense of possibility, a demand to imagine the world differently.[14]

Reading the Giroux Reader

Giroux's theoretical and practical work have been, from the start, devoted to investigating and bringing into being the conditions and relationships capable of supporting a more just and humane social order, a vision that Giroux came to align with the project of a *radical, inclusive democracy.* The theoretical traditions from which he has worked and reworked in the interests of this project have changed over time, and the categories stimulating Giroux's studies have differed from time to time. However, there are some categories, for example, critical pedagogy and the transformative or oppositional public intellectual, which have always figured in Giroux's research and which he has rethought in various moments.[15] For these reasons, the selections compiled in this volume are organized somewhat chronologically in thematic sections, according to both the theoretical-political evolution of Giroux's work and the primary categories he has investigated and theorized in the interests of promoting a radical, inclusive democracy.

The sections used to organize the selections in this volume are as follows, and in this order: Sociology of Education, Cultural Studies and Cultural Politics, The War against Youth, From Critical Pedagogy to Public Pedagogy, The Politics of Higher Education, and Public Intellectuals and Their Work. Of course, another scholar might have devised and used different categories, for instance, "film as public pedagogy" since Giroux has provided many studies on the subject. However, these have been addressed very well elsewhere.[16] Considering the magnitude of Giroux's publishing record, another scholar might have, similarly, selected any number of studies in place of one or, perhaps, all of them presented here. We all have our rationales. In addition to providing a sampling of Giroux's studies that speaks to the transformations and continuities in his theoretical work and the central categories that have impelled his research, I have attempted to provide selections that meet one or all of the following criteria: 1) provide theoretical and practical resources for teachers, students, and other citizens to use in their professional, academic, and everyday lives; 2) demonstrate a general intellectual contribution made by Giroux to social, political, cultural, and educational thought; and 3) have ongoing social, political, cultural and educational relevance. What's more, it is hoped that these selections and their ordering can assist in taking up Giroux's contributions as a whole or in parts by using specific sections of the volume as they fit particular course goals.

The Sociology of Education

Influenced strongly by the critical theory of the Frankfurt School, Giroux's first studies in the late 1970s and early 1980s dealt with a range of concerns, which were related but not limited to the social, historical, and philosophical foundations of education, curriculum studies, and citizenship education. These studies largely underpinned Giroux's development of a critical theory/ science of schooling and, in turn, a *critical pedagogy of learning*. For Giroux to devise a self-reflexive and socially critical mode of collective learning by which its limitations and possibilities for enabling critical thinking and analytical discourse were constantly made visible, open to *resistance* and transformation, he took a detour through the *sociology of education,* primarily that which emerged from studies affiliated with what became known as the New Sociology of Education. Through his dialectical treatment of cultural reproduction and production, accommodation and resistance, structural-institutional forms and concrete human agency, and intensive engagement with issues of ideology and hegemony, a singular, though provisional, critical theory of schooling emerged from Giroux's work at this time.[17] In contradistinction to both liberal and radical theories of schooling, Giroux defined schools as "contested terrains" that were neither foolproof conveyor belts of social mobility and harmony nor precision-built engines of domination free from the play of history, culture, and the intended and unintended consequences of power, but arenas in which competing and unequal social groups struggled to institute and legitimate their view of social order.[18] For this reason, teacher work itself had to be redefined, and Giroux began reformulating the role of the teacher as not merely a legislator or purveyor of given "truth," but as a "transformative intellectual," an interpreter of and key participant in the *production* of culture and, potentially, resistance, thus stripping the "intellectual" of his/her elitist regalia and pretensions to "scholarly" and political "neutrality," a reformulation that would remain central to Giroux's work as readers will learn in Chapters 7–8 and 12–13.

Beginning in the mid- to late 1980s and significantly in the early 1990s, Giroux's perspectives on culture, ideology, power and resistance began to integrate the key insights provided by cultural studies, critical feminism, and the moral and ethical work of liberation theology stemming from South America, in addition to the emerging theoretical discourses of postmodernism. Giroux also began to focus intensively on the political, cultural, and educational power of *popular culture* in a mass-mediated world that was undergoing rapid social and economic change. Both of these transformations in Giroux's work revised his understanding of the complexity of domination by extending it from merely class oppression to gender and racial injustices, seeing oppression as a multivalenced process operating on different groups and different individuals in different ways and at different times across the shifting "borders" in a social world that was marked by the fluid conditions of postmodernity.

These advances in Giroux's thought politicized popular culture. While Giroux retained the Frankfurt School's critical posture toward the ways in which capitalist relationships saturated the spheres of entertainment and leisure, he refused to abandon or belittle these spheres. He understood/ understands them to be contested terrains where battles were/are waged over the construction of subjectivities, and social, political, cultural, moral and, arguably, economic regulation occurred/s.[19] Consequently, Giroux's position on the power of schooling began to shift, understanding it in relation to the modes by which and the conditions under which people learn outside of the formal process of schooling. In this regard, Giroux came to see the production and regulation of desire that occurred through popular culture as a constitutive, "legitimate aspect of students' everyday lives" and a "primary force in shaping the various and often contradictory subject positions students take up."

Cultural Studies and Cultural Politics

The theoretical legacy and political thrust of cultural studies provided Giroux with the categories of investigation and modes of analysis for identifying, engaging, and redirecting the "educational force" of culture, assisting in further theorizing how schools occupy only one point in an intricate network of educational processes and social, political, and moral regulation. In particular, Giroux's appropriation of cultural studies and his articulation of it with critical pedagogy laid the basis for a radical or "insurgent" cultural pedagogy, that is, the understanding that "culture is intrinsically pedagogical; it forms, shapes, and cultivates individuals and groups and is, thus, an important site for radical democratic politics."[20] Subsequently, Giroux theorized more specifically how the processes of learning—in schools and by way of the educational force of culture—had to be constitutive of the processes of socially just transformation, extending an insight from cultural theorist Raymond Williams. To embrace critical pedagogy as cultural politics meant that, in addition to proliferating and legitimating the sites in which education occurs, literacy itself would then need to be pluralized. The idea of litera-*cies* suggested that in addition to being attentive to the pedagogical value of traditional print technologies and cultural artifacts, educators needed to engage just as seriously the cultural codes produced by youth and other citizens within asymmetrical relationships of power and *the images, sound texts, narratives, and (Hollywood) films* that pervaded increasingly commodified public cultures and which were circulated by the ever-changing new media technologies in a social field dominated by corporate interests.

These transformations in Giroux's theoretical work provided the tools with which he began to work on other sites, processes, and agencies of education in the interests of both expanding, that is, democratizing, the sites and processes of education in which people were entangled in their everyday lives *and* providing modes of analysis and resources capable of intervening in those *contexts* and, when necessary, changing them for the better. Amongst other substantive pedagogical sites, Giroux analyzed how corporations were not only involved in a *politics of representation,* but were also transforming the *representation of politics* in the early 1990s (Chapter 3, this volume), simultaneously riffing on captivating and formative social relationships in particular historical contexts, and educating citizens to construct new relationships in which their roles would be defined less by the demands of citizenship than by the allures of being loyal consumers of "responsible" corporations in a marketized social order.[21] Moreover, this crossing of cultural studies and critical pedagogy alerted Giroux to and allowed him to examine how the reordering of capitalism, the changing roles of the state, and the conditions of postmodernity began to impact youth, underscoring challenges besetting democratic public life more generally (Chapter 4, this volume).

The War against Youth

Giroux rarely asks comfortable questions. Particularly since the mid-1990s, he has mobilized his facility with multiple theoretical and public discourses to address the following questions: In what ways and how do the conditions to which youth are subjected and the various "crises" surrounding them constitute, by definition and in effects, *a war against youth?* How does the war against youth register iniquitously along *gender and racial* lines and across multiple, purportedly unrelated spheres (e.g., talk radio and social welfare policy, popular newspeak and public schools, or Hollywood films and education and criminal justice policy)? In turn, how does the war against youth both symbolize and constitute a war on the future and democratic public life itself? What tendencies of force with what latent and blatant consequences tie the two wars into a seemingly "natural" whole? Indeed, these are disturbing questions, and it is not accidental that Giroux started asking them in the mid-1990s and has returned to them at the beginning of the twenty-first century.

In part, Giroux's entry point to the war against youth was, counter intuitively, the public discourses of "innocence," and, more predictably, the syntax of abridgment that began to lock media image-narratives of people of color and "criminality" into a nearly impenetrable post–civil rights world-view. Giroux found that behind the pretensions to innocence and the panics about youth criminality in the 1990s was a set of wicked material practices, which were/are related to changes in social policy and public culture and have produced devastating consequences for a generation of youth. To put it differently, while a direct causal relationship might not necessarily exist between media representations of youth (of color) and changes in social policy, Giroux underscores the substantive resonances between the two sets of discourses and practices, as they mobilize the same codes of representation within the same historical-material conditions. Both sides of this relationship were/are related to a larger set of forces for Giroux: Between the *persistent and escalating corporate assault on public spaces and discourses,* a process which Giroux increasingly has come to associate with *neoliberal* economic philosophy and cultural politics, and *decreasing state responsibility* for social provisions such as public schools, social welfare, healthcare and so on, children and youth have become public enemy number one—not because they are dangerous, though an exceptionally rare few of them are from time to time, but because they are dependent upon the very public investments that neoliberals and social conservatives of the New Right have lambasted as public burdens and fiscal waste for the last 30 years. This makes children and youth, by default, not only private burdens, according to the New World Order(ing) of things, but also social dangers and wasteable or, in Giroux's term, *disposable* as both public coffers and public languages are emptied of any vestiges of social responsibility toward youth and the future—a social irresponsibility of sorts that is run through the distillery of "private" choice, "personal" responsibility or pathology, and "self-help."[22] In study after study, Giroux has mapped the territory of this harrowing set of social forces across numerous public and private sites. These forces are implicated in processes ranging from the *commercialization* of public schools and the *commodification* and *sexualization* of child and youth bodies (Chapter 5, this volume) to the *criminalization* of youth and the *militarization* of public space and culture (Chapter 6, this volume). Assuredly, for Giroux, these transformations in the conditions of public life and in adult responsibility toward youth bear consequences for all youth, but they also need to be understood and contested in terms of how they are refracted disproportionately through the modalities of race and gender and threaten the very promise of democracy.

From Critical Pedagogy to Public Pedagogy

As Giroux's conceptualizations and understandings of education, cultural politics, public culture, the profound and pervasive influences of (global) corporate culture and politics, and democracy both expanded and became more exacting, so too did his understanding of critical pedagogy. In recent years, Giroux has theorized critical pedagogy as *public pedagogy*. Public pedagogy is, as Giroux explains in Chapter 8, a strategy for engaging "more seriously how pedagogy functions on local and global levels to secure and challenge the ways in which power is deployed, affirmed, and resisted within and outside traditional discourses and cultural spheres." This reformulation of critical pedagogy, in broader terms as public pedagogy, has at least four consequences, making a significant contribution to social thought. One, Giroux again provides a rationale—and calls into being the set of relationships—for recognizing and extending, or transforming, the ways power operates, knowledge is produced, and subjectivities are secured or resisted under the conditions of a globalizing neoliberal capitalism and emerging global public sphere. This has the consequence of subjecting all knowledge forms and their modes of production to public engagement and contestation. Two, it requires that the historical legacy of cultural studies, and its relationship to public pedagogy, be rethought in light of altered historical conditions—by no means an easy task, but a necessary one all the same. Three, the *responsibility* of intellectuals takes on a new dimension and force, as the borders delineating official and unofficial sites of knowledge production either proliferate, become commodified, or become more porous due to ever-changing media and communications technologies and in accordance with the assault on all things public and democratic by the forces of neoliberalism. Intellectuals, that is, must renew and extend their practices and projects with a moral commitment to creating contexts—within *and* outside of dominant cultural institutions—in which education can be linked to "modes of political agency that promote critical citizenship and engage the ethical imperative to alleviate human suffering," as Giroux explains in Chapters 7 and 8 (this volume). Thus, as human suffering and grotesque power asymmetries have assumed global proportions that evade the limited reach of the modern nation-state's social side, citizenship itself must be calibrated to the "new social formations that the current political and social institutions of the nation-state cannot influence, contain, or control," and it must "invoke a broader notion of democracy in which the global becomes the space for exercising civic courage, social responsibility, politics, and compassion for the plight of others," Giroux explains in the intimate context of an interview with another international scholar (Chapter 7, this volume). (Intellectuals, it should be clear, play a critical role in either supporting or subverting such a global democratic project.) Four, considering the inordinate power that corporations wield on the representation of politics and the politics of representation, cultural production, and everyday life, public pedagogy underscores the profound necessity of educators and cultural workers to work with wider groups to both hold corporations publicly accountable for their impacts on public life and struggle for fundamental reform of economic, education, and media policy. In other words, corporations should be engaged for the public pedagogies they produce and the representational politics they employ, "forcing civic discourse and popular culture to rub ... against each other," as Giroux demonstrates in one of his many case studies of the Disney Corporation in Chapter 9 (this volume).[23]

The Politics of Higher Education

Despite Giroux's formulation of public pedagogy and forays into popular culture, he is still critically invested in the moral and ethical roles demanded of public schooling and higher education in educating critical, civic minded citizens and keeping the "promise" of democracy alive. To be more precise, and honest to Giroux's work, public pedagogy and popular culture, and public schooling and higher education, are not diametrically opposed or mutually exclusive spheres, and they cannot be if Giroux is, in fact, concerned with democratizing the processes of education and developing contexts in which learning processes can become the processes of social transformation. On the one hand, this understanding presents specific curricular and pedagogical challenges to educators and cultural workers working within institutions of public and higher education and, on the other, it demands sustained engagements with the structural-institutional and social changes (self-) imposed on institutions of higher education by the wider and often contradictory forces of neoliberalism and social conservativism.[24]

In the former case, this suggests, in part, that educators provide conditions and pedagogical relationships in which students can interrogate *public discourses* (e.g., Hollywood film, policy talk) as texts equally as legitimate as, and often more powerful than, traditional curricular devices and pedagogical modes. This does not mean that texts simply be "added" to existing curricular materials, but that they are added within a larger attempt to link critique with social action as part of developing the skills of and affective investments in critical citizenship. Educators and cultural workers must also be concerned with creating pedagogical conditions and relationships capable of not only bridging the gap between how the social world is represented within disciplinary gazes and how it is actually experienced by, for instance, people of color in this historical juncture, but also reordering the material and symbolic structures underpinning that gap and its threat to democratic public life (Chapter 10, this volume). In the latter case, it means to engage the crisis of higher education as being fundamentally related to the war being waged against youth and on democracy by corporate culture. There are at least two points of entry here, as Giroux explains in Chapter 11. One is the construction of and recommitment to *public time* in higher educa-tion. This is a structural-institutional concern. As universities are defined (define themselves?) more by instrumental and commercial desires than by their responsibilities to public needs, the temporal burdens operating in universities refigure academic labor, transform university space, undermine collegiality, and alter teacher-student relationships and, more broadly, the relationship between universities, democratic public life, and the future. Two, educators, cultural workers, and students crucially need to construct and deploy a *language of possibility* within a *politics of educated hope* that "makes concrete the possibility for transforming higher education into a practice and public event that confronts the flow of everyday experience and the weight of social suffering with the force of individual and collective resistance and the promise of an ongoing project of democratic social transformation" (Giroux, Chapter 11, this volume).

Public Intellectuals and Their Work

The intellectual has always featured prominently in Giroux's research. His earliest writings in *Ideology, Culture, and the Process of Schooling, Theory and Resis-tance in Education, Education under Siege* (with Stanley Aronowitz) (Bergin and Garvey, 1985), *Teachers as Intellectuals: Towards a Critical Pedagogy of Learning* (Bergin and Garvey, 1988), and the important *Schooling and the Struggle for Public Life: Critical Pedagogy in the Modern Age* (University of Minnesota Press, 1988), can be understood, in part, as "quest[s] to identify ... the role of the intellectual as a *participant* in social affairs" (Emphasis added).[25] This is a deceivingly simple quest. The intellectual was not always imagined across the 20th century to be a self-reflexive "participant" in social affairs, but a "scholar," an "academic," a mere "observer" unadulterated by the "outside" world, or a legislator of it vis-à-vis his/her "objective" descriptions of and prescriptions for it. Characteristic of Giroux's approach, he has sought in different mo-ments to give the intellectual critical and transformative, not affirmative and reproductive, roles and, more recently, an oppositional, engaged public set of moral and ethical commitments.[26] The intellectual is consequently redefined, in Giroux's work, from his/her role as transmitter of "universal truths" to an active *creator and innovator* within multiple, related communities who is capable of providing moral leadership and constructing formative alliances with other cultural workers within, against, and between dominant cultural institutions and on local and global levels. For Giroux, the intellectual thus must become a "border crosser," one capable of "reinvent[ing] traditions not within the discourse of submission, reverence, and repetition, but '[in one of] transformation and critique'" (Giroux, Chapter 12, this volume). For these reasons, Giroux's work on intellectuals investigates the politics of *the intellectual's location* and work, the *intellectual's public responsibility* as a result of his/her position in the division of labor, the ways intellectuals navigate the shoals of *crisis, criticism,* and *worldliness* (Chapter 13, this volume), and the intellectual's place in articulating a politics of educated hope with a public pedagogy capable of contesting "social relations that keep privilege and oppression alive as active constituting forces of daily life" (Giroux, Chapter 12, this volume).

A closing editorial consideration before the reader can address the task at hand: Since the intellectual has always maintained a central presence in Giroux's work, this section should have, perhaps, opened the volume, so as to give clearer insights to both the implicit and explicit values driving Giroux's commitment to the work he does. I have my rationale. *Respect, engagement, criticality, and a language of possibility* saturate Giroux's work on public intellectuals. This, I believe, in both personal and profound senses, is an important way to close *The Giroux Reader*—at least for now, since Giroux exhibits no signs of fatigue, lack of civic courage, or boredom with the ever-changing world around him ... and us. Closing this collection with Giroux's work on intellectuals will nod to the respect and language of possibility I have fortunately witnessed and experienced firsthand with Giroux, the mentor and teacher, and demonstrate Giroux's openness and critical posture, as an engaged public intellectual himself, toward the insights and actions of others. More importantly, I wish to leave readers mobilized by the same openness, criticality, and language of possibility that animate these selections on public intellectuals and suffuse the rest of this collection.

Notes

1. For more background information on Giroux, see Henry A. Giroux, *Disturbing Pleasures: Learning Popular Culture* (New York: Routledge, 1994), pp. ix–xi; *Breaking into the Movies: Film and the Culture of Politics* (Malden, MA: Blackwell, 2002), pp. 1–16; *Fugitive Cultures: Race, Youth, and Violence* (New York: Routledge, 1996), especially pp. 3–23.

2. See Stanley Aronowitz, "Preface," in H. A. Giroux, *Theory and Resistance in Education: Towards a Pedagogy for the Opposition* (Westport, CT: Bergin and Garvey, 2001), pp. xv–xviii.

3. See, for example, Livy Visano, *Crime and Culture: Refining the Traditions* (Toronto, ON: Canadian Scholars Press, 1998); Andrea Rose, "Music Education and the Formation of Social Consciousness," available at http://www.mun.ca/educ/faculty/mwatch/vol2/rose.html; Valerie Hill-Jackson, "The Culture of Lead Poisoning in Oppressed Communities: Steps Toward a Pedagogy of Possibility," *Journal of*

Multicultural Nursing and Health 10, no. 3 (2004): 55–60; Bradford T. Stull, *Amid the Fall, Dreaming of Eden: Du Bois, King, Malcolm X, and Emancipatory Composition* (Carbondale: Southern Illinois University Press, 1999); Zygmunt Bauman, *Wasted Lives: Modernity and Its Outcasts* (Malden, MA: Polity, 2004).

4. See, for instance, J. Martin Rochester, "Critical Demagogues," *Education Next* 3, no. 4 (2003): 77–82. In this essay, Rochester so egregiously misrepresents Giroux's work by claiming it is "Marxist" and his whole pedagogical project is to inculcate unwitting students with revolutionary scripture. In this volume, one can see and learn that nothing could be further from the crux of Giroux's work, especially that which has been published post-1995, which is founded in radical democratic theory, not revolutionary Marxism. Needless to say, this piece was published in a think tank rag that is edited by neoconservative restorationists. Another example of this type of misrepresentation comes from Fred Hess, an American Enterprise Institute fellow who is increasingly achieving acclaim in educational reform. Hess, in the typical New Right way, inverts the problematic. In this instance, Hess, whose education reform theories are underpinned by neoliberal market practices and ideology, hardly a democratic or even "conservative" framework, argues that the weakness in Giroux's work is that he is a "status quo reformer," impeding the change that schools and the wider American public "need." Giroux, it is clear, is about change, democratic change. Thus, the revolutionaries on the right, for whom social democracy is anti-democratic and inefficient, invert the script, while misrepresenting Giroux's work. See Frederick M. Hess, *Common Sense School Reform* (New York: Palgrave/Macmillan, 2004).

5. See Eric Weiner, "Making the Pedagogical (Re)Turn: Henry Giroux's Insurgent Cultural Pedagogy," *JAC* 21, no. 2 (2001): 434–451, especially p. 440.

6. To get insight to this type of criticism, see the otherwise insightful review of Giroux's *Stealing Innocence: Youth, Corporate Power, and the Politics of Culture* (New York: St. Martin's, 2000) written by Kysa Koerner Hubbard, "Stealing Innocence: Corporate Culture's War on Children," *Cultural Critique* 51: 246–250.

7. See Alan R. Sadovnik, "Postmodernism in the Sociology of Education: Closing the Rift among Theory, Practice, and Research," in G. Noblit and W. T. Pink, eds., *Continuity and Contradiction: The Futures of the Sociology of Education* (Cresskill, NJ: Hampton Press, 1995), pp. 309–326. To see how Giroux actively differentiates himself from postmodernism and modernism, see Henry A. Giroux, "Rethinking the Boundaries of Educational Discourse: Modernism, Postmodernism, and Feminism," *College Literature* 17, no. 2/3 (1990): 1–50. Additionally, some direct insights on how Giroux is, by all means, a critical theorist, but tied neither to postmodernism or modernism, can be found in Chapter 2, this volume.

8. These considerations of Giroux's research and the ways he goes about conducting it are not made to claim that Giroux's work should be left alone, left to "speak for itself," or that it has no shortcomings. None of these options is scarcely the case. None of them would be productive for intellectual work and public debate, or honest about Giroux's and others' research. To the contrary, these considerations indicate the need to subject his and other scholars' work to types of critical analysis that embrace the possibilities *and* limits of the work, so as to model and produce analytical discourses, vocabularies, and practices crucial to enriching wider public dialogue about the work and its potential effects on the social context from which it emerges and into which it intervenes.

9. To see the many ways this work was taken up and the implications it was thought to have presented for educational and social theory, see the following different engagements with this book: David W. Livingstone, "A Pedagogy of Hope: A Review of *Theory and Resistance*," *Boston University Journal of Education* 166, no. 3 (1984): 316–320; Michael Ryan, "Theory and Resistance in Education: A Pedagogy for the Opposition," *Curriculum Inquiry* 14, no. 4 (1984): 469–473; Jerald Zaslove, "Theory and Resistance in Education," *Boston University Journal of Education* 166, no. 3 (1984): 321–330.

10. Henry A. Giroux, *Public Spaces/Private Lives: Democracy beyond the Politics of Cynicism*, (Lanham, MD: Rowman and Littlefield, 2001), p. 83.

11. While discussing this anthology project with another professor and after telling him of the various reviews and citations that I found in reference to Giroux's *Border Crossings: Cultural Workers and the Politics of Education*, he replied, "That book was like Dylan's coming out electric at Newport," Patrick Shannon, personal communication (May 15, 2005). See Henry A. Giroux, *Border Crossings: Cultural Workers and the Politics of Education* (New York: Routledge, 1992).

12. An important theoretical exploration and antecedent to this understanding of the role of effective communication in a democracy can be found in Raymond Williams, *Culture and Society: 1780–1950* (New York: Columbia University Press, 1983), pp. 295–338.

13. See Henry A. Giroux, *The Terror of Neoliberalism: Authoritarianism and the Eclipse of Democracy* (Boulder, CO: Paradigm Publishers, 2004).

14. Chapters 12 and 13, this volume, eloquently address the relationship between critique, discourses of hope, and possibility, particularly as they might be addressed in higher education and by public intellectuals.

15. For informative summaries and analyses of Giroux's work at different times, see the following: Douglas Kellner, "Critical Pedagogy, Cultural Studies, and Radical Democracy at the Turn of the Millennium: Reflections on the Work of Henry Giroux," available at http://www.gseis.ucla.edu/faculty/kellner/essays/henrygiroux.pdf; Peter McLaren, "Foreword: Critical Theory and the Meaning of Hope," in Henry A. Giroux, *Teachers as Intellectuals: Towards a Critical Pedagogy of Learning* (Westport, CT: Bergin and Garvey, 1988), pp. ix–xxi.

16. See Henry A. Giroux, *Breaking into the Movies: Film and the Culture of Politics*, Op cit.

17. It should be noted that planted in these engagements with cultural production were the seeds of Giroux's fruitful studies to come.

18. See Peter McLaren, Op cit.

19. For a useful and concise explanation of Giroux's reworking of the Frankfurt School's position on popular culture, see Michael Peters and Nicholas C. Burbules, *Poststructuralism and Educational Research* (Lanham, MD: Rowman and Littlefield, 2004).

20. Douglas Kellner, "Critical Pedagogy," p. 12. The modifier "insurgent" comes from Eric Weiner. See Eric Weiner, "Making the Pedagogical Return."

21. It is suggested that one reads Chapter 3, this volume, with Naomi Klein's critically acclaimed and insightful study done nearly ten years later. See Naomi Klein, *No Logo: No Space, No Choice, No Jobs* (New York: Picador, 2002), especially pp. 87–105.

22. See also Lawrence Grossberg's important study, *Caught in the Crossfire: Kids, Politics, and America's Future* (Boulder, CO: Paradigm Publishers, 2005).

23. For a more specific look at public pedagogy and its relationship to neoliberal ideology and cultural politics, see Henry A. Giroux, "Public Pedagogy and the Politics of Neoliberalism: Making the Political More Pedagogical," *Policy Futures in Education* 2, no. 3/4 (2004): 494–503. For Giroux's sustained analysis of the Disney Corporation, see Henry A. Giroux, *The Mouse that Roared: Disney and the End of Innocence* (Lanham, MD: Rowman and Littlefield, 1999).

24. For such an effort, see Henry A. Giroux and Susan Searls Giroux, *Take Back Higher Education: Race, Youth, and the Crisis of Democracy in the Post–Civil Rights Era* (New York: Palgrave/Macmillan, 2004).

25. Thomas S. Popkewitz, "Intellectuals, Sciences, and Pedagogies: Critical Traditions and Instrumental Cultures," *American Journal of Education* 93, no. 3 (1985): 433. If the reader is not familiar with this review essay, it is highly recommended reading for its critical insights on not only Giroux's early work, but also the background history of social and political thought concerning schooling in the twentieth century.

26. See Henry A. Giroux, "Curriculum, Teaching, and the Resisting Intellectual," *Curriculum and Teaching* 1, no. 1/2 (1986): 33–42.

I
Sociology of Education

I
Theories of Reproduction and Resistance in the New Sociology of Education
Toward a Critical Theory of Schooling and Pedagogy for the Opposition

✦

In the last decade [between early 1970s and 1980s], Karl Marx's concept of reproduction has been one of the major organizing ideas informing socialist theories of schooling. Marx states that "every social process of production is, at the same time, a process of reproduction.... Capitalist production, therefore ... produces not only commodities, not only surplus-value, but it also produces and reproduces the capitalist relation, on the one side the capitalist, on the other the wage-labourer."[1] Radical educators have given this concept a central place in developing a critique of liberal views of schooling. Moreover, they have used it as the theoretical foundation for developing a critical science of education.[2] Thus far, the task has been only partially successful.

Contrary to the claims of liberal theorists and historians that public education offers possibilities for individual development, social mobility, and political and economic power to the disadvantaged and dispossessed, radical educators have argued that the main functions of schools are the reproduction of the dominant ideology, its forms of knowledge, and the distribution of skills needed to reproduce the social division of labor. In the radical perspective, schools as institutions could only be understood through an analysis of their relationship to the state and the economy. In this view, the deep structure or underlying significance of schooling could only be revealed through analyzing how schools functioned as agencies of social and cultural reproduction—that is, how they legitimated capitalist rationality and sustained dominant social practices.

Instead of blaming students for educational failure, radical educators blamed the dominant society. Instead of abstracting schools from the dynamics of inequality and class-race-gender modes of discrimination, schools were considered central agencies in the politics and processes of domination. In contrast to the liberal view of education as the great equalizer, radical

3

educators saw the objectives of schooling quite differently. As Paul Willis states, "Education was not about equality, but inequality.... Education's main purpose of the social integration of a class society could be achieved only by preparing most kids for an unequal future, and by insuring their personal underdevelopment. Far from productive roles in the economy simply waiting to be 'fairly' filled by the products of education, the 'Reproduction' perspective reversed this to suggest that capitalist production and its roles required certain educational outcomes."[3]

In my view, radical educators presented a serious challenge to the discourse and logic of liberal views of schooling. But they did more than that. They also tried to fashion a new discourse and set of understandings around the reproduction thesis. Schools were stripped of their political innocence and connected to the social and cultural matrix of capitalist rationality. In effect, schools were portrayed as reproductive in three senses. First, schools provided different classes and social groups with the knowledge and skills they needed to occupy their respective places in a labor force stratified by class, race, and gender. Second, schools were seen as reproductive in the cultural sense, functioning in part to distribute and legitimate forms of knowledge, values, language, and modes of style that constitute the dominant culture and its interests. Third, schools were viewed as part of a state apparatus that produced and legitimated the economic and ideological imperatives that underlie the state's political power.

Radical reproduction theorists have used these forms of reproduction to fashion a number of specific concerns that have shaped the nature of their educational research and inquiry. These concerns have focused on analyses of the relationships between schooling and the workplace,[4] class-specific educational experiences and the job opportunities that emerge for different social groups,[5] the culture of the school and the class-defined cultures of the students who attend them,[6] and the relationship among the economic, ideological, and repressive functions of the state and how they affect school policies and practices.[7]

Reproduction theory and its various explanations of the role and function of education have been invaluable in contributing to a broader understanding of the political nature of schooling and its relation to the dominant society. But it must be stressed that the theory has not achieved its promise to provide a comprehensive critical science of schooling. Reproduction theorists have overemphasized the idea of domination in their analyses and have failed to provide any major insights into how teachers, students, and other human agents come together within specific historical and social contexts in order to both make and reproduce the conditions of their existence. More specifically, reproduction accounts of schooling have continually patterned themselves after structural-functionalist versions of Marxism which stress that history is made "behind the backs" of the members of society. The idea that people do make history, including its constraints, has been neglected. Indeed, human subjects generally "disappear" amidst a theory that leaves no room for moments of self-creation, mediation, and resistance. These accounts often leave us with a view of schooling and domination that appears to have been pressed out of an Orwellian fantasy; schools are often viewed as factories or prisons, teachers and students alike act merely as pawns and role bearers constrained by the logic and social practices of the capitalist system.

By downplaying the importance of human agency and the notion of resistance, reproduction theories offer little hope for challenging and changing the repressive features of schooling. By ignoring the contradictions and struggles that exist in schools, these theories not only dissolve human agency, they unknowingly provide a rationale for *not* examining teachers and students in concrete school settings. Thus, they miss the opportunity to determine whether there is a substantial difference between the existence of various structural and ideological modes of domination and their actual unfolding and effects.

Recent research on schooling in the United States, Europe, and Australia has both challenged and attempted to move beyond reproduction theories. This research emphasizes the importance of human agency and experience as the theoretical cornerstones for analyzing the complex relationship between schools and the dominant society. Organized around what I loosely label as resistance theory, these analyses give central importance to the notions of conflict, struggle, and resistance.[8]

Combining ethnographic studies with more recent European cultural studies, resistance theorists have attempted to demonstrate that the mechanisms of social and cultural reproduction are never complete and always meet with partially realized elements of opposition.[9] In effect, resistance theorists have developed a theoretical framework and method of inquiry that restores the critical notion of agency. They point not only to the role that students play in challenging the most oppressive aspects of schools but also to the ways in which students actively participate through oppositional behavior in a logic that very often consigns them to a position of class subordination and political defeat.

One of the most important assumptions of resistance theory is that working-class students are not merely the by-product of capital, compliantly submitting to the dictates of authoritarian teachers and schools that prepare them for a life of deadening labor. Rather, schools represent contested terrains marked not only by structural and ideological contradictions but also by collectively informed student resistance. In other words, schools are social sites characterized by overt and hidden curricula, tracking, dominant and subordinant cultures, and competing class ideologies. Of course, conflict and resistance take place within asymmetrical relations of power which always favor the dominant classes, but the essential point is that there are complex and creative fields of resistance through which class-, race- and gender-mediated practices often refuse, reject, and dismiss the central messages of the schools.

In resistance accounts, schools are relatively autonomous institutions that not only provide spaces for oppositional behavior and teaching but also represent a source of contradictions that sometimes make them dysfunctional to the material and ideological interests of the dominant society. Schools are not solely determined by the logic of the workplace or the dominant society; they are not merely economic institutions but are also political, cultural, and ideological sites that exist somewhat independently of the capitalist market economy. Of course, schools operate within limits set by society, but they function in part to influence and shape those limits, whether they be economic, ideological, or political. Moreover, instead of being homogeneous institutions operating under the direct control of business groups, schools are characterized by diverse forms of school knowledge, ideologies, organizational styles, and classroom social relations. Thus, schools often exist in a contradictory relation to the dominant society, alternately supporting and challenging its basic assumptions. For instance, schools sometimes support a notion of liberal education that is in sharp contradiction to the dominant society's demand for forms of education that are specialized, instrumental, and geared to the logic of the marketplace. In addition, schools still strongly define their role via their function as agencies for social mobility even though they currently turn out graduates at a faster pace than the economy's capacity to employ them.

Whereas reproduction theorists focus almost exclusively on power and how the dominant culture ensures the consent and defeat of subordinate classes and groups, theories of resistance restore a degree of agency and innovation to the cultures of these groups. Culture, in this case, is constituted as much by the group itself as by the dominant society. Subordinate cultures, whether working-class or otherwise, partake of moments of self-production as well as reproduction; they are contradictory in nature and bear the marks of both resistance and reproduction. Such cultures are forged within constraints shaped by capital and its institutions, such as schools, but the conditions within which such constraints function vary from school to school and from neighborhood to neighborhood. Moreover, there are never any guarantees that capitalist values and ideologies will automatically succeed, regardless of how strongly they set the agenda. As Stanley Aronowitz reminds us, "In the final analysis, human praxis is not determined by its pre-conditions; only the boundaries of possibility are given in advance."[10]

In this rather brief and abstract discussion, I have juxtaposed two models of educational analysis to suggest that theories of resistance represent a significant advance over the important but limited theoretical gains of reproduction models of schooling. But it is important to emphasize that, in spite of more complex modes of analysis, resistance theories are also marred by a number of theoretical flaws. In part, these flaws stem from a failure to recognize the degree to which resistance theories themselves are indebted to some of the more damaging features of reproduction theory. At the same time, however, resistance theories have too readily ignored the most valuable insights of reproduction theory and, in doing so, have failed to examine and appropriate those aspects of the reproduction model that are essential to developing a critical science of education. Furthermore, despite their concrete differences, resistance and reproduction approaches to education share the failure of recycling and reproducing the dualism between agency and structure, a failure that has plagued educational theory and practice for decades, while simultaneously representing its greatest challenge. Consequently, neither position provides the foundation for a theory of education that links structures and institutions to human agency and action in a dialectical manner.

The basis for overcoming this separation of human agency from structural determinants lies in the development of a theory of resistance that both questions its own assumptions and critically appropriates those aspects of schooling that are accurately presented and analyzed in the reproduction model. In other words, the task facing resistance theorists is twofold: first, they must structure their own assumptions to develop a more dialectical model of schooling and society; and second, they must reconstruct the major theories of reproduction in order to abstract from them their most radical and emancipatory insights.

The remainder of this essay will first discuss three important theories that constitute various dimensions of the reproduction model of schooling: the economic-reproductive model, the cultural-reproductive model, and the hegemonic-state reproductive model. Since reproduction theorists have been the object of considerable criticism elsewhere, I shall focus primarily on the strengths of each of these models, and shall only summarize some of the general criticisms. Second, I shall look at what I generously call neo-Marxist theories of resistance that have recently emerged in the literature on education and schooling, examining their theoretical strengths and weaknesses, while at the same time analyzing how they are either positively or negatively informed by theories of reproduction. Finally, I shall attempt to develop a new theory of resistance and shall briefly analyze its implications for a critical science of schooling.

Schooling and Theories of Reproduction

Economic-Reproductive Model

The political-economy model of reproduction has exercised the strongest influence on radical theories of schooling. Developed primarily around the work of Samuel Bowles and Herbert Gintis, it has had a major influence on theories about the hidden curriculum,[11] educational policy studies,[12] and a wide range of ethnographic research.[13] At the core of the political-economy approach are two fundamentally important questions. The most important of these focuses on the relationship between schooling and society and asks, How does the educational system function within society? The second question points to a related but more concrete concern regarding the issue of how subjectivities actually get constituted in schools, asking, How do schools fundamentally influence the ideologies, personalities, and needs of students? While theorists who work within this model give different answers, they generally agree on the relationship between power and domination, on the one hand, and the relationship between schooling and the economy on the other.

Power in these accounts is defined and examined primarily in terms of its function to mediate and legitimate the relations of dominance and subordinance in the economic sphere. In this perspective, power becomes the property of dominant groups and operates to reproduce class, gender, and racial inequalities that function in the interests of the accumulation and expansion of capital. This becomes clear in the way economic-reproductive theorists analyze the relations between the economy and schooling.

Central to this position is the notion that schools can only be understood by analyzing the structural effects of the workplace on them. In Bowles and Gintis's work this notion becomes clear through their reliance on what they call the correspondence theory.[14] Broadly speaking, the correspondence theory posits that the hierarchically structured patterns of values, norms, and skills that characterize both the workforce and the dynamics of class interaction under capitalism are mirrored in the social dynamics of the daily classroom encounter. Through its classroom social relations, schooling functions to inculcate students with the attitudes and dispositions necessary to accept the social and economic imperatives of a capitalist economy.

In this view, the underlying experience and relations of schooling are animated by the power of capital to provide different skills, attitudes, and values to students of different classes, races, and genders. In effect, schools mirror not only the social division of labor but also the wider society's class structure. The theoretical construct that illuminates the structural and ideological connection between the schools and the workplace is the notion of the hidden curriculum. This term refers to those classroom social relations that embody specific messages which legitimize the particular views of work, authority, social rules, and values that sustain capitalist logic and rationality, particularly as manifested in the workplace. The power of these messages lies in their seemingly universal qualities—qualities that emerge as part of the structured silences that permeate all levels of school and classroom relations. The social relations that constitute the hidden curriculum provide ideological and material weight to questions regarding what counts as high versus low status knowledge (intellectual or manual), high versus low status forms of social organization (hierarchical or democratic), and, of course, what counts as high versus low status forms of personal interaction (interaction based on individual competitiveness or interaction based on collective sharing). The nature and meaning of the hidden curriculum is further extended through an understanding of how it contributes to the construction of student subjectivities—that is, those conscious and unconscious dimensions of experience that inform student behavior. Consideration of this issue leads into the work of the French social theorist, Louis Althusser.

Althusser also argues that schools represent an essential and important social site for reproducing capitalist relations of production.[15] In agreement with Bowles and Gintis, he argues that the school carries out two fundamental forms of reproduction: the reproduction of the skills and rules of labor power, and the reproduction of the relations of production.

The reproduction of the skills and rules of labor power is defined within the context of the formal curriculum and, in Althusser's terms, includes the kind of "know-how" students need in order to

> read, to write and to add—i.e., a number of techniques, and a number of other things as well, including elements of "scientific" or "literary culture," which are directly useful in the different jobs in production (one instruction for manual workers, another for technicians, a third for engineers, a final one for high management).... Children also learn the rules of good behaviour, i.e., the attitude that should be observed by every agent in the division of labor, according to the job he is "destined" for: rules of morality, civic and professional conscience, which actually means rules of respect for the socio-technical divisions of labour and ultimately the rules of the order established by class domination.[16]

Although both Althusser and Bowles and Gintis acknowledge the role that school knowledge plays in the reproductive process, it is not of much significance in their analyses. Domination and the reproduction of the work force as constitutive elements of the schooling process take place primarily "behind the backs" of teachers and students through the hidden curriculum of schooling. But it is at this point that these theorists provide important and differing explanations. Unlike Bowles and Gintis, who situate the hidden curriculum in social relations that are somehow internalized by (read imposed on) students, Althusser attempts to explain this "hidden" process of socialization through a systematic theory of ideology.

Althusser's theory of ideology has a dual meaning, which becomes clear in his analysis of how ruling-class domination is secured in schools. In its first meaning, the theory refers to a set of material practices through which teachers and students live out their daily experiences. Ideology has a material existence in the rituals, routines, and social practices that both structure and mediate the day-to-day workings of schools. This material aspect of ideology is clearly seen, for example, in the architecture of school buildings, with their separate rooms, offices, and recreational areas—each positing and reinforcing an aspect of the social division of labor. Space is arranged differently for the administrative staff, teachers, secretaries, and students within the school building. Further, the ideological nature of the ecology of the school is somewhat obvious in the seating arrangements in university halls, or, for that matter, in the classrooms of many urban schools.

This material aspect of Althusser's notion of ideology corresponds somewhat to Bowles and Gintis's notion of the hidden curriculum in pointing to the political nature and use of space, time, and social processes as they function within specific insitutional settings. Similarly, it also points to the class-specific source and control of power that bears down on ideological institutions such as schools—institutions deemed essential, according to Althusser, to the production of ideologies and experiences that support the dominant society.[17]

In the second meaning of Althusser's notion of ideology, the dynamics of the reproductive model unfold. In this sense, ideology is completely removed from any notion of intentionality, producing neither consciousness nor willing compliance. Instead, it is defined as those systems of meanings, representations, and values embedded in concrete practices that structure the unconsciousness of students. The effect of such practices and their mediations is to induce in teachers and students alike an "imaginary relationship ... to their real conditions of existence."[18] Althusser explains:

> It is customary to suggest that ideology belongs to the region of "consciousness".... In truth, ideology has very little to do with "consciousness".... It is profoundly unconscious, even when it presents itself in a reflected form. Ideology is indeed a system of representations, but in the majority of cases these representations have nothing to do with "consciousness": they are usually images and occasionally concepts, but it is above all as structures that they impose on the vast majority of men, not via their "consciousness." They are perceived-accepted-suffered cultural objects and they act functionally on one in a process that escapes them. Men "live" their ideologies as the Cartesian "saw" the moon at two hundred paces away: not at all as a form of consciousness, but as an object of their "world"—as their world itself.[19]

The economic-reproductive model gains an added dimension in the work of Christian Baudelot and Roger Establet.[20] Baudelot and Establet also stress that the principal function of the school can only be understood in terms of the role it plays in the production of labor power, the accumulation of capital, and in the reproduction of legitimating ideologies. Once again, schools are tied to the engine of domination and reproduction. But in this case, power does not collapse into an all-encompassing construct of ideological domination. Though still tied to the economic-reproductive model, Baudelot and

Establet are not willing to dissolve human *agency* under the heavy hand of a one-sided notion of domination. Domination, they claim, does manifest itself through the imposition of bourgeois ideology in French schools, but the ideology is sometimes opposed and resisted by working-class youths, particularly at the compulsory levels of schooling.

Several important but underdeveloped theoretical considerations begin to emerge in Baudelot and Establet's model of reproduction. First, schools are not viewed as sites that smoothly socialize working-class students into the dominant ideology. Instead, schools are seen as social sites informed by conflicting ideologies which are rooted, in part, in the antagonistic class relations and structured practices that shape the day-to-day workings of these institutions. But if schools are viewed as sites containing oppositional ideologies, the sources of these ideologies—which fuel student resistance—are to be found not only inside but outside the school as well. That is, the basis for both critique and resistance on the part of working-class students is partly produced through the knowledge and practices made available to them in schools, but the primary historical and material basis for such action is located in oppositional public spheres that exist outside of such institutions.

The question of the location of the basis of resistance leads to Baudelot and Establet's second major insight. They rightly argue that the source of working-class student consciousness cannot be limited to such spheres as the workplace and the school. Working-class student social formations—groups organized around specific cultural experiences, values, and class, gender, and racial relations—with their combination of hegemonic and oppositional ideologies, are primarily formed in the family, the neighborhood, and in the mass- and class-mediated youth cultures.[21] Social classes, in this account, are formed not through the primacy of their determined structural relation to the work-place, but through culture as well. Aronowitz captures this complex dynamic behind the construction of class formations in his comment, "The class's capacity for self-representation is marked by common conditions of life, including, but not limited to, a common relation to the ownership and control of the means of production. Among other things, classes are ... formed by culture, understood here as modes of discourse, a shared symbolic universe, rituals and customs that connote solidarity and distinguish a class from others."[22]

A third important but underdeveloped insight in Baudelot and Establet's analysis is that ideology is limited neither to the realm of the unconscious nor to a configuration of internalized personality traits. As I have mentioned elsewhere, Bowles and Gintis as well as Althusser have drawn accounts of schooling in which the logic of domination appears to be inscribed without the benefit of human mediation or struggle.[23] Baudelot and Establet modify these positions by giving ideology a more active nature. For them, ideology refers to that part of the realm of consciousness that produces *and* mediates the contradictory relations of capitalism and school life. Consequently, ideology becomes the locus of contradictory consciousness, informed by and containing both dominant and oppositional ideologies. This is evident in the contradictory logic exhibited in certain types of resistance. For example, some working-class students either resist or reject the notion of book learning and other forms of literacy in favor of subversive school behavior and a celebration of physicality and manual labor. In doing so, these students may undermine one of the fundamental ideologies of the school, but they do so at the cost of rejecting the possibility for developing modes of critical literacy that could be crucial to their own liberation.[24]

Cultural-Reproductive Model

Theories of cultural reproduction are also concerned with the question of how capitalist societies are able to reproduce themselves. Central to these theories is a sustained effort to develop a sociology of schooling that links culture, class, and domination. The mediating role of culture in reproducing class societies is given priority over the study of related issues, such as the source and consequences of economic inequality. The work of Pierre Bourdieu and his colleagues in France represents the most important perspective for studying the cultural-reproductive model.[25]

Bourdieu's theory of cultural reproduction begins with the notion that the logic of domination, whether manifested in schools or in other social sites, must be analyzed within a theoretical framework capable of dialectically linking human agents and dominant structures. Bourdieu rejects functionalist theories that either impute the effects of domination to a single, central apparatus or fail to see how the dominated participate in their own oppression. This rejection becomes clear in Bourdieu's theory of schooling in which he attempts to link the notions of structure and human agency through an analysis of the relationships among dominant culture, school knowledge, and individual biographies.[26] In his attempt to understand the role of culture in linking, first, schools to the logic of the dominant classes, and, second, the dynamics of capitalist reproduction to the subordinate classes, Bourdieu argues against the notion that schools simply mirror the dominant society. Instead, he claims that schools are relatively autonomous institutions that are influenced only indirectly by more powerful economic and political institutions. Rather than being linked directly to the power of an economic elite, schools are seen as part of a larger universe of symbolic institutions that do not overtly impose docility and oppression, but reproduce existing power relations more subtly through the production and distribution of a dominant culture that tacitly confirms what it means to be educated.

Bourdieu's theory of cultural reproduction begins with the assumption that class-divided societies and the ideological and material configurations on which they rest are partially mediated and reproduced through what he calls "symbolic violence." That is, class control is constituted through the subtle exercise of symbolic power waged by ruling classes in order "to impose a definition of the social world that is consistent with its interests."[27] Culture becomes the mediating link between ruling-class interests and everyday life. It functions to portray the economic and political interests of the dominant classes, not as arbitrary and historically contingent, but as necessary and natural elements of the social order.

Education is seen as an important social and political force in the process of class reproduction. By appearing to be an impartial and neutral "transmitter" of the benefits of a valued culture, schools are able to promote inequality in the name of fairness and objectivity. Through this argument Bourdieu rejects both the idealist position, which views schools as independent of external forces, and orthodox radical critiques, in which schools merely mirror the needs of the economic system. According to Bourdieu, it is precisely the relative autonomy of the educational system that "enables it to serve external demands under the guise of independence and neutrality, i.e., to conceal the social functions it performs and so to perform them more effectively."[28]

The notions of culture and cultural capital are central to Bourdieu's analysis of how the mechanisms of cultural reproduction function within schools. He argues that the culture transmitted by the school is related to the various cultures that make up the wider society in that it confirms the culture of the ruling classes while simultaneously disconfirming the cultures of other groups. This becomes more understandable through an analysis of the notion of cultural capital—the different sets of linguistic and cultural competencies that individuals inherit by way of the class-located boundaries of their family. A child inherits from his or her family those sets of meanings, qualities of style, modes of thinking, and types of dispositions that are assigned a certain social value and status in accordance with what the dominant classes label as the most valued cultural capital. Schools play a particularly important role in legitimating and reproducing dominant cultural capital. They tend to legitimize certain forms of knowledge, ways of speaking, and ways of relating to the world that capitalize on the type of familiarity and skills that only certain students have received from their family backgrounds and class relations. Students whose families have only a tenuous connection to the dominant cultural capital are at a decided disadvantage. Bourdieu sums up this process:

> The culture of the elite is so near that of the school that children from the lower middle class (and *a fortiori* from the agricultural and industrial working class) can acquire only with great effort something which is *given* to the children of the cultivated classes—style, taste, wit—in short, those aptitudes which seem natural in members of the cultivated classes and naturally expected of them precisely because (in the ethnological sense) they are the *culture* of that class.[29]

By linking power and culture, Bourdieu provides a number of insights into how the hegemonic curriculum works in schools, pointing to the political interests underlying the selection and distribution of those bodies of knowledge that are given top priority.[30] These bodies of knowledge not only legitimate the interests and values of the dominant classes, they also have the effect of marginalizing or disconfirming other kinds of knowledge, particularly knowledge important to feminists, the working class, and minority groups. For example, working-class students often find themselves subjected to a school curriculum in which the distinction between high-status and low-status knowledge is organized around the difference between theoretical and practical subjects. Courses that deal with practical subjects, whether they be industrial arts or culinary arts, are seen as marginal and inferior. In this case, working-class knowledge and culture are often placed in competition with what the school legitimates as dominant culture and knowledge. In the end, working-class knowledge and culture are seen not as different and equal, but as different and inferior. It is important to note that high-status knowledge often corresponds to bodies of knowledge that provide a stepping stone to professional careers via higher education. Such knowledge embodies the cultural capital of the middle and upper classes and presupposes a certain familiarity with the linguistic and social practices it supports. Needless to say, such knowledge is not only more accessible to the upper classes, but also functions to confirm and legitimate their privileged positions in schools. Thus, the importance of the hegemonic curriculum lies in both what it includes—with its emphasis on Western history, science, and so forth—and what it excludes—feminist history, black studies, labor history, critical courses in the arts, and other forms of knowledge important to the working class and other subordinate groups.[31]

Thus, schools legitimize the dominant cultural capital through the hierarchically arranged bodies of school knowledge in the hegemonic curriculum, and by rewarding students who use the linguistic style of the ruling class. Certain linguistic styles, along with the body postures and the social relations they reinforce (lowered voice, disinterested tone, non-tactile interaction), act as identifiable forms of cultural capital that either reveal or betray a student's social background. In effect, certain linguistic practices and modes of discourse become privileged by being treated as natural to the gifted, when in fact they are the speech habits of dominant classes and thus serve to perpetuate cultural privileges.

Class and power connect with the production of dominant cultural capital not only in the structure and evaluation of the school curriculum but also in the dispositions of the oppressed themselves, who sometimes actively participate in their own subjugation. This point is central to Bourdieu's theory of cultural reproduction and can be examined more closely through a discussion of his notions of habitat (positions) and habitus (dispositions).[32]

In Bourdieu's most recent writings, he examines the relationship between action and structure through forms of historical action that bring together two histories. The first is the habitat, or *objectified history,* "the history which has accumulated over the passage of time in things, machines, buildings, monuments, books, theories, customs, law, etc."[33] The second refers to the *embodied history* of the habitus, and points to a set of internalized competencies and structured needs, an internalized style of knowing and relating to the world that is grounded in the body itself. Habitus, then, becomes a "matrix of perceptions, appreciations and actions,"[34] "a system of durably acquired schemes of perception, thought and action, engendered by objective conditions but tending to persist even after an alteration of those conditions."[35] The habitus is a product of both socialization and embodied history, and differs for various dominant and subordinant groups within society. As principles inscribed deeply within the needs and dispositions of the body, the habitus becomes a powerful force in organizing an individual's experience and is the central category in situating human agency within practical activity.

It is in the dialectical relationship between institutions as objectified history and the habitus or dispositions of different classes that Bourdieu attempts to fashion a theory of domination and learning. Bourdieu explains the process of domination by arguing that it is often forged through a correlation between a certain disposition (habitus) and the expectations and interests embedded in the position of specific institutions (habitat). Thus, it is in this correspondence between the tacitly inscribed values and ideologies that make up the individual's disposition and the norms and ideologies embedded in the positions characterizing institutions such as schools that the dynamics of domination become manifest. Furthermore, for Bourdieu the notions of habitus and habitat reveal how domination is forged in a logic that draws together those corresponding ideologies and practices that constitute both agents and structures. "The dispositions inculcated by a childhood experience of the social world which, in certain historical conditions, can predispose young workers to accept and even wish for entry into a world of manual labor which they identify with the adult world, are reinforced by work experience itself and by all the consequent changes in their dispositions."[36]

The importance of the notion of habitus to a theory of schooling becomes evident in the expanded theory of learning that it suggests. Bourdieu argues that individuals from different social groups and classes undergo processes of socialization that are not only intellectual but also emotional, sensory, and physical. Learning, in this case, is actively situated in the practical activity of the body, senses, and emotions. It is organized around class-specific cultural practices that inscribe their messages beyond consciousness, in the materiality of the body and the values and dispositions it signifies. Bourdieu explains:

The principles embodied in [the habitus] ... are placed beyond the grasp of consciousness, and hence cannot be touched by voluntary deliberate transformation, cannot even be made explicit; nothing seems more ineffable, more incommunicable, more inimitable, and, therefore, more precious, than the values given body, *made* body by the transubstantiation achieved by the hidden persuasion of an implicit pedagogy, capable of instilling a whole cosmology, an ethic, a metaphysic, a political philosophy, through injunctions as insignificant as "stand up straight" as "don't hold your knife in your left hand."[37]

Bourdieu's work is significant in that it provides a theoretical model for understanding aspects of schooling and social control that have been virtually ignored in conservative and liberal accounts. Its politicization of school knowledge, culture, and linguistic practices formulates a new discourse for examining ideologies embedded in the formal school curriculum. Similarly, Bourdieu adds a new dimension to analyses of the hidden curriculum by focusing on the importance of the body as an object of learning and social control.[38] In effect, what emerges in this account are the theoretical rudiments of a cultural-reproductive model that attempts to take seriously the notions of history, sociology, and psychology.

Yet, Bourdieu's work is not without some serious theoretical flaws. The most glaring flaws concern the mechanistic notions of power and domination and the overly determined view of human agency that characterizes much of this work. For example, Bourdieu's formulation of the notion of habitus is based on a theory of social control and depth psychology that appears to be fashioned almost exclusively in the logic of domination. The following comment by Bourdieu is representative of this position.

The uses of the body, of languages, and of time are all privileged objects of social control: innumerable elements of explicit education—not to mention practical, mimetic transmission—relate to uses of the body ("sit up straight," "don't touch") or uses of language ("say this" or "don't say that"). Through bodily and linguistic discipline ... the choices constituting a certain relation to the world are internalized in the form of durable patternings not accessible to consciousness nor even, in part, amenable to will. Politeness contains a politics, a practical immediate recognition of social classifications and of hierarchies between the sexes, the generations, the classes, etc.[39]

Unfortunately, where the conceptual possibility for resistance does appear in Bourdieu's work—that is, in the mismatch between one's habitus and the position one occupies—the foundation for such action rests not on a notion of reflexivity or critical self-consciousness, but on the incompatability between two structures—the historical structure of the disposition and the historical structure embodied in the institution. Thus, resistance becomes the outcome of a conflict between two formalistic structures, one situated in the realm of the unconscious and the other situated in the social practices that make up institutions such as schools. The result is that the power of reflexive thought and historical agency are relegated to a minor theoretical detail in Bourdieu's theory of change.

Another theoretical flaw in Bourdieu's work is that culture represents a somewhat one-way process of domination. As a result, his theory suggests falsely that working-class cultural forms and knowledge are homogeneous and merely a pale reflection of dominant cultural capital. Working-class cultural production and its relation to cultural reproduction through the complex dynamics of resistance, incorporation, and accommodation are not acknowledged by Bourdieu. The collapse of culture and class into the processes of cultural reproduction raises a number of significant problems. First, such a portrayal eliminates conflict both within and between different classes, resulting in the loss of such notions as struggle, diversity, and human agency in a somewhat reductionist view of human nature and history. Second, by reducing classes to homogeneous groups whose only differences are based on whether they exercise or respond to power, Bourdieu provides no theoretical opportunity to unravel how cultural domination and resistance are mediated through the complex interface of race, gender, and class. What is missing from Bourdieu's work is the notion that culture is both a structuring and transforming process. David Davies captures this dynamic in his comment: "Culture refers paradoxically to conservative adaptation and lived subordination of classes and to opposition, resistance, and creative struggle for change.[40]

Bourdieu's analyses of schooling also suffer from a one-sided treatment of ideology.[41] While it is useful to argue, as Bourdieu does, that dominant ideologies are transmitted by schools and actively incorporated by students, it is equally important to remember that ideologies are also *imposed* on students, who occasionally view them as contrary to their own interests and either resist them openly or conform to them under pressure from school authorities. In other words, dominant ideologies are not just transmitted in schools nor are they practiced in a void. On the contrary, they are often met with resistance by teachers, students, and parents. Furthermore, it is reasonable to argue that in order to be successful, schools have to repress the production of counter-ideologies. Roger Dale illuminates this process in his discussion of how hegemony functions in schools, writing that "hegemony is not so much about winning approval for the status quo. . . . Rather what seems to be involved is the prevention of rejection, opposition or alternatives to the status quo through denying the use of the school for such purposes."[42] Similarly, it must be noted that schools are not simply static institutions that reproduce the dominant ideology; they are active agents in its construction as well. This is aptly portrayed in an ethnographic study of ruling class schools conducted by Robert Connell and his colleagues. They write:

The school generates practices by which the class is renewed, integrated and reconstituted in the face of changes in its own composition and in the general social circumstances in which it tries to survive and prosper. (This is an embracing practice, ranging from the school fete, Saturday sport and week-night dinners with parents, to the organization of a marriage market—e.g., inter-school dances—and informal networks in business and the professions, to the regulation of class membership, updating of ideology, and subordination of particular interests to those of class as a whole.) The ruling-class school is no mere agent of the class; it is an important and active part of it. In short, it is organic to its class. Bourdieu wrote a famous essay about the "school as conserver"; we would suggest an equal stress should be laid on the school as constructor.[43]

By failing to develop a theory of ideology that speaks to the way in which human beings dialectically create, resist, and accommodate themselves to dominant ideologies, Bourdieu excludes the active nature of both domination and resistance. In spite of his claims, it is important to argue that schools do not simply usurp the cultural capital of working-class families and neighborhoods. Complex relations develop between the schools and working-class families and they need to be analyzed in terms of the conflicts and struggles that inform them. This point is highlighted in an ethnographic study by R. Timothy Sieber that chronicles the history of a power struggle over an elementary school in New York City.[44]

This study reinforces one aspect of Bourdieu's analysis in revealing that middle-class students, with their respective cultural competencies and experiences, were accorded specific academic privileges and freedoms denied to working-class and Puerto Rican students in the same school. But the more interesting aspect of Sieber's study indicates that the "privileged standing" and educational benefits provided to middle-class students were the outcome of a long struggle between the middle-class segment of the community and its predominantly working-class residents. The predominance of middle-class culture in this school was the outcome of a political struggle, and contrary to Bourdieu's position, was actively and systematically developed "both inside and outside of the school" by middle-class parents.[45]

Finally, there is a serious flaw in Bourdieu's work regarding his unwillingness to link the notion of domination with the materiality of economic forces. There is no insight in Bourdieu's analyses regarding how the economic system, with its asymmetrical relations of power, produces concrete constraints on working-class students. Michel Foucault's notion that power works on the body, the family, sexuality, and the nature of learning itself serves to remind us that the relations of power weigh down on more than just the mind.[46] In other words, the constraints of power are not exhausted within the concept of symbolic violence. Domination as an objective, concrete instance cannot be ignored in any discussion of schooling. For instance, the privileged classes have a relationship to time that enables them to make long-term plans regarding their futures. In contrast, the children of the dispossessed, especially those who are in higher education, often are burdened by economic constraints that lock them into the present and limit their goals to short-term plans. Time is a privation, not a possession, for most working-class students.[47] It is the economic dimension that often plays a crucial role in the decision over whether a working-class student can go to school full or part time, or in some cases can afford to go at all, just as the economic issue is often the determining factor in deciding whether or not a student will have to work part time while attending school. Bourdieu appears to have forgotten that domination has to be grounded in something other than mere ideology, that it also has a material foundation. This is no small matter, because it points to a major gap in Bourdieu's reasoning regarding working-class failure. The internalization of dominant ideology is not the only force that motivates working-class students or secures their failure. Their behaviors, failures, and choices are also grounded in material conditions.

As a result of Bourdieu's one-sided emphasis on ruling-class domination and its attendant cultural practices, it becomes clear that both the concept of capital as well as the notion of class are treated as static categories. In my view, class involves a notion of social relations that are in opposition to each other. It refers to the shifting relations of domination and resistance and to capital and its institutions as they constantly regroup and attempt to reconstruct the logic of domination and incorporation. These oppositions are missing from Bourdieu's analyses.[48] What we are left with is a theory of reproduction that displays little faith in subordinate classes and groups and little hope in their ability or willingness to reconstruct the conditions under which they live, work, and learn. Consequently, most reproduction theories informed by Bourdieu's notion of domination ultimately fail to provide the comprehensive theoretical elements needed for a radical pedagogy.

Hegemonic-State Reproductive Model

Recently Marxist theorists have argued that understanding the role of the State is central to any analysis of how domination operates.[49] Thus, a major concern now among a number of educational theorists focuses on the complex role of state intervention in the educational system.[50] These theorists believe that educational change cannot be understood by looking only at capital's domination of the labor process or the way capitalist domination is reproduced through culture. Neither of these explanations, they claim, has given adequate attention to the underlying structural determinants of inequality that characterize the advanced industrial countries of the West. They argue that such accounts display little understanding of how political factors lead to State interventionist policies that serve to structure and shape the reproductive functions of education.

In spite of the agreement among reproductive theorists about the importance of the State, there are significant differences among them as to what the State actually is, how it works, and what the precise relationship is between the State and capital, on the one hand, and the State and education on the other. Michael Apple captures the complexity of this issue in his review of some of the major questions with which theorists of the State are currently grappling. He writes:

> Does the state only serve the interests of capital or is it more complex than that? Is the State instead an arena of class conflict and a site where hegemony must be worked for, not a foregone conclusion where it is simply imposed? Are schools—as important sites of the State—simply "ideological state apparatuses" (to quote Althusser), ones whose primary role is to reproduce the ideological and "manpower" requirements of the social relations of production? Or, do they also embody contradictory tendencies and provide sites where ideological struggles within and among classes, races, and sexes can and do occur?[51]

It is not my intent to unravel how different theorists of the State deal with these issues. Instead, I will focus on two major themes. First, I will explore some of the dynamics that characterize the relationship between the State and capitalism. Second, I will explore some of the underlying dynamics at work in the relationship between the State and schooling.

The State and capitalism. One of the major assumptions in Marxist accounts regarding the relationship between the State and capitalism has been developed around the work of the late Italian theorist, Antonio Gramsci.[52] For Gramsci, any discussion about the State had to begin with the reality of class relations and the exercise of hegemony by the dominant classes. Gramsci's dialectical formulation of hegemony as an ever-changing combination of force and consent provides the basis for analyzing the nature of the State in capitalist society.

Hegemony, in Gramsci's terms, appears to have two meanings. First, it refers to a process of domination whereby a ruling class exercises control through its intellectual and moral leadership over allied classes.[53] In other words, an alliance is formed among ruling classes as a result of the power and "ability of one class to articulate the interest of other social groups to its own."[54] Hegemony in this instance signifies, first, a pedagogic and politically transformative process whereby the dominant class articulates the common elements embedded in the world views of allied groups. Second, hegemony refers to the dual use of force and ideology to reproduce societal relations between dominant classes and subordinate groups. Gramsci strongly emphasizes the role of ideology as an active force used by dominant classes to shape and incorporate the commonsense views, needs, and interests of subordinate groups. This is an important issue. Hegemony in this account represents more than the exercise of coercion: it is a process of continuous creation and includes the constant structuring of consciousness as well as a battle for the control of consciousness. The production of knowledge is linked to the political sphere and becomes a central element in the State's construction of power. The primary issue for Gramsci centers around demonstrating how the State can be defined, in part, by referring to its active involvement as a repressive and cultural (educative) apparatus.

This brings us directly to Gramsci's definition of the State. Rejecting orthodox Marxist formulations of the State as merely the repressive tool of the dominant classes, Gramsci divides the State into two specific realms: political society and civil society. Political society refers to the state apparatuses of administration, law, and other coercive institutions whose primary, though not exclusive, function is based on the logic of force and repression. Civil society refers to those private and public institutions that rely upon meanings, symbols, and ideas to universalize ruling-class ideologies, while simultaneously shaping and limiting oppositional discourse and practice.

Two issues need to be stressed in conjunction with Gramsci's view of the State. All state apparatuses have coercive and consensual functions; it is the dominance of one function over the other that gives the apparatuses of either political or civil society their defining characteristic. Furthermore, as a mode of ideological control, hegemony—whether it takes place in the schools, the mass media, or the trade unions—must be fought for constantly in order to be maintained. It is not something "that simply consists of the projection of the ideas of the dominant classes into the heads of the subordinate classes."[55] The footing on which hegemony moves and functions has to shift ground in order to accommodate the changing nature of historical circumstances and the complex demands and critical actions of human beings. This view of the function of the State redefines class rule and the complex use of power. Power as used here is both a positive and a negative force. It functions negatively in the repressive and ideological apparatuses of the government and civil society to reproduce the relations of domination. It functions positively as a feature of active opposition and struggle, the terrain on which men and women question, act, and refuse to be incorporated into the logic of capital and its institutions.

In short, Gramsci provides a definition of the State that links power and culture to the traditional Marxist emphasis on the repressive aspects of the State. Gramsci is rather succinct on this issue: "The state is the entire complex of practical and theoretical activities with which the ruling class not only justifies and maintains its dominance, but manages to win the active consent of those over whom it rules."[56]

Gramsci's writings are crucial to an understanding of the meaning and workings of the State and have influenced a wide range of Marxist writers who argue that "all state formations under capitalism articulate class power."[57] The crucial starting point for many of these theorists is a sustained attack on the liberal assumption that the State is a neutral, administrative structure that operates in the interests of the general will. This attack generally takes the form of an historical critique that rejects the liberal notion of the State as a naturally evolving structure of human progress which stands above class and sectional interests. Marxist critics have argued in different ways that the State is a specific set of social relations linked historically to the conditions of capitalist production. In effect, the State is an organization, an embodiment of a changing pattern of class relations organized around the dynamics of class struggle, domination, and contestation. Furthermore, as a set of relations organized around class divisions, the State expresses ideological and economic interests through repressive as well as legitimating institutions. "The State is not a structure, it is an organization; or better, it is a complex of social forms organized so that it inflects all relations and ideas about relations in such a way that capitalist production, and all it entails, becomes thought of as lived and natural."[58]

This leads to a related and important issue concerning the defining features of the State's operation. Theorists such as Nicos Poulantzas have rightly argued that the State and its various agencies, including public schools, cannot be seen merely as tools manipulated at will by the ruling classes.[59] On the contrary, as the concrete representation of class relations, the State is constituted through continuing conflicts and contradictions, which, it can be argued, take two primary forms. First, there are conflicts among different factions of the ruling class, who often represent varied and competing approaches to social control and capital accumulation. But it is important to note that the relative autonomy of the State, secured partly through the existence of competing dominant classes, often tends to obscure what various factions of the ruling class have in common. That is, the State's short-term policies are firmly committed to maintaining the underlying economic and ideological structures of capitalist society. Thus, behind the discourse of diverging political, sectional, and social interests, there is the underlying grammar of class domination and structured inequality. Dominant classes may battle over the size of the military budget, monetary cutbacks in social services, and the nature of the tax structure, but they do not challenge basic capitalist production relations.

The definitive feature of the relative autonomy of the State is to be found, then, not in its chorus of oppositional discourses, but in its structured silences regarding the underlying basis of capitalist society. Moreover, the State is defined less by the interest of any one dominant group than by the specific set of social relations it mediates and sustains. Claus Offe and Volker Ronge summarize this position well: "What the State protects and sanctions is a set of rules and social relations which are presupposed by the class rule of the capitalist class. The State does not defend the interests of one class but the common interests of all members of a capitalist society."[60]

The second defining feature of the State centers around the relationship between the dominant and dominated classes. The State is not only an object of struggle among members of the ruling class, it is also a defining force in the production of conflict and struggle between the ruling class and other subordinate groups. The underlying logic of State formation is situated in the State's dual role of performing the often contradictory tasks of establishing the conditions for the accumulation of capital, on the one hand, and the ideological task of moral regulation on the other. In other words, the State has the task of meeting the basic needs of capital by providing, for instance, the necessary flow of workers, knowledge, skills, and values for the reproduction of labor power.[61] But at the same time, the State has the task of winning the consent of the dominated classes, which it attempts by legitimating the social relations and values that structure the capital accumulation process either through remaining silent about the class interests that benefit from such relations, or through marginalizing or disqualifying any serious critique or alternative to them. Furthermore, the State attempts to win the consent of the working class for its policies by making an appeal to three types of specific outcomes—economic (social mobility), ideological (democratic rights), and psychological (happiness). Philip Corrigan and his colleagues point to this issue in their argument:

> We stress that the State is constructed and fought over. Central to this is a two fold set of historical practices: (i) the constant "rewriting" of history to naturalize what has been, in fact, an extremely changeable set of State relations, to claim that there is, and has always been, one "optimal institutional structure" which is what "any" civilization needs; and (ii) to marginalize (disrupt, deny, destroy, dilute, "help") all alternative forms of State, particularly any which announces any form of organization that established difference at the level of the national social formation (or crime of all crimes!, that established any form of international solidarity along class lines).[62]

The contradictions that arise out of the differences between the reality and the promise of capitalist social relations are evident in a number of instances, some of which directly involve schooling. For example, schools often promote an ideology of social mobility that is at odds with high levels of unemployment and the overabundance of highly qualified workers. Furthermore, the ideology of the work ethic is often contradicted by the increasing number of routinized and alienating jobs. In addition, capitalism's appeal to the satisfaction of higher needs often rests on an image of leisure, beauty, and happiness, the fulfillment of which lies beyond the capabilities of the existing society.

What emerges from this analysis of the relationship between the State and the economy are a number of crucial issues that have a significant bearing on educational policy and practice. First, it is rightly claimed that the State is neither the instrument of any one dominant class faction nor simply a pale reflection of the needs of the economic system. Second, the State is accurately portrayed as a site marked by ongoing conflicts among and between various class, gender, and racial groups. Third, the State is not merely an expression of class struggle, it is primarily an organization that actively defends capitalist society through repressive as well as ideological means. Finally, in its capacity as an ideological and repressive apparatus, the State limits and channels the responses that schools can make to the ideology, culture, and practices that characterize the dominant society. The following section contains a more detailed examination of these issues.

The State and schooling. In order to adequately investigate the relationship between the State and schooling, two questions need to be posed and analyzed. How does the State exercise control over schools in terms of its economic, ideological, and repressive functions? How does the school function not only to further the interests of the State and the dominant classes but also to contradict and resist the logic of capital?

As part of the state apparatus, schools and universities play a major role in furthering the economic interests of the dominant classes. Several theorists have argued that schools are actively involved in establishing the conditions for capital accumulation, and they point specifically to a number of instances in which the State intervenes to influence this process.[63] For example, through state-established certification requirements, educational systems are heavily weighted toward a highly technocratic rationality that relies upon a logic drawn primarily from the natural sciences. The effects can be seen in the distinction schools at all levels make between high-status knowledge—usually the "hard sciences"—and low-status knowledge—subjects in the humanities. This bias also puts pressures on schools to utilize methods of inquiry and evaluation that stress efficiency, prediction, and the logic of the mathematical formula. The extent of State intervention is obvious in the favorable political orientation exercised through small- and large-scale government funding for educational research programs. Apple, for instance, illuminates this point:

> The state will take on the large initial cost of basic research and development. It then "transfers" the fruits of it back to the "private sector" once it becomes profitable. The state's role in capital accumulation is very evident in its subsidization of the production of technical/administrative knowledge.... Like the economy, examples of this pattern of intervention are becoming more visible. They include the emphasis on competency-based education, systems management, career education, futurism (often a code word for manpower planning), continued major funding for mathematics and science curriculum development (when compared to the arts), national testing programs.... All of these and more signal the sometimes subtle and sometimes quite overt role of state intervention into schooling to attempt to maximize efficient production of both the agents and the knowledge required by an unequal economy.[64]

The rationality that supports state intervention into schools also influences the development of curricula and classroom social relations the success of which is often measured against how well they "equip" different groups of students with the knowledge and skills they will need to perform productively in the workplace. Moreover, beneath the production of this type of curriculum and socialization there is the brute reality that schools function partly to keep students out of the labor force. As Dale points out, "schools keep children off the streets, and insure that for a large part of most days in the year they cannot engage in activities which might disrupt a social context amenable to capital accumulation but are exposed to attempts to socialize them into ways compatible with the maintenance of that context."[65]

State intervention is also manifested in the way policy is formulated outside of the control of teachers and parents. The economic interest underlying such policy is present not only in the rationality of control, planning, and other bureaucratic emphases on rule-following but also in the way in which the State funds programs to handle what Apple calls "negative outcomes" in the accumulation process.

> By defining large groups of children as deviant (slow learners, remedial problems, discipline problems, etc.), and giving funding and legislative support for special teachers and for "diagnosis" and for "treatment" the state will fund extensive remedial projects. While these projects seem neutral, helpful, and may seem aimed at increasing mobility, they will actually defuse the debate over the role of schooling in the reproduction of the knowledge and people "required" by society. It will do this in part by defining the ultimate causes of such deviance as within the child or his or her culture and not due to, say, poverty, the conflicts and disparities generated by the historically evolving cultural and economic hierarchies of the society, etc. This will be hidden from us as well by our assumption that schools are primarily organized as distribution agencies, instead of, at least in part, important agencies in the accumulation process.[66]

One of the major questions pursued by educational theorists studying the State focuses on the relationship between power and knowledge—specifically, how the State "exercises and imposes its power through the production of 'truth' and 'knowledge' about education."[67] Poulantzas, for example, argues that the production of dominant ideologies in the schools is to be found not only in the high-status knowledge and social relations sanctioned by the State bureaucracy but, more importantly, in the reproduction of the mental-manual division. The State appropriates, trains, and legitimates "intellectuals" who serve as experts in the production and conception of school knowledge, and who ultimately function to separate knowledge from both manual work and popular consumption. Behind this facade of credentialized expertise and professionalism lies a major feature of dominant ideology—the separation of knowledge from power. Poulantzas states, "The knowledge-power relationship finds expression in particular techniques of the exercise of power—exact devices inscribed in the texture of the State whereby the popular masses are permanently kept at a distance from the centres of decision making. These comprise a series of rituals and styles of speech, as well as structural modes of formulating and tackling problems that monopolise knowledge in such a way that the popular masses are effectively excluded."[68]

This separation becomes more pronounced in the special status that state certification programs and schools give to curriculum "experts"; the underlying logic of this status suggests that teachers should implement rather than conceptualize and develop curriculum approaches. The knowledge-power relation also finds expression in the active production and distribution of knowledge itself. For instance, one of the main roles of the schools is to valorize mental labor and disqualify manual labor. This division finds its highest representation in forms of tracking, classroom social relations, and other aspects of school legitimation that function to exclude and devalue working-class history and culture. Furthermore, this division between mental and manual labor underlies the school's socializing process which prepares working-class and other students for their respective places in the work force.

Schools, of course, do more than mediate the logic of domination, and this can be seen in the contradictions that emerge around the ideology of democratic rights often reproduced in the school curriculum. Schools play an active role in legitimating the view that politics and power are primarily defined around the issues of individual rights and through the dynamics of the electoral process. Central to this liberal ideology of democratic rights are assumptions that define the political sphere and the role of the State in that sphere. The importance of this ideology as a contradictory part of the hegemonic curriculum cannot be overstated. On the one hand, it functions to separate the issues of politics and democracy from the economic sphere and to displace the notion of conflict from its class-specific social context to the terrain of individual rights and struggle. On the other hand, there is a certain counter-logic in democratic liberal ideology that provides the basis for resistance and conflict. That is, liberal democratic ideology contains concerns for human rights that are often at odds with capitalist rationality, its ethos of commodity fetish, and its drive for profits.

Finally, it must be remembered that the most direct intervention exercised by the State is constituted by law. Though impossible to discuss here in detail, this intervention often takes forms which link schools to the logic of repression rather than ideological domination. One instance of this linkage is that the foundation of school policy is sometimes established in the courts, such as the push towards racial integration of public schooling. Another instance is that school attendance is established through the rule of law and provides the "legal" cement that brings students into the schools. Relatedly, it is the courts, the police, and other state agencies that attempt to enforce involuntary school attendance. Of course, involuntary school attendance does not guarantee student obedience, and in some respects becomes a major issue promoting student resistance, a fact often forgotten by resistance theorists.

In conclusion, it must be emphasized that theories of the State perform a theoretical service by adding to our understanding of how the processes of social and cultural reproduction function in the political sphere. They rightly draw our attention to the importance of the relative autonomy of the State and its apparatuses (such as schools), the contradictory character of the State, and the economic, ideological, and repressive pressures the State exerts on schooling. But it must be acknowledged that, as part of a wider theory of reproduction, hegemonic-state accounts exhibit some major theoretical failings. First, theories of the State focus primarily on macro and structural issues, resulting in a mode of analysis that points to contradictions and struggle, but says little about how human agency works through such conflicts at the level of everyday life and concrete school relations. A second failing is that some theories of the State display little understanding of culture as a relatively autonomous realm with its own inherent counter-logic. For instance, Poulantzas's heavy-handed notion of the school as merely an ideological state apparatus provides no theoretical space for investigating the emergence and dynamics of student counter-cultures as they develop in the interplay of concrete, antagonistic school relations.[69] Culture is, however, both the subject and object of resistance; the driving force of culture is contained not only in how it functions to dominate subordinate groups, but also in the way in which oppressed groups draw from their own cultural capital and set of experiences to develop an oppositional logic. Despite theoretical lip service to the contrary, this dialectical view of culture is often subsumed within a view of power that leans too heavily on the logic of domination in defining culture simply as an *object* of resistance rather than its *source*. In order to obtain a more concrete view of the dynamics of resistance and struggle as they inform subordinate school cultures operating under the ideological and material constraints partly constructed by the State, it is necessary to turn to theories of resistance.

Schooling and Theories of Resistance

The concept of resistance is relatively new in educational theory. The reasons behind this theoretical neglect can be traced partly to the failings of both conservative and radical approaches to schooling. Conservative educators analyzed oppositional behavior primarily through psychological categories that served to define such behavior not only as deviant, but more importantly, as disruptive and inferior—a failing on the part of the individuals and social groups that exhibited it. Radical educators, on the other hand, have

27

generally ignored the internal workings of the school and have tended to treat schools as "black boxes." Beneath a discourse primarily concerned with the notions of domination, class conflict, and hegemony, there has been a structured silence regarding how teachers, students, and others live out their daily lives in schools. Consequently, there has been an overemphasis on how structural determinants promote economic and cultural inequality, and an underemphasis on how human agency accommodates, mediates, and resists the logic of capital and its dominating social practices.

More recently, a number of educational studies have emerged that attempt to move beyond the important but somewhat limited theoretical gains of reproduction theory. Taking the concepts of conflict and resistance as starting points for their analyses, these accounts have sought to redefine the importance of mediation, power, and culture in understanding the complex relations between schools and the dominant society. Consequently, the work of a number of theorists has been instrumental in providing a rich body of detailed literature that integrates neo-Marxist social theory with ethnographic studies in order to illuminate the dynamics of accommodation and resistance as they work through countercultural groups both inside and outside schools.[70]

Resistance, in these accounts, represents a significant critique of school as an institution and points to social activities and practices whose meanings are ultimately political and cultural. In contrast to a vast amount of ethnographic literature on schooling in both the United States and England, neo-Marxist resistance theories have not sacrificed theoretical depth for methodological refinement.[71] That is, recent neo-Marxist studies have not followed the method of merely providing overly-exhaustive descriptive analyses of the internal workings of the school. Instead, they have attempted to analyze how determinant socioeconomic structures embedded in the dominant society work through the mediations of class and culture to shape the antagonistic experiences of students' everyday lives. Rejecting the functionalism inherent in both conservative and radical versions of educational theory, neo-Marxist accounts have analyzed curricula as a complex discourse that not only serves the interests of domination but also contains aspects which provide emancipatory possibilities.

The attempt to link social structures and human agency in order to explore the way they interact in a dialectical manner represents a significant advance in educational theory. Of course, neo-Marxist resistance theories are also beset with problems, and I will mention some of the more outstanding ones here. Their singular achievement is the primary importance they allot to critical theory and human agency as the basic categories to be used in analyzing the daily experiences that constitute the internal workings of the school.

Central to theories of resistance is an emphasis on the tensions and conflicts that mediate relationships among home, school, and workplace. For example, Willis demonstrates in his study of the "lads"—a group of working class males who constitute the "counterculture" in an English secondary school—that much of their opposition to the labels, meanings, and values of the official and hidden curriculum is informed by an ideology of resistance, the roots of which are in the shop-floor cultures occupied by their family members and other members of their class.[72] The most powerful example of this mode of resistance is exhibited by the lads in their rejection of the primacy of mental over manual labor. Not only do the lads reject the alleged superiority of mental labor, they also reject its underlying ideology that respect and obedience will be exchanged for knowledge and success. The lads oppose this ideology because the counter-logic embodied in the families, workplaces, and street life that make up *their* culture points to a different and more convincing reality. Thus, one major contribution that has emerged from resistance studies is the insight that the mechanisms of reproduction are never complete and are always faced with partially realized elements of opposition.

Furthermore, this work points to a dialectical model of domination, one that offers valuable alternatives to many of the radical models of reproduction analyzed previously. Instead of seeing domination as simply the by-product of external forces—for example, capital or the State—resistance theorists have developed a notion of reproduction in which working-class subordination is viewed not only as a result of the structural and ideological constraints embedded in capitalist social relationships, but also as part of the process of self-formation within the working class itself.

One key issue posed by this notion of domination is the question, How does the logic that promotes varied forms of resistance become implicated in the logic of reproduction? For example, theories of resistance have attempted to demonstrate how students who actively reject school culture often display a deeper logic and view of the world that confirms rather than challenges existing capitalist social relations. Two illustrations demonstrate this point. Willis's lads rejected the primacy of mental labor and its ethos of individual appropriation, but in doing so they closed off any possibility of pursuing an emancipatory relationship between knowledge and dissent. By rejecting intellectual labor, the lads discounted the power of critical thinking as a tool of social transformation.[73]

The same logic is displayed by the students in Michelle Fine's study of dropouts from alternative high schools in New York City's South Bronx.[74] Fine had assumed that the students who dropped out of these schools were victims of "learned helplessness," but she discovered instead that they were the most critical and politically astute students in the alternative schools: "Much to our collective surprise (and dismay) the dropouts were those students who were most likely to identify injustice in their social lives and at school, and most ready to correct injustice by criticizing or challenging a teacher. The dropouts were least depressed, and had attained academic levels equivalent to students who remained in school."[75] There is a certain irony here: while such students were capable of challenging the dominant ideology of the school, they failed to recognize the limits of their own resistance. By leaving school, these students placed themselves in a structural position that cut them off from political and social avenues conducive to the task of radical reconstruction.

Another important and distinctive feature of resistance theories is their emphasis on the importance of culture and, more specifically, cultural production. In the concept of cultural production we find the basis for a theory of human agency, one that is constructed through the active, ongoing, collective medium of oppressed groups' experiences. In a more recent work, Willis elaborates on this issue, arguing that the notion of cultural production

> insists on the active, transformative natures of cultures and on the collective ability of social agents, not only to think like theorists, but to act like activists. Life experiences, individual and group projects, secret illicit and informal knowledge, private fears and fantasies, the threatening anarchic power arising from irreverent association are not merely interesting additions.... These things are central: determined but also determining. They must occupy, fully fledged in their own right, a vital theoretical and political transformative stage in our analyses. This is, in part, the project of showing the capacities of the working class to generate albeit ambiguous, complex, and often ironic, collective and cultural forms of knowledge not reducible back to the bourgeois forms and the importance of this as one of the bases for political change.[76]

As Willis suggests, theories of resistance point to new ways of constructing a radical pedagogy by developing analyses of the ways in which class and culture combine to offer the outlines for a "cultural politics." At the core of such a politics is a semiotic reading of the style, rituals, language, and systems of meaning that inform the cultural terrains of subordinate groups. Through this process, it becomes possible to analyze what counterhegemonic elements such cultural fields contain, and how they tend to become incorporated into the dominant culture and subsequently stripped of their political possibilities. Implicit in such an analysis is the need to develop strategies in schools in which oppositional cultures might be rescued from the processes of incorporation in order to provide the basis for a viable political force. An essential element of such a task, which has been generally neglected by radical educators, is the development of a radical pedagogy that links a politics of the concrete not just with the processes of reproduction but also with the dynamics of social transformation. The possibility for such a task already exists and is present in the attempt by resistance theorists to view the cultures of subordinate groups as more than simply the by-product of hegemony and defeat.[77]

Another important feature of resistance theory is a deeper understanding of the notion of relative autonomy. This notion is developed through a number of analyses that point to those nonreproductive moments that constitute and support the critical notion of human agency. As I have mentioned, resistance theory assigns an active role to human agency and experience as key mediating links between structural determinants and lived effects. Consequently, there is the recognition that different spheres or cultural sites—schools, families, mass media—are governed by complex ideological properties that often generate contradictions both within and among them. At the same time, the notion of ideological domination as all-encompassing and unitary in its form and content is rejected, and it is rightly argued that dominant ideologies themselves are often contradictory, as are different factions of the ruling classes, the institutions that serve them, and the subordinate groups under their control.

In considering the weaknesses in theories of resistance, I will make several criticisms which represent starting points for the further development of a critical theory of schooling. First, although studies of resistance point to those social sites and "spaces" in which the dominant culture is encountered and challenged by subordinate groups, they do not adequately conceptualize the historical development of the conditions that promote and reinforce contradictory modes of resistance and struggle. What is missing in this perspective are analyses of those historically and culturally mediated factors that produce a *range* of oppositional behaviors, some of which constitute resistance and some of which do not. Put simply, not all oppositional behavior has "radical significance," nor is all oppositional behavior a clear-cut response to domination. The issue here is that there have been too few attempts by educational theorists to understand how subordinate groups embody and express a combination of reactionary and progressive behaviors—behaviors that embody ideologies both underlying the structure of social domination and containing the logic necessary to overcome it.

Oppositional behavior may not be simply a reaction to powerlessness, but might be an expression of power that is fueled by and reproduces the most powerful grammar of domination. Thus, on one level, resistance may be the simple appropriation and display of power, and may manifest itself through the interests and discourse of the worst aspects of capitalist rationality. For example, students may violate school rules, but the logic that informs such behavior may be rooted in forms of ideological hegemony such as racism and sexism. Moreover, the source of such hegemony often originates outside of the school. Under such circumstances, schools become social sites where oppositional behavior is simply played out, emerging less as a critique of schooling than as an expression of dominant ideology.

This becomes clearer in Angela McRobbie's account of sixth-form female students in England who, by aggressively asserting their own sexuality, appear to be rejecting the official ideology of the school with its sexually repressive emphasis on neatness, passivity, compliance, and "femininity."[78] Their opposition takes the form of carving boyfriends' names on school desks, wearing makeup and tight-fitting clothes, flaunting their sexual preferences for older, more mature boys, and spending endless amounts of time talking about boys and boyfriends. It could be argued that this type of oppositional behavior, rather than suggesting resistance, primarily displays an oppressive mode of sexism. Its organizing principle appears to be linked to social practices informed by the objective of developing a sexual, and ultimately successful, marriage. Thus, it appears to underscore a logic that has little to do with resistance to school norms and a great deal to do with the sexism that characterizes working-class life and mass culture in general. This is not to say that such behavior can simply be written off as reactionary. Obviously, the fact that these young women are acting collectively and attempting to define for themselves what they want out of life contains an emancipatory moment. But in the final analysis, this type of opposition is informed by a dominating, rather than liberating, logic.

This leads to a related issue. Resistance theories have gone too far in viewing schools as institutions characterized exclusively by forms of ideological domination. Lost from this view is an insight provided by theorists who deal with the hegemonic-state reproductive model: the notion that schools are also repressive institutions that use various coercive state agencies, including the police and the courts, to enforce involuntary school attendance. The point here is that resistance theories must recognize that in some cases students may be totally indifferent to the dominant ideology of the school with its respective rewards and demands. Their behavior in school may be fueled by ideological imperatives that signify issues and concerns that have very little to do with school directly. School simply becomes the place where the oppositional nature of these concerns is expressed.

In short, oppositional behaviors are produced amid contradictory discourses and values. The logic that informs a given act of resistance may, on the one hand, be linked to interests that are class-, gender-, or race-specific. On the other hand, it may express the repressive moments inscribed in such behavior by the dominant culture rather than a message of protest against their existence. To understand the nature of such resistance, we must place it in a wider context to see how it is mediated and articulated in the culture of such oppositional groups. Because of a failure to understand the dialectical nature of resistance, most theories of education have treated the concept somewhat superficially. For instance, when domination is stressed in such studies, the portrayals of schools, working-class students, and classroom pedagogy often appear too homogeneous and static to be taken seriously. When resistance is discussed, its contradictory nature is usually not analyzed seriously, nor is the contradictory consciousness of the students and teachers treated dialectically.[79]

A second weakness in theories of resistance is that they rarely take into account issues of gender and race. As a number of feminists have pointed out, resistance studies, when analyzing domination, struggle, and schooling, generally ignore women and gender issues and focus instead on males and class issues.[80] This has meant that women are either disregarded altogether or are included only in terms that echo the sentiments of the male counter-cultural groups being portrayed. This raises a number of important problems that future analyses must resolve. One problem is that such studies have failed to account for the notion of patriarchy as a mode of domination that both cuts across various social sites and mediates between men and women within and between different social class formations. The point here, of course, is that domination is not singularly informed or exhausted by the logic of class oppression, nor does it affect men and women in similar ways. Women, though in different degrees, experience dual forms of domination in both the home and the workplace. How the dynamics of these forms are interconnected, reproduced, and mediated in schools represents an important area of continuing research. Another problem is that these studies contain no theoretical room for exploring forms of resistance that are race- and gender-specific, particularly as these mediate the sexual and social divisions of labor in various social sites such as schools. The failure to include women and racial minorities in such studies has resulted in a rather uncritical theoretical tendency to romanticize modes of resistance even when they contain reactionary racial and gender views. The irony here is that a large amount of neo-Marxist work on resistance, although allegedly committed to emancipatory concerns, ends up contributing to the reproduction of sexist and racist attitudes and practices.

A third weakness characterizing theories of resistance, as Jim Walker points out, is that they have focused primarily on overt acts of rebellious student behavior.[81] By so limiting their analyses, resistance theorists have ignored less obvious forms of resistance among students and have often misconstrued the political value of overt resistance. For example, some students minimize their participation in routine school practices while simultaneously displaying outward conformity to the school's ideology, opting for modes of resistance that are quietly subversive in the most immediate sense, but that have the potential to be politically progressive in the long run. These students may use humor to disrupt a class, use collective pressure to draw teachers away from class lessons, or purposely ignore the teacher's directions while attempting to develop collective spaces that allow them to escape the ethos of individualism permeating school life. Each type of behavior can indicate a form of resistance if it emerges out of a latent or overt ideological condemnation of the underlying repressive ideologies that characterize schools in general. That is, if we view these acts as practices involving a conscious or semiconscious political response to school-constructed relations of domination, then these students are resisting school ideology in a manner that gives them the power to reject the system on a level that will not make them powerless to protest it in the future. They have not renounced access to knowledge and skills that may allow them to move beyond the class-specific positions of dead-end, alienating labor that most of the showy rebels will eventually occupy.[82]

What resistance theorists have failed to acknowledge is that some students are able to see through the lies and promises of the dominant school ideology but decide not to translate this insight into extreme forms of rebelliousness. In some cases the reason for this decision may be an understanding that overt rebelliousness may result in powerlessness now and in the future. Needless to say, they may also go through school on their own terms and still face limited opportunities in the future. But what is of major importance here is that any other alternative seems ideologically naive and limits whatever transcendent hopes for the future these students may have.[83]

It is the tension between the present reality of their lives and their willingness to dream of a better world that makes such students potential political leaders. Of course, in some cases students may not be aware of the political grounds of their position toward school, except for a general awareness of its dominating nature and the need to somehow escape from it without relegating themselves to a future they do not want. Even this vague understanding and its attendant behavior portend a politically progressive logic, a logic that needs to be incorporated into a theory of resistance.

A fourth weakness of theories of resistance is that they have not given enough attention to the issue of how domination reaches into the structure of personality itself. There is little concern with the often contradictory relation between understanding and action. Part of the solution to this problem may lie in uncovering the genesis and operation of those socially constructed needs that tie people to larger structures of domination. Radical educators have shown a lamentable tendency to ignore the question of needs and desires in favor of issues that center around ideology and consciousness. A critical psychology is needed that points to the way in which "un-freedom" reproduces itself in the psyche of human beings. We need to understand how dominating ideologies prevent many-sided needs from developing in the oppressed, or, in other words, how hegemonic ideologies function to exclude oppressed groups from creating needs that extend beyond the instrumental logic of the market. I am concerned here with such radical needs as those that represent the vital drive toward new relationships between men and women, the generations, different races, and humanity and nature. More specifically, we need to understand how to substitute radical needs organized around the desire for meaningful work, solidarity, an aesthetic sensibility, eros, and emancipatory freedoms for the egoistic, aggressive, calculable greed of capitalist interests. Alienating need structures—those dimensions of our psyche and personality that tie us to social practices and relationships that perpetuate systems of exploitation and the servitude of humanity—represent one of the most crucial areas from which to address a radical pedagogy.

The question of the historical genesis and transformation of needs constitutes, in my mind, the most important basis for a theory of radical educational praxis. Until educators can point to possibilities for the development "of radical needs that both challenge the existing system of interest and production and point to an emancipated society,"[84] it will be exceptionally difficult to understand how schools function to incorporate people, or what that might mean to the establishment of a basis for critical thinking and responsible action. Put another way, without a theory of radical needs and critical psychology, educators have no way of understanding the grip and force of alienating social structures as they manifest themselves in the lived but often nondiscursive aspects of everyday life.[85]

Toward a Theory of Resistance

Resistance is a valuable theoretical and ideological construct that provides an important focus for analyzing the relationship between school and the wider society. More importantly, it provides a new means for understanding the complex ways in which subordinate groups experience educational failure, pointing to new ways of thinking about and restructuring modes of critical pedagogy. As I have noted, the current use of the concept of resistance by radical educators suggests a lack of intellectual rigor and an overdose of theoretical sloppiness. It is imperative that educators be more precise about what resistance actually is and what it is not, and be more specific about how the concept can be used to develop a critical pedagogy. It is also clear that a rationale for employing the concept needs to be considered more fully. I will now discuss these issues and briefly outline some basic theoretical concerns for developing a more intellectually rigorous and politically useful foundation for pursuing such a task.

In the most general sense, resistance must be grounded in a theoretical rationale that provides a new framework for examining schools as social sites which structure the experiences of subordinate groups. The concept of resistance, in other words, represents more than a new heuristic catchword in the language of radical pedagogy; it depicts a mode of discourse that rejects traditional explanations of school failure and oppositional behavior and shifts the analysis of oppositional behavior from the theoretical terrains of functionalism and mainstream educational psychology to those of political science and sociology. Resistance in this case redefines the causes and meaning of oppositional behavior by arguing that it has little to do with deviance and learned helplessness, but a great deal to do with moral and political indignation.

Aside from shifting the theoretical ground for analyzing oppositional behavior, the concept of resistance points to a number of assumptions and concerns about schooling that are generally neglected in both traditional views of schooling and radical theories of reproduction. First, it celebrates a dialectical notion of human agency that rightly portrays domination as a process that is neither static nor complete. Concomitantly, the oppressed are not seen as being simply passive in the face of domination. The notion of resistance points to the need to understand more thoroughly the complex ways in which people mediate and respond to the connection between their own experiences and structures of domination and constraint. Central categories that emerge in a theory of resistance are intentionality, consciousness, the meaning of common sense, and the nature and value of nondiscursive behavior. Second, resistance adds new depth to the notion that power is exercised on and by people within different contexts that structure interacting relations of dominance and autonomy. Thus, power is never unidimensional; it is exercised not only as a mode of domination, but also as an act of resistance. Last, inherent in a radical notion of resistance is an expressed hope for radical transformation, an element of transcendence that seems to be missing in radical theories of education which appear trapped in the theoretical cemetery of Orwellian pessimism.

In addition to developing a rationale for the notion of resistance, there is a need to formulate criteria against which the term can be defined as a central category of analysis in theories of schooling. In the most general sense, I think resistance must be situated in a perspective that takes the notion of emancipation as its guiding interest. That is, the nature and meaning of an act of resistance must be defined by the degree to which it contains possibilities to develop what Herbert Marcuse termed "a commitment to an emancipation of sensibility, imagination and reason in all spheres of subjectivity and objectivity."[86] Thus, the central element of analyzing any act of resistance must be a concern with uncovering the degree to which it highlights, implicitly or explicitly, the need to struggle against domination and submission. In other words, the concept of resistance must have a revealing function that contains a critique of domination and provides theoretical opportunities for self-reflection and struggle in the interest of social and self-emancipation. To the degree that oppositional behavior suppresses social contradictions while simultaneously merging with, rather than challenging, the logic of ideological domination, it does not fall under the category of resistance, but under its opposite—accommodation and conformism. The value of the concept of resistance lies in its critical function and in its potential to utilize both the radical possibilities embedded in its own logic and the interests contained in the object of its expression. In other words, the concept of resistance represents an element of difference, a counter-logic, that must be analyzed to reveal its underlying interest in freedom and its rejection of those forms of domination inherent in the social relations against which it reacts. Of course, this is a rather general set of standards upon which to ground the notion of resistance, but it does provide a notion of interest and a theoretical scaffold upon which to make a distinction between forms of oppositional behavior that can be used for either the amelioration of human life or for the destruction and denigration of basic human values.

Some acts of resistance reveal quite visibly their radical potential, while others are rather ambiguous; still others may reveal nothing more than an affinity for the logic of domination and destruction. It is the ambiguous area that I want to analyze briefly, since the other two areas are self-explanatory. Recently, I heard a "radical" educator argue that teachers who rush home early after school are, in fact, committing acts of resistance. She also claimed that teachers who do not adequately prepare for their classroom lessons are participating in a form of resistance as well. Of course, it is equally debatable that the teachers in question are simply lazy or care very little about teaching, and that what in fact is being displayed is not resistance but unprofessional and unethical behavior. In these cases, there is no logical, convincing response to either argument. The behaviors displayed do not speak for themselves. To call them resistance is to turn the concept into a term that has no analytical precision. In cases like these, one must either link the behavior under analysis with an interpretation provided by the subjects themselves, or dig deeply into the historical and relational conditions from which the behavior develops. Only then will the interest embedded in such behavior be revealed.

It follows from my argument that the interests underlying a specific form of behavior may become clear once the nature of that behavior is interpreted by the person who exhibits it. But I do not mean to imply that such interests will automatically be revealed. Individuals may not be able to explain the reasons for their behavior, or the interpretation may be distorted. In this case, the interest underlying such behavior may be illuminated against the backdrop of social practices and values from which the behavior emerges. Such a referent may be found in the historical conditions that prompted the behavior, the collective values of a peer group, or the practices embedded in other social sites such as the family, the workplace, or the church. I want to stress that the concept of resistance must not be allowed to become a category indiscriminately hung over every expression of "oppositional behavior." On the contrary, it must become an analytical construct and mode of inquiry that is self-critical and sensitive to its own interests—radical consciousness-raising and collective critical action.

Let us now return to the question of how we define resistance and view oppositional behavior, and to the implications for making such distinctions. On one level, it is important to be theoretically precise about which forms of oppositional behavior constitute resistance and which do not. On another level, it is equally important to argue that all forms of oppositional behavior represent a focal point for critical analysis and should be analyzed to see if they represent a form of resistance by uncovering their emancipatory interests. This is a matter of theoretical precision and definition. On the other hand, as a matter of radical strategy, *all* forms of oppositional behavior, whether actually resistance or not, must be examined for their possible use as a basis for critical analysis. Thus, oppositional behavior becomes the object of both theoretical clarification and the subject of pedagogical considerations.

On a more philosophical level, I want to stress that the theoretical construct of resistance rejects the positivist notion that the meaning of behavior is synonymous with a literal reading based on immediate action. Instead, resistance must be viewed from a theoretical starting point that links the display of behavior to the interest it embodies, going beyond the immediacy of behavior to the interest that underlies its often hidden logic, a logic that also must be interpreted through the historical and cultural mediations that shape it. Finally, I want to emphasize that the ultimate value of the notion of resistance must be measured not only by the degree to which it promotes critical thinking and reflective action but, more importantly, by the degree to which it contains the possibility of galvanizing collective political struggle among parents, teachers, and students around the issues of power and social determination.

I will now briefly discuss the value of a dialectical notion of resistance for a critical theory of schooling. The pedagogical value of resistance lies, in part, in the connections it makes between structure and human agency on the one hand and culture and the process of self-formation on the other. Resistance theory rejects the idea that schools are simply instructional sites by not only politicizing the notion of culture, but also by analyzing school cultures within the shifting terrain of struggle and contestation. In effect, this represents a new theoretical framework for understanding the process of schooling which places educational knowledge, values, and social relations within the context of antagonistic relations and examines them within the interplay of dominant and subordinate school cultures. When a theory of resistance is incorporated into radical pedagogy, elements of oppositional behavior in schools become the focal point for analyzing different, and often antagonistic, social relations and experiences among students from dominant and subordinate cultures. Within this mode of critical analysis, it becomes possible to illuminate how students draw on the limited resources at their disposal in order to reaffirm the positive dimensions of their own cultures and histories.

Resistance theory highlights the complexity of student responses to the logic of schooling. Thus, it highlights the need for radical educators to unravel how oppositional behavior often emerges within forms of contradictory consciousness that are never free from the reproductive rationality embedded in capitalist social relations. A radical pedagogy, then, must recognize that student resistance in all of its forms represents manifestations of struggle and solidarity that, in their incompleteness, both challenge and confirm capitalist hegemony. What is most important is the willingness of radical educators to search for the emancipatory interests that underlie such resistance and to make them visible to students and others so that they can become the object of debate and political analysis.

A theory of resistance is central to the development of a radical pedagogy for other reasons as well. It helps bring into focus those social practices in schools whose ultimate aim is the control of both the learning process and the capacity for critical thought and action. For example, it points to the ideology underlying the hegemonic curriculum, to its hierarchically organized bodies of knowledge, and particularly to the way in which this curriculum marginalizes or disqualifies working-class knowledge as well as knowledge about women and minorities. Furthermore, resistance theory reveals the ideology underlying such a curriculum, with its emphasis on individual rather than collective appropriation of knowledge, and how this emphasis drives a wedge between students from different social classes. This is particularly evident in the different approaches to knowledge supported in many working-class and middle-class families. Knowledge in the working-class culture is often constructed on the principles of solidarity and sharing, whereas within middle-class culture, knowledge is forged in individual competition and is seen as a badge of separateness.

In short, resistance theory calls attention to the need for radical educators to unravel the ideological interests embedded in the various message systems of the school, particularly those embedded in its curriculum, systems of instruction, and modes of evaluation. What is most important is that resistance theory reinforces the need for radical educators to decipher how the forms of cultural production displayed by subordinate groups can be analyzed to reveal both their limitations and their possibilities for enabling critical thinking, analytical discourse, and learning through collective practice.

Finally, resistance theory suggests that radical educators must develop a critical rather than a pragmatic relationship with students. This means that any viable form of radical pedagogy must analyze how the relations of domination in schools originate, how they are sustained, and how students, in particular, relate to them. This means looking beyond schools. It suggests taking seriously the counter-logic that pulls students away from schools into the streets, the bars, and the shopfloor culture.[87] For many working-class students, these realms are "real time" as opposed to the "dead time" they often experience in schools. The social spheres that make up this counter-logic may represent the few remaining terrains that provide the oppressed with the possibility of human agency and autonomy. Yet, these terrains appear to represent less a form of resistance than an expression of solidarity and self-affirmation.

The pull of this counter-logic must be critically engaged and built into the framework of a radical pedagogy. Yet, this is not to suggest that it must be absorbed into a theory of schooling. On the contrary, it must be supported by radical educators and others from both inside and outside of schools. But as an object of pedagogical analysis, this counter-logic must be seen as an important theoretical terrain in which one finds fleeting images of freedom that point to fundamentally new structures in the public organization of experience.

Inherent in the oppositional public spheres that constitute a counter-logic are the conditions around which the oppressed organize important needs and relations. Thus, it represents an important terrain in the ideological battle for the appropriation of meaning and experience. For this reason, it provides educators with an opportunity to link the political with the personal in order to understand how power is mediated, resisted, and reproduced in daily life. Furthermore, it situates the relationship between schools and the larger society within a theoretical framework informed by a fundamentally political question, How do we develop a radical pedagogy that makes schools meaningful so as to make them critical, and how do we make them critical so as to make them emancipatory?

In short, the basis for a new radical pedagogy must be drawn from a theoretically sophisticated understanding of how power, resistance, and human agency can become central elements in the struggle for critical thinking and learning. Schools will not change society, but we can create in them pockets of resistance that provide pedagogical models for new forms of learning and social relations—forms which can be used in other spheres more directly involved in the struggle for a new morality and view of social justice. To those who would argue that this is a partisan goal, I would reply that they are right, for it is a goal that points to what should be the basis of all learning—the struggle for a qualitatively better life for all.

Notes

1. Marx, *Capital,* I (Moscow: Progress Publishers, 1969), pp. 531, 532.

2. For a critical analysis of the significance of Marx's notion of reproduction in social theory, see Henri Lebevre, *The Survival of Capitalism,* trans. Frank Bryant (New York: St. Martin's Press, 1973). For a critical review of the literature on schooling that takes the notion of reproduction as its starting point see Michael Apple, *Ideology and Curriculum* (London: Routledge & Kegan Paul, 1979); Henry A. Giroux, *Ideology, Culture and the Process of Schooling* (Philadelphia: Temple Univ. Press, 1981); Geoff Whitty and Michael Young, ed., *Society, State, and Schooling* (Sussex, Eng.: Falmer Press, 1977); Len Barton, Roland Meighan, and Stephen Walker, ed., *Schooling, Ideology and Curriculum* (Sussex, Eng.: Falmer Press, 1980); Samuel Bowles and Herbert Gintis, *Schooling in Capitalist America* (New York: Basic Books, 1977).

3. Willis, "Cultural Production and Theories of Reproduction," in *Race, Class and Education,* ed. Len Barton and Stephen Walker (London: Croom-Helm, 1983), p. 110.

4. Bowles and Gintis.

5. Jean Anyon, "Social Class and the Hidden Curriculum of Work," *Journal of Education, 162* (1980), 67–92.

6. Pierre Bourdieu and Jean Claude Passeron, *Reproduction in Education, Society, and Culture* (Beverly Hills, Calif.: Sage, 1977).

7. Nicos Poulantzas, *Classes in Contemporary Society* (London: Verso Books, 1978).

8. Representative examples include Michael Apple, *Education and Power* (London: Routledge & Kegan Paul, 1982); Richard Bates, "New Developments in the New Sociology of Education," *British Journal of Sociology of Education,* 1 (1980), 67–79; Robert W. Connell, Dean J. Ashenden, Sandra Kessler, and Gary W. Dowsett, *Making the Difference* (Sydney: Allen & Unwin, 1982); Geoff Whitty, *Ideology, Politics, and Curriculum* (London: Open Univ. Press, 1981); Henry A. Giroux, *Theory and Resistance in Education* (South Hadley, Mass.: Bergin and Garvey, 1983).

9. Paul Willis, *Learning to Labour* (Lexington: Heath, 1977); Women's Study Group, Centre for Contemporary Cultural Studies, ed., *Women Take Issue* (London: Hutchinson, 1978); David Robins and Philip Cohen, *Knuckle Sandwich: Growing Up in a Working-Class City* (London: Pelican Books, 1978); Paul Corrigan, *Schooling and the Smash Street Kids* (London: Macmillan, 1979); Angela McRobbie and Trisha McCabe, *Feminism for Girls* (London: Routledge & Kegan Paul, 1981); Thomas Popkewitz, B. Robert Tabachnick, and Gary Wehlage, *The Myth of Educational Reform* (Madison, Wis.: Univ. of Wisconsin Press, 1982); Robert B. Everhart, "Classroom Management, Student Opposition, and the Labor Process" in *Ideology and Practice in Schooling,* ed. Michael Apple and Lois Wiess (Philadelphia: Temple Univ. Press, forthcoming); Paul Olson, "Inequality Remade: The Theory of Correspondence and the Context of French Immersion in Northern Ontario," *Journal of Education, 165* (1983), 75–78.

10. Aronowitz, "Marx, Braverman, and the Logic of Capital," *The Insurgent Sociologist, 8* (1977), 126–146.

11. Michael Apple, "The Hidden Curriculum and the Nature of Conflict," *Interchange, 2* (1971), 27–40; Henry A. Giroux and Anthony N. Penna, "Social Education in the Classroom: The Dynamics of the Hidden Curriculum," *Theory and Research in Social Education, 7 (1979), 21–42;* Henry A. Giroux and David Purpel, ed., *The Hidden Curriculum and Moral Education* (Berkeley, Calif.: McCutchan, 1983).

12. Martin Carnoy and Henry Levin, *The Limits of Educational Reform* (New York: McKay, 1976); W. Timothy Weaver, *The Contest for Educational Resources* (Lexington, Mass.: Lexington Books, 1982).

13. Kathleen Wilcox and Pia Moriarity, "Schooling and Work: Social Constraints on Educational Opportunity," in *Education: Straitjacket or Opportunity,* ed. James Benet and Arlene Kaplan Daniels (New York: Transaction Books, 1980); Roslyn Arlin Mickelson, "The Secondary School's Role in Social Stratification: A Comparison of Beverly Hills High School and Morningside High School," *Journal of Education, 162* (1980), 83–112; Jean Anyon, "Social Class and School Knowledge," *Curriculum Inquiry, 11* (1981), 3–42.

14. Bowles and Gintis, p. 131.

15. Althusser, *For Marx* (New York: Vintage Books, 1969), *Reading Capital* (London: New Left Books, 1970), and "Ideology and the Ideological State Apparatuses," in his *Lenin and Philosophy, and Other Essays,* trans. Ben Brewster (New York: Monthly Review Press, 1971).

16. Althusser, "Ideological State Apparatuses," p. 132.

17. Althusser, "Ideological State Apparatuses," pp. 148–158.

18. Althusser, "Ideological State Apparatuses," p. 162.

19. Althusser, *For Marx*, p. 233.

20. Baudelot and Establet, *L'Ecole Capitaliste en France* (Paris: Maspero, 1971).

21. *Hegemonic* as it is used here refers to elements of unconsciousness, common sense, and consciousness that are compatible with ideologies and social practices that perpetuate existing practices of domination and oppression. This is discussed in greater detail in Giroux, *Theory and Resistance*.

22. Aronowitz, "Cracks in the Bloc: American Labor's Historic Compromise and the Present Crisis," *Social Text, 5* (1982), 22–52.

23. See Henry A. Giroux, "Hegemony, Resistance, and the Paradox of Educational Reform," *Interchange, 12* (1981), 3–26.

24. James Donald, "How Illiteracy Became a Problem and Literacy Stopped Being One," *Journal of Education, 165* (1983), 35–52.

25. Bourdieu and Passeron, *Reproduction;* Bourdieu, *Outline of Theory and Practice* (Cambridge, Eng.: Cambridge Univ. Press, 1977). It must be noted that the pioneering work in this area was done by Paulo Freire, *Pedagogy of the Oppressed* (New York: Seabury Press, 1970).

26. Bourdieu and Passeron, *Reproduction;* Bourdieu, "Symbolic Power," *Critique of Anthropology, 4* (1979), 77–85.

27. Bourdieu, "Symbolic Power," p. 30.

28. Bourdieu and Passeron, *Reproduction,* p. 178.

29. Bourdieu, "The School as a Conservative Force: Scholastic and Cultural Inequalities," in *Contemporary Research in the Sociology of Education,* ed. John Eggleston (London: Methuen, 1974), p. 39.

30. The hegemonic curriculum refers to the way in which "schools are organized around a particular organization of learning and content.... The crucial features of this curriculum are hierarchically-organized bodies of academic knowledge appropriated in individual competition" (Connell et al., *Making the Difference,* p. 120). The curriculum is hegemonic in that it functions to exclude large numbers of students who are from subordinate classes. Connell et al. were the first to use the term, while Bourdieu and his associates have demonstrated how the hegemonic curriculum works in France's system of higher education.

31. For an illuminating analysis of this issue see Jean Anyon, "Ideology and United States History Textbooks," *Harvard Educational Review, 49* (1979), 361–386; and Joshua Brown, "Into the Minds of Babes: A Journey Through Recent Children's History Books," *Radical History Review, 25* (1981), 127–145.

32. Bourdieu, *Outline of Theory and Practice;* Bourdieu, "Men and Machines," in *Advances in Social Theory and Methodology,* ed. Karin Knorr-Cetina and Aaron V. Cicourel (London: Routledge & Kegan Paul, 1981).

33. Bourdieu, "Men and Machines," p. 305.

34. Bourdieu, *Outline of Theory and Practice,* p. 83.

35. Pierre Bourdieu and Jean-Claude Passeron, *The Inheritors: French Students and Their Relation to Culture* (Chicago: Univ. of Chicago Press. 1979).

36. Bourdieu, "Men and Machines," p. 314.

37. Bourdieu, *Outline of Theory and Practice,* p. 94.

38. It must be stressed that the most important work on the politics of the body is to be found in Maurice Merleau-Ponty, *Phenomenology of Perception* (London: Routledge & Kegan Paul, 1962), esp. pp. 67–199.

39. Bourdieu, "The Economics of Linguistic Exchanges," *Social Science Information, 16* (1977), 645–668.

40. Davies, *Popular Culture, Class, and Schooling* (London: Open Univ. Press, 1981), p. 60.

41. This is particularly true in Bourdieu and Passeron's Reproduction.

42. Dale, "Education and the Capitalist State: Contributions and Contradictions," in *Cultural and Economic Reproduction in Education*, ed. Michael Apple (London: Routledge & Kegan Paul, 1982), p. 157.

43. Robert W. Connell, Dean J. Ashenden, Sandra Kessler, and Gary W. Dowsett, "Class and Gender Dynamics in a Ruling Class School," *Interchange, 12* (1981), 102–117.

44. Sieber, "The Politics of Middle-Class Success in an Inner-City School," *Journal of Education, 164* (1981), 30–47.

45. Sieber, p. 45.

46. Foucault, *Power and Knowledge: Selected Interviews and Other Writings,* ed. Colin Gordon (New York: Pantheon, 1980).

47. Noelle Bisseret, *Education, Class Language, and Ideology* (London: Routledge & Kegan Paul, 1979).

48. See esp. Bourdieu, "Cultural Reproduction and Social Reproduction," in *Power and Ideology in Education*, ed. Jerome Karabel and Albert H. Halsey (New York: Oxford Univ. Press, 1979); and Bourdieu and Passeron, Reproduction.

49. Some representative examples include Ralph Miliband, *The State and Capitalist Society* (New York: Basic Books, 1969); James O'Connor, *The Fiscal Crisis of the State* (New York: St. Martin's Press, 1973); Nicos Poulantzas, *Political Power and Social Classes* (London: New Left Books, 1973), and *Classes in Contemporary Society;* Goran Therbom, *What Does the Ruling Class Do When It Rules* (London: New Left Books, 1978); Philip Corrigan, ed., *Capitalism, State Formation, and Marxist Theory* (London: Quartet Books, 1980).

50. This is a small but growing and important body of literature. Among the more recent works are Roger Dale, Geoff Easland, and Madeleine Macdonald, ed., *Education and the State, I and II* (Sussex, Eng.: Falmer Press, 1980); Mariam E. David, *The State, the Family, and Education* (London: Routledge & Kegan Paul, 1980); Madan Sarup, *Education, State and Crisis* (London: Routledge & Kegan Paul, 1982); Apple, *Education and Power.*

51. Apple, "Reproduction and Contradiction in Education," in *Cultural and Economic Reproduction in Education*, p. 14.

52. Gramsci, *Selections from Prison Notebooks*, ed. and trans. Quintin Hoare and Geoffrey Smith (New York: International Publishers, 1971).

53. Gramsci, pp. 57–58.

54. Chantal Mouffe, "Hegemony and Ideology in Gramsci," in *Gramsci and Marxist Theory*, ed. Chantal Mouffe (London: Routledge & Kegan Paul, 1979), pp. 182–183. It is important to stress that hegemony is not a static concept; on the contrary, hegemony is an active process realized as an uneven and tenuous situation and outcome through which oppositional forces are either accommodated, constrained, or defeated. The

relationship between hegemony and political education is treated extensively in Walter Adamson, *Hegemony and Revolution: A Study of Antonio Gramsci's Political and Cultural Theory* (Berkeley: Univ. of California Press, 1980); see also Philip Wexler and Tony Whitson, "Hegemony and Education," *Psychology and Social Theory, 3* (1982), 31–42.

55. Kenneth Neild and John Seed, "The Theoretical Poverty or the Poverty of Theory," *Economy and Society, 8* (1979), 383–416.

56. Gramsci, p. 244.

57. Philip Corrigan, Harvie Ramsey, and Derek Sayer, "The State as a Relation of Production," in *Capitalism, State Formation and Marxist Theory,* ed. Philip Corrigan (London: Quartet Books, 1980), p. 21.

58. Corrigan, Ramsey, and Sayer, p. 10.

59. Poulantzas, *Classes in Contemporary Society.* For an important discussion of Marxist theories of the State and the issue of relative autonomy, see Ralph Miliband, "State Power and Class Interests," *New Left Review, 138* (1983), 57–68.

60. Offe and Ronge, "Thesis on the Theory of the State," *New German Critique, 6* (1975), 137–147.

61. Althusser, "Ideological State Apparatuses," pp. 127–186.

62. Corrigan, Ramsey, and Sayer, p. 17.

63. See esp. Martin Carnoy, "Education, Economy and the State"; Roger Dale, "Education and the Capitalist State," in *Cultural and Economic Reproduction in Education.*

64. Apple. *Education and Power,* pp. 54–55.

65. Dale, pp. 146–147.

66. Apple, *Education and Power,* p. 95.

67. James Donald, "Green Paper: Noise of a Crisis," *Screen Education, 30* (1979), 13–49.

68. Poulantzas, quoted in Donald, "Green Paper," p. 21.

69. Poulantzas, *Classes in Contemporary Society,* pp. 259–270.

70. See, for example, Willis, *Learning to Labour;* McRobbie and McCabe, *Feminism for Girls;* Robins and Cohen, *Knuckle Sandwich;* Dick Hebdige, *Subculture: The Meaning of Style* (London: Methuen, 1980).

71. Representative examples of the ethnographic literature in the United States include Howard Becker, *Boys in White* (Chicago: Univ. of Chicago Press, 1961); Arthur Stinchombe, *Rebellion in a High School* (New York: Quadrangle Books, 1964); Harry Wolcott, *The Man in the Principal's Office: An Ethnography* (New York: Holt, Rinehart and Winston, 1973); George Spindler, ed., *Ethnography of Schooling* (New York: Holt, Rinehart and Winston, 1982). Works from England include David Hargreaves, *Social Relations in a Secondary School* (London: Routledge & Kegan Paul, 1967); Colin Lacey, *Hightown Grammar* (Manchester: Manchester Univ. Press, 1970); Peter Woods, *The Divided School* (London: Routledge & Kegan Paul, 1979); Stephen Ball, *Beachside Comprehensive: A Case Study of Secondary Schooling* (London: Cambridge Univ. Press, 1981).

72. Willis, *Learning to Labour,* pp. 99–116.

73. Willis, *Learning to Labour,* pp. 89–116.

74. Fine, "Examining Inequity: View from Urban Schools," Univ. of Pennsylvania, Unpublished Manuscript, 1982.

75. Fine, p. 6.

76. Willis, "Cultural Production and Theories of Reproduction," p. 114.

77. It is important to stress that the opposition displayed by a subordinate group must be seen not only as a form of resistance but also as an expression of a group's struggle to constitute its social identity.

78. Angela McRobbie, "Working Class Girls and the Culture of Femininity," in *Women Take Issue.*

79. A representative example of the work I am criticizing can be found in Nancy King, "Children's Play as a Form of Resistance in the Classroom," *Journal of Education, 164* (1982), 320–329; Valerie Suransky, "Tale of Rebellion and Resistance: The Landscape of Early Institutional Life," *Journal of Education* (forthcoming). There is a certain irony in that these articles are organized around the concept of resistance without ever providing a rigorous theoretical definition of what the term means.

80. See, for example, Angela McRobbie, "Settling Accounts with Subcultures," *Screen Education, 34* (1980), 37–49.

81. Walker, "Rebels with Our Applause: A Critique of Resistance Theories," *Journal of Education* (forthcoming).

82. Willis, *Learning to Labour,* pp. 190–137.

83. See Willis, *Learning to Labour,* chs. 8 and 9; Connell et al., *Making the Difference,* ch. 5.

84. Jean Cohen, review of *Theory and Need in Marx,* by Agnes Heller, *Telos, 33* (1977), 170–184.

85. For an excellent analysis of the relationship between Marxist theory and psychoanalysis, see the differing interpretations by Richard Lichtman, *The Production of Desire* (New York: Free Press, 1982); and Russell Jacoby, *Social Amnesia* (Boston: Beacon Press, 1973).

86. Marcum, *The Aesthetic Dimension* (Boston: Beacon Press, 1977).

87. I am indebted to a conversation with Stanley Aronowitz for this insight regarding the idea of counter-logic. For an elaborated analysis of this idea, see his *Crisis in Historical Materialism* (New York: Preager, 1981).

2
Border Pedagogy in the Age of Postmodernism

⌁

Within the last two decades, the varied discourses known as postmodernism have exercised a strong influence on the nature of intellectual life both in and out of the university. As a form of cultural criticism, postmodernism has challenged a number of assumptions central to the discourse of modernism. These include modernism's reliance on metaphysical notions of the subject, its advocacy of science, technology, and rationality as the foundation for equating change with progress, its ethnocentric equation of history with the triumphs of European Civilization, and its globalizing view that the industrialized Western countries constitute "a legitimate center—a unique and superior position from which to establish control and to determine hierarchies" (Richard, 1987/1988, p. 6). From the postmodernist perspective, modernism's claim to authority partly serves to privilege Western, patriarchal culture, on the one hand, while simultaneously repressing and marginalizing the voices of those who have been deemed subordinate and/or subjected to relations of oppression because of their color, class, ethnicity, race, or cultural and social capital. In postmodernist terms, the political map of modernism is one in which the voice of the other is consigned to the margins of existence, recognition, and possibility. At its best, a critical postmodernism wants to redraw the map of modernism so as to effect a shift in power from the privileged and the powerful to those groups struggling to gain a measure of control over their lives in what is increasingly becoming a world marked by a logic of disintegration (Dews, 1987). Postmodernism not only makes visible the ways in which domination is being prefigured and redrawn, it also points to the shifting configurations of power, knowledge, space, and time that characterize a world that is at once more global and more differentiated.

One important aspect of postmodernism is its recognition that, as we move into the 21st century, we find ourselves no longer constrained by modernist images of progress and history. In the postmodern era, the elements of discontinuity, rupture, and difference provide alternative sets of referents by which to understand modernity as well as challenge and modify it. This is a world in which capital no longer is restricted by the imperatives of nationalism; it is a culture in which the production of electronic information radically alters traditional notions of time, community, and history while simultaneously blurring the distinction between reality and image. In the postmodern age, it becomes more difficult not only to define cultural differences in hegemonic colonialist notions of worth and possibility but also to define meaning and knowledge through the master narratives of "great men!" Similarly, the modernist emphasis on totality and mastery has given way to a more acute understanding of suppressed and local histories along with a deeper appreciation for struggles that are contextual and specific in scope. In addition, in the age of instant information and global networking, the old distinction between high and popular culture collapses as the historically and socially constructed nature of meaning can no longer be privileged by universalizing claims to history, truth, or class. All culture is worthy of investigation, and no aspect of cultural production can escape its own history within socially constructed hierarchies of meaning.

Another important aspect of postmodernism is that it provides a series of referents both for problematizing some of the most basic elements of modernism and for redrawing and rewriting how individual and collective experience might be struggled over, understood, felt, and shaped. For example, postmodernism presents itself as a critique of all forms of representations and meanings that claim transcendental and transhistorical status. It rejects universal reason as a foundation for human affairs, and, as an alternative, poses forms of knowing that are partial, historical, and social in nature. In addition, postmodernism points to a world in which the production of meaning has become as important as the production of labor in shaping the boundaries of human existence. In this view, how we are constituted in language is no less important than how we are constructed as subjects within relations of production. The political economy of the sign does not displace political economy; it simply assumes its rightful place as a primary category for understanding how identities are forged within particular relations of privilege, oppression, and struggle. Similarly, postmodernism serves to deterritorialize the map of dominant cultural understanding. That is, it rejects the European tradition as the exclusive referent for judging what constitutes historical, cultural, and political truth. There is no tradition or story that can speak with authority and certainty for all of humanity. In contrast, critical postmodernism argues that traditions should be valued for their attempts to name the partial, the particular, the specific; in this view, traditions demonstrate the importance of constituting history as a dialogue among a variety of voices as they struggle within asymmetrical relations of power. Traditions are not valued for their claims to truth or authority, but for the ways in which they serve to liberate and enlarge human possibilities. Tradition does not represent the voice of an all-embracing view of life; instead, it serves to place people self-consciously in their histories by making them aware of the memories constituted in difference, struggle, and hope. Tradition in postmodern terms is a form of counter-memory that points to the fluid and complex identities that constitute the social and political construction of public life.

Finally, and at the risk of great simplification, a postmodernism of resistance challenges the liberal, humanist notion of the unified, rational subject as the bearer of history. In this view, the subject is neither unified nor can such a subject's action be guaranteed in metaphysical or transhistorical terms. Postmodernism not only views the subject as contradictory and multilayered; it rejects the notion that individual consciousness and reason are the most important determinants in shaping human history. It posits instead a faith in forms of social transformation that understand the historical, structural, and ideological limits that shape the possibility for self-reflection and action. It points to solidarity, community, and compassion as essential aspects of how we develop and understand the capacities we have for how we experience the world and ourselves in a meaningful way. More specifically, postmodernism offers a series of referents for rethinking how we are constituted as subjects within a rapidly changing set of political, social, and cultural conditions.

What does this suggest for the way we look at the issue of pedagogy? I believe that by combining the best insights of modernism and postmodernism, educators can deepen and extend what is generally referred to as critical pedagogy. We need to combine the modernist emphasis on the capacity of individuals to use critical reason to address the issue of public life with a critical postmodernist concern with how we might experience agency in a world constituted in differences unsupported by transcendent phenomena or metaphysical guarantees. In that way, critical pedagogy can reconstitute itself in terms that are both transformative and emancipatory. This is not to suggest that critical pedagogy constitutes a monolithic discourse and corresponding set of robotlike methods. In fact, the discourse of critical pedagogy as it has developed over the last decade incorporates a variety of theoretical positions that differ in both methodological focus and ideological orientation (Apple & Beyer, 1988; Giroux & McLaren, 1989; Pinar, 1988).

At its worst, critical pedagogy as a form of educational criticism has been overly shaped by the discourse of modernism. Increasingly reduced to a modernist emphasis on technique and procedure, some versions of critical pedagogy reduce its liberatory possibilities by focusing almost exclusively on issues of dialogue, process, and exchange. In this form, critical pedagogy comes perilously close to emulating the liberal-progressive tradition in which teaching is reduced to getting students to merely express or assess their own experiences (e.g., Shor, 1979). Teaching collapses in this case into a banal notion of facilitation, and student experience becomes an unproblematic vehicle for self-affirmation and self-consciousness. Within this perspective, it is assumed that student experience produces forms of understanding that escape the contradictions that inform them. Understanding the limits of a particular position, engaging its contradictory messages, or extending its insights beyond the limits of particular experiences is lost in this position. This position both over-privileges the notion of student voice and simultaneously refuses to engage its contradictory nature. Moreover, this position lacks any sense of its own political project as a starting point from which to define both the role of the teacher in such a pedagogy and the role that the school should play with respect to the larger society. In this version of critical pedagogy, there is a flight from authority and a narrow definition of politics that abandons the utopian project of educating students to both locate themselves in their particular histories and simultaneously confront the limits of their own perspectives as part of a broader engagement with democratic public life.

At its best, critical pedagogy is developed as a cultural practice that enables teachers and others to view education as a political, social, and cultural enterprise. That is, as a form of engaged practice, critical pedagogy calls into question forms of subordination that create inequities among different groups as they live out their lives. Likewise, it rejects classroom relations that relegate difference as an object of condemnation and oppression, and it refuses to subordinate the purpose of schooling to narrowly defined economic and instrumental considerations. This is a notion of critical pedagogy that equates learning with the creation of critical rather than merely good citizens. This is a pedagogy that links schooling to the imperatives of democracy, views teachers as engaged and transformative intellectuals, and makes the notion of democratic difference central to the organization of curriculum and the development of classroom practice.

In what follows, I want to advance the most useful and transformative aspects of this version of critical pedagogy by articulating a theory of what I call a border pedagogy of postmodern resistance. Within this perspective, the issue of critical pedagogy is located within those broader cultural and political considerations that are beginning to redefine our traditional view of community, language, space, and possibility. It is a pedagogy that is attentive to developing a democratic public philosophy that respects the notion of difference as part of a common struggle to extend the quality of public life. In short, the notion of border pedagogy presupposes not merely an acknowledgment of the shifting borders that both undermine and reterritorialize different configurations of power and knowledge; it also links the notion of pedagogy to a more substantive struggle for a democratic society. It is a pedagogy that attempts to link an emancipatory notion of modernism with a postmodernism of resistance.

Border Pedagogy as a Counter-text

Border pedagogy offers the opportunity for students to engage the multiple references that constitute different cultural codes, experiences, and languages. This means educating students not only to read these codes critically but also to learn the limits of such codes, including the ones they use to construct their own narratives and histories. Partiality becomes, in this case, the basis for recognizing the limits built into all discourses and necessitates taking a critical view of authority. Within this discourse, a student must engage knowledge as a border-crosser, as a person moving in and out of borders constructed around coordinates of difference and power (Hicks, 1988). These are not only *physical* borders, they are *cultural* borders historically constructed and socially organized within maps of rules and regulations that limit and enable particular identities, individual capacities, and social forms. In this case, students cross over into borders of meaning, maps of knowledge, social relations, and values that are increasingly being negotiated and rewritten as the codes and regulations which *organize* them become destabilized and reshaped. Border pedagogy decenters as it remaps. The terrain of learning becomes inextricably linked to the shifting parameters of place, identity, history, and power.

Within critical social theory, it has become commonplace to argue that knowledge and power are related, though the weight of the argument has often overemphasized how domination works through the intricacies of this relationship (Foucault, 1977b). Border pedagogy offers a crucial theoretical and political corrective to this insight. It does so by shifting the emphasis of the knowledge/power relationship away from the limited emphasis on the mapping of domination to the politically strategic issue of engaging the ways in which knowledge can be remapped, reterritorialized, and de-centered in the wider interests of rewriting the borders and coordinates of an oppositional cultural politics. This is not an abandonment of critique as much as it is an extension of its possibilities. In this case, border pedagogy not only incorporates the postmodern emphasis on criticizing official texts and using alternative modes of representation (mixing video, photography, and print); it also incorporates popular culture as a serious object of politics and analysis and makes central to its project the recovery of those forms of knowledge and history that characterize alternative and oppositional Others (Said, 1983). How these cultural practices might be taken up as pedagogical practices has been demonstrated by a number of theorists (Brodkey & Fine, 1988; Cherryholmes, 1988; Giroux & Simon, 1988; Scholes, 1985).

For example, Robert Scholes (1985) develops elements of a "border pedagogy" around the notion of textual power. According to Scholes, texts have to be seen in historical and temporal terms and not treated as a sacred vehicle for producing eternal truths. Instead of simply imparting information to students, Scholes argues that teachers should replace teaching texts with what he calls textuality. What this refers to pedagogically is a process of textual study that can be identified by three forms of practice: reading, interpretation, and criticism, which roughly correspond to what Scholes calls reading within, upon, and against a text. In brief, reading within a text means identifying the cultural codes that structure an author's work. But it also has the pedagogical value of illuminating further how such codes function as part of a student's own attempt "to produce written texts that are 'within' the world constructed by their reading" (p. 27). This is particularly important, Scholes adds, in giving students the opportunity to "retell the story, to summarize it, and to expand it!" Interpretation means reading a text along with a variety of diverse interpretations that represent a second commentary on the text. At issue here is the pedagogical task of helping students to analyze texts within "a network of relations with other texts and institutional practices" so as to make available to students "the whole intertextual system of relations that connects one text to others—a system that will finally include the student's own writing" (Scholes, 1985, p. 30). The first two stages of Scholes's pedagogical practice are very important because they demonstrate the need for students to sufficiently engage and disrupt the text. He wants students to read the text in terms that the author might have intended so as not to make the text merely a mirror image of the student's own subjective position, but at the same time he wants students to open the text up to a wide variety of readings so it can be "sufficiently other for us to interpret it and, especially to criticize it" (Scholes, 1985, p. 39). Finally, Scholes wants students to explode the cultural codes of the text through the assertion of the reader's own textual power, to analyze the text in terms of its absences, to free "ourselves from [the] text [by] finding a position outside the assumptions upon which the text is based" (p. 62). Scholes combines the best of postmodern criticism with a notion of modernity in his notion of pedagogy. He wants, on the one hand, to engage texts as semiotic objects but, on the other, he employs a modernist concern for history by arguing that the point of such an interrogation is to "liberate us from the empirical object whether institution, event, or individual work—by displacing our attention to its constitution as an object and its relationship to the other objects constituted" (Scholes, 1985, p. 84).

Another example of how a postmodern pedagogy of resistance might inform the notion of border pedagogy can be found in some of the recent work being done on educational theory and popular culture (Giroux & Simon, 1988; Giroux & Simon, 1989). Two important issues are being worked out. First, there is a central concern for understanding how the production of meaning is tied to emotional investments and the production of pleasure. In this view, it is necessary for teachers to incorporate into their pedagogies a theoretical understanding of how the production of meaning and pleasure become mutually constitutive of who students are, how they view themselves, and how *they* construct a particular vision of their future. Second, rethinking the nature of how students make semantic and emotional investments needs to be theorized within a number of important pedagogical considerations.

One such consideration is that the production and regulation of desire must be seen as a crucial aspect of how students mediate, relate, resist, and create particular cultural forms and forms of knowing. Another concern is that popular culture be seen as a legitimate aspect of the everyday lives of students and be analyzed as a primary force in shaping the various and often contradictory subject positions that students take up. Finally, popular culture needs to become a serious object of study in the official curriculum. This can be done by treating popular culture either as a distinct object of study within particular academic disciplines such as media studies or by drawing upon the resources it produces for engaging various aspects of the official curriculum (Simon & Giroux, 1988).

In both of these examples, important elements of a border pedagogy informed by postmodern criticism point to ways in which those master narratives based on white, patriarchal, and class-specific versions of the world can be challenged critically and effectively deterritorialized. That is, by offering a theoretical language for establishing new boundaries with respect to knowledge most often associated with the margins and the periphery of the cultural dominant, postmodern discourses open up the possibility for incorporating into the curriculum a notion of border pedagogy in which cultural and social practices need no longer be mapped or referenced solely on the basis of the dominant models of Western culture. In this case, knowledge forms emanating from the margins can be used to redefine the complex, multiple, heterogeneous realities that constitute those relations of difference that make up the experiences of students who often find it impossible to define their identities through the cultural and political codes of a single, unitary culture.

The sensibility which informs this view of knowledge emphasizes a pedagogy in which students need to develop a relationship of non-identity with respect to their own subject positions and the multiple cultural, political, and social codes which constitute established boundaries of power, dependency, and possibility. In other words, such a pedagogy emphasizes the non-synchronous relationship between one's social position and the multiple ways in which culture is constructed and read. That is, there is no single, predetermined relationship between a cultural code and the subject position that a student occupies. One's class, racial, gender, or ethnic position may influence but does not irrevocably predetermine how one takes up a particular ideology, reads a particular text, or responds to particular forms of oppression. Border pedagogy recognizes that teachers, students, and others often "read and write culture on multiple levels" (Kaplan, 1987, p. 187). Of course, the different subject positions and forms of subjugation that are constituted within these various levels and relations of culture have the potential to isolate and alienate instead of opening up the possibility for criticism and struggle. What is at stake here is developing a border pedagogy that can fruitfully work to break down those ideologies, cultural codes, and social practices that prevent students from recognizing how social forms at particular historical conjunctures operate to repress alternative readings of their own experiences, society, and the world.

Border Pedagogy as Counter-Memory

Postmodernism charts the process of deterritorialization as part of the break-down of master narratives. It celebrates, in part, the loss of certainty and experience of *defamiliarization* even as it produces alienation and the displace-ment of identities (Deleuze & Guattari, 1986). In opposition to conservative readings of this shifting destabilizing process, I believe that such a disruption of traditional meaning offers important insights for developing a theory of border pedagogy based on a postmodernism of resistance. But this language runs the risk of undercutting its own political possibilities by ignoring how a language of difference can be articulated with critical modernist concerns for developing a discourse of public life. It also ignores the possibilities for developing, through the process of counter-memory, new and emancipatory forms of political identity. In what follows, I address some of the important work being done in radical public philosophy and feminist theory paying particular attention to the issues of identity and counter-memory. The brief final section of this paper will offer some considerations of how the critical insights of a postmodernism of resistance can be deepened within a theory of border pedagogy.

Postmodernism has launched a major attack on the modernist notion of political universality (Ross, 1988). By insisting on the multiplicity of social positions, it has seriously challenged the political closure of modernity with its divisions between the center and the margins and in doing so has made room for those groups generally defined as the excluded others. In effect, postmodernism has reasserted the importance of the partial, the local, and the contingent, and in doing so it has given general expression to the demands of a wide variety of social movements. Postmodernism has also effectively challenged the ways in which written history has embodied a number of assumptions that inform the discourse of Eurocentrism. More specifically, it has rejected such Eurocentric assumptions as the pretentious claim to "speak" for all of mankind *(sic)* and the epistemological claims to foundationalism.

Laclau (1988) rightfully argues that an adequate approximation of the postmodern experience needs to be seen as part of a challenge to the discourses of modernity, with their "pretension to intellectually dominate the foundation of the social, to give a rational context to the notion of the totality of history, and to base in the latter the project of global human emancipation" (pp. 71–72). But Laclau also points out that the postmodern

challenge to modernity does not represent the abandonment of its emancipatory values so much as it opens them up to a plurality of contexts and
an indeterminacy "that redefines them in an unpredictable way" (p. 72).
Chantal Mouffe (1988) extends this insight and argues that modernity has
two contradictory aspects: its political project is rooted in a conception of
the struggle for democracy, while its social project is tied to a foundationalism which fuels the process of social modernization under "the growing
domination of relations of capitalist production" (p. 32). For Mouffe, the
modernist project of democracy must be coupled with an understanding of
the various social movements and the new politics that have emerged with
the postmodern age. At the heart of this position is the need to rearticulate
the tradition of liberty and justice with a notion of radical democracy; similarly, there is a need to articulate the concept of difference as more than a
replay of liberal pluralism or a pastiche of diverse strands of interests with
no common ground to hold them together.

This is not a liberal call to harmonize and resolve differences, as critics
like Elizabeth Ellsworth (1988) wrongly argue, but an attempt to understand
differences in terms of the historical and social grounds on which they are organized. By locating differences in a particular historical and social location,
it becomes possible to understand how they are organized and constructed
within maps of rules and regulations and located within dominant social
forms which either enable or disable such differences. Differences only exist
relative to the social forms in which they are enunciated, that is, in relation
to schools, workplaces, families, as well as in relationship to the discourses
of history, citizenship, sex, race, gender, and ethnicity. To detach them from
the discourse of democracy and freedom is to remove the possibility of either
articulating their particular interests as part of a wider struggle for power or
understanding how their individual contradictory interests are developed
with historically specific conjunctures. At stake here is the need for educators
to fashion a critical politics of difference not outside but within a tradition of
radical democracy. Similarly, it is imperative for critical educators to develop
a discourse of counter-memory, not as an essentialist and closed narrative, but
as part of a utopian project that recognizes "the composite, heterogeneous,
open, and ultimately indeterminate character of the democratic tradition"
(Mouffe, 1988, p. 41). The pedagogical issue here is the need to articulate
difference as part of the construction of a new type of subject, one which
would be both multiple and democratic. Chantal Mouffe (1988) is worth
quoting at length on this issue:

> If the task of radical democracy is indeed to deepen the democratic revolution
> and to link together diverse democratic struggles, such a task requires the cre-
> ation of new subject-positions that would allow the common articulation, for
> example, of antiracism, antisexism, and anticapitalism. These struggles do not

spontaneously converge, and in order to establish democratic equivalences, a new "common sense" is necessary, which would transform the identity of different groups so that the demands of each group could be articulated with those of others according to the principle of democratic equivalence. For it is not a matter of establishing a mere alliance between given interests but of actually modifying the very identity of these forces. In order that the defense of workers' interests is not pursued at the cost of the rights of women, immigrants, or consumers, it is necessary to establish an equivalence between these different struggles. It is only under these circumstances that struggles against (authoritarian) power become truly democratic. (p. 42)

How might the issue of democracy and difference be taken up as part of a border pedagogy informed by a project of possibility? I want to argue that the discourses of democracy and difference can be taken up as pedagogical practices through what Foucault calls the notion of counter-memory. For Foucault (1977a), counter-memory is a practice which "transforms history from a judgment on the past in the name of the present truth to a 'counter-memory' that combats our current modes of truth and justice, helping us to understand and change the present by placing it in a new relation to the past" (pp. 160, 163–164). Counter-memory represents a critical reading of not only how the past informs the present but how the present reads the past. Counter-memory provides a theoretical tool to restore the connection between the language of public life and the discourse of difference. It represents an attempt to rewrite the language of resistance in terms that connect human beings within forms of remembrance that dignify public life while at the same time allowing people to speak from their particular histories and voices. Counter-memory refuses to treat democracy as merely inherited knowledge; it attempts, instead, to link democracy to notions of public life that "afford both agency and sources of power or empowering investments" (De Lauretis, 1987, p. 25). It also reasserts as a pedagogical practice the rewriting of history through the power of student voice. This points to the practice of counter-memory as a means of constructing democratic social forms that enable and disable particular subjectivities and identities; put another way, democracy in this instance becomes a referent for understanding how public life organizes differences and what this means for the ways in which schools, teachers, and students define themselves as political subjects, as citizens who operate within particular configurations of power.

In effect, the language of radical democracy provides the basis for educators not only to understand how differences are organized but also how the ground for such difference might be constructed within a political identity rooted in a respect for democratic public life (Giroux, 1988b). What is being suggested here is the construction of a project of possibility in pedagogical terms which is connected to a notion of democracy capable of mobilizing a variety of groups to develop and struggle for what Linda Alcoff (1988) calls a positive alternative vision. She writes, "As the Left should by now have learned, you cannot mobilize a movement that is only and always against: you must have a positive alternative, a vision of a better future that can motivate people to sacrifice their time and energy toward its realization" (Alcoff, 1988, pp. 418–419). If the notion of radical democracy is to function as a pedagogical practice, educators need to allow students to comprehend democracy as a way of life that consistently has to be fought for, has to be struggled over, and has to be rewritten as part of an oppositional politics. This means that democracy has to be viewed as a historical and social construction rooted in the tension between what Bruce James Smith (1985) calls remembrance and custom. I want to extend Smith's argument by developing remembrance as a form of counter-memory and custom as a form of reactionary nostalgia rooted in the loss of memory.

Custom, as Smith (1985) argues, constructs subjects within a discourse of continuity in which knowledge and practice are viewed as a matter of inheritance and transmission. Custom is the complex of ideologies and social practices that views counter-memory as subversive and critical teaching as unpatriotic. It is the ideological basis for forms of knowledge and pedagogy which refuse to interrogate public forms and which deny difference as a fundamental referent for a democratic society. According to Smith (1985), custom can be characterized in the following manner:

> The affection it enjoys and the authority it commands are prescriptive. The behavior of the person of custom is, by and large, habitual. To the question "why?" he (sic) is apt to respond simply, "This is the way it has always been done." ... A creature of habit, the person of custom does not reflect upon his condition. To the extent that a customary society "conceives" of its practice, it is likely to see it, says Pocock, as "an indefinite series of repetitions!" If the customary society is, in reality, a fluid order always in the process of adaptation, its continuity and incrementalism give rise to perceptions of changelessness and of the simple repetition of familiar motions.... Indeed, ... custom operates as if it were a second nature.... Custom is at once both more and less inclusive than remembrance. It includes things that are remembered and things that are forgotten. It is almost a definition of custom that its beginnings are lost. (pp. 15–16)

Remembrance is directed more toward specificity and struggle, it resurrects the legacies of actions and happenings, it points to the multitude of voices that constitute the struggle over history and power. Its focus is not on the ordinary but the extraordinary. Its language presents the unrepresentable, not merely as an isolated voice, but as a subversive interruption, a discursive space, that moves "against the grain" as it occupies "a view... carved in the interstices of institutions and in the chinks and cracks of the power-knowledge apparati" (De Lauretis, 1987, p. 25). Remembrance is part of a language of public life that promotes an ongoing dialogue between the past, present, and future. It is a vision of optimism rooted in the need to bear witness to history, to reclaim that which must not be forgotten. It is a vision of public life which calls for an ongoing interrogation of the past that allows different groups to locate themselves in history while simultaneously struggling to make it.

Counter-memory provides the ethical and epistemological grounds for a politics of solidarity within difference. At one level, it situates the notion of difference and the primacy of the political firmly within the wider struggle for broadening and revitalizing democratic public life. At the same time, it strips reason of its universal pretensions and recognizes the partiality of all points of view. In this perspective, the positing of a monolithic tradition that exists simply to be revered, reaffirmed, reproduced, or resisted is unequivocally rejected. Instead, counter-memory attempts to recover communities of memory and narratives of struggle that provide a sense of location, place, and identity to various dominant and subordinate groups. Counter-memory as a form of pedagogical practice is not concerned with simply marking difference as a historical construct; rather, it is concerned with providing the grounds for self-representation and the struggle for justice and a democratic society. Counter-memory resists comparison to either a humanist notion of pluralism or a celebration of diversity for its own sake. As both a pedagogical and political practice, it attempts to alter oppressive relations of power and to educate both teachers and students to the ways in which they might be complicitous with dominant power relations, victimized by them, and how they might be able to transform such relations. Abdul JanMohamed and David Lloyd (1987) are instructive on what counter-memory might mean as part of discourse of critique and transformation:

> Ethnic or gender difference must be perceived as one among a number of residual cultural elements which retain the memory of practices which have had to be and still have to be repressed in order that the capitalist economic subject may be more easily produced...! "Becoming minor" is not a question of essence but a question of positions—a subject-position that can only be defined, in the final analysis, in "political" terms, that is, in terms of the effects of economic exploitation, political disfranchisement, social manipulation, and ideological domination on the cultural formation of minority subjects and discourses. It is one of the central tasks of the theory of minority discourse to define that subject-position and explore the strengths and weaknesses, the affirmations and negations that inhere in it. (p. 11)

Remembrance as a form of counter-memory attempts to create for students the limits of any story that makes claims to predetermined endings and to expose how the transgressions in those stories cause particular forms of suffering and hardship. At the same time, remembrance as counter-memory opens up the past not as nostalgia but as the invention of stories, some of which deserve a retelling, and which speak to a very different future—one in which democratic community makes room for a politics of both difference and solidarity, for otherness stripped of subjugation, and for others fighting to embrace their own interests in opposition to sexism, racism, ethnocentrism, and class exploitation. Counter-memory is tied in this sense to a vision of public life that both resurrects the ongoing struggle for difference and situates difference within the broader struggle for cultural and social justice.

Counter-memory provides the basis and rationale for a particular kind of pedagogy but it cannot on its own articulate the specific classroom practices that can be constructed on the basis of such a rationale. The formation of democratic citizens demands forms of political identity which radically extend the principles of justice, liberty, and dignity to public spheres constituted by difference and multiple forms of community. Such identities have to be constructed as part of a pedagogy in which difference becomes a basis for solidarity and unity rather than for hierarchy, denigration, competition, and discrimination. It is to that issue that I will now turn.

Border Pedagogy and the Politics of Difference

If the concept of border pedagogy is to be linked to the imperatives of a critical democracy, as it must, it is important that educators possess a theoretical grasp of the ways in which difference is constructed through various representations and practices that name, legitimate, marginalize, and exclude the cultural capital and voices of subordinate groups in American society.

As part of this theoretical project, a theory of border pedagogy needs to address the important question of how representations and practices that name, marginalize, and define difference as the devalued Other are actively learned, interiorized, challenged, or transformed. In addition, such a pedagogy needs to address how an understanding of these differences can be used in order to change the prevailing relations of power that sustain them. It is also imperative that such a pedagogy acknowledge and critically interrogate how the colonizing of differences by *dominant* groups is expressed and sustained through representations: in which Others are seen as a deficit, in which the humanity of the Others is either cynically posited as problematic or ruthlessly denied. At the same time, it is important to understand how the experience of marginality at the level of everyday life lends itself to forms of oppositional and transformative consciousness. This is an understanding based on the need for those designated as Others to both reclaim and remake their histories, voices, and visions as part of a wider struggle to change those material and social relations that deny radical pluralism as the basis of democratic political community. For it is only through such an understanding that teachers can develop a border pedagogy, one which is characterized by what Teresa De Lauretis (1987) calls "an ongoing effort to create new spaces of discourse, to rewrite cultural narratives, and to define the terms of another perspective—a view from 'elsewhere'" (p. 25). This suggests a pedagogy in which occurs a critical questioning of the omissions and tensions that exist between the master narratives and hegemonic discourses that make up the official curriculum and the self-representations of subordinate groups as they might appear in "forgotten" or erased histories, texts, memories, experiences, and community narratives.

Border pedagogy both confirms and critically engages the knowledge and experience through which students author their own voices and construct social identities. This suggests taking seriously the knowledge and experiences that constitute the individual and collective voices by which students identify and give meaning to themselves and others and drawing upon what they know about their own lives as a basis for criticizing the dominant culture. In this case, student experience has to be first understood and recognized as the accumulation of collective memories and stories that provide students with a sense of familiarity, identity, and practical knowledge. Such experience has to be both affirmed and critically interrogated. In addition, the social and historical construction of such experience has to be affirmed and understood as part of a wider struggle for voice. But it must also be understood that while past experiences can never be denied, their most debilitating dimensions can be engaged through a critical understanding of what was at work in their construction. It is in their critical engagement that such experiences can be remade, reterritorialized in the interest of a social imagery that dignifies the best traditions and possibilities of those groups who are learning to speak from a discourse of dignity and self-governance. In her analysis of the deterritorialization of women as Other, Caren Kaplan (1987) astutely articulates this position:

> Recognizing the minor cannot erase the aspects of the major, but as a mode of understanding it enables us to see the fissures in our identities, to unravel the seams of our totalities.... We must leave home, as it were, since our homes are often sites of racism, sexism, and other damaging social practices. Where we come to locate ourselves in terms of our specific histories and differences must be a place with room for what can be salvaged from the past and made anew. What we gain is a reterritorialization; we reinhabit a world of our making (here "our" is expanded to a coalition of identities—neither universal nor particular). (pp. 187–188)

Furthermore, it is important to extend the possibilities of the often contradictory values that give meaning to students' lives by making them the object of critical inquiry—and by appropriating in a similarly critical fashion, when necessary, the codes and knowledges that constitute broader and less familiar historical and cultural traditions. At issue here is the development of a pedagogy that replaces the authoritative language of recitation with an approach that allows students to speak from their own histories, collective memories, and voices while simultaneously challenging the grounds on which knowledge and power are constructed and legitimated. Such a pedagogy contributes to making possible a variety of social forms and human capacities which expand the range of social identities that students may carry and become. It points to the importance of understanding in both pedagogical and political terms how subjectivities are produced within those social forms in which people move but of which they are often only partially conscious. Similarly, it raises fundamental questions regarding how students make particular investments of meaning and affect, how they are constituted within a triad of relationships of knowledge, power, and pleasure, and why students should be indifferent to the forms of authority, knowledge, and values that we produce and legitimate within our classrooms and university. It is worth noting that such a pedagogy not only articulates a respect for a diversity of student voices, it also provides a referent for developing a public language rooted in a commitment to social transformation.

Central to the notion of border pedagogy are a number of important pedagogical issues regarding the role that teachers might play within the interface of modern and postmodern concerns that have been taken up in this essay. Clearly, the concept of border pedagogy suggests that teachers exist within social, political, and cultural boundaries that are both multiple and historical in nature and that place particular demands on a recognition and pedagogical appropriation of differences. As part of the process of developing a pedagogy of difference, teachers need to deal with the plethora of voices, and the specificity and organization of differences that constitute any course, class, or curriculum so as to make problematic not only the stories that give meanings to the lives of their students, but also the ethical and political lineaments that inform their students' subjectivities and identities.

In part this suggests a pedagogy which does more than provide students with a language and context by which to critically engage the plurality of habits, practices, experiences, and desires that define them as part of a particular social formation within ongoing relations of domination and resistance. Border pedagogy provides opportunities for teachers to deepen their own understanding of the discourse of various others in order to effect a more dialectical understanding of their own politics, values, and pedagogy. What border pedagogy makes undeniable is the relational nature of one's own politics and personal investments. But at the same time, border pedagogy emphasizes the primacy of a politics in which teachers assert rather than retreat from the pedagogies they utilize in dealing with the various differences represented by the students who come into their classes. For example, it is not enough for teachers to merely affirm uncritically their students' histories, experiences, and stories. To take student voices at face value is to run the risk of idealizing and romanticizing them. The contradictory and complex histories and stories that give meaning to the lives of students are never innocent and it is important that they be recognized for their contradictions as well as for their possibilities. Of course, it is crucial that critical educators provide the pedagogical conditions for students to give voice to how their past and present experiences place them within existing relations of domination and resistance. Central to this pedagogical process is the important task of affirming the voices that students bring to school and challenging the separation of school knowledge from the experience of everyday life (Fine, 1987). But it is crucial that critical educators do more than allow such stories to be heard. It is equally important for teachers to help students find a language for critically examining the historically and socially constructed forms by which they live. Such a process involves more than "speaking" one's history and social formation, it also involves engaging collectively with others within a pedagogical framework that helps to reterritorialize and rewrite the complex narratives that make up one's life. This is more than a matter of rewriting stories as counter-memories, it is what Frigga Haug (1987) and her colleagues call memory-work, a crucial example of how the pedagogical functions to interrogate and retrieve rather than to merely celebrate one's voice. She writes:

> By excavating traces of the motives for our past actions, and comparing these with our present lives, we are able to expand the range of our demands and competences. Admittedly, this is not as easy as it sounds. Our stories are expressed in the language we use today. Buried or abandoned memories do not speak loudly; on the contrary we can expect them to meet us with obdurate silence. In recognition of this, we must adopt some method of analysis suited to the resolution of a key question for women; a method that seeks out the unnamed, the silent and the absent. Here too, our experience of education maps out a ready-made path of analysis; we have been taught to content ourselves with decoding texts, with search for truth in textual analysis, complemented at best by the author's own analysis. "Relearning" in this context means seeing what is not said as interesting, and the fact that it was not said as important; it involves a huge methodological leap, and demands more than a little imagination. (p. 65)

The different stories that students from all groups bring to class need to be interrogated for their absences as well as their contradictions, but they also need to be understood as more than simply a myriad of different stories. They have to be recognized as being forged in *relations of opposition* to the *dominant structures* of power. At the same time, differences among students are not merely antagonistic as Liz Ellsworth (1988) has argued. She suggests not only that there is little common ground for addressing these differences, but that separatism is the only valid political option for any kind of pedagogical and political action. Regrettably, this represents less an insight than a crippling form of political disengagement. It reduces one to paralysis in the face of such differences. It ignores the necessity of exploring differences for the specific, irreducible interests they represent, for the excesses and reactionary positions they may produce, and for the pedagogical possibilities they contain for helping students to work with other groups as part of a collective attempt at developing a radical language of democratic public life. Moreover, Ellsworth's attempt to delegitimate the work of other critical educators by claiming rather self-righteously the primacy and singularity of her own ideological reading of what constitutes a political project appears to ignore both the multiplicity of contexts and projects that characterize critical educational work and the tension that haunts all forms of teacher authority, a tension marked by the potential contradiction between being theoretically or ideologically correct and pedagogically wrong. By ignoring the dynamics of such a tension and the variety of struggles being waged under historically specific educational conditions, she degrades the rich complexity of theoretical and pedagogical processes that characterize the diverse discourses in the field of critical pedagogy. In doing so, she succumbs to the familiar academic strategy of dismissing others through the use of strawman tactics and excessive simplifications which undermine not only the strengths of her own work, but also the very nature of social criticism itself. This is "theorizing" as a form of "bad faith," a discourse imbued with the type of careerism that has become all too characteristic of many left academics.

At stake here is an important theoretical issue that is worth repeating. Knowledge and power come together not merely to reaffirm difference but also to interrogate it, to open up broader theoretical considerations, to tease out its limitations, and to engage a vision of community in which student voices define themselves in terms of their distinct social formations and their broader collective hopes. As teachers we can never inclusively speak as the Other (though we may be the Other with respect to issues of race, class, or gender), but we can certainly work with diverse Others to deepen their understanding of the complexity of the traditions, histories, knowledges, and politics that they bring to the schools. This means, as Abdul JanMohemad and David Lloyd (1987) point out, that educators need to recognize the importance of developing a theory of minority discourse which not only explores the strengths and weaknesses, affirmations, and negations that inhere in the subject positions of subordinate groups but also "involves drawing our solidarities in the form of similarities between modes of repression and modes of struggle which all minorities separately experience, and experience precisely as minorities" (JanMohamed & Lloyd, 1987, p. 11). To assume such a position is not to practice forms of gender, racial, or class-specific imperialism as Ellsworth suggests; rather, it is to create conditions within particular institutions that allow students to locate themselves and others in histories that mobilize rather than destroy their hopes for the future.

The theoretical sweep may be broad, the sentiment utopian, but it is better than wallowing in guilt or refusing to fight for the possibility of a better world. Sentimentality is no excuse for the absence of any vision for the future. Like Klee's angel in the painting "Angelus Novus," modernity provides a faith in human agency while recognizing that the past is often built on the suffering of others. In the best of the Enlightenment tradition, reason at least offers the assumption and hope that men and women can change the world in which they live. Postmodernism frays the boundaries of that world and makes visible what has often been seen as unrepresentable. The task of modernity with its faith in reason and emancipation can perhaps renew its urgency in a postmodern world, a world where difference, contingency, and power can reassert, redefine, and in some instances collapse the monolithic boundaries of nationalism, sexism, racism, and class oppression. In a world whose borders have become chipped and porous, new challenges present themselves not only to educators but to all those for whom contingency and loss of certainty do not mean the inevitable triumph of nihilism and despair but rather a state of possibility in which destiny and hope can be snatched from the weakening grasp of modernity. We live in a postmodern world that no longer has any firm—but has ever flexing—boundaries. It is a time when reason is in crisis and new political and ideological conditions exist for fashioning forms of struggle defined in a radically different conception of politics. For educators, this is as much a pedagogical issue as it is a political one. At best, it points to the importance of rewriting the relationship between knowledge, power, and desire. It points as well to the necessity of redefining the importance of difference while at the same time seeking articulations among subordinate groups and historically privileged groups committed to social transformations that deepen the possibility for radical democracy and human survival.

References

Alcoff, L. (1988). Cultural feminism vs. poststructuralism: The identity crisis in feminist theory. *Signs, 13,* 405–436.

Apple, M., & Beyer, L. (Eds.) (1988). *The curriculum: Problems, politics and possibilities.* Albany: State University of New York Press.

Brodkey, L., & Fine, M. (1988). Presence of mind in the absence of body. *Journal of Education* (this issue).

Cherryholmes, C. (1988). *Power and criticism: Poststructural investigations in education.* New York: Teachers College Press.

Deleuze, G., & Guattari, F. (1986). *Toward a minor literature.* Minneapolis: University of Minnesota Press.

De Lauretis, T. (1987). *Technologies of gender.* Bloomington: Indiana University Press.

Dews, P. (1987). *Logics of disintegration.* London: Verso Books.

Ellsworth, E. (1988). *Why doesn't this feel empowering? Working through the repressive myths of critical pedagogy.* Paper presented at the Tenth Conference on Curriculum Theory and Classroom Practice, Bergamo Conference Center, Dayton, Ohio, October 26–29, 1988.

Fine, M. (1987). Silencing in the public schools. *Language Arts, 64*(2), 157–174.

Foucault, M. (1977a). *Language, counter-memory, practice: Selected essays and interviews* (D. Bouchard, Ed.). Ithaca: Cornell University Press.

Foucault, M. (1977b). *Power and knowledge: Selected interviews and other writings* (G. Gordon, Ed.). New York: Pantheon.

Giroux, H. (1988a). *Schooling and the struggle for public life.* Minneapolis: University of Minnesota Press.

Giroux, H. (1988b). *Teachers as intellectuals.* Granby, MA: Bergin & Garvey.

Giroux, H., & McLaren, P. (1989). Introduction. In H. Giroux & P. McLaren (Eds.), *Critical pedagogy, the state, and cultural struggle.* Albany: State University of New York Press.

Giroux, H., & Simon, R. (1988). Critical pedagogy and the politics of popular culture. *Cultural Studies, 2,* 294–320.

Giroux, H., & Simon, R. (1989). *Popular culture, schooling, and everyday life.* Boston: Bergin & Garvey Press.

Haug, F., et al. (1987). *Female sexualization: A collective work of memory.* London: Verso Press.

Hicks, E. (1988). Deterritorialization and border writing. In R. Merrill (Ed.), *Ethics/ aesthetics: Post-modern positions* (pp. 47–58). Washington, DC: Maisonneuve Press.

Jameson, F. (1984). Postmodernism or the cultural logic of late capitalism. *New Left Review, No. 146,* pp. 53–93.

JanMohamed, A. (1987). Introduction: Toward a theory of minority discourse. *Cultural Critique, No. 6,* pp. 5–11.

JanMohamed, A., & Lloyd, D. (1987). Introduction: Minority discourse—what is to be done? *Cultural Critique, No. 7,* 5–17.

Kaplan, C. (1987). Deterritorialisations: The rewriting of home and exile in western feminist discourse. *Cultural Critique, No. 6,* 187–198.

Kellner, D. (1988). Postmodernism as social theory: Some challenges and problems. *Theory, Culture and Society, 5*(2 & 3), 239–269.

Kellner, D. (1989). Boundaries and borderlines: Reflections on Jean Baudrillard and critical theory. In *Jean Baudrillard: From Marxism to Postmodernism and Beyond.* Oxford: Polity Press.

Kolb, D. (1986). *The critique of pure modernity: Hegel, Heidegger, and after.* Chicago: University of Chicago Press.

Laclau, E. (1988). Politics and the limits of modernity. In A. Ross (Ed.), *Universal abandon? The politics of postmodernism* (pp. 63–82). Minneapolis: University of Minnesota Press.

Laclau, E., & Mouffe, C. (1985). *Hegemony and socialist strategy.* London: Verso Books.

Lash, S., & Urry, J. (1987). *The end of organized capitalism.* Madison: University of Wisconsin Press.

Lunn, E. (1982). *Marxism and modernism.* Berkeley: University of California Press.

Lyotard, J. (1984). *The postmodern condition.* Minneapolis: University of Minnesota Press.

McLaren, P. (1986). Postmodernism and the death of politics: A Brazilian reprieve. *Educational Theory, 36,* 389–401.

McLaren, P. (1988). *Life in schools.* New York: Longman.

Morris, M. (1988). *The pirate's fiancee: Feminism, reading, postmodernism.* London: Verso Press.

Mouffe, C. (1988). Radical democracy: Modern or postmodern? In A. Ross (Ed.), *Universal abandon? The politics of postmodernism* (pp. 31–45). Minneapolis: University of Minnesota Press.

Peller, G. (1987). Reason and the mob: The politics of representation. *Tikkun, 213,* 28–31, 92–95.

Pinar, W. (Ed.). (1988). *Contemporary curriculum discourses.* Scottsdale, AZ: Gorsuch Scarisbrick.

Richard, N. (1987/1988). Postmodernism and periphery. *Third Text, No. 2,* pp. 5–12.

Ross, A. (Ed.). (1988). *Universal abandon? The politics of postmodernism.* Minneapolis: University of Minnesota Press.

Said, E. (1983). Opponents, audiences, constituencies, and community. In H. Foster (Ed.), *The anti-aesthetic; Essays on postmodern culture* (pp. 135–139). Port Townsend, WA: Bay Press.

Scholes, R. (1985). *Textual power.* New Haven: Yale University Press.

Shor, I. (1979). *Critical teaching and everyday life.* Boston: South End Press.

Smith, B. J. (1985). *Politics and remembrance.* Princeton: Princeton University Press.

II
Cultural Studies and Cultural Politics

3
Consuming Social Change
The "United Colors of Benetton"

⤜

Diversity is good ... your culture (whoever you are) is as important as our culture (whoever we are).[1]

In spite of the alleged collapse of postmodernism as yet another theoretical fashion, the politics of representation that has occupied the center of its analysis has become indispensable for understanding how politics reaches into everyday life to mobilize particular lived experiences, desires and forms of agency. While certain versions of postmodernism may have over-estimated the degree to which the boundaries between images and reality have become blurred, it does not underestimate the expanding power of representations, texts, and images in producing identities and shaping the relationship between the self and society in an increasingly commodified world. If postmodern theory used concepts such as the "decentered subject" or "plural identities" to analyze the emergence of broader cultural and so-cial changes, mass market advertisers have seized upon the cultural logic of postmodernism to rearticulate politics and difference into the stylized world of aesthetics and consumption. Situated in a vortex of globally produced images and representations, consumer postmodernism produces meanings mediated through claims to truth represented in images that circulate in an electronic, informational hyperspace, which disassociates itself from history, context, and struggle. Images that shocked people in the past have become "the most effective way of selling commodities today."[2]

There is a certain irony in the fact that while many social theorists claim that postmodernism is dead, mass advertisers have seized upon the postmodern condition with its celebration of images, its proliferation of differences, and its fragmented notion of the subject to create pedagogical practices that offer a sense of unity amid a world increasingly devoid of any substantive discourse of community and solidarity. It is its concerted and often pernicious efforts to rearticulate the relationship among difference, human agency, and community that mass advertising increasingly succeeds in its promotional mission: to disguise the political nature of everyday life and appropriate the vulnerable new terrain of insurgent differences in the interests of a crass consumerism.

But there is more at stake here than advertising and commerce combining in the postmodern age to commodify through the ritualization of fashion that which has previously escaped its reach. More importantly, mass advertising has become the site of a representational politics that powerfully challenges our understanding of what constitutes pedagogy, the sites in which it takes place, and who speaks under what conditions through its authorizing agency. With the emergence of advertising as a global enterprise, we are witnessing a new form of violence against the public. By this I do not mean simply the intrusion of violence into designated public spheres as much as I am suggesting a "public whose essential predicate would be violence."[3] At the core of this violence are constituting principles that accentuate individualism and difference as central elements of the marketplace. Underlying this violence of the public is a notion of the social bereft of ethics, social justice, and any viable notion of democratic public cultures. Put another way, mass advertising and its underlying corporate interests represent a new stage in an effort to abstract the notion of the public from the language of ethics, history and democratic community.

The rearticulation and new intersection of advertising and commerce, on the one hand, and politics and representational pedagogy on the other, can be seen in the emergence of Benetton as one of the leading manufacturers and retailers of contemporary clothing. Benetton is important not only because of its marketing success, but also because it has taken a bold stance in attempting to use advertising as a forum to address highly charged social and political issues. Through its public statements and advertising campaigns, Benetton has brought a dangerously new dimension to corporate appropriation as a staple of postmodern aesthetics. Inviting the penetration of aesthetics into everyday life, Benetton has utilized less deterministic and more flexible approaches to design, technology, and styling. Such postmodern approaches to marketing and layout privilege contingency, plurality, and the poetics of the photographic image in an attempt to rewrite the relationship among aesthetics, commerce, and politics. Instead of depoliticizing or erasing images that vividly and, in some cases, shockingly depict social and political events, Benetton has attempted to redefine the link between commerce and politics by emphasizing both the politics of representation and the representation of politics. In the first instance, Benetton has appropriated for its advertising campaign actual news photos of social events that portray various calamities of the time. These include pictures of a duck covered with thick oil, a bloodied mafia murder victim, depictions of child labor, and a terrorist car bombing. As part of a representation of politics, Benetton struggles to reposition itself less as a producer of commodities and market retailer than as a corporate voice for a particular definition of public morality, consensus, coherence, and community. This has been more recently revealed in an advertisement campaign that depicts Senator Luciano Benetton posing nude, the accompanying text urging people of wealth to give away their "old" clothes to charity. Benetton justifies the ad by arguing, "[B]usiness has to go on for everybody. Rich people should buy new stuff and be pleased that others can profit from [their old clothes]."[4] Justice in this case is appropriated less to regulate the production of consumerism than to legitimate it.

Within Benetton's worldview, the relationship among identity formation, commerce, pedagogy, and politics is being reworked. That is, such a relationship is now used to highlight how pedagogy can be conscripted into the service of relations of identity and difference that promote an apolitical egalitarianism. The result is that Benetton offers itself as the promotional mediator of a version of the social that abstracts ethics from a history informed by diverse forms of resistance and collective struggle. Social consciousness and activism in this worldview are about purchasing merchandise, not changing oppressive relations of power.

In what follows, I want to provide a brief introduction to the history of Benetton's advertising campaign. Second, I want to analyze the structural relations and ideological rationale that inform the emergence of Benetton as a major distributor of clothing in the post-Fordist age and as a corporate advocate for a particular approach to multiculturalism and diversity. Third, I will examine in some detail what I will call the Benetton pedagogy of representation, focusing on its claim to realism and its politics of de/contextualism. In addition, I will attempt to deconstruct three of its more politically charged photo-journalistic advertisements. In conclusion, I will attempt to analyze briefly how cultural workers might challenge the implications of Benetton's pedagogy and cultural politics.

Small Beginnings and Global Controversies

All over the world Benetton stands for colorful sportswear, multiculturalism, world peace, racial harmony, and now, a progressive approach toward serious social issues.[5]

In 1965, Luciano Benetton and three siblings established a small business, Fratelli Benetton, near Treviso, Italy. Originally designed to produce colorful sweaters, the business expanded into a full range of clothing apparel and eventually developed into a $2 billion fashion empire producing 80 million pieces of clothing a year for 7,000 franchise stores in over 100 countries.

Benetton's advertising campaign over the last decade has been instrumental to its success in the fashion world. The advertising campaign is important not merely as a marker for assessing Benetton commercial success in extending its name recognition, it is crucial for understanding how the philosophy of the company has attempted to reinscribe its image within a broader set of political and cultural concerns. In 1984, Benetton hired Oliviero Toscani, an award-winning photographer, to head its advertising campaign. Given a free hand with the advertising budget, Toscani's early work focused on culturally diverse young people dressed in Benetton attire and engaging in a variety of seemingly aimless and playful acts. Linking the colors of Benetton clothes to the diverse "colors" of their customers from all over the world, Toscani attempted to use the themes of racial harmony and world peace as an articulating principle to register such differences within a wider unifying articulation. In 1990, Toscani adopted the United Colors of Benetton as a unifying trademark to promote the Benetton ideology. In 1991, Toscani initiated a publicity campaign that removed Benetton merchandise from the firm's advertising, and started using its $80 million global ad budget to publish controversial and disturbing photographs in magazines and billboards. Taking full control of the ad blitz, Toscani actually photographed many of the images that dominated the 1991 Benetton campaign. These included a number of compelling photographs that created a provocative effect: variously colored, blown-up condoms floating in the air, a nun kissing a priest on the lips, a row of test tubes filled with blood, and a newborn baby girl covered in blood and still attached to her umbilical cord. In 1992, Toscani added his most dramatic approach to combining high fashion and politics in the service of promoting the Benetton name. He selected a series of highly charged, photojournalistic images depicting, among other things, the AIDS crisis, environmental disaster, political violence, war, exile, and natural catastrophe. All of these images appeared in various journals, magazines, and billboards without commentary except for the conspicuous insertion of the green and white United Colors of Benetton logo located in the margins of the photograph.

Benetton's shift in advertising strategy between 1983 and 1991 needs to be taken up as part of a wider politics and pedagogy of representation. The earlier photographs representing children of diverse races and colors dressed in Benetton clothing have a "netherworld quality that gives the viewers the impression they're glimpsing some fashionable heaven."[6] Depicted in these photographs of children hugging and holding hands is a portrayal of racial harmony and difference that appears both banal and sterile. The studio-touched clarity and primary colors used in the advertisements render racial unity as a purely aesthetic category while eliminating racial conflict completely. In addition, these colorful images appear almost too comfortable, and seem at odds with a world marked by political, economic, and cultural conflict. Benetton's attempt to subordinate racial difference to the unifying dictates of harmony and consensus, a two-dimensional land of make believe, appears to play itself out in a pedagogical strategy that seems to be hopelessly out of touch with how racial differences are constructed within the realities of everyday life. Difference in the early ads is largely subordinated to the logic of the marketplace and commerce. In fact, such differences often depict a mocking quality towards concrete racial, social, and cultural differences as they are constituted amid hierarchical relations of struggle, power, and authority. Benetton's corporate image in this case seems strangely at odds with its own market research, which indicated that its "target customers—18–34 year old women—are more socially active and aware than any generation that precedes them."[7]

The switch in the ad campaign to the use of controversial photo-journalistic images reflects an attempt on the part of Benetton to redefine its own corporate image. In order to define itself as a company concerned with social change, Benetton suspended its use of upscale representations in its mass advertising campaign, especially in a world where "denial in the service of upbeat consumerism is no longer a workable strategy as we are continually overwhelmed by disturbing and even cataclysmic events."[8] In a postmodern world caught in the disruptive forces of nationalism, famine, violence, and war, such representations linked Benetton's image less to the imperatives of racial harmony than to the forces of cultural uniformity and yuppie colonization. Moreover, Benetton's move away from an appeal to utility to one of social responsibility provides an object lesson in how promotional culture increasingly uses pedagogical practices to shift its emphasis from selling a product to selling an image of corporate responsibility.[9] Given the increase in sales, profits, and the widespread publicity Benetton has received, the campaign appears to have worked wonders.

The response to the campaign inaugurated in 1991 was immediate. Benetton was both condemned for its appropriation of serious issues to sell goods and praised for incorporating serious social concerns into its advertising campaign. In many cases, a number of the Benetton ads were either banned from particular countries or refused by specific magazines. One of the most controversial ads portrayed AIDS patient David Kirby, surrounded by his family shortly before he died. The Kirby ad became the subject of heated debate among a variety of groups in a number of countries. While consumers and critics of Benetton's advertising campaign have complained that the company is exploiting human tragedy, Benetton has aggressively defended its policies by either condemning the criticism as a form of censorship or criticizing other ad companies for producing advertising that merely engages in the most reductionistic forms of pragmatism. In spite of the criticism and perhaps in part due to it, the company's profits have risen 24 percent, to $132 million, worldwide in 1991. The Benetton name has even infiltrated popular literary culture, with Douglas Coupland in his novel, *Shampoo Planet,* coining the phrase "Benetton Youth" to refer to global kids whose histories, memories, and experiences began in the Reagan era of greed and consumption. *Adweek* reports that because of the success of the Benetton campaign, Toscani has become something of a commercial "star," and has been asked by American Express to develop marketing concepts for them. Benetton's stock is up because of the visibility of the company, and David Roberts, an analyst with Nomura International/London, clams that Benetton's "name recognition is approaching that of Coca-Cola."[10]

Benetton's response to the controversy has been threefold. First, Benetton and its spokespersons have reacted aggressively within a number of public forums and debates in order to defend its advertising policies. Second, it has used the debate to reorder its identity as a corporate force for social responsibility. Third, it has seized upon the controversy itself as a pretext for further marketing its ideology in the form of books, magazines, talks, interviews, articles, and the use of stars such as Spike Lee to endorse its position in the debate.[11] In what follows, I want to focus primarily on the legitimating claims Benetton has used to defend its policies and to examine such claims in the context of some broader economic considerations and a politics of difference that informs its worldview.

Benetton has attempted to articulate and defend its position through material found in its campaign copy, particularly the Fall/Winter and Spring/Summer 1992 versions. Moreover, it has attempted to defray criticism of its advertising campaign by allowing selected executives to speak in interviews, the public press, and various popular magazines. The three major spokespersons for Benetton have been Luciano Benetton, founder and managing director, Oliviero Toscani, creative director, and Peter Fressola, Benetton's director of communications in North America. All three provide different versions of a similar theme: Benetton is not about selling sweaters but social responsibility, and it is a company that represents less a product than a lifestyle, worldview, and idea.

Recently elected as a Senator to the Italian Parliament, Luciano Benetton is the principle ideologue in the Benetton apparatus. He is chiefly responsible for the structuring principles that guide Benetton as both a corporate identity and ideological force. His own political beliefs are deeply rooted in the neoliberal language of the free market, privatization, the removal of government from the marketplace, and the advocacy of business principles as the basis for an elective community of possibility. Hence, it is not surprising that in addition to defending the ads for their focusing of public opinion on controversial issues, Luciano Benetton readily admits that the advertising campaign "has a traditional function ... to make Benetton known around the world and to introduce the product to consumers."[12] More than any other spokesperson, Luciano Benetton rearticulates the relationship between commerce and art, and serves as a constant reminder that the bottom line for the company is profit and not social justice.

Peter Fressola, on the other hand, promotes the ideological position, and claims that the ad campaign does not reflect the company's intention to sell sweaters. He argues, "We're not that stupid. We're doing corporate communication. We're sponsoring these images in order to change people's minds and create compassion around social issues. We think of it as art with a social message."[13] Of course, the question at stake here is whose minds Benetton wants to shape? In part, the answer lies in its own advertising copy material, which makes it quite clear that "Various studies have shown that in 1992 consumers are as concerned by what a company stands for as they are about the price/value relationship of that company's product."[14] There is nothing in Fressola's message that challenges the legacy of the corporate use of communications to advance, if only tacitly, "some kind of self-advantaging exchange."[15]

On one level, logos permeate our everyday world to such a degree that they have become commonplace symbols that blur the line between art, politics, and commodification. As a new form of cultural capital they distinguish upscale or trendy corporations from less prominent corporate players. But more importantly, they constitute the borders within which cultural objects and practices are constituted as a form of capital. Logos in this sense do not simply signify goods; they serve as a marker to remind us that there are no public spheres, desires, practices, and goods that can escape commodification. Logos have become central to a politics of identity in which they provide people with forms of representation in which they can identify themselves and their relationship to others. The political and cultural implications of the use of logos to connect identities to the dictates of corporate ideologies are captured by Susan Willis in her analysis of the Disney logo:

> In late twentieth-century America, the cultural capital of corporations has replaced many of the human forms of cultural capital. As we buy, wear, and eat logos, we become the henchmen and admen of the corporations, defining ourselves with respect to the social standing of the various corporations. Some would say that this is a new form of tribalism, that in sporting corporate logos we ritualize and humanize them, we redefine the cultural capital of corporations in human social terms. I would say that a state where culture is indistinguishable from logo and where the practice of culture risks infringement of private property is a state that values the corporate over the human.[16]

Benetton's response to such criticism is either to occupy the moral high ground or to displace the wider political and ideological significance of the logo by making a pragmatic appeal to the results of extensive market research. For example, when questioned about the use of the Benetton logo imprinted on all of the photographs, Fressola, Toscani and other spokespersons respond by generally evading the question and pointing to the use of such photographs as part of their support for art, controversy, and public dialogue around social issues. But the presence of the Benetton logo is no small matter. In light of their market research, which stresses what Raymond Loewy called the need for designer corporate symbols to index visual memory retention, the presence of the Benetton logo carries with it a powerful advertising legacy. It asserts that regardless of the form it takes, the purpose of advertising is to subordinate all values to the imperatives of profit and commercialization. Loewy's argument that "We want anyone who has seen the logotype, even fleetingly, to never forget it, or at least to forget it slowly"[17] provides a powerful indictment of the Benetton logo and the claim that Benetton is engaging in a new form of corporate communication. By refusing to rupture or challenge this haunting and revealing legacy of designer logos, communication in these terms appears to do nothing more than link the commodification of human tragedy with the imperatives of brand recognition while simultaneously asserting the discourse of aesthetic freedom and the moral responsibility of commerce. This is captured in part in a statement that appeared in the Fall/Winter 1992 Advertising Campaign literature. It reads: "Among the various means available to achieve the brand recognition that every company must have, we at Benetton believe our strategy for communication to be more effective for the company and more useful to society than would be yet another series of ads showing pretty girls wearing pretty clothes."[18] Toscani goes so far as to separate his economic role as the director of advertising from what he calls the process of communication by claiming rather blithely, "I am responsible for the company's communications; I am not really responsible for its economics."[19] Toscani's appeal in this case is to the moral high ground, one that he suggests is untarnished by the commercial context that informs the deep structure of his job. Should we assume that Benetton's market research in identifying target audiences has nothing to do with Mr. Toscani's creative endeavors? Or, perhaps, Mr. Toscani has found a way to avoid linking his own corporate success to the rise of Benetton's name recognition in a global marketplace? Mr. Toscani is well aware of the relationship between representation and power, not to mention his own role in giving a new twist to the advertising of commodities as cultural signs ordered to promote a particular system of exchange.

Post-Fordism and the Politics of Difference

> Capital has fallen in love with difference; advertising thrives on selling us things that will enhance our uniqueness and individuality.... From World Music to exotic holidays in Third World locations, ethnic TV dinners to Peruvian knitted hats, cultural difference sells.[20]

In the world of international capital, difference is a contentious and paradoxical concept. On the one hand, as individuals increasingly position themselves within and across a variety of identities, needs, and lifestyles, capital seizes upon such differences in order to create new markets and products. Ideas that hold the promise of producing social criticism are insinuated into products in an attempt to subordinate the dynamics of social struggle to the production of new lifestyles. On the other hand, difference is also a dangerous marker for those historical, political, social, and cultural borderlands where people who are considered the "other" are often policed, excluded, and oppressed. Between the dynamics of commodification and resistance, difference becomes a site of conflict and struggle over bodies, desires, land, labor, and the distribution of resources. It is within the space between conflict and commercial appeal that difference carries with it the legacy of possible disruption and political struggle as well as the possibility for colonizing diverse markets. Within the logic of restructured capital and global markets, cultural differences have to be both acknowledged and depoliticized in order to be contained. In a world riddled with conflicts over cultural, ethnic, and racial differences, Benetton defines difference in categorical rather than relational terms and in doing so accentuates a warmed up diet of liberal pluralism, harmony, and consensus.

Central to Benetton's celebration of cultural differences is the dynamic of a shifting economy and its own rise from a local business venture to a global marketing conglomerate. Benetton's commercial success and the legitimating ideology upon which it constructs its "United Colors of Benetton" world view derives, in part, from its aggressive adaptation to the shifting economic and cultural cartography of what has been called post-Fordism.

Although post-Fordism is not an unproblematic term for designating the changes that have taken place in manufacturing and retailing in the advanced industrial countries of the world since 1950, it does focus attention on a number of economic and ideological tendencies that alert us to the need for new descriptions and analyses of the "shifting social and technical landscapes of modern industrial production regimes" that are refiguring the relationship between capital and everyday life.[21] Stuart Hall has succinctly described some of the most salient characteristics of post-Fordism:

"Post-Fordism" is a broader term, suggesting a whole new epoch distinct from the era of mass production.... It covers at least some of the following characteristics: a shift to the new information "technologies"; more flexible, decentralized forms of labor process and work organization; decline of the old manufacturing base and the growth of the "sunrise," computer-based industries; the hiving off or contracting out of functions and services; a greater emphasis on choice and product differentiation, on marketing, packaging, and design, on the "targeting" of consumers by lifestyle, taste, ad culture rather than by the categories of social class; a decline in the proportion of the skilled, male, manual working class, the rise of the service and white-collar classes and the "feminization" of the work force; an economy dominated by the multinationals, with their new international division of labor and their greater autonomy from nation-state control; and the "globalization" of the new financial markets, linked by the communications revolution.[22]

Capitalizing on global shifts in the order of economic and cultural life, Benetton has seized upon post-Fordist production techniques and methods of retailing that integrate various aspects of production, design, distribution, and labor flexibility into a single coordinated system. With great skill and ingenuity, Benetton uses its computerized planning systems, flexible technology, and marketing resources to both forecast and respond immediately to consumer demands from all over the world. Once consumer orders are tallied at the end of the day from various Benetton retailers, they are sent to a centralized computer system that allows the orders to be filled within days. Benetton's concern with difference is in part rooted in the hard realities of a global market and its need to serve various consumer needs. But difference is more than just a marker of commerce; it is also about social movements, dangerous memories, and the struggle on the part of subordinate groups to reclaim their histories and collective voices. It is in response to the latter that Benetton has developed a representational politics in the service of a corporate narrative whose purpose is to harness difference as part of an ideology of promotion and political containment.

In this case, Benetton's post-Fordist economic policies are underwritten by a neoconservative politics that supports minimum state intervention in the world of commerce, accentuates privatization in the form of subcontracting, wages a full-fledged assault on unionized labor, and dramatically expands the service sector. While preaching the gospel of social responsibility, Benetton has become a "corporate model" for new post-Fordist production techniques in which workers are increasingly forced to take on jobs with less security, benefits, and wages. In the new world of subcontracting more and more "office and factory employees are getting transplanted overnight to a temporary or subcontracting nether world [in order] to save the mother company paperwork and cost."[23]

This assault on workers is coupled with a call for less state intervention in regulating business. As a Senator in the Italian Parliament, Luciano Benetton has made it clear that he would promote "lesser State presence in the economy," and apply the logic of business to the larger world of politics.[24] Within this scenario, Benetton's discourse of social justice contradicts its conglomerate building management practices, increasing use of temporary workers at the expense of a full-time, unionized workforce, and aggressive attempts to subordinate all aspects of political and cultural discourse to the logic of capital and commerce.[25]

The economic mandates of Benetton's post-Fordism are informed by an underlying ideological imperative: the need to contain potentially antagonistic cultural differences and an insurgent multiculturalism through a representational politics that combines pluralism with a depoliticized appeal to world harmony and peace. This becomes clearer by recognizing that Benetton's politics of difference intersects with diverse vectors of representation. Economically, its post-Fordist organizational structure supports cultural difference as a vehicle for expanding its range of markets and goods; diversity in the commercial sense signals the move away from standardized markets and the intrusion of business into the postmodern world of plural identities as part of a market driven attempt to expand its production of a variety of clothing apparel for vastly different individuals, groups, and markets. Benetton's corporate ideology, therefore, bespeaks the need to construct representations that not only affirm differences but at the same time deny their radical possibilities within a corporate ideology that speaks to global concerns. Difference in this sense poses the postmodern problem of maintaining the particularity of diverse groups while unifying such differences within Benetton's concept of a "world without borders."

Benetton addresses this problem in both pedagogical and political terms. Pedagogically, it takes up the issue of difference through the representations of fashion, style, and spectacle. Adapting its widely circulated magazine *Colors* to an MTV format, it uses the journal to focus on transnational issues such as music, sex, birth control, and a wide range of issues that incorporate popular culture while depoliticizing it. Popular culture in this sense becomes the pedagogical vehicle through which Benetton addresses the everyday concerns of youth while blurring the lines between popular cultures of resistance and the culture of commerce and commercialization. Interspersed with its commentary on music, art, rock stars, and the biographies of various Benetton executives, *Colors* parades various racial and ethnic youth wearing Benetton apparel. In this context, difference is stripped of all social and political antagonisms and becomes a commercial symbol for what is youthfully chic, hip, and fashionable. At the same time, *Colors* appears to take its cue from the many concerns that inform the daily lives of teenagers all over the industrialized world.

But *Colors* does more than signify the commodification of popular culture; it also signifies Benetton's attempt both to rewrite the content of ads and to blur the boundaries and cultural codes that structure their very forms. Within this context, the distinctions between "the news," advertising, mass communication, public events, editorials, and feature stories breaks down. Subordinated to the logic of the spectacle, the selling of fantasies, and the pleasures of buying, the distinctions between these genres disappear. Back and Quaade's analysis of *Colors* is worth quoting at length:

> The paper constantly crosses the line between forms of mass communication, provides commodity information (adverts) and news information ("the news"), but takes on the usual form of a newspaper, with editorial and features stories.

Its format is that of the non-tabloid morning paper, divided into eight sections dealing with familiar and newsworthy global problems, including waste disposal, North-South inequality, and the plight of refugees and immigrants. It also includes more style-oriented issues like music, hairstyles and subcultures. Benetton turn [sic] the usual relationship between advertising and news media inside out. Unlike conventional newspapers, where advertising is carried as an income-generated appendix to the news, *Colors* uses its news as Benetton's advertising. The news stories are elided with the philosophy of the paper, which is, in turn, associated with the brand quality of its products.[26]

Politically, Benetton develops a politics of containment through advertising practices using journalistic photos that address consumers through stylized representations whose structuring principles are shock, sensationalism, and voyeurism. In these images, Benetton's motives are less concerned with selling particular products than with offering its publicity to diverse public cultures as a unifying discourse for solving the great number of social problems that threaten to uproot difference from the discourses of harmony, consensus, and fashion. In substituting the "manufactured" studio shot for the hyperrealism of photodocumentary images, Benetton collapses the boundaries between the lucid fantasies that promote consumption and those visions that compel social responsibility.

Representations of Hopelessness

Many people have asked why we didn't include a text that would explain the image. But we preferred not to because we think the image is understandable by itself.[27]

I think to die is to die. This is a human situation, a human condition....But we know this death happened. This is the real thing, and the more real the thing is, the less people want to see it. It's always intrigued me why fake has been accepted and reality has been rejected. At Benetton, we are trying to create an awareness of issues. AIDS is one of today's major modern problems in the world, so I think we have to show something about it.[28]

In defense of the commercial use of sensational, photojournalistic images that include a dying AIDS patient surrounded by his family, a terrorist car bombing, and a black soldier with a gun strapped over his shoulder holding part of the skeletal remains of another human being, Benetton's spokespeople combine the discourse of universalism with the politics of realism. Arguing that such images serve as a vehicle for social change by calling attention to the real world, Benetton suggests that its advertising campaign is informed by a representational politics in which the truth-content of such images is guaranteed by their purchase on reality. In this perspective, "shock photos" are used to register rather than engage an alleged unmediated notion of the truth. This appeal to the unmediated "truth-effects" of images is coupled with a claim to universalism ("to die is to die") that serves to deny the historical, social, and political specificity of particular events. Ideologically, this suggests that the value of Benetton's photos resides in their self-referentiality, that is, their ability to reflect both the unique vision of its sponsor and their validation of a certain construction of reality. Suppressed in this discourse is an acknowledgment that the meaning of such photos resides in their uses within particular contexts.

Before discussing specific examples from Benetton's advertising campaign, I want to comment briefly on some of the structuring devices at work in the construction of the use of the photo-journalistic images. All of Benetton's images reveal the double movement between decontextualization and re-contextualization. To accomplish the first move, the photos militate against a reading in which the context and content of the photo are historically and relationally situated. Overdetermined by the immediacy of the logic of the spectacle, Benetton's photos become suspended in what Stewart Ewen has called "memories of style."[29] That is, by dehistoricizing and decontextualizing the photos, Benetton attempts to render ideology innocent by blurring the conditions of production, circulation, and commodification that present such photos as unproblematically real and true. By denying the specificity of its images, Benetton suppresses their history and in doing so limits the range of meanings that might be brought into play in viewing the texts. At stake here is a denial of how shifting contexts give an image different meanings. Of course, the depoliticization that is at work here is not innocent. By failing to rupture the ideological codes that structure what I call Benetton's use of hyperventilating realism, the ads simply register rather than challenge the dominant social relations reproduced in the photographs.

The viewer is afforded no sense of how the aesthetic of realism works to mask "the codes and structures which give photographs meaning as well as the historical contingencies (e.g., patriarchal structures which normalize notions of looking) which give such codes salience."[30] There is no sense here of how the operations of power inform the construction the social problems depicted in the Benetton ads; nor is there a recognition of the diverse struggles of resistance which attempt to challenge such problems. Within this aestheticization of politics, spectacle foregrounds our fascination with the hyper-real and positions the viewer within a visual moment that simply registers horror and shock without critically responding to it. Roland Barthes has referred to this form of representation as one that positions the viewer within the "immediacy of translation."[31] According to Barthes, this is a form of representational politics that functions as myth, because:

it abolishes the complexity of human acts, it gives them the simplicity of essences, it does away with all dialectics, with any going back beyond what is immediately visible, it organizes a world which is without contradictions because it is without depth, a world wide open and wallowing in the evident, it establishes a blissful clarity: things appear to mean something by themselves.[32]

Isolated from historical and social contexts, Benetton's images are stripped of their political possibilities and reduced to a spectacle of fascination, horror, and terror that appears to primarily privatize one's response to social events. That is, the form of address both reproduces dominant renderings of the image and translates the possibility of agency to the privatized act of buying goods rather than engaging forms of self and social determination. This becomes clearer in analyzing one of Benetton's more controversial ads in which David Kirby, an AIDS patient is portrayed on his deathbed as he is surrounded by his grieving family.

As I noted above, this image involves a double movement. On the one hand, it suppresses the diversity of lifestyles, struggles, and realities of diverse individuals in various stages of living with AIDS. In doing so, it reinforces in the Kirby image dominant representations of people with AIDS. The Benetton AIDS ad reproduces, what Douglas Crimp, in another context, refers to as "what we have already been told or shown about people with AIDS: that they are ravaged, disfigured, and debilitated by the syndrome (and that) they are generally ... desperate, but resigned to their inevitable deaths."[33] The appeal to an aesthetic of realism does little to rupture the social and ideological force of such inherited representations. On the contrary, by not providing an analysis of AIDS as a de facto death sentence and by relying instead on the clichés enforced through dominant images and their social effects, the Benetton ad reproduces rather than challenges conventional representations that portray people with AIDS as helpless victims.

The politics at work in the Benetton photographs is also strikingly revealed in its use of photojournalistic images that are decontextualized from any meaningful historical and social context and then recontextualized through the addition of the United Colors of Benetton logo. In the first instance, the use of the logo produces a representational "zone of comfort" that confirms a playfulness which allows the viewer to displace any ethical or political understanding of the images contained in the Benetton ads. The logo serves largely to position the audience within a combination of realism and amusement. Public truths revealed in Benetton's images, regardless of how horrifying or threatening, are offered up "as a kind of joke in which the reader is invited to participate (the 'joke' is how low can we go?), but its potential dangers are also pretty clear: today aliens from Mars kidnap joggers, yesterday Auschwitz didn't happen, tomorrow who cares what happens."[34] Of course, the "joke" here is that anything is for sale and social commitment is just another gimmick for selling goods. In this type of representational politics, critical engagement is largely rendered ineffective by turning the photo and its political referent into an advertisement. If the possibility of social criticism is suggested by the ad it is quickly dispelled by the insertion of the logo which suggests that any complicity between the viewer and the event it depicts is merely ironic since the image ultimately references nothing more than a safe space where the logic of the commodity and the marketplace generate the demand to buy rather than struggle over social injustices and conflicts. In the case of the AIDS ad, the use of the Benetton logo juxtaposes human suffering and promotional culture so as to invite the viewer to position him or herself between the playfulness of commodification and an apocalyptic image in which social change seems either ironic or unimaginable. This serves less to position the viewer to critically mediate social reality and its attendant problems than to subordinate it to the demands and aesthetic of commerce. Stuart Ewen has captured one consequence of such a position. He states: "By reducing all social issues to matters of perception, it is on the perceptual level that social issues are addressed. Instead of social change, there is image change. Brief shows of flexibility at the surface mask intransigence at the core."[35]

In the second instance, recontextualization appeals to an indeterminacy in which it is suggested that such images can be negotiated by different individuals in multiple and varied ways. Hence, Benetton's claim that such photos generate diverse interpretations. While such an assumption rightly suggests that viewers always mediate and rewrite images differently from particular ideologies and histories, it also, when unqualified, overlooks how specific contexts privilege some reading formations over others. In other words, while individuals produce rather than merely receive meanings, the choices they make and the meanings they produce are not free floating. Such meanings and mediations are, in part, formed within wider social and cultural determinations that offer a range of reading practices that are privileged within dominant and subordinate relations of power. The reading of any text cannot be understood independently of the historical and social experiences that construct how audiences interpret other texts. It is this notion of reading formation that is totally missing from Benetton's defense and use of its endless images of death, pain, danger, and shock. Tony Bennett is helpful on this issue: "The concept of reading formation ... is an attempt to think context as a set of discursive and intertextual determinations, operating on material and institutional supports, which bear in upon a text not just externally, from the outside in, but internally, shaping it—in the historically concrete forms in which it is available as a text-to-be-read—from the inside out."[36]

This point can be illustrated by examining two of Benetton's racially marked ads. The first depicts a black woman feeding a white baby. The second portrays two hands, one black, and one white, handcuffed together. In the former ad, one is presented with the torso of a robust black woman breast feeding a white baby. A crimson cable-knit cardigan is pulled down over her shoulders to reveal her breasts. Her hands reveal a trace of scar tissue, and her nails are trimmed short. This is not a traditional Benetton model. How might one decipher these potent, overdetermined sets of signifiers? I say overdetermined in the double sense; first, the racial coding of the image is so overdetermined that it is difficult to escape from a privileged dominant racial reading. It seems difficult to believe that this black woman nursing a long, pale pink baby is the child's mother. Given the legacy of colonialism and racism that informs this image, I believe that the photo privileges a range of dominant readings that suggest the ingrained racial stereotype of the black/slave/wet nurse or mammy.[37] There are no signifiers in this photo, outside of the logo, which would threaten or rupture such a dominant imperialist coding that informs this representation. It is precisely the absent referents of resistance, rupture, and critique that allow the reader to be perfectly comfortable with such a configuration of race and class while accepting the image as nothing more than a "playful" ad.

In the second ad, there is a calculated and false equality at work in presenting an image of a black and white hand handcuffed together. Is the viewer in the United States, England, France, or South Africa to believe that the black hand is the signifier of law, order, and justice? Or, given the legacy of white racism in all of these countries is it more probable to believe that the image, at least at the level of the unconscious, reproduces the racist assumption that social issues regarding crime, turmoil, and lawlessness are essentially a black problem? Restaging race relations in these terms exploits the racially charged tensions that underlie current racial formations in the Western industrial countries while simultaneously reducing the historical legacy of white supremacy to a representation of mere equality between the races. The emotionally charged landscape of race relations, in this instance, becomes another example of how social problems become "packaged" in order to "reinject the real into our lives as spectacle."[38]

Conclusion: Pedagogy and the Need for Critical Public Cultures

The new postmodern pedagogy of mass advertising poses a central challenge to the role cultural workers might play in deepening their own politics through a broader understanding of how knowledge is produced, identities shaped, and values articulated as a pedagogical practice that takes place in multiple sites outside of the traditional institution of schooling. The struggle over meaning is no longer one that can be confined to the struggle over programs and curricula. Moreover, the struggle over identity can no longer be seriously considered outside of the politics of representation and the new formations of consumption. Culture is increasingly constituted by commerce, and the penetration of commodified relations into every facet of daily life has become the major axis of exchange relations through which corporations actively produce new forms of address that are increasingly more effective in their inscription of both subjects and markets.

This is not to suggest that the politics of consumption in its various circuits of power constitutes an unadulterated form of domination. Such a view is often more monolithically defensive than dialectical and has less interest in understanding the complex process by which people desire, choose, and act in everyday life than it does with shielding the guardians of high modernism who have always despised popular culture for its vulgarity and association with the masses.[39] What is at stake in the new intersection of commerce, advertising, and consumption is the very definition and survival of critical public cultures. I am referring here to those public spaces predicated on the multiplication of spheres of daily life where people can debate the meaning and consequences of public truths, inject a notion of moral responsibility into representational practices, and collectively struggle to change dominating relations of power. Central to my argument has been the assumption that the new forms of advertising and consumption do not deny politics, they simply reappropriate it. This is a politics that "actively creates one version of the social," one that exists in harmony with market ideologies and initiatives.[40] Such a politics offers no resistance to a version of the social as largely a "democracy of images," a public media extravaganza in which politics is defined largely through the "consuming of images."[41]

Cultural workers need to reformulate the concept resistance usually associated with these forms of colonization. Such a formulation has to begin with an analysis of how a postmodern pedagogy works by problematizing the intersection of power and representation in an ever expanding democraticization of images and culture. Representations in the postmodern world reach deeply into daily life, contributing to the increasing fragmentation and decentering of individual and collective subjects. Not only are the old categories of race, gender, age, and class increasingly rewritten in highly differentiating and often divisive terms, but the space of the social is further destabilized through niche marketing which constructs identities around lifestyles, ethnicity, fashion, and a host of other commodified subject positions. Central here is the issue of how power has become an important cultural and ideological form, particularly within the discourse of difference and popular culture.

Cultural workers need a new map for registering and understanding how power works to inscribe desires and identities and create multiple points of antagonism and struggle. In serious need of consideration is the creation of a new kind of politics and pedagogy, one organized more deeply through guiding narratives that link global and local social contexts, provide new articulations for engaging popular culture within rather than outside of the new technologies and regimes of representation, and offer a moral language for expanding the struggle over democracy and citizenship to ever-widening spheres of daily life. Clearly more is at issue here than understanding how representations work to construct their own systems of meaning, social organizations, and cultural identifications. In part this means that cultural workers must investigate the new politics of commerce not merely as an economic issue, that is, as symptomatic of the new configurations of a post-Fordist world, but as a reaction to the emergence and "assertion of new ethnicities, problems of racism, problems of nationality, of law, of discrimination, and the assertion of particular communities."[42] This further suggests the need for cultural workers to reformulate a politics and pedagogy of difference around an ethical discourse of multiplicity, one that both challenges the ideological grounds and representations of commerce but at the same time limits those public spheres it attempts to appropriate. If a politics of difference is to be linked to not merely registering "otherness" but identifying the conditions through which other become critical agents, the ethic of consumerism must be challenged by exposing its limits.

Cultural workers need to take up the challenge of teaching ourselves, students, and others to both acknowledge our and their complicity in the discourse and practice of consumerism while bringing the hope mobilized in such practices to a principled and persistent crisis. This is not to invoke a vulgar critique of the real pleasures and joys of buying. Neither is it meant to underestimate the diverse ways in which people negotiate the terrain of the market or reappropriating goods through resisting and oppositional practices. Rather the issue here is to recognize the political and pedagogical limits of consumerism, its often active involvement in creating new identities, and its ongoing assault on the notion of insurgent differences and a multicultural and multiracial democracy. Individual and collective agency is about more than buying goods, and social life in its most principled forms points beyond the logic of the market as a guiding principle. It is up to cultural workers and other progressive educators to address this challenge directly as part of a postmodern political and pedagogical challenge.

Notes

1. *Colors 1* (Fall–Winter 1991–1992): 63.
2. David Bailey and Stuart Hall, "The Vertigo of Displacement," *Ten.8* 2:3 (1992): 15.
3. Andrew Payne and Tom Taylor, "Introduction—The Violence of the Public," *Public 6* (1992): 10.
4. Sharon Waxman, "Benetton Laid Bar," *Miami Herald* Living Section, February 8, 1993, p. 1C.
5. Quoted in Benetton's spring/summer 1992 advertising campaign copy, p. 5.
6. Michael Stevens, "Change the World, Buy a Sweater," *Chicago Tribune,* December 11, 1992, p. 33.
7. Cited in Benetton's spring/summer 1992 advertising campaign copy, p. 4.

8. Carol Squires, "Violence at Benetton," *Artforum 30* (May 1992): 18–19.

9. On the issue of promotional culture, an excellent text can be found in Andrew Warnick, *Promotional Culture* (Newbury Park, CA: Sage, 1991).

10. Noreen O'Leary, "Benetton's True Colors," *Adweek* (August 24, 1992): 28.

11. Benetton not only published with Ginko Press a book appropriately titled, *United Colors of Benetton*, which "vividly display[ed] the Benetton corporate philosophy," it also came out with a book in 1994 titled, *What's the Relationship between AIDS and Selling a Sweater*, which chronicled various responses to the controversial Benetton ads. Both books appropriate the controversy over Benetton's ads to both spread the company's name and generate profits. It seems that nothing is capable of existing outside of Benetton's high-powered commercialism and drive for profits. Spike Lee is one of the most high-profile celebrities to endorse Benetton's campaign. See the interview with Spike Lee, which was sponsored as an advertisement in "United Colors of Benetton," in *Rolling Stone 643* (November 12, 1992).

12. Ingrid Sischy, "Advertising Taboos: Talking to Luciano Benetton and Oliviero Toscani," *Interview* (April 1992): 69.

13. Fressola quoted in Carol Squires, "Violence at Benetton," *Artforum 30* (May 1992): 18.

14. Cited in Benetton's spring/summer 1992 advertising campaign copy, p. 2.

15. Andrew Warnick, *Promotional Culture*, op. cit., p. 181.

16. Susan Willis, "Disney World: Public Use/Private State," *South Atlantic Quarterly 92*:1 (1983): 133.

17. Loewy cited in Stuart Ewen, *All Consuming Images* (New York: Basic Books, 1988), p. 247.

18. Cited in Benetton's fall/winter 1992 advertising campaign copy, p. 2.

19. Ingrid Sischy, "Advertising Taboos," op. cit., p. 69.

20. Cited in Martin Davidson, *The Consumerist Manifesto* (New York: Routledge, 1992), p. 199.

21. Stuart Hall, "The Meaning of New Times," in Stuart Hall and Martin Jacques, eds. *New Times: The Changing Face of Politics in the 1990s* (London: Verso Press, 1990), p. 117.

22. Stuart Hall, "Brave New World," *Socialist Review 91*:1 (1991): 57–58.

23. Clare Ansberry, "Workers are Forced to Take More and More Jobs with Fewer Benefits," *Wall Street Journal LXXIV*:103 (March 11, 1993): 1. See also Robin Murray, "Benetton Britain: The New Economic Order," in Stuart Hall and Martin Jacques, eds., *New Times: The Changing Face of Politics in the 1990s* (London: Verso Press, 1990), pp. 54–64.

24. Interview with Luciano Benetton in "News," an insert in *Colors 3* (Fall–Winter, 1992–1993): 2.

25. For a succinct analysis of the relationship between post-Fordism and capitalism, see David Harvey, "Flexibility: Threat or Opportunity? *Socialist Review 91*:1 (1991): 65–75.

26. Les Back and Vibeke Quaade, "Dream Utopias, Nightmare Realties: Imaging Race and Culture within the World of Benetton Advertising," *Third Text 22*(1993): 77.

27. Luciano Benetton cited in Ingrid Sischy, "Advertising Taboos: Talking to Luciano Benetton and Oliviero Toscani," *Interview* (April 1992): 69.

28.   Oliviero Toscani cited in Ingrid Sischy, "Advertising Taboos: Talking to Luciano Benetton and Oliviero Toscani," *Interview* (April 1992): 69.

29.   Stuart Ewen, *All Consuming Images* (New York: Basic Books, 1988), p. 248.

30.   Abigail Solomon-Godeau, *Photography at the Dock* (Minneapolis: University of Minnesota Press, 1991), p. 145.

31.   Roland Barthes, "Shock-Photos," in *The Eiffel Tower* (New York: Hill and Wang, 1979), p. 72.

32.   Roland Barthes, *Mythologies* (New York: Noonday, 1972), p. 143.

33.   Douglas Crimp, "Portraits of People with AIDS," in Lawrence Grossberg, et al., eds. *Cultural Studies* (New York: Routledge, 1992), p. 118.

34.   Dick Hebdige, "After the Masses," in Stuart Hall and Martin Jacques, eds. *New Times,* op. cit., p. 83.

35.   Stuart Ewen, op. cit., p. 264.

36.   Tony Bennett, "Texts in History: The Determinations of Readings and Their Texts," in Derek Atridge, et al., eds., *Poststructuralism and the Question of History* (Cambridge: Cambridge University Press, 1987), p. 72.

37.   This issue of the legacy of racial representations and their affect on shaping cultural practices can be seen in K. Sue Jewell, *From Mammy to Miss America and Beyond* (New York: Routledge, 1993).

38.   Hal Foster, *Recordings: Art Spectacle, Cultural Politics* (Seattle: Bay Press, 1985), pp. 6–7.

39.   On the dialectics of consumerism, see Mike Featherstone, *Consumer Culture and Postmodernism* (Newbury Park: Sage Publications, 1991); Mica Nava, *Changing Cultures: Feminism, Youth and Consumerism* (Newbury Park: Sage Publications, 1992).

40.   Dick Hebdige, "After the Masses," in Stuart Hall and Martin Jacques, eds., *New Times: The Changing Fact of Politics in the 1990s* (London: Verso Press, 1990), p. 89.

41.   I have taken this idea from the transcript of the television show, *The Public Mind* with Bill Moyers (New York/WNET Public Affairs Television, 1989), p. 14.

42.   David Bannet and Terry Collits, "Homi Bhabha Interviewed by David Bannet and Terry Collits—the Postcolonial Critic," *Arena 96* (Spring 1991): 47–48.

4
Doing Cultural Studies
Youth and the Challenge of Pedagogy

⊸

> In our society, youth is present only when its presence is a problem, or is
> regarded as a problem. More precisely, the category "youth" gets mobilized
> in official documentary discourse, in concerned or outraged editorials
> and features, or in the supposedly disinterested tracts emanating from the
> social sciences at those times when young people make their presence felt
> by going "out of bounds," by resisting through rituals, dressing strangely,
> striking bizarre attitudes, breaking rules, breaking bottles, windows, heads,
> issuing rhetorical challenges to the law.[1]

A commentary in the *Chronicle of Higher Education* claimed that the field of
cultural studies is "about the hottest thing in humanities and social science
research right now, but it's largely peopled by scholars in literature, film and
media, communications, and philosophy."[2] Given the popularity of cultural
studies for a growing number of scholars, I have often wondered why so few
academics have incorporated cultural studies into the language of educational reform. If educators are to take seriously the challenge of cultural
studies, particularly its insistence on generating new questions, models, and
contexts in order to address the central and most urgent dilemmas of our
age, they must critically address the politics of their own location. This means
understanding not only the ways in which institutions of higher education,
in part, shape the work we do with students but also the ways in which our
vocation as educators supports, challenges, or subverts institutional practices
that are at odds with democratic processes and the hopes and opportunities we provide for the nation's youth. In what follows, I want to explore not
only why educators refuse to engage the possibilities of cultural studies but
also why scholars working within a cultural studies framework often refuse
to take seriously pedagogy and the role of schools in the shaping of democratic public life.

Educational theorists demonstrate as little interest in cultural studies as
cultural studies scholars do in the critical theories of schooling and pedagogy.

For educators, this indifference may be explained, in part, by the narrow technocratic models that dominate mainstream reform efforts and structure education programs. Within such a tradition, management issues become more important than understanding and furthering schools as democratic public spheres.[3] Hence, the regulation, certification, and standardization of teacher behavior is emphasized over creating the conditions for teachers to undertake the sensitive political and ethical roles they might assume as public intellectuals who selectively produce and legitimate particular forms of knowledge and authority. Similarly, licensing and assimilating differences among students is more significant than treating students as bearers of diverse social memories with a right to speak and represent themselves in the quest for learning and self-determination. While other disciplines have appropriated, engaged, and produced new theoretical languages in keeping with changing historical conditions, colleges of education have maintained a deep suspicion of theory and intellectual dialogue and thus have not been receptive to the introduction of cultural studies.[4] Other considerations in this willful refusal to know would include a history of educational reform which has been overly indebted to practical considerations that often support a long tradition of anti-intellectualism. Moreover, educators frequently pride themselves on being professional, scientific, and objective.

Cultural studies challenges the ideological and political nature of such claims by arguing that teachers always work and speak within historically and socially determined relations of power.[5] Put another way, educators whose work is shaped by cultural studies do not simply view teachers and students either as chroniclers of history and social change or recipients of culture, but as active participants in its construction.

The resistance to cultural studies may also be due to the fact that it reasserts the importance of comprehending schooling as a mechanism of culture and politics, embedded in competing relations of power that attempt to regulate and order how students think, act, and live.[6] Since cultural studies is largely concerned with the critical relationship among culture, knowledge, and power, it is not surprising that mainstream educators often dismiss cultural studies as being too ideological, or simply ignore its criticisms regarding how education generates a privileged narrative space for some social groups and a space of inequality and subordination for others.

Historically schools and colleges of education have been organized around either traditional subject-based studies (math education) or into largely disciplinary/administrative categories (curriculum and instruction). Within this type of intellectual division of labor, students generally have had few opportunities to study larger social issues. This slavish adherence to structuring the curriculum around the core disciplinary subjects is at odds with the field of cultural studies whose theoretical energies are largely focused on interdisciplinary issues, such as textuality and representation refracted through the dynamics of gender, sexuality, subordinate youth, national identity, colonialism, race, ethnicity, and popular culture.[7] By offering educators a critical language through which to examine the ideological and political interests that structure reform efforts in education such as nationalized testing, standardized curriculum, and efficiency models, cultural studies incurs the wrath of mainstream and conservative educators who often are silent about the political agendas that underlie their own language and reform agendas.[8]

Cultural studies also rejects the traditional notion of teaching as a technique or set of neutral skills and argues that teaching is a cultural practice that can only be understood through considerations of history, politics, power, and culture. Given its concern with everyday life, its pluralization of cultural communities, and its emphasis on knowledge that is multidisciplinary, cultural studies is less concerned with issues of certification and testing than it is with how knowledge, texts, and cultural products are produced, circulated, and used. In this perspective, culture is the ground "on which analysis proceeds, the object of study, and the site of political critique and intervention."[9] This in part explains why some advocates of cultural studies are increasingly interested in "how and where knowledge needs to surface and emerge in order to be consequential" with respect to expanding the possibilities for a radical democracy.[10]

Within the next century, educators will not be able to ignore the hard questions that schools will have to face regarding issues of multiculturalism, race, identity, power, knowledge, ethics, and work. These issues will play a major role in defining the meaning and purpose of schooling, the relationship between teachers and students, and the critical content of their exchange in terms of how to live in a world that will be vastly more globalized, high tech, and racially diverse than at any other time in history. Cultural studies offers enormous possibilities for educators to rethink the nature of educational theory and practice as well as what it means to educate future teachers for the twenty-first century.[11]

At the same time, it is important to stress that the general indifference by many cultural studies theorists to the importance of critical pedagogy as a form of cultural practice does an injustice to the politically charged history of cultural studies, one which points to the necessity for combining self-criticism with a commitment to transforming existing social and political problems. It is not my intention here to replay the debate regarding what the real history of cultural studies is, though this is an important issue. Instead, I want to focus on the importance of critical pedagogy as a central aspect of cultural studies and cultural work as a pedagogical practice. This suggests analyzing cultural studies for the insights it has accrued as it has moved historically from its previous concerns with class and language to its more recent analysis of the politics of race, gender, identity, and ethnicity. This is not meant to suggest that the history of cultural studies needs to be laid out in great detail as some sort of foundational exegesis. On the contrary, cultural studies needs to be approached historically as a mix of founding moments, transformative challenges, and self-critical interrogations.[12] And it is precisely the rupturing spirit that informs elements of its interdisciplinary practice, social activism, and historical awareness that prompts my concern for the current lacunae in cultural studies regarding the theoretical and political importance of pedagogy as a founding moment in its legacy.

In what follows, I want to take up these concerns more concretely as they bear on what Dick Hebdige calls the "problem of youth"[13] and the necessary importance of this issue for educators and other cultural workers. In constructing this line of thought I begin by making the case that pedagogy must become a defining principle of any critical notion of cultural studies. This position is developed, in part, to expand the meaning and relevance of pedagogy for those engaged in cultural work both in and outside of the university. I then argue for the pedagogical practice of using films about youth not only as legitimate objects of social knowledge that offer representations in which youth can identify their desires and hopes, but also as pedagogical texts that play a formative role in shaping the social identities of youth. Through an analysis of four Hollywood films about youth I hope to show how the more progressive elements of critical pedagogical work can inform and be informed by cultural studies' emphasis on popular culture as a terrain of significant political and pedagogical importance. I will conclude by developing the implications cultural studies might have for those of us who are concerned about reforming schools and colleges of education.

The Absence of Pedagogy in Cultural Studies

It is generally argued that cultural studies is largely defined through its analysis of culture and power, particularly with regard to its "shifting of the terrain of culture toward the popular"[14] while expanding its critical reading of the production, reception, use, and effects of popular texts. Texts in this case constitute a wide range of aural, visual, and printed signifiers; moreover, such texts are often taken up as part of a broader attempt to analyze how individual and social identities are mobilized, engaged, and transformed within circuits of power informed by issues of race, gender, class, ethnicity, and other social formations. All of these concerns point to the intellectual and institutional borders that produce, regulate, and engage meaning as a site of social struggle. Challenging the ways in which the academic disciplines have been used to secure particular forms of authority, cultural studies has opened up the possibility for both questioning how power operates in the construction of knowledge while redefining the parameters of the form and content of what is being taught in institutions of higher education. In this instance, struggles over meaning, language, and textuality have become symptomatic of a larger struggle over the meaning of cultural authority, the role of public intellectuals, and the meaning of national identity. While cultural studies proponents have provided an enormous theoretical service in taking up the struggle over knowledge and authority particularly as it effects the restructuring of the curriculum in many colleges and universities, what is often overlooked in such struggles are some of the major concerns that have been debated by various theorists who work within the diverse traditions of critical pedagogy. This is especially surprising since cultural studies draws its theoretical and political inspiration from feminism, postmodernism, postcolonialism, and a host of other areas that have at least made a passing reference to the importance of pedagogy.

I want to argue that cultural studies is still too rigidly tied to the modernist, academic disciplinary structures that it often criticizes. This is not to suggest that it does not adequately engage the issue of academic disciplines. In fact, this is one of its most salient characteristics.[15] What it fails to do is critically address a major prop of disciplinarity, which is the notion of pedagogy as an unproblematic vehicle for transmitting knowledge. Lost here is the attempt to understand pedagogy as a mode of cultural criticism for questioning the very conditions under which knowledge and identities are produced. Of course, theorists such as Gayatri Spivak, Stanley Aronowitz, and others do engage the relationship between cultural studies and pedagogy, but they constitute a small minority.[16] The haunting question here is what is it about pedagogy that allows cultural studies theorists to ignore it?

One answer may lie in the refusal of cultural studies theorists to either take schooling seriously as a site of struggle or to probe how traditional pedagogy produces particular social histories, how it constructs student identities through a range of subject positions. Of course, within radical educational theory, there is a long history of developing critical discourses of the subject around pedagogical issues.[17]

Another reason cultural studies theorists have devoted little attention to pedagogy may be due to the disciplinary policing that leaves the marks of its legacy on all areas of the humanities and liberal arts. Pedagogy is often deemed unworthy of being taken up as a serious project; in fact, even popular culture has more credibility than pedagogy. This can be seen not only in the general absence of any discussion of pedagogy in cultural studies texts, but also in those studies in the humanities that have begun to engage pedagogical issues. Even in these works there is a willful refusal to acknowledge some of the important theoretical gains in pedagogy that have gone on in the last twenty years.[18] Within this silence lurk the seductive rewards of disciplinary control, a refusal to cross academic borders, and a shoring up of academic careerism, competitiveness, and elitism. Of course, composition studies, one of the few fields in the humanities that does take pedagogy seriously, occupies a status as disparaging as the field of education.[19] Hence, it appears that the legacy of academic elitism and professionalism still exercises a strong influence on the field of cultural studies, in spite of its alleged democratization of social knowledge.

Cultural Studies and Pedagogy

In what follows, I want to make a case for the importance of pedagogy as a central aspect of cultural studies. In doing so, I first want to analyze the role that pedagogy played in the early founding stages of the Birmingham Center for Cultural Studies.[20] I then want to define more specifically the central dimensions of pedagogy as a cultural practice. But before I address these two important moments of critical pedagogy as a form of cultural politics, I think it is important to stress that the concept of pedagogy must be used with respectful caution. Not only are there different versions of what constitutes critical pedagogy, but there is no generic definition that can be applied to the term. At the same time, there are important theoretical insights and practices that weave through various approaches to critical pedagogy. It is precisely these insights which often define a common set of problems that serve to delineate critical pedagogy as a set of conditions articulated within the shifting context of a particular political project. These problems include but are not limited to the relationship between knowledge and power, language and experience, ethics and authority, student agency and transformative politics, and teacher location and student formations.

Richard Hoggart and Raymond Williams addressed the issue of pedagogy in a similar manner in their early attempts to promote cultural studies in Britain. As founding figures in the Birmingham Centre for Cultural Studies, Hoggart and Williams believed that pedagogy offered the opportunity to link cultural practice with the development of radical cultural theories. Not only did pedagogy connect questions of form and content, it also introduced a sense of how teaching, learning, textual studies, and knowledge could be addressed as political issues which foreground considerations of power and social agency. According to Williams, the advent of cultural studies in the 1930s and 1940s directly emerged out of the pedagogical work that was going on in Adult Education. The specificity of the content and context of adult education provided cultural studies with a number of issues that were to direct its subsequent developments in Birmingham. These included the refusal to accept the limitations of established academic boundaries and power structures, the demand for linking literature to the life situations of adult learners, and the call that schooling be empowering rather than merely humanizing.[21]

For Williams there is more at stake here than reclaiming the history of cultural studies; he is most adamant in making clear that the "deepest impulse [informing cultural studies] was the desire to make learning part of the process of social change itself."[22] It is precisely this attempt to broaden the notion of the political by making it more pedagogical that reminds us of the importance of pedagogy as a cultural practice. In this context, pedagogy deepens and extends the study of culture and power by addressing not only how culture is produced, circulated, and transformed but also how it is actually negotiated by human beings within specific settings and circumstances. In this instance, pedagogy becomes an act of cultural production, a process through which power regulates bodies and behaviors as "they move through space and time."[23] While pedagogy is deeply implicated in the production of power/knowledge relationships and the construction of values and desires, its theoretical center of gravity begins not with a particular claim to new knowledge, but with real people articulating and rewriting their lived experiences within rather than outside of history. In this sense pedagogy, especially in its critical variants, is about understanding how power works within particular historical, social, and cultural contexts in order to engage and when necessary to change such contexts.[24]

The importance of pedagogy to the content and context of cultural studies lies in the relevance it has for illuminating how knowledge and social identities are produced in a variety of sites in addition to schools. For Raymond Williams one of the founding concepts of cultural studies was that cultural education was just as important as labor, political, and trade union education. Moreover, Williams believed that limiting the study of culture to higher education ran the risk of depoliticizing it. Williams believes that education in the broad, political sense was essential not only for engaging, challenging, and transforming policy, but also the necessary referent for stressing the pedagogical importance of work shared by all cultural workers who engage in the production of knowledge. This becomes clear in Williams' notion of permanent education. He writes:

> This idea [permanent education] seems to me to repeat, in a new and important idiom, the concepts of learning and of popular democratic culture which underlie the present book. What it valuably stresses is the educational force of our whole social and cultural experience. It is therefore concerned, not only with continuing education, of a formal or informal kind, but with what the whole environment, its institutions and relationships, actively and profoundly teaches. To consider the problems of families, or of town planning, is then an educational enterprise, for these, also, are where teaching occurs. And then the field of this book, of the cultural communications which, under an old shadow, are still called mass communications, can be integrated, as I have always intended, with a whole social policy. For who can doubt, looking at television or newspapers, or reading the women's magazines, that here, centrally, is teaching, and teaching financed and distributed in a much larger way than in formal education?[25]

Building upon Williams' notion of permanent education, pedagogy, in this sense, provides a theoretical discourse for understanding how power and knowledge mutually inform each other in the production, reception, and transformation of social identities, forms of ethical address, and "desired versions of a future human community."[26] By refuting the objectivity of knowledge and asserting the partiality of all forms of pedagogical authority, critical pedagogy initiates an inquiry into the relationship between the form and content of various pedagogical sites and the authority they legitimate in securing particular cultural practices.

I want to be more specific about the importance of pedagogy for cultural studies and other emerging forms of interdisciplinary work by analyzing how youth are increasingly being addressed and positioned through the popular media, changing economic conditions, an escalating wave of violence, and the emergence of discourse that Ruth Conniff has aptly called the culture of cruelty.[27] I will then address both theoretically and through examples of my own teaching how the pedagogy implicit in a spate of Hollywood films about youth culture reinforces dominant racist and cultural stereotypes, but in doing so also creates the conditions for rewriting such films through diverse critical pedagogical strategies.

Mass Culture and the Representation of Youth(s)

Youth have once again become the object of public analysis. Headlines proliferate like dispatches from a combat zone frequently coupling youth and violence in the interests of promoting a new kind of causal relationship. For example, gangster rap artist Snoop Doggy Dogg is featured on the front cover of a recent issue of *Newsweek*.[28] This message is that young black men are selling violence to the mainstream public through their music. But according to *Newsweek*, the violence is not just in the music, it is also embodied in the lifestyles of the rappers who produce it. The potential victims in this case are a besieged white majority of male and female youth. Citing a wave of arrests among prominent rappers, the story reinforces the notion that crime is a racially coded word for associating black youth with violence.[29]

The statistics on youth violence point to social and economic causes that lie far beyond the reach of facile stereotypes. On a national level American society is witnessing the effects of a culture of violence in which "close to 12 U.S. children aged 19 and under die from gun fire each day. According to the National Center for Health Statistics, 'Firearm homicide is the leading cause of death of African American teenage boys and the second leading cause of death of high school age children in the United States.'"[30] What is missing from these reports is any critical commentary on underlying causes that produce the representations of violence that saturate the mass media; nor is there any mention of the high toll of life taken every year by the infants and children killed through "poverty-related malnutrition and disease" nor is the American public informed in the popular press about "the gruesome toll of the drunk driver who is typically White."[31] But the bad news doesn't end with violence.

The representations of white youth produced by dominant media within recent years have increasingly portrayed them as lazy, sinking into a self-indulgent haze, and oblivious to the middle-class ethic of working hard and getting ahead. Of course, what the dominant media do not talk about are the social conditions that are producing a new generation of youth steeped in despair, violence, crime, poverty, and apathy. For instance, to talk about black crime without mentioning that the unemployment rate for black youth exceeds 40 percent in many urban cities, primarily serves to make invisible a major cause of youth unrest. Or to talk about apathy among white youth without analyzing the junk culture, poverty, social disenfranchisement, drugs, lack of educational opportunity, and commodification that shape daily life removes responsibility from a social system that often sees youth as simply another market niche.

A failing economy that offers most youth the promise of service sector jobs, dim prospects for the future, a world of infinite messages and images designed to sell a product or to peddle senseless violence as another TV spectacle, in part, constitute the new conditions of youth. In light of radically altered social and economic conditions, educators need to fashion alternative analyses in order to understand what is happening to our nation's youth. Such a project seems vital in light of the rapidity in which market values and a commercial public culture have replaced the ethical referents for developing democratic public spheres. For example, since the 1970s millions of jobs have been lost to capital flight, and technological change has wiped out millions more. In the last twenty years alone, the U.S. economy lost more than 5 million jobs in the manufacturing sector.[32] In the face of extremely limited prospects for economic growth over the next decade, schools will be faced with an identity crisis regarding the traditional assumption that school credentials provide the best route to economic security and class mobility for a large proportion of our nation's youth. As Stanley Aronowitz and I have pointed out elsewhere:

> The labor market is becoming increasingly bifurcated: organizational and technical changes are producing a limited number of jobs for highly educated and trained people-managers, scientific and technological experts, and researchers. On the other hand, we are witnessing the disappearance of many middle-level white collar subprofessions.... And in the face of sharpening competition, employers typically hire a growing number of low paid, part-time workers.... Even some professionals have become free-lance workers with few, if any, fringe benefits. These developments call into question the efficacy of mass schooling for providing the "well-trained" labor force that employers still claim they require.[33]

Rather than blaming youth for the economic slump, the culture of racially coded violence, or the hopelessness that seems endemic to dominant versions of the future, it makes more sense for educators to reexamine the mission of the school and the changing conditions of youth in light of these shattering shifts in economic and cultural life.

But rethinking the conditions of youth is also imperative in order to reverse the mean-spirited discourse of the 1980s, a discourse that has turned its back on the victims of American society and has resorted to both blaming and punishing them for their social and economic problems. This is evident in states such as Michigan and Wisconsin, which subscribe to "Learnfare" programs designed to penalize a single mother with a lower food allowance if her kids are absent from school. In other states, welfare payments are reduced if single mothers do not marry. Micky Kaus, an editor at the *New Republic,* argues that welfare mothers should be forced to work at menial jobs and, if they refuse, Kaus suggests that the state remove their children from them. Illiterate women, Kaus argues, could work raking leaves.[34] There is indifference and callousness in this kind of language that now spills over to talking about youth. Instead of providing economic and social conditions that provide the nation's youth, especially those who are poor and live on the margins of hope, without food, shelter, access to decent education, and safe environments, conservatives such as William Bennett, the former Secretary of Education, talk about imposing national standards on public schools, creating voucher systems that benefit middle class parents, and doing away with the concept of the public altogether. There is more at work here than simply ignorance and neglect.

It is in the dominant discourse on values that one gets a glimpse of the pedagogy at work in the culture of mean-spiritedness. For instance, Bennett in his book, *The Book of Virtues: A Treasury of Great Moral Stories,* finds hope in "Old Mr. Rabbit's Thanksgiving Dinner," in which the rabbit instructs us that there is more joy in being helpful than in being helped. The discourse of moral uplift may provide soothing and inspirational help for children whose parents send them to private schools, establish trust-fund annuities for their future, and connect them to the world of political patronage, but it says almost nothing about the culture of compressed and concentrated human suffering that many children have to deal with daily in this country. In what follows, I want to draw from a number of insights provided by the field of cultural studies to chart out a different cartography that might be helpful for educators to address what might be called the changing conditions of youth.

Framing Youth

The programmed instability and transitoriness characteristically widespread among a diverse generation of 18- to 25-year-old youth is inextricably rooted in a larger set of postmodern cultural conditions informed by the following assumptions: a general loss of faith in the modernist narratives of work and emancipation; the recognition that the indeterminacy of the future warrants confronting and living in the immediacy of experience; an acknowledgment that homelessness as a condition of randomness has replaced the security, if not misrepresentation, of home as a source of comfort and security; an experience of time and space as compressed and fragmented within a world of images that increasingly undermine the dialectic of authenticity and universalism. For many youth, plurality and contingency, whether mediated through the media or through the dislocations spurned by the economic system, the rise of new social movements, or the crisis of representation and authority, have resulted in a world with few secure psychological, economic, or intellectual markers. This is a world in which one is condemned to wander within and between multiple borders and spaces marked by excess, otherness, and difference. This is a world in which old certainties are ruptured and meaning becomes more contingent, less indebted to the dictates of reverence and established truth. While the circumstances of youth vary across and within terrains marked by racial and class differences, the modernist world of certainty and order that has traditionally policed, contained, and insulated such difference has given way to a shared postmodern culture in which representational borders collapse into new hybridized forms of cultural performance, identity, and political agency. As the information highway and MTV condense time and space into what Paul Virilio calls "speed space,"[35] new desires, modes of association, and forms of resistance inscribe themselves into diverse spheres of popular culture. Music, rap, fashion, style, talk, politics, and cultural resistance are no longer confined to their original class and racial locations. Middle class white kids take up the language of gangsta rap spawned in neighborhood turfs far removed from their own lives. Black youth in the urban centers produce a bricolage of style fashioned amid a combination of sneakers, baseball caps, and oversized clothing that integrates forms of resistance and style later to be appropriated by suburban kids whose desires and identities resonate with the energy and vibrancy of the new urban funk. Music displaces older forms of textuality and references a terrain of cultural production that marks the body as a site of pleasure, resistance, domination, and danger.[36] Within this postmodern culture of youth, identities merge and shift rather than become more uniform and static. No longer belonging to any one place or location, youth increasingly inhabit shifting cultural and social spheres marked by a plurality of languages and cultures.

Communities have been refigured as space and time mutate into multiple and overlapping cyberspace networks. Bohemian and middle class youth talk to each other over electronic bulletin boards in coffee houses in North Beach, California. Cafes and other public salons, once the refuges of beatniks, hippies, and other cultural radicals, have given way to members of the hacker culture. They reorder their imaginations through connections to virtual reality technologies, and produce forms of exchange through texts and images that have the potential to wage a war on traditional meaning, but also run the risk of reducing critical understanding to the endless play of random access spectacles.

This is not meant to endorse a Frankfurt School dismissal of popular culture in the postmodern age. On the contrary, I believe that the new electronic technologies with their proliferation of multiple stories and open-ended forms of interaction have altered not only the pedagogical context for the production of subjectivities, but also how people "take in information and entertainment."[37] Produced from the centers of power, mass culture has spawned in the name of profit and entertainment a new level of instrumental and commodified culture. On the other hand, popular culture offers resistance to the notion that useful culture can only be produced within dominant regimes of power. This distinction between mass and popular culture is not meant to suggest that popular culture is strictly a terrain of resistance. Popular culture does not escape commodification, racism, sexism, and other forms of oppression, but it is marked by fault lines that reject the high/low culture divide while attempting to affirm a multitude of histories, experiences, cultural forms, and pleasures. Within the conditions of postmodern culture, values no longer emerge unproblematically from the modernist pedagogy of foundationalism and universal truths, or from traditional narratives based on fixed identities with their requisite structure of closure. For many youths, meaning is in route, media has become a substitute for experience, and what constitutes understanding is grounded in a decentered and diasporic world of difference, displacement, and exchanges.

The intersection among cultural studies and pedagogy can be made clearer through an analysis of how the pedagogy of Hollywood has attempted in some recent films to portray the plight of young people within the conditions of a postmodern culture. I will focus on four films: *River's Edge* (1986), *My Own Private Idaho* (1991), *Slacker* (1991), and *Juice* (1992). These films are important as arguments and framing devices that in diverse ways attempt to provide a pedagogical representation of youth. These films point to some of the economic and social conditions at work in the formation of different racial and economic strata of youth, but they often do so within a narrative that combines a politics of despair with a fairly sophisticated depiction of the alleged sensibilities and moods of a generation of youth growing up amid the fracturing and menacing conditions of a postmodern culture. The challenge for progressive educators is to question how might a critical pedagogy be employed to appropriate the more radical and useful aspects of cultural study in addressing the new and different social, political, and economic contexts that are producing the twenty-something generation. At the same time, there is the issue of how a politics and project of pedagogy might be constructed to create the conditions for social agency and institutionalized change among diverse sectors of youth?

White Youth and the Politics of Despair

For many youth, showing up for adulthood at the fin de siècle means pulling back on hope and trying to put off the future rather than take up the modernist challenge of trying to shape it.[38] Popular cultural criticism has captured much of the ennui among youth and has made clear that "What used to be the pessimism of a radical fringe is now the shared assumption of a generation."[39] Cultural studies has helped to temper this broad generalization about youth in order to investigate the more complex representations at work in the construction of a new generation of youth that cannot be simply abstracted from the specificities of race, class, or gender. And yet, cultural studies theorists have also pointed to the increasing resistance of a twenty-something generation of youth who seem neither motivated by nostalgia for some lost conservative vision of America nor at home in the New World Order paved with the promises of the expanding electronic information highway.[40] While "youth" as a social construction has always been mediated, in part, as a social problem, many cultural critics believe that postmodern youth are uniquely "alien," "strange" and disconnected from the real world. For instance, in Gus Van Sant's film, *My Own Private Idaho,* the main character, Mike, who hustles his sexual wares for money, is a dreamer lost in fractured memories of a mother who deserted him as a child. Caught between flashbacks of Mom shown in 8mm color, and the video world of motley, street hustlers and their clients, Mike moves through his existence by falling asleep in times of stress only to awake in different geographic and spatial locations. What holds Mike's psychic and geographic travels together is the metaphor of sleep, the dream of escape, and the ultimate realization that even memories cannot fuel hope for the future. Mike becomes a metaphor for an entire generation of lower, middle-class youth forced to sell themselves in a world with no hope, a generation that aspires to nothing, works at degrading McJobs, and lives in a world in which chance and randomness rather than struggle, community, and solidarity drive their fate.

A more disturbing picture of white, working class youth can be found in *River's Edge.* Teenage anomie and drugged apathy are given painful expression in the depiction of a group of working class youth who are casually told by John, one of their friends, that he has strangled his girlfriend, another of the group's members, and left her nude body on the riverbank. The group at different times visits the site to view and probe the dead body of the girl. Seemingly unable to grasp the significance of the event, the youths initially hold off in informing anyone of the murder and with different degrees of concern initially try to protect John, the teenage sociopath, from being caught by the police. The youths in *River's Edge* drift through a world of broken families, blaring rock music, schooling marked by dead time, and a general indifference to life in general. Decentered and fragmented, they view death like life itself as merely a spectacle, a matter of style rather than substance. In one sense, these youth share the quality of being "asleep" that is depicted in *My Own Private Idaho*. But what is more disturbing in *River's Edge* is that lost innocence gives way not merely to teenage myopia, but to a culture in which human life is experienced as a voyeuristic seduction, a video game, good for passing time and diverting oneself from the pain of the moment. Despair and indifference cancel out the language of ethical discriminations and social responsibility while elevating the immediacy of pleasure to the defining moment of agency. In *River's Edge*, history as social memory is reassembled through vignettes of 1960s types portrayed as either burned out bikers or as the ex-radical turned teacher whose moralizing relegates politics to simply cheap opportunism. Exchanges among the young people in *River's Edge* appear like projections of a generation waiting either to fall asleep or to commit suicide. After talking about how he murdered his girlfriend, John blurts out "You do shit, it's done, and then you die." Another character responds, "It might be easier being dead." To which her boyfriend, a Wayne's world type, replies, "Bullshit you couldn't get stoned anymore." In this scenario, life imitates art when committing murder and getting stoned are given equal moral weight in the formula of the Hollywood spectacle, a spectacle which in the end flattens the complex representations of youth while constructing their identities through ample servings of pleasure, death, and violence.

River's Edge and *My Own Private Idaho* reveal the seamy and dark side of a youth culture while employing the Hollywood mixture of fascination and horror to titillate the audiences drawn to these films. Employing the postmodern aesthetic of revulsion, locality, randomness, and senselessness, youth in these films appear to be constructed outside of a broader cultural and economic landscape. Instead, they become visible only through visceral expressions of psychotic behavior or the brooding experience of a self-imposed comatose alienation.

One of the more celebrated white, youth films of the 1990s is Richard Linklater's *Slacker*. A decidedly low-budget film, *Slacker* attempts in both form and content to capture the sentiments of a twenty-something generation of middle-class, white youth who reject most of the values of the Reagan/Bush era but have a difficult time imagining what an alternative might look like. Distinctly nonlinear in its format, *Slacker* takes place in a 24-hour time frame in the college town of Austin, Texas. Building upon an antinarrative structure, *Slacker* is loosely organized around brief episodes in the lives of a variety of characters, none of whom are connected to each other except that each provides the pretext to lead the audience to the next character in the film. Sweeping through bookstores, coffee shops, auto parts yards, bedrooms, and rock music clubs, *Slacker* focuses on a disparate group of young people who possess little hope in the future and drift from job to job speaking a hybrid argot of bohemian intensities and new age–pop cult babble.

The film portrays a host of young people who randomly move from one place to the next, border crossers with no sense of where they have come from or where they are going. In this world of multiple realities, youth work in bands with the name "Ultimate Loser," talk about being forcibly put in hospitals by their parents, and one neopunker attempts to sell a Madonna pap smear to two acquaintances she meets in the street. "Check it out, I know it's kind of disgusting, but it's like sort of getting down to the real Madonna." This is a world in which language is wedded to an odd mix of nostalgia, popcorn philosophy, and MTV babble. Talk is organized around comments like: "I don't know ... I've traveled ... and when you get back you can't tell whether it really happened to you or if you just saw it on TV." Alienation is driven inward and emerges in comments like "I feel stuck." Irony slightly overshadows a refusal to imagine any kind of collective struggle. Reality seems too despairing to care about. This is humorously captured in one instance by a young man who suggests: "You know how the slogan goes, workers of the world, unite? We say workers of the world, relax?" People talk, but appear disconnected from themselves and each other, lives traverse each other with no sense of community or connection. There is a pronounced sense in *Slacker* of youth caught in the throes of new information technologies that both contain their aspirations while at the same time holding out the promise of some sense of agency.

At rare moments in the films, the political paralysis of narcissistic forms of refusal is offset by instances in which some characters recognize the importance of the image as a vehicle for cultural production, as a representational apparatus that can not only make certain experiences available but can also be used to produce alternative realities and social practices. The power of the image is present in the way the camera follows characters throughout the film, at once stalking them and confining them to a gaze that is both constraining and incidental. In one scene, a young man appears in an apartment surrounded by televisions that he claims he has had on for years. He points out that he has invented a game called a "Video Virus" in which through the use of a special technology he can push a button and insert himself onto any screen and perform any one of a number of actions. When asked by another character what this is about, he answers: "Well, we all know the psychic powers of the televised image. But we need to capitalize on it and make it work for us instead of working for it." This theme is taken up in two other scenes. In one short clip, a history graduate student shoots the video camera he is using to film himself, indicating a self-consciousness about the power of the image and the ability to control it at the same time. In another scene which concludes the film, a carload of people, each equipped with their Super 8 cameras, drive up to a large hill and they throw their cameras into a canyon. The film ends with the images being recorded by the cameras as they cascade to the bottom of the cliff in what suggests a moment of release and liberation.

In many respects, these movies largely focus on a culture of white, male youth who are both terrified and fascinated by the media, who appear overwhelmed by "the danger and wonder of future technologies, the banality of consumption, the thrill of brand names, [and] the difficulty of sex in alienated relationships."[41] The significance of these films rests, in part, in their attempt to capture the sense of powerlessness that increasingly affects working class and middle class white youth. But what is missing from these films along with the various books, articles, and reportage concerning what is often called the "Nowhere Generation," "Generation X," "13thGen," or "Slackers" is any sense of the larger political, racial, and social conditions in which youth are being framed as well as the multiple forms of resistance and racial diversity that exists among many different youth formations. What in fact should be seen as a social commentary about "dead-end capitalism" emerges simply as a celebration of refusal dressed up in a rhetoric of aesthetics, style, fashion, and solipsistic protests. Within this type of commentary, postmodern criticism is useful but limited because of its often theoretical inability to take up the relationship between identity and power, biography and the commodification of everyday life, or the limits of agency in an increasingly globalized economy as part of a broader project of possibility linked to issues of history, struggle, and transformation.[42]

In spite of the totalizing image of domination that structures *River's Edge* and *My Own Private Idaho,* and the lethal hopelessness that permeates *Slacker,* all of these films provide opportunities for examining the social and cultural context to which they refer in order to enlarge the range of strategies and understandings that students might bring to them to create a sense of resistance and transformation. For instance, many of my students who viewed *Slacker* did not despair over the film, but interpreted it to mean that "going slack" was viewed as a moment in the lives of young people when, with the proper resources, offered them a period in which to think, move around the country, and chill out in order to make some important decisions about their lives. Going slack became increasingly more oppressive as the slack time became drawn out far beyond their ability to end or control it. The students also pointed out that this film was made by Linklater with his friends with a great deal of energy and gusto that offers in itself a pedagogical model for young people to take up in developing their own narratives.

Black Youth and the Violence of Race

With the explosion of rap music into the sphere of popular culture and the intense debates that have emerged around the crisis of black masculinity, the issue of black nationalism, and the politics of black urban culture, it is not surprising that the black cinema has produced a series of films about the coming of age of black youth in urban America. What is unique about these films is that unlike the black exploitation films of the 1970s which were made by white producers for black audiences, the new wave of black cinema is being produced by black directors and aimed at black audiences.[43] With the advent of the 1990s, Hollywood has cashed in on a number of young talented black directors such as Spike Lee, Allen and Albert Hughes, Julie Dash, Ernest Dickerson, and John Singleton. Films about black youth have become big business as exemplified by the fact that in 1991 *New Jack City* and *Boys 'N the Hood* pulled in over 100 million dollars between them. Largely concerned with the inequalities, oppression, daily violence, and diminishing hope that plagues black communities in the urban war zone, the new wave of black films has attempted to accentuate the economic and social conditions that have contributed to the construction of "black masculinity and its relationship to the ghetto culture in which ideals of masculinity are nurtured and shaped."[44]

Unlike many of the recent films about white youth whose coming of age narratives are developed within traditional sociological categories such as alienation, restlessness, and anomie, black film productions such as Ernest Dickerson's *Juice* (1992) depict a culture of nihilism that is rooted directly in a violence whose defining principles are homicide, cultural suicide, internecine warfare, and social decay. It is interesting to note that just as the popular press has racialized crime, drugs, and violence as a black problem, some of the most interesting films to appear recently about black youth have been given the Hollywood imprimatur of excellence and have moved successfully as crossover films to a white audience. In what follows, I want to briefly probe the treatment of black youth and the representations of masculinity and resistance in the exemplary black film, *Juice.*

Juice (street slang for "respect") is the story of four young Harlem African American youth who are first portrayed as kids who engage in the usual antics of skipping school, fighting with other kids in the neighborhood, clashing with their parents about doing homework, and arguing with their siblings over using the bathroom in the morning. If this portrayal of youthful innocence is used to get a general audience to comfortably identify with these four black youths, it is soon ruptured as the group, caught in a spiraling wave of poverty and depressed opportunities, turn to crime and violence as a way to both construct their manhood and solve their most immediate problems. Determined to give their lives some sense of agency, the group moves from ripping off a record store to burglarizing a grocery market to the ruthless murder of the store owner and eventually each other. Caught in a world in which the ethics of the street is mirrored in the spectacle of TV violence, Bishop, Quincy, Raheem, and Steel (Tupac Shakur, Omar Epps, Kahalil Kain, and Jermaine Hopkins) decide after watching James Cagney go up in a blaze of glory in *White Heat* to take control of their lives by buying a gun and sticking up a neighborhood merchant who once chased them out of his store. Quincy is hesitant about participating in the stickup because he is a talented disc jockey and is determined to enter a local deejay contest in order to take advantage of his love of rap music and find a place for himself in the world.

Quincy is the only black youth in the film who models a sense of agency that is not completely caught in the confusion and despair exhibited by his three friends. Trapped within the loyalty codes of the street and in the protection it provides, Quincy reluctantly agrees to participate in the heist. Bad choices have major consequences in this typical big city ghetto, and Quincy's sense of hope and independence is shattered as Bishop, the most violent of the group, kills the store owner and then proceeds to murder Raheem and hunt down Quincy and Steele since they no longer see him as a respected member of the group. Quincy eventually buys a weapon to protect himself and in the final scene of the film confronts Bishop on the roof where a struggle ensues and Bishop plunges to his death. As the film ends, one of onlookers tells Quincy "You got the juice," but Quincy rejects the accolade ascribing power and prestige to him and walks away.

Juice reasserts the importance of rap music as the cultural expression of imaginable possibilities in the daily lives of black youth. Not only does rap music provide the musical score which frames the film, it also plays a pivotal role by providing a social context for the desires, rage, and independent expression of black, male, artistic expression. For Quincy, rap music offers him the opportunity to claim some "juice" among his peers while providing him with a context to construct an affirmative identity along with the chance for real employment. Music in this context becomes a major referent for understanding how identities and bodies come together in a hip-hop culture that at its most oppositional moment is testing the limits of the American dream. But *Juice* also gestures, through the direction of Ernest Dickerson, that if violence is endemic to the black ghetto its roots lie in a culture of violence that is daily transmitted through the medium of television. This is suggested in one powerful scene in which the group watches on television both the famed violent ending of James Cagney's *White Heat,* and the news bulletin announcing the death of a neighborhood friend as he attempted to rip off a local bar. In this scene, Dickerson draws a powerful relationship between what the four youths see on television and their impatience over their own lack of agency and need to take control of their lives. As Michael Dyson points out:

> Dickerson's aim is transparent: to highlight the link between violence and criminality fostered in the collective American imagination by television, the consumption of images through a medium that has replaced the Constitution and the Declaration of Independence as the unifying fiction of national citizenship and identity. It is also the daily and exclusive occupation of Bishop's listless father, a reminder that television's genealogy of influence unfolds from its dulling effects

in one generation to its creation of lethal desires in the next, twin strategies of destruction when applied in the black male ghetto.[45]

While Dyson is right in pointing to Dickerson's critique of the media, he overestimates the importance given in *Juice* to the relationship between black-on-black violence and those larger social determinants which black urban life both reflects and helps to produce. In fact, it could be argued that the violence portrayed in *Juice* and similar films such as *Boys N' the Hood, New Jack City*, and especially *Menace II Society*, "feeds the racist national obsession that black men and their community are the central locus of the American scene of violence."[46]

Although the violence in these films is traumatizing as part of its efforts to promote an antiviolence message, it is also a violence that is hermetic, sutured, and sealed within the walls of the black urban ghetto. The counterpart of this type of violence in controversial, white films such as *Reservoir Dogs* is taken up by most critics as part of an avant garde aesthetic, but the violence in the recent wave of black youth films often reinforces for middle-class viewers the assumption that such violence is endemic to the black community and the only salvation gained in portraying such inner city hopelessness is that it be noticed so that it can be stopped from spreading like a disease into the adjoining suburbs and business zones that form a colonizing ring around black ghettoes. Because films such as *Juice* do not self-consciously rupture dominant stereotypical assumptions that make race and crime synonymous, they often suggest a kind of nihilism that Cornel West describes as "the lived experience of coping with a life of horrifying meaninglessness, hopelessness and (most important) lovelessness."[47]

Unfortunately, West's notion of nihilism is too tightly drawn and while it may claim to pay sufficient attention to the loss of hope and meaning among black youth, it fails to connect the specificity of black nihilism to the nihilism of systemic inequality, calculated injustice, and moral indifference that operates daily as a regime of brutalization and oppression for so many youth of color and class in this country. Itabari Njeri forcefully captures the failure of such an analysis and the problems that films such as *Juice*, in spite of the best intentions of their directors, often reproduce. Commenting on another coming-of-age black youth film, *Menace II Society*, he writes:

The nation cannot allow nearly 50 percent of black men to be unemployed, as is the case in many African American communities. It cannot let schools systematically brand normal black children as uneducable for racist reasons, or permit the continued brutalization of blacks by police, nor have black adults take out their socially engendered frustrations on each other and their children and not yield despair and dysfunction. This kind of despair is the source of the nihilism Cornel West described. Unfortunately, the black-male-as-menace film genre often fails to artfully tie this nihilism to its poisonous roots in America's system of inequality. And because it fails to do so, the effects of these toxic forces are seen as causes.[48]

In both pedagogical and political terms, the reigning films about black youth that have appeared since 1990 may have gone too far in producing narratives that employ the commercial strategy of reproducing graphic violence and then moralizing about its effects. Violence in these films is tied to a self-destructiveness and senselessness that shocks but often fails to inform the audience about either its wider determinations or the audience's possible complicity in such violence. The effects of such films tend to reinforce for white middle-class America the comforting belief that nihilism as both a state of mind and a site of social relations is always somewhere else in that strangely homogenized social formation known as "black" youth.

Of course, it is important to note that *Juice* refrains from romanticizing violence, just as it suggests at the end of the film that Quincy does not want the juice if it means leading a life in which violence is the only capital that has any exchange value in African American communities. But these sentiments come late and are too underdeveloped. One pedagogical challenge presented by these films is for educators and students to theorize why Hollywood is investing in films about black youth that overlook the complex representations that structure African American communities. Such an inquiry can be taken up by looking at the work of black feminist film makers such as Julie Dash and the powerful and complex representations she offers black women in *Daughters of the Dust* or the work of Leslie Harris, whose film *Just Another Girl on the IRT* challenges the misogyny that structures the films currently being made about black, male youth. Another challenge involves trying to understand why large numbers of black, urban, male youth readily identify with the wider social representations of sexism, homophobia, misogyny, and gaining respect at such a high cost to themselves and the communities in which they live. Films about black youth are important to engage in order to both understand the pedagogies that silently structure their representations and how such representations pedagogically work to educate crossover white audiences. Most importantly, these films should not be dismissed because they are reductionistic, sexist, or one dimensional in their portrayal of the rite of passage of black, male youth; at most, they become a marker for understanding how complex representations of black youth get lost in racially coded films that point to serious problems in the urban centers but do so in ways that erase any sense of viable hope, possibility, resistance, and struggle.

Contemporary films about black youth offer a glimpse into the specificity of otherness, that is, they cross a cultural and racial border and in doing so perform a theoretical service in making visible what is often left out of the dominant politics of representations. And it is in the light of such an opening that the possibility exists for educators and other cultural workers to take up the relationship among culture, power, and identity in ways that grapple with the complexity of youth and the intersection of race, class, and gender formations.

Combining cultural studies with pedagogical theory would suggest that students take these films seriously as legitimate forms of social knowledge that reveal different sets of struggles among youths within diverse cultural sites. For white youth, these films mimic a coming-of-age narrative that indicts the aimlessness and senselessness produced within a larger culture of commercial stupefaction; on the other hand, black youth films posit a "not-coming-of-age" narrative that serves as a powerful indictment of autogenocide among African American youths. Clearly, educators can learn from these films and in doing so bring these different accounts of the cultural production of youth together within a common project that addresses the relationship between pedagogy and social justice, on the one hand, and democracy and the struggle for equality on the other. Clearly these films suggest that educators need to ask new questions, develop new models, and new ways of producing an oppositional pedagogy that is capable of understanding the different social, economic, and political contexts that produce youth differently within varied sets and relations of power.

Another pedagogical challenge offered by these films concerns how teachers can address the desires that different students bring to these popular cultural texts. In other words, what does it mean to mobilize the desires of students by using forms of social knowledge that constitute the contradictory field of popular culture? In part, it means recognizing that while students are familiar with such texts, they bring different beliefs, political understandings, and affective investments to such a learning process. Hence, pedagogy must proceed by acknowledging that conflict will emerge regarding the form and content of such films and how students address such issues. For such a pedagogy to work, Fabienne Worth argues that "students must become visible to themselves and to each other and valued in their differences."[49] This suggests giving students the opportunity to decenter the curriculum by structuring, in part, how the class should be organized and how such films can be addressed without putting any one student's identity on trial. It means recognizing the complexity of attempting to mobilize students' desires as part of a pedagogical project that directly addresses representations that affect certain parts of their lives, and to acknowledge the emotional problems that will emerge in such teaching.

At the same time, such a pedagogy must reverse the cycle of despair that often informs these accounts and address how the different postmodern conditions and contexts of youth can be changed in order to expand and deepen the promise of a substantive democracy. In part, this may mean using films about youth that capture the complexity, sense of struggle, and diversity that marks different segments of the current generation of young people.

In this case, cultural studies and pedagogical practice can mutually inform each other by using popular cultural texts as serious objects of study that can be used to address the limits and possibilities that youth face in different social, cultural, and economic contexts; equally important is the need to read popular cultural texts as part of a broader pedagogical effort to develop a sense of agency in students based on a commitment to changing oppressive contexts by understanding the relations of power that inform them.

The pedagogical challenge represented by the emergence of a postmodern generation of youth has not been lost on advertisers and market research analysts. According to a 1992 Roper Organization, Inc. study, the current generation of 18–29 year olds has an annual buying power of 125 billion dollars. Addressing the interests and tastes of this generation, "McDonald's, for instance, has introduced hip-hop music and images to promote burgers and fries, ditto Coca-Cola, with its frenetic commercials touting Coca-Cola Classic."[50] Benetton, Esprit, The Gap, and other companies have followed suit in their attempts to identify and mobilize the desires, identities, and buying patterns of a new generation of youth.[51] What appears as a despairing expression of the postmodern condition to some theorists becomes for others a challenge to invent new market strategies for corporate interests. In this scenario, youth may be experiencing the indeterminacy, senselessness, and multiple conditions of postmodernism, but corporate advertisers are attempting to theorize a pedagogy of consumption as part of a new way of appropriating postmodern differences among youth in different sites and locations. The lesson here is that differences among youth matter politically and pedagogically, but not as a way of generating new markets or registering difference simply as a fashion niche.

What educators need to do is to make the pedagogical more political by addressing both the conditions through which they teach and what it means to learn from a generation that is experiencing life in a way that is vastly different from the representations offered in modernist versions of schooling. This is not to suggest that modernist schools do not attend to popular culture but they do so on very problematic terms, which often confine it to the margins of the curriculum. Moreover, modernist schools cannot be rejected outright. As I have shown elsewhere, the political culture of modernism with its emphasis on social equality, justice, freedom, and human agency needs to be refigured within rather than outside of an emerging postmodern discourse.[52]

The emergence of the electronic media coupled with a diminishing faith in the power of human agency has undermined the traditional visions of schooling and the meaning of pedagogy. The language of lesson plans and upward mobility and the forms of teacher authority on which it was based has been radically delegitimated by the recognition that culture and power are central to the authority/knowledge relationship. Modernism's faith in the past has given way to a future for which traditional markers no longer make sense.

Cultural Studies and Youth: The Pedagogical Issue

Educators and cultural critics need to address the effects of emerging postmodern conditions on a current generation of young people who appear hostage to the vicissitudes of a changing economic order with its legacy of diminished hopes, on the one hand, and a world of schizoid images, diminishing public spaces and an increasing fragmentation, uncertainty, and randomness that structure postmodern daily life on the other. Central to this issue is whether educators are dealing with a new kind of student forged within organizing principles shaped by the intersection of the electronic image, popular culture, and a dire sense of indeterminacy.

What cultural studies offers educators is a theoretical framework for addressing the shifting attitudes, representations, and desires of this new generation of youth being produced within the current historical, economic, and cultural juncture. But it does more than simply provide a lens for resituating the construction of youth within a shifting and radically altered social, technological, and economic landscape; it also provides elements for rethinking the relationship between culture and power, knowledge and authority, learning and experience, and the role of teachers as public intellectuals. In what follows, I want to point to some of the theoretical elements that link cultural studies and critical pedagogy and speak briefly to their implications for cultural work.

First, cultural studies is premised on the belief that we have entered a period in which the traditional distinctions that separate and frame established academic disciplines cannot account for the great diversity of cultural and social phenomena that has come to characterize an increasingly hybridized, postindustrial world. The university has long been linked to a notion of national identity that is largely defined by and committed to transmitting traditional, Western culture.[53] Traditionally, this has been a culture of exclusion, one which has ignored the multiple narratives, histories, and voices of culturally and politically subordinated groups. The emerging proliferation of diverse social movements arguing for a genuinely multicultural and multiracial society have challenged schools that use academic knowledge to license cultural differences in order to regulate and define who they are and how they might narrate themselves. Moreover, the spread of electronically mediated culture to all spheres of everyday intellectual and artistic life has shifted the ground of scholarship away from the traditional disciplines designed to preserve a "common culture" to the more hybridized fields of comparative and world literature, media studies, ecology, society and technology, and popular culture.

Second, advocates of cultural studies have argued strongly that the role of culture, including the power of the mass media with its massive apparatuses of representation and its regulation of meaning, is central to understanding how the dynamics of power, privilege, and social desire structure the daily life of a society.[54] This concern with culture and its connection to power has necessitated a critical interrogation of the relationship between knowledge and authority, the meaning of canonicity, and the historical and social contexts that deliberately shape students' understanding of accounts of the past, present, and future. But if a sea change in the development and reception of what counts as knowledge has taken place, it has been accompanied by an understanding of how we define and apprehend the range of texts that are open to critical interrogation and analysis. For instance, instead of connecting culture exclusively to the technology of print and the book as the only legitimate academic artifact, there is a great deal of academic work going on which analyzes how textual, aural, and visual representations are produced, organized, and distributed through a variety of cultural forms such as the media, popular culture, film, advertising, mass communications, and other modes of cultural production.[55]

At stake here is the attempt to produce new theoretical models and methodologies for addressing the production, structure, and exchange of knowledge. This approach to inter/postdisciplinary studies is valuable because it addresses the pedagogical issue of organizing dialogue across and outside of the disciplines in order to promote alternative approaches to research and teaching about culture and the newly emerging technologies and forms of knowledge. For instance, rather than organize courses around strictly disciplinary concerns arising out of English and social studies courses, it might be more useful and relevant for colleges of education to organize courses that broaden students' understanding of themselves and others by examining events that evoke a sense of social responsibility and moral accountability. A course on "Immigration and Politics in Fin-de-Siecle America" could provide a historical perspective on the demographic changes confronting America and how such changes are being felt within the shifting dynamics of education, economics, cultural identity, and urban development. A course on the Los Angeles uprisings could incorporate the related issues of race, politics, economics, and education to address the multiple conditions underlying the violence and despair that produced such a tragic event.

Third, in addition to broadening the terms and parameters of learning, cultural studies rejects the professionalization of educators and the alienating and often elitist discourse of professionalism and sanitized expertise. Instead, it argues for educators as public intellectuals. Stuart Hall is instructive on this issue when he argues that cultural studies provides two points of tension that intellectuals need to address:

First, cultural studies constitutes one of the points of tension and change at the frontiers of intellectual and academic life, pushing for new questions, new models, and new ways of study, testing the fine lines between intellectual rigor and social relevance....But. secondly ... cultural studies insists on what I want to call the vocation of the intellectual life. That is to say, cultural studies insists on the necessity to address the central, urgent, and disturbing questions of a society and a culture in the most rigorous intellectual way we have available.[56]

In this view, intellectuals must be accountable in their teaching for the ways in which they address and respond to the problems of history, human agency, and the renewal of democratic public life. Cultural studies strongly rejects the assumption that teachers are simply transmitters of existing configurations of knowledge. As public intellectuals, academics are always implicated in the dynamics of social power through the experiences they organize and provoke in their classrooms. In this perspective, intellectual work is incomplete unless it self-consciously assumes responsibility for its effects in the larger public culture while simultaneously addressing the most profoundly and deeply inhumane problems of the societies in which we live. Hence, cultural studies raises questions about what knowledge is produced in the university and how it is consequential in extending and deepening the possibilities for democratic public life. Equally important is the issue of how to democratize the schools so as to enable those groups who in large measure are divorced from or simply not represented in the curriculum to be able to produce their own representations, narrate their own stories, and engage in respectful dialogue with others. In this instance, cultural studies must address how dialogue is constructed in the classroom about other cultures and voices by critically addressing both the position of the theorists and the institutions in which such dialogues are produced. Peter Hitchcock argues forcefully that the governing principles of any such dialogic exchange should include some of the following elements:

1) attention to the specific institutional setting in which this activity takes place; 2) self-reflexivity regarding the particular identities of the teacher and students who collectively undertake this activity; 3) an awareness that the cultural identities at stake in "other" cultures are in the process-of-becoming in dialogic interaction and are not static as subjects; but 4) the knowledge produced through this activity is always already contestable and by definition is not the knowledge of the other as the other would know herself or himself.[57]

Fourth, another important contribution of cultural studies is its emphasis on studying the production, reception, and use of varied texts, and how they are used to define social relations, values, particular notions of community, the future, and diverse definitions of the self. Texts in this sense do not merely refer to the culture of print or the technology of the book, but to all those audio, visual, and electronically mediated forms of knowledge that have prompted a radical shift in the construction of knowledge and the ways in which knowledge is read, received, and consumed. It is worth repeating that contemporary youth increasingly rely less on the technology and culture of the book to construct and affirm their identities; instead, they are faced with the task of finding their way through a decentered cultural landscape no longer caught in the grip of a technology of print, closed narrative structures, or the certitude of a secure economic future. The new emerging technologies that construct and position youth represent interactive terrains that cut across "language and culture, without narrative requirements, without character complexities....Narrative complexity [has given] way to design complexity; story [has given] way to a sensory environment."[58] Cultural studies is profoundly important for educators in that it focuses on media not merely in terms of how it distorts and misrepresents reality, but also on how media plays "a part in the formation, in the constitution, of the things they reflect. It is not that there is a world outside, 'out there,' which exists free of the discourse of representation. What is 'out there' is, in part, constituted by how it is represented."[59]

I don't believe that educators and schools of education can address the shifting attitudes, representations, and desires of this new generation of youth within the dominant disciplinary configurations of knowledge and practice. On the contrary, as youth are constituted within languages and new cultural forms that intersect differently across and within issues of race, class, gender, and sexual differences, the conditions through which youth attempt to narrate themselves must be understood in terms of both the context of their struggles and through a shared language of agency that points to a project of hope and possibility. It is precisely this language of difference, specificity, and possibility that is lacking from most attempts at educational reform.

Fifth, it is important to stress that when critical pedagogy is established as one of the defining principles of cultural studies, it is possible to generate a new discourse for moving beyond a limited emphasis on the mastery of techniques and methodologies. Critical pedagogy represents a form of cultural production implicated in and critically attentive to how power and meaning are employed in the construction and organization of knowledge, desires, values, and identities. Critical pedagogy in this sense is not reduced to the mastering of skills or techniques, but is defined as a cultural practice that must be accountable ethically and politically for the stories it produces, the claims it makes on social memories, and the images of the future it deems legitimate. As both an object of critique and a method of cultural production, it refuses to hide behind claims of objectivity, and works effortlessly to link theory and practice to enabling the possibilities for human agency in a world of diminishing returns. It is important to make a distinction here that challenges the liberal and conservative criticism that since critical pedagogy attempts both to politicize teaching and teach politics that it represents a species of indoctrination. By asserting that all teaching is profoundly political and that critical educators and cultural workers should operate out of a project of social transformation, I am arguing that as educators we need to make a distinction between what Peter Euben calls political and politicizing education.

Political education, which is central to critical pedagogy, refers to teaching "students how to think in ways that cultivate the capacity for judgment essential for the exercise of power and responsibility by a democratic citizenry....A political, as distinct from a politicizing education would encourage students to become better citizens to challenge those with political and cultural power as well as to honor the critical traditions within the dominant culture that make such a critique possible and intelligible."[60] A political education means decentering power in the classroom and other pedagogical sites so the dynamics of those institutional and cultural inequalities that marginalize some groups, repress particular types of knowledge, and suppress critical dialogue can be addressed. On the other hand, politicizing education is a form of pedagogical terrorism in which the issue of what is taught, by whom, and under what conditions is determined by a doctrinaire political agenda that refuses to examine its own values, beliefs, and ideological construction. While refusing to recognize the social and historical character of its own claims to history, knowledge, and values, a politicizing education silences in the name of a specious universalism and denounces all transformative practices through an appeal to a timeless notion of truth and beauty. For those who practice a politicizing education, democracy and citizenship become dangerous in that the precondition for their realization demands critical inquiry, the taking of risks, and the responsibility to resist and say no in the face of dominant forms of power.

Conclusion

Given its challenge to the traditional notion of teachers as merely transmitters of information and its insistence that teachers are cultural producers deeply implicated in public issues, cultural studies provides a new and transformative language for educating teachers and administrators around the issue of civic leadership and public service. In this perspective, teacher education is fashioned not around a particular dogma, but through pedagogical practices which address the changing contexts and conditions for students to be critically attentive to the historical and socially constructed nature of the locations they occupy within a shifting world of representations and values. Cultural studies requires that teachers be educated to be cultural producers, to treat culture as an activity, unfinished, and incomplete. This suggests that they should be critically attentive to the operations of power as it is implicated in the production of knowledge and authority in particular and shifting contexts. This means learning how to be sensitive to considerations of power as it is inscribed on every facet of the schooling process.

The conditions and problems of contemporary youth will have to be engaged through a willingness to interrogate the world of public politics while appropriating modernity's call for a better world and abandoning its linear narratives of Western history, unified culture, disciplinary order, and technological progress. In this case, the pedagogical importance of uncertainty and indeterminacy can be rethought through a modernist notion of the dream world in which youth and others can shape, without the benefit of master narratives, the conditions for producing new ways of learning, engaging, and positing the possibilities for social struggle and solidarity. Critical educators cannot subscribe either to an apocalyptic emptiness or to a politics of refusal that celebrates the abandonment of authority or the immediacy of experience over the more profound dynamic of social memory and moral outrage forged within and against conditions of exploitation, oppression, and the abuse of power.

The intersection of cultural studies and critical pedagogy offers the possibilities for educators to confront history as more than simulacrum and ethics as something other than the casualty of incommensurable language games. Educators need to assert a politics that makes the relationship among authority, ethics, and power central to a pedagogy that expands rather than closes down the possibilities of a radical democratic society. Within this discourse, images do not dissolve reality into simply another text; on the contrary, representations become central to revealing the structures of power relations at work in the public, schools, society, and the larger global order. Pedagogy does not succumb to the whims of the market place in this logic nor to the latest form of educational chic; instead, critical pedagogy engages cultural studies as part of an ongoing movement towards a shared conception of justice and a radicalization of the social order. This is a task that not only recognizes the multiple relationships between culture and power, but also makes critical pedagogy one of its defining principles.

Notes

1. Dick Hebdige, *Hiding in the Light* (New York: Routledge, 1988), pp. 17–18.
2. "Footnotes," *Chronicle of Higher Education* (December 1, 1993): A8.
3. I provide a detailed critique of this issue in Henry A. Giroux, *Schooling and the Struggle for Public Life,* 2nd ed. (Boulder: Paradigm Publishers, 2005). See also Stanley Aronowitz and Henry A. Giroux, *Education Still under Siege* (Westport, CT: Bergin and Garvey Press, 1993).
4. I take this issue up in detail in Henry A. Giroux, *Disturbing Pleasures: Learning Popular Culture* (New York: Routledge, 1994).
5. Feminist theorists have been making this point for years. For an example of some of this work as it is expressed at the intersection of cultural studies and peda-

gogy; see the various articles in Henry A. Giroux and Peter McLaren, eds., *Between Borders: Pedagogy and the Politics of Cultural Studies* (New York: Routledge, 1993).

6. The relationship between cultural studies and relations of government are taken up in Tony Bennett, "Putting Policy into Cultural Studies," *Cultural Studies* (New York: Routledge, 1992), pp. 23–34.

7. For representative example of the diverse issues taken up in the field of cultural studies, see Lawrence Grossberg, Cary Nelson, and Paula Treichler, eds., *Cultural Studies* (New York: Routledge, 1992) and Simon During, ed. *The Cultural Studies Reader* (New York: Routledge, 1993).

8. This is especially true of some of the most ardent critics of higher education. A representative list includes: William J. Bennett, *To Reclaim a Legacy: A Report on the Humanities in Higher Education* (Washington, DC: National Endowment for the Humanities, 1984); Stephen H. Balch and Herbert London, "The Tenured Left," *Commentary 82*:4 (October 1986): 41–51; Lynne V. Cheney, *Tyrannical Machines: A Report on Education Practices Gone Wrong and Our Best Hopes for Setting Them Right* (Washington, DC: National Endowment for the Humanities, 1990); Roger Kimball, *Tenured Radicals: How Politics Has Corrupted Our Higher Education* (New York: Harper and Row, 1990); Dinesh D'Souza, *Illiberal Education: The Politics of Race and Sex on Campus* (New York: Free Press, 1991). For a highly detailed analysis of the web of conservative money, foundations, and ideologies that connect the above intellectuals, see Ellen Messer-Davidow, "Manufacturing the Attack on Liberalized Higher Education," *Social Text 36* (Fall 1993): 40–80.

9. Cary Nelson, Paula Treichler, and Lawrence Grossberg, "Cultural Studies: An Introduction," in Cary Nelson, Paula Treichler, and Lawrence Grossberg, eds., *Cultural Studies* (New York: Routledge, 1992), p. 5.

10. Tony Bennett, "Putting Policy into Cultural Studies," in Grossberg, et al., eds., ibid., p. 32.

11. I take up these issues in more detail in Henry A. Giroux, *Border Crossings* (New York: Routledge, 1992) and in *Disturbing Pleasures: Learning Popular Culture* (New York: Routledge, 1994).

12. Cary Nelson, "Always Already Cultural Studies," op. cit., p. 32.

13. Dick Hebdige, *Hiding in the Light* (New York: Routledge, 1988), pp. 17–18.

14. Stuart Hall, "What is this 'Black' in Popular Culture?" in Gina Dent, ed. *Black Popular Culture* (Seattle: Bay Press, 1992), p. 22.

15. As a representative example of this type of critique, see any of the major theoretical sources of cultural studies, especially the Center for Contemporary Cultural Studies in Birmingham. For example, Stuart Hall, "Cultural Studies: Two Paradigms," *Media Culture, and Society 2* (1980): 57–72; "Cultural Studies and the Center: Some Problematics and Problems," in Hall, et al., eds. *Culture, Media, Language: Working Paper in Cultural Studies* (London: Hutchinson, 1980); Richard Johnson, "What Is Cultural Studies Anyway?" *Social Text 6*:1 (1987): 38–40; and Meaghan Morris, "Banality in Cultural Studies," *Discourse 10*:2 (1988): 3–29.

16. See Stanley Aronowitz, *Roll over Beethoven: Return of Cultural Strife* (Hanover, NH: University Press of New England, 1993) and Gayatri C. Spivak, *Outside in the Teaching Machine* (New York: Routledge, 1993). See also a few articles in Grossberg, et al., eds., *Cultural Studies*. Also, see various issues of *College Literature* under the editorship of Kostas Mrysiades. It is quite revealing to look into some of the latest

books on cultural studies and see no serious engagement of pedagogy as a site of theoretical and practical struggle. In David Punter, ed., *Introduction to Contemporary Cultural Studies* (New York: Longman, 1986), there is one chapter on identifying racism in textbooks. For more recent examples, see Patrick Brantlinger, *Crusoe's Footprints: Cultural Studies in Britain and America* (New York: Routledge, 1990); Graeme Turner, *British Cultural Studies* (London: Unwin Hyman, 1990); John Clarke, *New Times and Old Enemies* (London: HarperCollins, 1991); and Sarah Franklin, Celia Lury, and Jackie Stacey, eds. *Off-Centre: Feminism and Cultural Studies* (London: HarperCollins, 1991). In the following books published in 1993, there is not one mention of pedagogy: Simon During, ed., *The Cultural Studies Reader* (New York: Routledge, 1993) and Valda Blundell, John Shepherd, and Ian Taylor, eds., *Relocating Cultural Studies* (New York: Routledge, 1993).

17.   While there are too many sources to cite here, see R. W. Connell, D. J. Ashenden, S. Kessler, and G. W. Dowsett, *Making the Difference* (Boston: Allen and Unwin, 1982); Julian Henriques, Wendy Hollway, Cathy Urwin, Couze Venn, and Valerie Walkerdine, *Changing the Subject* (London: Methuen, 1984); James T. Sears, *Growing Up Gay in the South: Race, Gender, and Journeys of the Spirit* (New York: Harrington Park Press, 1991); Michelle Fine, *Framing Dropouts* (Albany: SUNY Press,1991); Roger I. Simon, *Teaching Against the Grain* (New York: Bergin and Garvey Press, 1992); and James Donald, *Sentimental Education* (London: Verso Press, 1992).

18.   For instance, while theorists such as Jane Tompkins, Gerald Graff, Gregory Ulmer, and others address pedagogical issues, they do it solely within the referenced terrain of literary studies. Moreover, even those theorists in literary studies who insist on the political nature of pedagogy generally ignore, with few exceptions, the work that has gone on in the field for twenty years. See, for example, Shoshana Felman and Dori Lamb, *Testimony: Crisis of Witnessing in Literature, Psychoanalysis, and History* (New York: Routledge, 1992); Bruce Henricksen and Thais E. Morgan, *Reorientations: Critical Theories and Pedagogies* (Urbana: University of Illinois Press, 1990); Patricia Donahue and Ellen Quahndahl, eds., *Reclaiming Pedagogy: The Rhetoric of the Classroom* (Carbondale: Southern Illinois University Press, 1989); Gregory Ulmer, *Applied Grammatology* (Baltimore: Johns Hopkins University Press, 1985); Barbara Johnson, ed., *The Pedagogical Imperative: Teaching as a Literary Genre* (New Haven: Yale University Press, 1983).

19.   One interesting example of this occurred when Gary Olson, the editor of the *Journal of Advanced Composition,* interviewed Jacques Derrida. He asked Derrida, in the context of a discussion about pedagogy and teaching, if he knew of the work of Paulo Freire. Derrida responded with "This is the first time I've heard his name" (Gary Olson, "Jacques Derrida on Rhetoric and Composition: A Conversation," in Gary Olson and Irene Gale, eds. *(Inter)views: Cross-Disciplinary Perspectives on Rhetoric and Literacy* [Carbondale: Southern Illinois University Press, 1991], p. 133). It is hard to imagine that a figure of Freire's international stature would not be known to someone in literary studies who is one of the major proponents of deconstruction. So much for crossing boundaries. Clearly, Derrida does not read the radical literature in composition studies, because if he did he could not miss the numerous references to the work of Paulo Freire and other critical educators. See, for instance, C. Douglas Atkins and Michael L. Johnson, *Writing and Reading Differently: Deconstruction and the Teaching of Composition and Literature* (Lawrence: University of Kansas Press,

1985); Linda Brodkey, *Academic Writing as a Social Practice* (Philadelphia, PA: Temple University Press, 1987); C. Mark Hurlbert and Michael Blitz, eds., *Composition and Resistance* (Portsmouth, NH: Heinemann, 1991).

20. It is worth noting that the term *cultural studies* derives from the Centre for Contemporary Cultural Studies at the University of Birmingham. Initially influenced by the work of Richard Hoggart, Raymond Williams, and E.P. Thompson, the center's ongoing work in cultural studies achieved international recognition under the direction of Stuart Hall in the 1970s and later under Richard Johnson in the 1980s. For a useful history of the center written from the theoretical vantage point of one of its American supporters, see Lawrence Grossberg, "The Formations of Cultural Studies: An American in Birmingham," in Valda Blundell, John Shepherd, and Ian Taylor, eds., *Relocating Cultural Studies: Developments in Theory and Research* (New York: Routledge, 1993), pp. 21–66.

21. Williams is quite adamant in refuting "encyclopedia articles dating the birth of cultural studies from this or that book in the late fifties." He goes on to say that: "the shift of perspective about the teaching of art and literature and their relation to history and to contemporary society began in adult education, it didn't happen anywhere else. It was when it was taken across by people with that experience to the universities that it was suddenly recognized as a subject. It is in these and other similar ways that the contribution of the process itself to social change itself, and specifically to learning, has happened." Cited in Raymond Williams, "Adult Education and Social Change," in *What I Came to Say* (London: Hutchinson-Radus, 1989), pp. 157–166. See also Raymond Williams, "The Future of Cultural Studies," in Raymond Williams, *The Politics of Modernism* (London: Verso, 1989), pp. 151–162.

22. Williams, ibid., p. 158.

23. John Fiske, *Power Plays, Power Works* (London: Verso Press, 1994), p. 20.

24. Larry Grossberg goes so far as to argue that cultural studies "sees both history and its own practice as the struggle to produce one context out of another, one set of relations out of another." Lawrence Grossberg, "Cultural Studies and/in New Worlds," *Critical Studies in Mass Communications* (March 1993), p. 4.

25. Raymond Williams, *Communications*, rev. ed. (New York: Barnes and Noble, 1967), pp. 14–15.

26. Roger I. Simon, *Teaching Against the Grain* (New York: Bergin and Garvey, 1992), p. 15.

27. Ruth Conniff, "The Culture of Cruelty," *Progressive* (September 16, 1992): 16–20.

28. See the November 29, 1993 issue of *Newsweek*. Of course, the issue that is often overlooked in associating gangsta rap with violence is that "gangsta rap does not appear in a cultural vacuum, but, rather, is expressive of the cultural crossing, mixing, and engagement of black youth culture with the values, attitudes, and concerns of the white majority." Quoted in bell hooks, "Sexism and Misogyny: Who Takes the Rap?" *Z Magazine* (February 1994): 26. See also Greg Tate's spirited defense of rap in Greg Tate, "Above and Beyond Rap's Decibels," *New York Times*, Sunday, March 6, 1994, pp. 1, 36.

29. This is most evident in the popular media culture where analysis of crime in the United States is almost exclusively represented through images of black youth. For example, in the May 1994 issue of *Atlantic Monthly*, the cover of the magazine

shows a black urban youth, absent a shirt, with a gun in his hand, staring out at the reader. The story the image is highlighting is about inner city violence. The flurry of articles, magazines, films, and news stories about crime produced in 1994 focus almost exclusively on black youth both discursively and representationally.

30. Camille Colatosti, "Dealing Guns," *Z Magazine* (January 1994): 59.

31. Holly Sklar, "Young and Guilty by Stereotype" *Z Magazine* (July/August 1993): 52.

32. Stanley Aronowitz, "A Different Perspective on Educational Inequality," *Review of Education/Pedagogy/Cultural Studies* 16:2 (1994): 15.

33. Stanley Aronowitz and Henry A. Giroux, *Education Still under Siege* (Westport, CT: Bergin and Garvey Press, 1993), pp. 4–5.

34. These quotes and comments are taken from a stinging analysis of Kaus in Jonathan Kozol, "Speaking the Unspeakable," unpublished manuscript. The context for Kaus' remarks is developed in Mickey Kaus, *The End of Equality* (New York: Basic Books, 1992).

35. Paul Virilio, *Lost Dimension*, trans. Daniel Moshenberg (New York: Semiotext(e), 1991).

36. Andrew Ross and Tricia Rose, eds., *Microphone Fiends: Youth Music and Youth Culture* (New York: Routledge, 1994).

37. Walter Parkes, "Random Access, Remote Control," *Omni* (January 1994): 54.

38. This section of the paper draws from: Henry A. Giroux, "Slacking Off: Border Youth and Postmodern Education," *Journal of Advanced Composition* 3:2 (1994).

39. Carol Anshaw, "Days of Whine and Poses," *Village Voice* (November 1992): 27.

40. For a critique of the so-called twenty-something generation as defined by *Time, U.S. News and World Report, Money, Newsweek,* and the *Utne Reader,* see Chris de Bellis, "From Slackers to Baby Busters," *Z Magazine* (December 1993): 8–10.

41. Andrew Kopkind, "Slacking toward Bethlehem," *Grand Street* 44 (1992): 183.

42. The contours of this type of criticism are captured in a comment by Andrew Kopkind, a keen observer of slacker culture.

> The domestic and economic relationship that have created the new consciousness are not likely to improve in the few years left in this century, or in the years of the next, when the young slackers will be middle-agers. The choices for young people will be increasingly constricted. In a few years, a steady job at a mall outlet or a food chain may be all that's left for the majority of college graduates. Life is more and more like a lottery—is a lottery—with nothing but the luck of the draw determining whether you get a recording contract, get your screenplay produced, or get a job with your M.B.A. Slacking is thus a rational response to casino capitalism, the randomization of success, and the utter arbitrariness of power. If no talent is still enough, why bother to hone your skills? If it is impossible to find a good job, why not slack out and enjoy life?

Andrew Kopkind, "Slacking toward Bethlehem," *Grand Street 44* (1992): 187.

43. For an analysis of African American cinema in the 1990s, see Ed Guerrero, "Framing Blackness: The African-American Image in the Cinema of the Nineties," *Cineaste 20*:2 (1993): 24–31.

44. Michael Dyson, "The Politics of Black Masculinity and the Ghetto in Black Film," in Carol Becker, ed., *The Subversive Imagination: Artists, Society, and Social Responsibility*" (New York: Routledge, 1994), p. 155.

45. Michael Dyson, "The Politics of Black Masculinity and the Ghetto in Black Film," in Carol Becker, ed., *The Subversive Imagination* (New York: Routledge, 1994), p. 163.

46. Itabari Njeri, "Untangling the Roots of the Violence around Us—On Screen and Off," *Los Angeles Times Magazine,* August 29, 1993, p. 33.

47. Cornel West, "Nihilism in Black America," in Gina Dent, ed., *Black Popular Culture* (Seattle: Bay Press, 1992), p. 40.

48. Itabari Njeri, "Untangling the Roots of the Violence around Us—On Screen and Off," op. cit., p. 34.

49. Fabienne Worth, "Postmodern Pedagogy in the Multicultural Classroom: For Inappropriate Teachers and Imperfect Spectators," *Cultural Critique 25* (Fall 1993): 27.

50. Pierce Hollingsworth, "The New Generation Gaps: Graying Boomers, Golden Agers, and Generation X," *Food Technology 47*:10 (October, 1993): 30.

51. I have called this elsewhere the pedagogy of commercialism. See Henry A. Giroux, *Disturbing Pleasures: Learning Popular Culture* (New York: Routledge, 1994).

52. For an analysis of the relationship among modernist schooling, pedagogy, and popular culture, see Henry A. Giroux and Roger I. Simon, "Popular Culture as a Pedagogy of Pleasure and Meaning," in Henry A. Giroux and Roger Simon, eds., *Popular Culture, Schooling, and Everyday Life* (Granby, MA: Bergin and Garvey, 1989), pp. 1–30; Giroux and Simon, "Schooling, Popular Culture, and a Pedagogy of Possibility," ibid., pp. 219–236.

53. Anyone who has been following the culture wars of the last eight years is well aware of the conservative agenda for reordering public and higher education around the commercial goal of promoting economic growth for the nation while simultaneously supporting the values of Western civilization as a common culture designed to undermine the ravages of calls for equity and multiculturalism. For a brilliant analysis of the conservative attack on higher education, see Ellen Messer-Davidow, "Manufacturing the Attack on Liberalized Higher Education," *Social Text 36* (Fall 1993): 40–80.

54. This argument is especially powerful in the work of Edward Said, who frames the reach of culture as a determining pedagogical force against the backdrop of the imperatives of colonialism. See Edward Said, *Culture and Imperialism* (New York: Alfred A. Knopf, 1993).

55. Selective examples of this work include: Carol Becker, ed., *The Subversive Imagination* (New York: Routledge, 1994); Henry Giroux and Peter McLaren, eds., *Between Borders: Pedagogy and the Politics of Cultural Studies* (New York: Routledge, 1994); Roger Simon, *Teaching Against the Grain* (Westport, CT: Bergin and Garvey, 1992); David Trend, *Cultural Pedagogy: Art/Education/Politics* (Westport, CT: Bergin and Garvey, 1992); James Schwoch, Mimi White, and Susan Reilly, eds., *Media Knowledge: Readings in Popular Culture, Pedagogy, and Critical Citizenship* (Albany: SUNY Press, 1992); and Lawrence Grossberg, *We Gotta Get Out of This Place: Popular Conservatism and Postmodern Culture* (New York: Routledge, 1992). See also Douglas Kellner, *Media Culture* (New

York: Routledge, 1995); Jeanne Brady, *Schooling Young Children* (Albany, SUNY Press, 1995).

56. Stuart Hall, "Race, Culture, and Communications: Looking Backward and Forward at Cultural Studies," *Rethinking Marxism* 5:1 (Spring 1992): 11.

57. Peter Hitchcock, "The Othering of Cultural Studies," *Third Text* 25 (Winter 1993–1994): 12.

58. Walter Parkes, "Random Access, Remote Control: The Evolution of Storytelling." *Omni* (January 1994): 50.

59. Stuart Hall, "Race, Culture, and Communications," ibid., p. 14.

60. Peter Euben, "The Debate over the Canon," *Civic Arts Review* 7:1 (Winter 1994): 14–15.

III
The War against Youth

5
Nymphet Fantasies
Child Beauty Pageants and the Politics of Innocence

∾

Only in a climate of denial could hysteria over satanic rituals at daycare centers coexist with a failure to grasp the full extent of child abuse. (More than 8.5 million women and men are survivors.) Only in a culture that represses the evidence of the senses could child pageantry grow into a $5 billion industry without anyone noticing. Only in a nation of promiscuous puritans could it be a good career move to equip a six-year-old with bedroom eyes.[1]

The Disappearing Child and the Politics of Innocence

The notion of the disappearing child and the myth of childhood innocence often mirror and support each other. Constructed within the myth of innocence, children are often portrayed as inhabiting a world that is untainted, magical, and utterly protected from the harshness of adult life. Innocence in this scenario not only erases the complexities of childhood and the range of experiences different children encounter but it also offers an excuse for adults to ignore responsibility for how children are firmly connected to and shaped by social and cultural institutions run largely by adults. Innocence in this instance makes children invisible except as projections of adult fantasies—fantasies that allow adults to believe that children do not suffer from their greed, recklessness, perversions of will and spirit, that they are, in the final analysis, unaccountable.[2]

If innocence provides the moral ethos that distinguishes children from adults, the discourse of the disappearing child signals that childhood is being threatened by forces that tend to collapse that distinction. For example, in cultural critic Neil Postman's thoroughly modernist view of the world, the electronic media, especially television, presents a threat to the existence of children and the civilized culture bequeathed to the West by the Enlightenment.[3] Not only does the very character of television—with its fast paced format, sound byte worldview, information overload, and narrative organization—undermine the very possibility for children to engage in critical thinking, but its content works to expel images of the child from its programming by both "adultifying" the child and promoting the rise of the "childified" adult.[4] But Postman is quick to extend his thesis to other spheres and notes, for example, the disappearance of children's clothing, children's games, the entry of children into professional sports, and the increasing willingness of the criminal justice system to treat children as miniature adults. Postman's lament represents less a concern with preserving childhood innocence than with bemoaning the passing of a world in which high culture is threatened by popular culture, and the culture of print loses its hold on a restricted notion of literacy and citizenship training. The loss of childhood innocence in this scenario registers the passing of a historical and political juncture in which children could be contained and socialized under the watchful tutelage of dominant regulatory institutions such as the family, school, and church.

Many politicians eager to establish themselves as protectors of childhood innocence have also appropriated the specter of the child as an endangered species. Numerous politicians, including President Clinton, who, in their rush to implement new social and economic policies, hold up children as both the inspiration and prime beneficiaries of their reforms. Lacking opportunities to vote, mobilize, or register their opinions, young children become an easy target and referent in the discourse of moral uplift and social legitimation. They also become pawns and victims. Far from benefiting children, many of the programs and government reforms enacted by Clinton and the Republican-led Congress represent what Senator Edward Kennedy has called "legislative child abuse."[5] Protecting the innocence of children in this case has a direct connection with the disappearing child, though not in the sense predicted by Neil Postman. The "draconian" cuts in social welfare, it is estimated, will result in eleven million families losing income under the new welfare bill, with more than eight million being families with children. Moreover, it is predicted that the new welfare reform measure will be responsible for moving "2.6 million people, including 1.1 million children, into poverty."[6] In this instance, children are indeed disappearing—right into the hole of poverty, suffering, and despair.[7]

Removed from its original concern with the welfare of all children, politicians have little interest in the welfare of kids who are poor and nonwhite. Under these circumstances, innocence emerges less as a trope to highlight the disappearance of kids than as metaphor for advancing a conservative political agenda and a conservative notion of "family values" in which white and middle-class children are viewed as more valued and deserving of the material resources and cultural goods of the larger society.[8] In this selective appropriation, innocence turns with a vengeance on its humanitarian impulse: the everyday experience of childhood is held hostage to the realities of power and the disingenuous rhetoric of political pragmatism.

As the rhetoric of child welfare heats up in the public consciousness, innocence is increasingly being redeployed to rearticulate what specific children are deserving of entitlements and adult protection and what forces pose a threat to such children. Shot through with political and ideological values, innocence is not merely selective about which children are endangered and need to be protected, it also is used to signal who and what constitutes a threat to children.

As the child is increasingly used as a moral yardstick by politicians, the popular press, and media, it becomes more difficult for adults to elide responsibility for what they do to kids. Consequently, childhood innocence appears both threatened and threatening. According to popular wisdom, the enemies of children are not to be found in the halls of Congress, in the poisonous advertisements that commodify and sexualize young children, or even in the endless media bashing that blames children for all of society's ills.[9] On the contrary, the biggest threat to children is to be found in the child molesters, pedophiles, abductors, and others who prey on children in the most obscene ways imaginable. In this instance, the discourse of childhood innocence does more than produce the rhetoric of political opportunism; it also provides the basis for moral panics. Both conservatives and liberals have fed off the frenzy of fear associated with a decade of revelations of alleged child abuse. Starting with the 1987 McMartin preschool case, a wave of fear-inspired legislation has swept the nation in order to protect children from pedophiles, child molesters, predatory priests and teachers, and anyone else who might be labeled as a sexual deviant posing a threat to the innocence of children.[10] Child abuse in this scenario is reduced to the individual pathology of the molester and pedophile, and the fear and anger it arouses is so great that the Supreme Court is even willing to suspend certain constitutional liberties in order to keep sexual predators locked up even after they finish serving their sentences.[11]

But the issue of widespread child abuse has done more than inspire a national fear of child molesters, it also points beyond the language of individual pathology to the more threatening issue of how society is treating its children and opens up the door to questions probing the degree to which society has failed to provide children with the security and resources necessary to insure their safety and well-being. The most disturbing threat to innocence may be child abuse, but it is not a form of abuse that can only be assessed through the horrible behavior of sexual predators. Such abuse needs to be situated within a broader set of political, economic, and social considerations, considerations that probe deeply into the cultural formations that not only make children visible markers of humanity and public responsibility but also see children as a menacing enemy, or as merely a market to be exploited. The social investment in children's innocence may be at the center of political rhetoric in the halls of Congress, but there are other forces in American society that aggressively breed hatred and disregard for children, especially those who are marginalized because of their class, race, gender, or status as non–U.S. citizens.

Innocence may have mythic invoking powers, but it also is a marker of privilege and discrimination. When Debra McMahon, a vice president for Mercer Management Consulting, gleefully asserts that "Kids are the most pure consumers you could have….They tend to interpret your ad literally. They are infinitely open," she is focusing on innocence as a weakness for manipulating children into consumers, and barely raises an eyebrow about the ethical implications of such an act.[12] Innocence in this instance becomes a metaphor for powerlessness.

In what follows, I want to argue that the central threat to childhood innocence lies not in the figure of the pedophile or sexual predator, but can be found in the diminishing public spheres available for children to experience themselves as critical agents. As cities become increasingly ghettoized because of the ravaging effects of deindustrialization, the loss of revenue, and white flight, children are left with fewer services to fulfill their needs and desires. As the public schools are abandoned or surrendered to the dictates of the market, children increasingly find themselves isolated and removed from the discourse of community and compassion. As the state is hallowed out and only the most brutal state apparatuses remain intact, children have fewer opportunities to protect themselves from an adult world that offers them dwindling resources, dead-end jobs, and diminished hopes for the future.[13] At the same time, children are increasingly subjected to social and economic forces that exploit them through the dynamics of sexualization, commodification, and commercialization throughout vast segments of the culture.[14]

JonBenet, Race, and the Perils of Home

While the concept of innocence may incite adults to publicly proclaim their support for future generations, it more often than not protects them from the reality of society and the influence they have in contributing to the ever increasing impoverishment of children's lives. Of course, there are often flash points in a society that signal that children are in danger and that certain elements in the culture pose a threat to their innocence. Conservatives, for example, have focused on the dangers to children presented by rap music, cinematic violence, and drugs to launch an attack on Hollywood films, the fashion world, single teen moms, and what it calls the cultural elite. But rarely do conservatives and the dominant press focus on social practices that locate the ongoing threats to children at the center of dominant economic, political, and cultural institutions. Poverty, racism, sexism, and the dismantling of the welfare state do great harm to children and some of the stories exemplifying the effects of these social conditions either do not get reported in the press or, if they do, prompt little public discussion and self-examination.

One recent exception can be found in the case of JonBenet Ramsey, the six-year-old girl who was found strangled in her wealthy parents' Boulder, Colorado home the day after Christmas. Throughout the first half of 1997, the case became a fixation in the press. Major media networks, newspapers, and tabloids besieged the public with photographs and television footage of JonBenet, dubbed as the slain little beauty queen, posing coquettishly in a tight dress, wearing bright red lipstick, her hair a highlighted blonde. The JonBenet Ramsey case revealed once again that the media gravitates towards victims that fit the dominant culture's image of itself. Children who are white, blond, and middle class are not only invested with more humanity, they become emblematic of a social order that banishes from consciousness any recognition of abused children who "don't fit the image of purity defiled."[15]

Consider the case of a nine-year-old, African American child, labeled in the press as Girl X. Girl X was raped, beaten, blinded, and dumped in a stairwell in the rundown Cabrini Green Housing Project in Chicago. The brutal murder aroused a great deal of publicity in Chicago, but not as much as the JonBenet Ramsey investigation. The case was virtually ignored by the national media. Race and poverty relegated the case of Girl X to a nonentity. But there is something equally disturbing about the JonBenet case. Innocence is primarily applied to children who are white and middle class, often tucked away in urban townhouses and the safe sanctuaries of segregated suburban America. Innocence also mystifies the sexualization and commodifcation of young girls who are being taught to identify themselves through the pleasures and desires of the adult gaze. The child becomes the principle incitement to adult desire, but the pedagogical and commercial practices at work in such a construction remain unexamined because they take place within acceptable cultural forms such as children's beauty pageants. JonBenet's murder jolts the public because it shatters the assumption that the primary threat to innocence lies outside the family in the image of the sexual pervert. The death of the young beauty queen raises serious questions about those forces at work in the cultural practices and institutions of every day life that organize children's lives, often in ways that undermine the possibility for children to enter adulthood free of violence, intimidation, and abuse along the way.

I will argue that the beauty pageant is an exemplary site for examining critically how the discourse of innocence mystifies the appropriation of children's bodies in a society that increasingly sexualizes and commodifies them. In pursuing this argument, I will examine how the culture of child beauty pageants functions as a pedagogical site where children learn about pleasure, desire, and the roles they might assume in an adult society. I also will examine how such pageants are rationalized, how they are upheld by commercial and ideological structures within the broader society, and how they are reproduced, reinforced, and sustained in related spheres such as advertising and fashion photography—spheres that also play an important role in marketing children as objects of pleasure, desire, and sexuality. Underlying this project is the attempt to challenge such rituals as innocent, to reconsider the role they play as part of a broader cultural practice in which children are reified and objectified. This is not meant to suggest that all child beauty pageants engage in a form of child abuse. Pageants vary in both the way they are constructed and how they interact with local and national audiences. Moreover, their outcomes are variable and contingent. But as sites of representation, identity formation, consumption, and regulation, the dominant and assigned meanings attached to these events have to be understood in terms of how they articulate and resonate with other cultural sites engaged in the production and regulation of youth, the packaging of desire, and the sexualized body.

Beauty Pageants and the Shock of the Real

Reality sometimes defies the ideological and institutional forces that attempt to keep it at bay. This seems to have been the case during the blitz of media coverage following the brutal murder of six-year-old JonBenet Ramsey. On one level, JonBenet's case attracted national attention because it fed into the frenzy and moral panic Americans are experiencing over the threat of child abuse—fueled by horrific crimes like the kidnap and murder of Polly Klaas in California. Similarly, it resonated with the highly charged public campaigns by various legislators and citizen groups calling for the death penalty for sex offenders such as Jesse Timmendequas, the child molester who killed seven-year-old Megan Kanka. On another level, it opened to public scrutiny another high-profile example of a child succeeding at the make-believe game of becoming an adult. Not unlike Jessica Dubroff, the seven-year-old and would-be Amelia Earhart who, while attempting to be the youngest pilot to cross the United States, died tragically in a plane crash, JonBenet Ramsey also projected the aura of a child with the uncanny ability to present herself as an adult. But if the boundary between innocence and impurity, child and adult, became blurred in both cases, JonBenet's notoriety as an object of public fascination revealed a dark and seamy element in the culture.

Night after night the major television networks aired videotapes of little JonBenet Ramsey wearing tight off-the-shoulder dresses, bright red lipstick, and curled, teased, and bleached blond hair pulling a feathered Mardi Gras mask almost seductively across her eyes as she sashayed down a runway. Playing the role of an alluring sex kitten, JonBenet's image seemed to belie the assumption that the voyeuristic fascination with the sexualized child was confined to the margins of society—inhabited largely by freaks and psychopaths.

The JonBenet Ramsey case revealed not only how regressive notions of femininity and beauty are redeployed in this conservative era to fashion the fragile identities of young girls, but also how easily adults will project their own fantasies onto children, even if it means selling them on the beauty block. The JonBenet case offered the public a spectacle in which it became both a voyeur and a witness to its refusal to address the broader conditions that contribute to the sexualization and commodifcation of kids in the larger culture. With the recent attention generated by celebrities such as Roseanne and Oprah Winfrey, the general public has come to recognize that child abuse often takes place at home and that the image of the child molester as strictly an outsider has become less credible. The image of the home as a safe space for children was also made problematic as it became clear that the Ramsey family imposed their own strange fantasies on their daughter and in doing so denied her an identity suitable for a six-year-old. Instead, they positioned her within a child beauty pageant culture that stripped her of her innocence by blurring the boundary between child and adult. Not allowed to be a child, JonBenet was given the unfortunate job of projecting herself through a degrading aesthetic that sexualized and commodified her.

Images of six-year-olds cosmetically transformed into sultry, Lolita-like waifs are difficult to watch. Such images strike at the heart of a culture beset by a deep disturbance in its alleged respect for children and decency. Whereas the blame for the often violent consequences associated with this eroticized costuming is usually placed on young women, the JonBenet Ramsey affair makes it difficult to blame kids for this type of objectification and commodifcation. The usual demonization and attack on kids in the public mind suggesting they are responsible for society's ills breaks down in this case as it becomes more difficult for adults to elide responsibility for what they do to children—their own and others.[16] Painted up like a miniature Pamela Anderson wannabe, JonBenet's image violently transgresses a sacred responsibility associated with protecting the innocence of children. Writ large across the media coverage of the JonBenet case was the disturbing implication and recognition that childhood innocence is assaulted when children can no longer expect from adults "protection ... consistency and some sort of dignity."[17]

The JonBenet Ramsey case prompted an unusual debate in the media and national press. Lacking the theoretical tools or political will to analyze the institutional and ideological forces in the culture that generate such disregard for children, the media focused on what was often termed "the strange subculture of child beauty pageants," and more often than not suggested that the abuse children suffered in such pageants was due to overbearing mothers trying to control their daughters' lives. It seems that if young girls are unavailable for scapegoating, their mothers make up for the loss. Rarely did the media raise the larger issue of how young girls are being educated to function within a limited notion of public life or how such a regressive education for young girls was more often than not the norm rather than the exception.

The traditional moral guardians of children's culture who would censor rap lyrics, remove "dangerous" videos and CDs from public circulation, boycott Disney for pro–gay and lesbian labor practices, and empty school libraries of many of their classic texts have had little to say about the sexualization of young children in a social form as American as apple pie as children's beauty pageants. Amidst the silence by conservatives and the family values crowd, liberal and progressive reporters began to raise some important questions. For example, CBS anchorman Dan Rather criticized the television networks for running the JonBenet tapes on the air, claiming that they amounted to nothing less than kiddy porn. Frank Rich wrote a courageous piece in the *New York Times* in which he argued that the "strange world of kids' pageantry" is not a "subculture"—it's our culture. But as long as we call it a subculture, it can remain a problem for somebody else."[18] Richard Goldstein followed up Rich's insights with a three-part series in the *Village Voice* in which he argued that the marketing of the sexual child has a long history in the United States and the JonBenet case "brings to the surface both our horror at how effectively a child can be constructed as a sexual being and our guilt at the pleasure we take in such a sight."[19] For Goldstein, the JonBenet case challenges the American public to confront the actual nature of child abuse which is all too often a part of family life and further legitimated in the hateful practices of a culture willing to capitalize on children as the new arena for the production of pleasure and commodification.

All of these critiques raise valid concerns about the role of child beauty pageants and how they produce particular notions of beauty, pleasure, and femininity that are as culturally gender specific as they are degrading; such criticisms also prompted a debate about the nature of adult needs and desires that push kids into pageants, and how such pageants resonate with other social practices that "silently" reproduce roles for children that undermine the notion of child innocence and reinforce particular forms of child abuse. In what follows, I want to examine these issues in detail by focusing on the scope and popularity of children's beauty pageants, what they attempt to teach young girls, and the broader commercial forces that sustain them. I also want to locate the phenomenon of child beauty pageants within a broader and related set of cultural practices, including the world of high fashion advertising and the rise of the teenage model in the world of high fashion.

Beauty and the Beast: A Genealogy of Child Beauty Pageants

Frank Rich insightfully argues that child beauty pageants represent more than a subculture in American society. Ted Cohen, president of World Pageants Inc, which publishes an international directory of pageants, estimates that the pageantry industry represents a billion-dollar-a-year industry, and includes such sponsors as Procter and Gamble, Black Velvet, and Hawaiian Tropics.[20] It is estimated that more than 3,000 pageants a year are held in the United States in which more than 100,000 children under the age of twelve compete.[21] In some cases, children as young as eight months old are entered in pageants. California, Florida, and New York hold the most pageants, and the number of pageants in the United States appears to be growing, in spite of the fact that many contests, especially at the national level, charge contestants between $250 and $800 to enter.[22]

Pageants are a lucrative business. Promoters market pleasure and rake in big dividends, with some making as much as $100,000 on each event. In addition, child beauty pageants have produced an offshoot of support industries, "including costume designers, grooming consultants, interview coaches, photographers, and publishers,"[23] not to mention the cosmetics weight reduction and other "beauty aid industries." Trade magazines such as *Pageant Life,* which has a circulation of 60,000, offer their readers a range of images and advertisements celebrating ideals of femininity, glamour, and beauty while marketing young girls in the image of adult drives and desires. In some cases, parents invest big money for makeup artists, hair stylists, and coaches to teach prepubescent kids particular modeling styles and tornado spins.[24] One story that appeared in *Life* magazine in 1994 featured Blaire, an eleven-year-old, as a seasoned beauty pageant performer. Blaire's fortunes at winning got better when her mom and dad hired Tony, a voice coach and makeup artist, at $40 an hour, to completely redesign her. When Blaire's father was asked why he was so involved with entering Blaire in child beauty pageants, he answered: "I am a plastic surgeon only from the neck up. I enjoy the beauty of the face. No doubt that's why I am so involved with Blaire."[25] The article reported that "Bruce is captivated by his daughter's beauty but prefers it enhanced: He apologizes to strangers when she is not wearing makeup. Some parents have accused Bruce of enhancing Blaire's looks with surgery."[26] Blaire indicates that she loves pageants, which are her only interests. The article ends by pointing out that Blaire lacks a child's spontaneity, and then conjectures that she "shows so little offstage emotion because she's so busy editing herself with adults."[27]

Blaire's case may appear to some as a caricature of pageant life narrowly depicting parents who push their kids too hard. That is, adults impose their own interests and desires on children too small to judge or refuse whether they want to actually participate in the pageants. But the popular literature on child beauty pageants is replete with such stories. For instance, there are endless examples in the media of little girls caked with makeup, adorned in dyed, coiffed helmet-like hair, performing childish burlesque-like routines under the direction of overbearing parents who seem totally oblivious to roles they are insisting their children assume.[28] There appears to be little concern on the part of many of these parents to the possible negative consequences of dressing their children up in provocative clothing, capping their teeth, putting fake eyelashes on them, and having them perform before audiences in a manner that suggests sexuality well beyond their years.

The popular literature that supports the child beauty pageant culture lacks any self-consciousness or recognition of the notion that "Sexualized images of little girls may have dangerous implications in a world where 450,000 American children were reported as victims of sexual abuse in 1993."[29] Trade house magazines such as *Pageant Life* and *Babette's Pageant and Talent Gazette* are filled with ads sponsored by companies such as Hawaiian Tropic in which toddlers strike suggestive poses. Full-page spreads of contest finalists often include young girls ranging from two-year-old to twenty-four-year-old adult contestants. All of the entrants are defined by the same aesthetic. The makeup, pose, smile, and hairstyles of the six-year-olds are no different from those of the much older contestants. Within the beauty pageant aesthetic, the line between children and adults is blurred, and all of the images depict the cool estrangement of sexual allure that has become a trademark in the commodities industries. In addition, the magazine is filled with ads addressing prepubescent youth that hawk pageant and talent clothes from designers such as "Hollywood Babe" and "Little Starlet Fashions"—with many ads invoking the warning "Don't Be Left Behind."[30] All the prepubescent children portrayed in the magazines I examined between 1992 and 1997 are dressed suggestively, wearing shocking red lipstick and teased hair, and with few exceptions, are white. Success stories for the younger age set (four- to eight-year-olds) consistently focused on the thrill of competition, winning titles, and the successful modeling careers of the pageant winners.

Parents and sponsors who participate in these pageants often respond to public criticisms by arguing that the press overreacted to JonBenet Ramsey's death by unfairly focusing on the beauty pageant as somehow being implicated in her murder. Others legitimate the child beauty pageant culture as a productive route to get their kids into lucrative careers such as modeling, or to win college scholarships, financial awards, and other prizes. The most frequently used rationale for defending pageants is that they build self-esteem in children, "help them to overcome shyness, and [teach them how] to grow up."[31] One pageant director in Murrieta, California, refuted the criticism that pageants are detrimental for young girls. She argued that "many young girls look at pageants as a protracted game of dress up, something most young girls love."[32] Another pageant participant, Pam Griffin, whose daughter trained JonBenet Ramsey, remarked that "more girls are trying pageants after seeing how much fun JonBenet had."[33] Even *Vogue* reporter, Ellen Mark, concluded that most kids who participate in beauty pageants end up as success stories.

The reason for their success, according to Mark, is that "pageants made them feel special....Little girls like to look pretty."[34]

Appropriating the discourse of liberal feminism, this argument is often associated with attributes affirming self-direction, autonomy, and a strong competitive spirit. But what is often missing from such critiques is the recognition that self-esteem is being defined within a very narrow standard of autonomy, one that appears impervious to how gender is continually made and remade on the body within a politics of appearance that is often reduced to the level of a degrading spectacle. Self-esteem in this context means embracing rather than critically challenging a gender code that rewards little girls for their looks, submissiveness, and sex appeal. Coupled with the ways in which the broader culture, through television, music, magazines, and advertising, consistently bombards young girls with a sexualized ideal of femininity "from which all threatening elements have been purged,"[35] self-esteem often becomes a euphemism for self-hatred, rigid gender roles, and powerlessness.

There is a certain irony in appropriating the language of self-esteem in defending child beauty pageants, especially since the latter provide young children with standards of beauty that one of 40,000 young women will actually meet. Must we ask what's wrong with young girls wanting to become fashion models (a la Kate Moss) who increasingly look as if they will never grow up, and for whom beauty is not only defined by the male gaze but appears to be one of the few requisites to enter "into the privileged male world"?[36] Naomi Wolf is right in arguing that the problem with linking standardized notions of sexualized beauty to self-esteem is that it doesn't present young girls or adult women with many choices, especially when issues regarding sexual pleasure and self-determination are held hostage to notions of femininity in which it becomes difficult for women to grow up and express themselves in a variety of public spaces.[37] Moreover, on the other side of the cheap glamorization of the waif-child as the fashion icon of beauty is the reality of a patriarchal society in which the nymphet fantasy reveals a "system by which men impose their authority on women and children alike."[38]

In short, rarely do the defenders of child beauty pageants comment critically about the consequences of stealing away a child's innocence by portraying her in the suggestive pose of a sexualized nymphet. Once again, little is said about what children are actually learning in pageants, how a child might see herself and mediate her relationship to society when her sense of self-worth is defined largely through a notion of beauty that is one-dimensional and demeaning. Nor does there seem to be much self-reflection on the part of parents and other pageant participators in allowing children to be sponsored by corporations. The pedagogical message that often informs such relations is that the identities of the young girls who enter the pageants become meaningful only when tied to the logic of the market. What a young girl learns in this case is that "in order to enter [the] contest she must represent someone other than herself."[39]

Unlike pageants that took place ten or fifteen years ago, pageants now offer bigger prizes and are backed by corporate sponsors, especially the national pageants. Moreover, as the commercial interests and level of investment in such pageants have risen, so has the competitive nature of the pageants along with the hype and glitzy nature of the spectacle. V. J. LaCour, publisher of *Pageant Life* and a firm supporter of child beauty pageants, thinks that many parents have resorted to makeup and other "extreme" measures because "the parents are trying to get a competitive edge."[40] In some cases, parents resort to measures mentally punitive and physically cruel to get their kids to perform "properly." Lois Miller, owner of the Star Talent Management in Allentown, Pennsylvania, reports that she has "seen parents who have pinched their children for messing up their dress or not looking appropriate or not wiggling enough or not throwing kisses."[41] Parents often respond to such criticisms by claiming that their kids are doing exactly what they want to do and enjoy being in the pageants. This argument appears strained when parents enter children as young as eight months old into pageants, or when parents decide, as reported in *Money* magazine, that their four-year-old child needed a talent agent in order to ensure that she made the right connections outside of the beauty pageants.

Sixty Minutes, the television program highly acclaimed for its investigative reporting, aired a segment on child beauty pageants on May 18, 1997 in the aftermath of the JonBenet Ramsey controversy. The premise of the program, announced by Morley Safer at the beginning of the segment, was to explore if "child beauty pageants exploit children to satisfy ambitions of parents, mothers." In order to provide a historical perspective on such pageants, *Sixty Minutes* aired cuts from child beauty pageants that had been seen on the program in 1977 and then presented videotaped shots of JonBenet and other children performing in a recent pageant. The contrast was both obscene and informative. The children in the 1977 pageants wore little girl dresses, ribbons in their hair, and embodied a kind of childlike innocence in their appearance as they displayed their little girl talents—singing, tap, and baton twirling. Not so with the JonBenet pageant shots. The contestants did not look like little girls, but rather coquettish, young women whose talents were reduced to their ability to move suggestively across the stage. Clearly, as Morley Safer indicated, "By today's beauty pageant standards, innocence seems to have vanished." To prove his point, he then asked one of the stage mothers who had appeared in the 1977 program what she thought of today's pageants. She responded that she recently went to a child beauty pageant and "walked in the door and walked out. It was disgusting to see the beaded dresses and blown up hair on kids." *Sixty Minutes*'s take on child beauty pageants was critical, yet it failed to consider the broader social practices, representations, and relations of power that provide the context for such pageants to flourish in the United States. Nor did it analyze the growing popularity of the pageants as part of a growing backlash against feminism reproduced in the media, culture, and fashion industries as well as in a growing number of conservative economic and political establishments.[42] What Morley Safer was clear about was the assumption that the root of such abuse towards children was to be placed squarely on the shoulders of overly ambitious and exploitative mothers.

But the feminist backlash has not stopped more informed criticisms from emerging. For example, some child psychologists argue that the intense competition at pageants along with the nomadic lifestyle of traveling from one hotel to another when school is not in session makes it difficult for young children to make friends and puts them at risk for developing a number of problems in their social interactions with other children. Other child specialists argue that it is developmentally inappropriate to "teach a 6 year old to pose like a 20 year old model as it is to allow her to drive [and] drink alcohol."[43] Of course, there is also the stress of the competition and the danger of undermining a child's self-confidence, especially when they lose, if the message they receive is that how they look is the most important aspect of who they are. Renowned psychologist David Elkind argues that parents used to be concerned with the ethical behavior of kids. A decade ago, when kids got home from school their parents asked them if they were good. Now parents are fearful that their kids will be losers because of the new economic realities of downsizing and deindustrialization. Marly Harris writes that the "massive restructuring of the economy creates a winner-take-all society in which parents believe that if kids don't end up as one of the few winners they will join the ranks of the many losers."[44] The question kids get when they come home in the nineties is no longer "Have you been good?", but "Did you win?" Another criticism is that the money spent on child pageants by parents, up to $10,000 per child in a year in some cases, could be invested in more productive ways for kids. Not the least of which could be a saving plan established to help young people alleviate the cost of a college education. Not only are kids objectified in this scenario, but the attributes accentuated in defining their identities and self-esteem offer them limited opportunities to develop and express themselves.

In spite of such criticisms, child beauty pageants are enormously popular in the United States and their popularity is growing; moreover, they have their defenders.[45] In part, such popularity can be explained by their potential to make money for promoters, but there is more to the story. Children's beauty contests also represent places where the rituals of small town America combine with the ideology of mass consumer culture. Pageants with titles such as "Miss Catfish Queen" and "Miss Baby Poultry Princess" along with "The Snake Charmer Queen Ritual Competition" suggest that such rituals are easily adapted to "local meanings and familiar symbols, values, and aesthetics—those relevant to the producers, performers, and consumers of the contest."[46] Such rituals are easy to put on, are advertised as a legitimate form of family entertainment, resonate powerfully with dominant Western models of femininity, beauty, and culture, and play a crucial role at the local and national levels of reproducing particular notions of citizenship and national identity. As American as apple pie, child beauty pageants are often embraced as simply good, clean entertainment and defended for their civic value to the community. Moreover, while adult beauty contests such as the annual Miss America pageant have been the object of enormous amounts of feminist criticism,[47] few academics and cultural critics have focused on child beauty pageants as a serious object of cultural analysis.[48]

Beyond the Politics of Child Abuse

Any attempt to challenge the sexist practices and abuses at work in children's beauty pageants must begin with the recognition that pageants represent more than trivial entertainment. Not only do such pageants occupy a reputable public space in which preadolescent girls are offered particular subject positions and identities, they also suggest the degree to which viable public spheres are diminishing for children. As public funding decreases, support services dry up, and extracurricular activities are eliminated from schools because of financial shortages, young people find themselves in a society in which there are very few decommodified public spheres for them to identify with and experience. As market relations expand their control over public space, corporations increasingly provide the public spheres for children to experience themselves as consuming subjects and commodities with limited opportunities to learn how to develop their full range of intellectual and emotional capacities to be critical citizens.

While many progressives are well aware that the struggle over culture is tantamount to the struggle over meaning and identity, it is also important to recognize that any viable cultural politics must also locate specific cultural texts within wider semiotic, material, and social relations of power that shape everyday life. Understood within a broader set of relations, children's beauty pageants become an important object of critical analysis for a number of reasons. First, the conservative and rigid gender roles that are legitimated at many child beauty pageants must be analyzed both in terms of the specific ideologies they construct for children, and how these ideologies find expression in other parts of the culture. This suggests that the values and dominant motifs that shape beauty pageants gain their meaning and appeal precisely because they find expression in related cultural spheres throughout American society. For instance, by examining how the ideologies at work in beauty pageants circulate in advertising campaigns such as those used by Calvin Klein or in the increasing use of advertising that represents the ideal modern American female as young, anorexic, sexually alluring, and available, it becomes clear that the processes at work in the sexualization and commodifcation of young children are not altogether different from the social relations that take place in other sites in which the bodies and body parts of young girls are used to market desire and sell commodities. What often makes such connections untenable in the public eye is that innocence as a trope for doing what is best for children is appropriated by beauty pageants in the name of dominant family values even though it is precisely in its name that practices that might be seen in other contexts as abusive to children are defined within the dominant culture as simply good, clean, family entertainment.

Whereas in advertisements for Calvin Klein's Obsession or his more recent jean ads, innocence becomes a fractured sign and is used unapologetically to foreground children as the objects of desire and adults as voyeurs. Innocence in this instance feeds into enticing images of childlike purity as it simultaneously sexualizes and commodifies them. Sexualizing children may be the final frontier in the fashion world and it can be seen in the rise of models such as Kate Moss who portray women as waifs—stick-like, expressionless, and blank-eyed.[49] Or it simply makes celebrities out of teenage models and film stars such as Ivanka Trump and Liv Tyler, who are left wondering in their waning teen years if they are too old to have a career in those culture industries that reduce a woman's talents to illusive and short-lived standards of desire, sexuality, and beauty. What connects the beauty pageants to the world of advertising and fashion modeling is that young girls are being taught to become little women while in the adult society women are being taught to assume the identities of powerless, child-like waifs. In this instance, Lolita grows up only to retreat into her youth as a model for what it means to be a woman.[50] Innocence reveals a dark quality in these examples and suggests not only that youth are being assaulted across a variety of public spaces but that their identities, especially those of young women, are being appropriated in different ways in diverse public sites for the high pleasure quotient they evoke in satisfying adult desires and needs.

As an ethical referent, innocence humanizes the child and makes a claim on adults to provide them with security and protection. But innocence gains its meaning from a complex set of semiotic, material, and social registers. And the reality of what is happening to children in cultural spheres as seemingly unrelated as child beauty pageants and the world of advertising and fashion modeling suggests how vulnerable children actually are to learning the worse social dimensions of our society: misogyny, sexism, racism, and violence. Innocence needs to be understood dialectically as a metaphor that is subject to diverse appropriations and whose effects can be both positive and devastating for children. If innocence is to become a useful category for social analysis, the term must be treated as an ideological practice that can only be understood politically and ethically through the ways in which it is represented and used within everyday life as it is shaped in the intersection of language, representations, and the technologies of power. Central to such a task is the need to address why, how, and under what conditions the marketing of children's bodies increasingly permeates diverse elements of society. Similarly, the answer to such a task demands uncovering not only the political and ideological interests and relations of power at work in such processes but also the actual ways in which cultural practices influence how children and adults learn about themselves and their relationship to others.

Innocence becomes both a mystifying ideology and a vehicle for commercial profit. In the first instance, innocence is a highly charged term for promoting moral panics in the popular imagination by pointing to pedophiles and sexual perverts as the most visible threat to children in our society. Such a restricted notion of innocence fails to understand how child abuse connects and works its way through the most seemingly benign of cultural spheres such as the beauty pageant. Under such circumstances, the beauty pageant is not only ignored as a serious object of social analysis, it is dismissed as simply a subculture. Innocence in this case protects a particular notion of family values that is class specific and racially coded. Moreover, it offers no language for understanding how the conditions under which children learn in specific sites such as the beauty pageant resonate and gain legitimacy through their connection to other cultural sites.

In the second instance, innocence falls prey to the logic of the market and the successful pedagogical operations of consumerism. The myth of innocence is increasingly appropriated through a transgressive aesthetics in which children provide the sexualized bait that creates images and representations that tread close to the border of pornography. In this scenario, children's sense of play and social development are transformed through marketing strategies and forms of consumer education that define the limits of their imaginations, identities, and sense of possibility while providing through the electronic media a "kind of entertainment that subtly influence the way we see [children], ourselves, and our communities."[51]

Concerned educators, parents, and activists must begin to challenge and counter such representations, ideologies, and social practices as part of a cultural politics that makes issues of pedagogy and power central to its project. This means taking seriously how beauty pageants and other popular cultural sites position children in terms of how they are taught to think of themselves through the images, values, and discourses offered to them.[52] It also means expanding our understanding of how pedagogy is played out on the bodies of young children in pageants and how this pedagogical practice resonates with what children are taught in other cultural spheres. Central to such a challenge is the political necessity for educators and other cultural workers to pressure schools and other educational sites to treat popular culture as a serious object of analysis in the curriculum so kids and adults can learn how to both demystify such images and learn the knowledge and skills that enable them to be cultural producers capable of creating public spheres informed by representations that honor and critically engage their traditions and experiences. In ideological terms, it is crucial that forms of cultural pedagogy be developed that provide students and others with texts, resources, and performative strategies that provide a complex range of subject positions that they can address, inhabit, mediate, and experiment with. Developing pedagogical practices and theoretical discourses that address how the operations of power work in sites such as beauty pageants also suggests teaching students and adults how to organize social movements at the local and national levels to pressure and boycott companies that engage in abusive practices toward children. Underlying this merging of the political and the pedagogical is the overt "political" goal of "enabling people to act more strategically in ways that may change their context for the better"[53] and, "pedagogically," finding ways for diverse groups to work together to transform popular public spheres into educational sites that address social problems by way of democratic, rather than merely market, considerations.

In short, the socialization of children must be addressed within a larger discourse about citizenship and democracy, one that resists what Adorno calls the "obscene merger of aesthetics and reality."[54] What Adorno means here is precisely the refutation of those ideologies and social practices that attempt to subordinate, if not eliminate, forms of identity that are fundamental to public life to an economy of bodies and pleasures that is all surface and spectacle. Such a discourse not only calls into question the conditions under which kids learn, what they learn, and how it shapes their identities and behavior; it also raises questions about the material and institutional relations of power that are fundamental for maintaining the integrity of public life—a condition that is essential for all children to learn to be critical participants in the shaping of their lives and the larger social order. Child abuse comes in many forms, and it has become a disturbing feature of American society. The current assault being waged on children through retrograde policy, the dismantling of the welfare state, and the pervasive glut of images that cast children as the principle incitements to adult desire suggest that democracy is in the throes of a major crisis. Surely, if democracy is to carry us forward into the next century, it will be based on a commitment to improving the lives of children, but not within the degrading logic of a market that treats their bodies like a commodity and their futures as a tradeoff for capital accumulation. On the contrary, critical educators and other progressives need to create a cultural vision along with strategies of understanding, representation, and transformation informed by "the rhetoric of political, civic, and economic citizenship."[55] The challenge to take up that commitment has never been so strained and never so urgent to confront and carry out.

Notes

1. Richard Goldstein, "The Killer Inside Me: Shirley Temple Meets the Demon Dad," *Village Voice* (June 24, 1997): 48.

2. For an insightful analysis of the myth of innocence, see Marina Warmer, *Six Myths of Our Time*, especially chapter 3: "Little Angels, Little Monsters: Keeping Childhood Innocent" (New York: Vintage, 1995), pp. 43–62. Of course, the concept of childhood innocence as a historical invention as has been pointed out by a number of theorists. See, for example, Philip Aries, *Centuries of Childhood* (Harmondsworth, Penguin, 1979); and Lloyd deMause, ed., *The Evolution of Childhood* (New York: Psychohistory Press, 1974).

3. Neil Postman, *The Disappearance of Childhood* (New York: Vintage, 1982, 1994).

4. Ibid., see chapter 8, "The Disappearing Child," pp. 120–142. The notion that television and popular culture represent the main threat to childhood innocence is central to the conservative call for censorship, limiting sex education in the schools, restricting aids education, redefining the home as the most important source of moral education, and the "Gumping" of American history in which the sixties are often seen as the source of the country's current social ills. The quintessential expression of this position can be found in the speeches, press releases, and writings of former Secretary of Education and "drug czar" William Bennett. It can also be found in legislation supported by groups such as the Christian Coalition, especially the Parental Rights and Responsibilities Act of 1995. Examples of the conservative position on child abuse, the loss of innocence, and the "poisonous" effects of popular culture abound in the popular press. See, for example, Jeff Stryker, "The Age of Innocence Isn't What It Once Was," *New York Times,* July 13, 1997, p. E3.

5. Senator Kennedy cited in Peter Edelman, "The Worst Thing Bill Clinton Has Done," *Atlantic Monthly* (March 1997): 45.

6. Peter Edelman, "The Worst Thing Bill Clinton Has Done," *Atlantic Monthly* (March 1997): 46.

7. For specific statistics on the state of youth in the United States, see Children's Defense Fund, *The State of America's Children Yearbook 1997* (Washington, DC: Children's Defense Fund, 1997); and Ruth Sidel, *Keeping Women and Children Last* (New York: Penguin, 1996).

8. For an analysis of the ideological underpinnings of the right wing family value crusade, see Judith Stacey, "The New Family Values Crusaders," *Nation* (July 25/August 1, 1994): 119–122; and Judith Stacey, *In the Name of the Family: Rethinking Family Values in the Postmodern Age* (Boston: Beacon Press, 1996).

9. For an analysis of the widespread assault currently being waged against children, see: Henry A. Giroux, *Channel Surfing: Race Talk and the Destruction of Today's Youth* (New York: St. Martin's Press, 1997); Mike A. Males, *The Scapegoat Generation: America's War on Adolescents* (Monroe, Maine: Common Courage Press, 1996); Charles R. Acland, *Youth, Murder, Spectacle: The Cultural Politics of "Youth in Crisis"* (Boulder, CO: Westview Press, 1995); Holly Sklar, "Young and Guilty by Stereotype," *Z Magazine* (July/August 1993): 52–61; and Deena Weinstein, "Expendable Youth: The Rise and Fall of Youth Culture," in Jonathan S. Epstein, ed., *Adolescents and Their Music* (New

York: Garland, 1994), pp. 67–83. See also various articles in Andrew Ross and Tricia Rose, eds., *Microphone Fiends* (New York: Routledge, 1994).

10. For a brilliant analysis of how the image of the sexual predator is used to preclude from public discussion the wide range of social factors at work in causing child abuse, see James R. Kincaid, *Child-Loving: The Erotic Child and Victorian Culture* (New York: Routledge, 1992).

11. For an analysis of the Supreme Court's decision, see Linda Greenhouse, "Likely Repeaters May Stay Confined," *New York Times,* June 24, 1997, p. A19.

12. Cited in Larry Armstrong, "Hey Kid, Buy This," *Business Week* (June 30, 1997): 66.

13. The concept of the hollow state comes from Stanley Aronowitz, *The Death and Birth of American Radicalism* (New York: Routledge, 1996).

14. The literature on advertising and the marketing of children's desires is too extensive to cite, but one of the best examples include: Stephen Kline, *Out of the Garden: Toys, TV, and Children's Culture in the Age of Marketing* (London: Verso Press, 1993).

15. Richard Goldstein, "The Girl in the Fun Bubble: The Mystery of JonBenet," *Village Voice* (June 10, 1997): 41.

16. For a sustained treatment of the current assault in kids, especially those who are poor, nonwhite, and live in the cities, see Henry A. Giroux, *Fugitive Cultures* (New York: Routledge, 1996).

17. Annie Gottlieb, "First Person Sexual," *Nation* (June 9, 1997): 26.

18. Frank Rich, "Let Me Entertain You," *New York Times,* January 18, 1997, Section 1, p. 23.

19. Richard Goldstein, "The Girl in the Fun Bubble: The Mystery of JonBenet," *Village Voice* (June 10, 1997): 41.

20. Cited in Karen de Witt, "All Dolled Up," *New York Times,* January 12, 1997, Section 4, p. 4.

21. While the statistics on children's beauty pageants vary, a number of sources cite similar figures to the ones I cite here. See, for example, Frank Rich, "Let Me Entertain You," *New York Times,* January, 18, 1997, Section 1, p. 23; Ellen Mark, "Pretty Babies," *Vogue* (June 1997): 240; Beverly Stoeltje, "The Snake Charmer Queen Ritual Competition, and Signification in American Festival," in Colleen Ballerino, Richard Wilk, and Beverly Stoeltje, eds., *Beauty Queens* (New York: Routledge, 1996), p. 13.

22. Cited in Pat Jordan, "The Curious Childhood of an 11–Year-Old," *Life* (April 1994): 38.

23. Ellen Mark, "Pretty Babies," *Vogue* (June 1997): 240.

24. Linda Caillouet echoes a point made by many academics and journalists across the country: "Pageants have changed over the past 30 years. Grade-schoolers are wearing makeup, modeling swim wear and sashaying down runways.... Today's little girls' parents often invest big money in coaches to teach the children the pro-am modeling style and tornado spins. They pay for makeup artists and hair stylists to accompany the children to pageants. Some of the kids use tanning beds. Seven-year-olds have reportedly worn false teeth, false eyelashes, and colored contact lenses." Cited in Linda Caillouet, "Slaying Has Child Pageants on Defensive," *Arkansas Democrat-Gazette,* April 14, 1997, p. 1A.

25. Ibid., p. 62.

26. Ibid., p. 62.

27. Ibid., p. 68.

28. One of the most disturbing examples of this can be found in the *Sixty Minutes* footage used in their analysis of child beauty pageants aired on May 18, 1997. Also see the BBC documentary show *Under the Sun,* which aired "Painted Babies" on Wednesday, January 31, 1996. This was an equally disturbing portrait of child beauty pageants.

29. Michael F. Jacobson, and Laurie Ann Mazur, *Marketing Madness* (Boulder, CO: Westview Press, 1995), p. 79.

30. Cited in ad for "Debbrah's: Nation's Top Pageant Designers," *Pageant Life 4,* no. 3 (Winter, 1996): 26.

31. Elliot Zaren, "Eyebrows Lift at Child Strutting in Sexy Dresses, Makeup," *Tampa Tribune,* January 14, 1997, p. 4.

32. Cited in Jodi Duckett, "In the Eyes of the Beholder: Child Beauty Pageants Get Mixed Reviews," *Morning Call,* April 6, 1997, p. E1.

33. Ibid., p. E1.

34. Ellen Mark, "Pretty Babies," *Vogue* (June 1997): 283.

35. Susan Bordo, *Unbearable Weight: Feminism, Western Culture, and the Body* (Berkeley: University of California Press, 1993), p. 162.

36. Ibid., p. 179.

37. Naomi Wolf, *The Beauty Myth* (New York: Anchor Books, 1992).

38. Richard Goldstein, "Nymph Mania: Honoring Innocence in the Breach," *Village Voice* (June 17, 1997), p. 71. This is not to suggest that women and children don't mediate and resist such domination as much as to make clear the determinate relations of power that lie behind the resurrection of the nymphet in the culture.

39. Stoeltje, "The Snake Charmer," p. 23.

40. Cited in Linda Caillouet, "Slaying Has Child Pageants on Defensive," *Arkansas Democrat-Gazette,* April 14, 1997, p. 1A.

41. Cited in Jodi Duckett, "In the Eyes of the Beholder: Child Beauty Pageants Get Mixed Reviews," *Morning Call,* April 6, 1997, p. E1.

42. See, for example, Susan Faludi, *Backlash: The Undeclared War against American Women* (New York: Anchor Books, 1991).

43. This paragraph relies heavily on comments by pediatric psychologists cited in Rebecca A. Eder, Ann Digirolamo, and Suzanne Thompson, "Is Winning a Pageant Worth a Lost Childhood?" *St. Louis Post-Dispatch,* February 24, 1997, p. 7B.

44. Marly Harris, "Trophy Kids," *Money* (March 1997): 102.

45. For an academic defense of beauty pageants as simply an acting out of community standards, see Michael T. Marsden, "Two Northwestern Ohio Beauty Pageants: A Study in Middle America's Cultural Rituals," in Ray B. Browne and Michael T. Marsden, eds., *The Cultures of Celebration* (Bowling Green, OH: Bowling Green State University Press, 1994). Marsden is so intent in focusing on pageants as ritualistic performances that he doesn't notice how ideological his own commentary is when focusing on some of the most sexist aspects of the pageant practices. Hence, for Marsden, bathing suit competitions simply prove that "beauty can be art." For a more complex analysis, see Robert H. Lavender, " 'It's Not a Beauty Pageant!' Hybrid

Ideology in Minnesota Community Queen Pageants," in Colleen Ballerino, Richard Wilk, and Beverly Stoeltje, eds. *Beauty Queens*, pp. 31–46.

46.   Beverly Stoeltje, "The Snake Charmer Queen Ritual Competition, and Significa- tion in American Festival," in Colleen Ballerino, Richard Wilk, and Beverly Stoeltje, eds., *Beauty Queens* (New York: Routledge, 1996), p. 13.

47.   For a brilliant analysis of the different critical approaches to beauty and the politics of appearance that feminists have taken since the appearance of the first Miss America pageant in 1968, see Annette Corrigan, "Fashion, Beauty and Feminism," *Meanjin* 51, no. 1 (1992). What is so interesting about this piece is that nothing is said about child beauty pageants. This is especially relevant since many of the conceptual approaches dealing with the politics of appearance simply don't apply to six-year- olds. For instance, the notion that beauty can be appropriated as an act of resistance and turned against the dominant culture seems a bit far fetched when talking about children who can barely read.

48.   One exception can be found in the collection of essays in Colleen Ballerino Cohen, Richard Wilk, and Beverly Stoeltje, eds. *Beauty Queens* (New York: Routledge, 1996).

49.   While I haven't developed in this paper the implications such depictions have for women, many feminists have provided some excellent analysis. See especially, Susan Bordo, *Unbearable Weight: Feminism, Western Culture, and the Body* (Berkeley: University of California Press, 1993). For a shameful defense of thinness as an aes- thetic in the fashion industry, see Rebecca Johnson, "The Body," *Vogue* (September 1997): 653–658. Johnson goes a long way to legitimate some of the most misogynist aspects of the beauty industry, but really reaches into the bottom of the barrel in claiming resentment is the primary reason that many women criticize the image of waif-like models permeating the media. Claiming that thinness is only an aesthetic and not a morality, Johnson seems to forget that within the dominant invocation of thinness as a standard of beauty there is the suggestion that overweight women are slovenly, older women are ugly, and nonwhite women are not as beautiful as the ever present blond-hair waif models who populate the media. Sadly, the notion that thinness generates a politically charged discourse in the media teaching young kids that thinness is a principal measure of a woman's worth also seems to have been lost on Ms. Johnson.

50.   The classic on this issue is Mary Pipher, *Reviving Ophelia: Saving the Selves of Adolescent Girls* (New York: Ballantine Books, 1994). See also Nicole Peradotto, "Little Women: A New Generation of Girls Growing Up before Their Time," *Buffalo News,* Sunday, January 26, 1997.

51.   Colleen Ballerino Cohen, Richard Wilk, and Beverly Stoeltje, "Introduction," in Colleen Ballerino, et al., Op. Cit., p. 10.

52.   For a brilliant analysis of how young girls are represented in popular culture and what is learned by them, see Valerie Walkerdine, *Daddy's Girl* (Cambridge: Har- vard University Press, 1997).

53.   Lawrence Grossberg, "Toward a Genealogy of the State of Cultural Studies," in Cary Nelson and Dilip Parameshwar Gaonkar, eds., *Disciplinarity and Dissent in Cultural Studies* (New York: Routledge, 1996), p.143.

54.   Adorno cited in Geoffrey Hartman, "Public Memory and Its Discontents," *Raritan 8*, no. 4 (Spring 1994): 27.

55.   Stanley Aronowitz, "A Different Perspective on Inequality," in Henry A. Giroux and Patrick Shannon, eds., *Education and Cultural Studies: Toward a Performative Practice* (New York: Routledge, 1998), p. 193.

6
Disposable Youth and the Politics
of Domestic Militarization
Mis/Education in the Age of Zero Tolerance

⊸

There is growing evidence in American life that citizenship is being further emptied of any critical social and political content. Of course, citizenship itself is a problematic and contested concept; even in its best moments historically, when it was strongly aligned with concerns for human rights, equality, justice, and freedom as social provisions, it never completely escaped from the exclusionary legacies of class, gender, and racial inequality.[1] Yet, in spite of such drawbacks, social citizenship contained, even within the watered down version characteristic of liberal democracy, the *possibility* for both reflecting critically upon its own limitations and implementing the promises of radical democracy. Accentuating the importance of public issues, social citizenship provided a referent, however limited, for individuals to think of themselves as active citizens and not merely taxpayers and homeowners. Moreover, as the site of many diverse struggles, citizenship often foregrounded models of political agency in which people were encouraged to address public issues that would benefit the larger collective good. Substantive citizenship also recognized that for democracy to work, individuals must feel a connection with each other that transcends the selfishness, competitiveness, and brutal self-interests unleashed by an ever-expanding market economy. In this context, the state was forced at times to offer a modicum of social services and forums designed to meet basic social needs. State-supported social provisions paralleled modest efforts to affirm public goods such as schools and to provide public spaces in which diverse individuals had the opportunity to debate, deliberate, and acquire the know-how to be critical and effective citizens. This is not meant to suggest that before neoliberalism's current onslaught on all things public that liberal democratic culture encouraged widespread critical thinking and inclusive debate. On the contrary, liberal democracy offered little more than the swindle of formalistic, ritualized democracy, but at least it contained a "referent" for addressing the deep gap between the promise of a radical democracy and the existing reality. With the rise of neoliberalism, referents for imagining even a weak democracy, or for that matter understanding the tensions between capitalism and democracy, which animated political discourse for the first half of the twentieth century, appear to be overwhelmed by market discourses, identities, and practices. Democracy has now been reduced to a metaphor for the alleged "free" market. It is not that a genuine democratic public space once existed in some ideal form and has now been corrupted by the values of the market, but that these democratic public spheres, even in limited forms, seem to no longer be animating concepts for making visible the contradiction and tension between what Jacques Derrida refers to as the reality of existing democracy and "the promise of a democracy to come."[2]

With the advent of neoliberalism, corporate culture has made efforts to privatize all things social, stripping citizenship of its emancipatory possibilities. As a result, the state has been hollowed out as its police functions increasingly overpower and mediate its diminishing social functions. Consequently, the government at all levels is largely abandoning its support for child protection, healthcare for the poor, and basic social services for the aged.[3] The government is now discounted as a means of addressing basic economic, educational, environmental, and social problems. Market-based initiatives are touted as the only avenue for resolving issues such as unemployment, education, housing, and poverty. Public goods are now disparaged in the name of privatization, and those public forums in which association and debate thrive are being replaced by what Paul Gilroy calls an "infotainment telesector" industry driven by dictates of the marketplace.[4]

Consumerism increasingly drives the meaning of citizenship as the principles of self-preservation and self-interest sabotage political agency, if not public life itself. As the public sector is remade in the image of the market, commercial values replace social values and the spectacle of politics gives way to the politics of the spectacle. For example, in the summer of 2000 the prime time entertainment hit *Survivor* drew an audience of over 50 million viewers in its final show, twice the amount of those viewers who tuned in on the best night to watch either the Republican or Democratic national party conventions. New "reality"-staged TV spectacles, with their aggressive celebration of individualism, competitiveness, and social Darwinism do more than mimic the market and put into place notions of agency that assist the transformation of the political citizen into a consumer. They also signify the death of those public forums where private troubles can be translated into public concerns by gradually displacing those noncommodified spaces that offer resources and possibilities for resisting the dissolution of civic culture, democratic politics, and social citizenship itself. This is not to suggest that neoliberalism's celebration of commercial and hyperindividualism simply turns everybody into a customer or merely expresses itself in the rise of a sensation-seeking public searching for relief from its alienation and boredom in mass-produced spectacles. But it does create, on the whole, a depoliticized citizenry by drastically limiting not only the access to, but also the capacity for imagining those public spheres and democratic cultures that might offer the skills, knowledge, and values necessary to engage human suffering, define responsible public action as an enabling quality, and provide public forums, spaces, and events "where the occupants of different residential areas [can] meet face-to-face, engage in casual encounters, accost and challenge one another, talk, quarrel, argue or agree, lifting their private problems to the level of public issues and making public issues into matters of private concerns."[5]

In what follows, I want to examine the social and political costs neoliberal and neoconservative policies are exacting on a generation of youth who increasingly are being framed as a generation of suspects. In addressing the interface between youth and public policy, especially the rapid growth of zero tolerance policies within public schools, I consider some broader questions about how the growing popular perception of youth as a threat to public life is connected to the collapse of public discourse, the increasing militarization of public space, and the rise of a state apparatus bent on substituting policing functions for social services. I then examine the implications these shifts in public discourse have for rethinking the relationship between pedagogy, political agency, and the imperatives of an energized and vibrant culture and radical democracy.

Privatizing and Commodifying Youth

In the summer of 2000, *The New York Times Sunday Magazine* ran two major stories on youth within a three-week period between the latter part of July and the beginning of August. The stories are important because they signify not only how youth fare in the politics of representation but also what identifications are made available for them to locate themselves in public discourse. The first article to appear, "The Backlash Against Children" by Lisa Belkin, is a feature story forecasted on the magazine's cover with a visually disturbing, albeit familiar, close-up of a young boy's face. The boy's mouth is wide open in a distorted manner, and he appears to be in the throes of a tantrum. The image goes right to that subliminal place that conjures up the ambiguities adults feel in the presence of screaming children, especially when they appear in public places, such as R-rated movies or upscale restaurants, where their presence is seen as an intrusion on adult life. The other full-page image that follows the opening text is even more grotesque, portraying a young boy dressed in a jacket and tie with chocolate cake smeared all over his face. His hands, covered with the gooey confection, reach out towards the viewer, capturing the child's mischievous attempt to grab some hapless adult by the lapels and add a bit of culinary dash to his or her wardrobe. The images match the text.

According to Belkin, a new movement is on the rise in American culture, one founded by individuals who don't have children, militantly describing themselves as "child free," and who view the presence of young people as an intrusion on the private space and their rights. Belkin charts this growing phenomenon with the precision of an obsessed accountant. She commences with an ethnographic account of thirty-one-year-old California software computer consultant Jason Gill, who is looking for a new place to live because the couple who have moved in next door to him have a new baby and he can hear "every wail and whimper." Even more calamitous for the yuppie consultant, the fence he replaced to prevent another neighbor's children from peering through at him is now used by the kids as a soccer goal, "often while Gill is trying to read a book or have a quiet glass of wine."[6] But Belkin doesn't limit her analysis to such anecdotal evidence, she also points to the emergence of national movements such as an organization called No Kidding!, which sets up social events only for those who remain childless. She reports that No Kidding! had only two chapters in 1995 but has 47 today. In addition, she comments on the countless number of online "child-free" sites with names like "Brats!" and a growing number of hotels that do not allow children under 18 unless they are paying guests.[7]

Of course, many parents and nonparents alike desire, at least for a short time, a reprieve from the often chaotic space of children, but Belkin takes such ambivalences to new heights. To be sure, her real ambition has very little to do with providing a space for adult catharsis. Rather it is to give public voice to a political and financial agenda captured by Elinor Burkett's *The Baby Boon: How Family-Friendly America Cheats the Childless*—an agenda designed to expose and rewrite governmental policies that relegate "the Childless to second-class citizens."[8] Included in Burkett's laundry list of targets are: the federal tax code and its dependent deductions, dependent care credits, child tax credits among "dozens of bills designed to lighten the tax burden of parents" and, "most absurd of all," an executive order prohibiting discrimination against parents in all areas of federal employment. Her position is straightforward enough: to end "fancy" benefits (e.g., on-site childcare and health insurance for dependents) which privilege parents *at the expense of the childless* and to bar discrimination on the basis of family status. "Why not make it illegal to presuppose that a nonparent is free to work the night shift or presuppose that nonparents are more able to work on Christmas than parents?" Burkett demands.[9] Indeed, in an era marked by zero tolerance policies, why should the government provide any safety nets for the nation's children at all? Why should whole communities be taxed to pay for the education and health of other people's children? In the face of such irresponsible claims, it seems all too obvious to suggest that society nurture children because they will be our future leaders and workers and parents—they are the nation's future who will in turn support a generation of elderly (parents and "child free" alike), who will pay taxes for Medicare, social security, and those other "fancy perks" provided to senior citizens. Ironically, Burkett's arguments are as childish and thoughtless as the worst offenders in the group she attempts to mobilize public sentiment against.

Belkin modifies her somewhat sympathetic encounter with the child free world view by interviewing Sylvia Ann Hewlett, a Harvard educated economist, who is a nationally known spokesperson for protecting the rights of parents and the founder of the National Parenting Association. Hewlett argues that parents have become yet another victimized group who are being portrayed by the media as the enemy. Hewlett translates her concerns into a call for parents to organize in order to wield more economic and political power. As important as Hewlett's comments are, they occupy a minor commentary in the text that overwhelmingly privileges the voices of those individuals and groups that view children and young people as a burden, a personal irritant, rather than a social good.

The notion that children should be understood as a crucial social resource who present for any healthy society important ethical and political considerations about the quality of public life, the allocation of social provisions, and the role of the state as a guardian of public interests appears to be lost in Belkin's article. Instead, Belkin ignores the social gravity and implications of these issues and focuses on youth exclusively as a private consideration rather than as part of a broader public discourse about democracy and social justice. In addition, she participates in an assault on youth, buttressed by two decades of a Reagan-Bush New Right neoconservatism and a more recent period of neoliberalism and hyper capitalism in which the language of the social, democracy, and solidarity are subordinated to the ethos of self-interest and self-preservation in the relentless pursuit of private satisfactions and pleasures. In this sense, the backlash against children that Belkin attempts to chronicle are symptomatic of an attack on public life itself, on the very legitimacy of those noncommercial values that are critical to defending a just and substantive democratic society.

I have spent some time on Belkin's article because it highlights, though uncritically, how market pressures work in society to undermine social structures and public spaces capable of raising questions about how particular groups such as youth are being abstracted from the language of justice, reciprocity, and compassion; and how the institutional and collective structures that once protected such groups are also being privatized, displaced, and defined almost entirely through the logic of the market. As the language of the public is emptied of its social considerations, private troubles and personal pathologies occupy center stage, and matters of resistance and struggle are displaced by the spectacle of a competitive war-against-all ethos that may offer fodder for prime time television but proves disastrous for children, the poor, the aged, and those groups consigned to the margins of society.

The second article to appear in the *New York Times Sunday Magazine* is titled "Among the Mooks" by RJ Smith.[10] According to the author, there is an emerging group of poor white males called "mooks" whose cultural style is fashioned out of an interest in fusing the transgressive languages, sensibilities, and styles that cut across and connect the worlds of rap and heavy metal music, ultra violent sports such as professional wrestling, and the misogyny rampant in the subculture of pornography. For Smith, the kids who inhabit this cultural landscape are losers from broken families, working-class fatalities whose anger and unexamined bitterness translates into bad manners, antisocial music, and uncensored rage.

Smith appears uninterested in contextualizing the larger forces and conditions that give rise to this matrix of cultural phenomena—deindustrialization, economic restructuring, domestic militarization, poverty, joblessness.[11] The youth portrayed in Smiths's account live in a historical, political, and economic vacuum. The ideological, cultural, and institutional forces that work on and through these teens simply disappear. Moreover, the teens represented by Smith have little recourse to adults who try to understand and help them navigate a complex and rapidly changing cultural landscape in which they must attempt to locate and define themselves. Along with the absence of adult protection and guidance, there is a lack of serious critique and social vision in dealing with the limits of youth culture. No questions are raised about the relationship between the popular forms teens inhabit and the ongoing commercialization and commodification of youth culture, or what the relationship might be between the subject positions young people invest in and those mainstream, commercially saturated dreamscapes of affect and representation that increasingly eat up social space and displace noncommodified public spheres. There is no understanding in Smith's analysis of how market-driven politics and established forms of power increasingly eliminate noncommodified social domains through which young people might learn an oppositional language for challenging those adult ideologies and institutional forces that both demonize them and limit their sense of dignity and capacity for political agency.

Of course, vulgarity, pathology, and violence are not limited to the spaces inhabited by the hypermasculine worlds of gangsta rap, porn, extreme sports, and professional wrestling. But Smith ignores all of this because he is much too interested in depicting today's teens, and popular culture in general, as the embodiment of moral decay and bad cultural values, an assessment that mimics the retrograde neoconservative ideological attacks on youth that have taken place since the 1980s.[12] Smith suggests that poor white kids are nothing more than semi-Nazis with a lot of pent up rage. There are no victims in his analysis, as social disorder is reduced to individualized pathology, and any appeal to injustice is viewed as mere whining. Smith is too intent on reinforcing images of demonization and ignorance that resonate comfortably with right-wing moral panics about youth culture. He succeeds, in part, by focusing on the icons of this movement in terms that move between caricature and scapegoating. For instance, The Insane Posse is singled out for appearing on cable access porn shows; the group Limp Bizkit is accused of using their music to precipitate a gang rape at the recent Woodstock melee; and the performer Kid Rock is defined in racially coded terms as a "vanilla version of a blackploitation pimp" whose concerts inspire fans to commit vandalism and prompts teenage girls to "pull off their tops as the boys whoop."[13] It gets worse.

At one level, "mooks" are portrayed as poor, working class, white kids who have seized upon the crudest aspects of popular culture in order to provide an outlet for their rage. But for Smith, the distinctive form this culture takes with its appropriation of the transgressive symbolism of rap music, porn, and wrestling does not entirely explain its descent into pathology and bad taste. Rather, Smith charges that black youth culture is largely responsible for the self-destructive, angst-ridden journey that poor white male youth are making through the cultural landmines of hypermasculinity, unbridled violence, "ghetto" discourse, erotic fantasy, and drugs. Smith points an accusing finger at the black "underclass," and the recent explosion of hip hop which allegedly offers poor white kids both an imaginary alternative to their trailer park boredom and a vast array of transgressive resources which they proceed to fashion through their own lived experiences and interests. Relying upon all too common racist assumptions about black urban life, Smith argues that black youth culture offers white youth

> a wide-screen movie of ghetto life, relishing the details, relating the intricacy of topics like drug dealing, brawling, pimping and black-on-black crime. Rap makes these things seem sexy, and makes life on the street seem as thrilling as a Playstation game. Pimping and gangbanging equal rebellion, especially for white kids who aren't going to get pulled over for driving while black, let alone die in a hail of bullets (as Tupac and B.I.G. both did).[14]

Trading substantive analysis for right-wing clichés, Smith is indifferent to both the complexity of rap as well as the "wide array of complex cultural forms" that characterize black urban culture.[15] Smith alleges that if poor white youth are in trouble it is not because of regressive government policies, the growing militarization of urban space, the attack on basic social provisions for the poor and young, the disinvestment in public goods such as public schools, or the growing criminalization of social policy.[16] On the contrary, the problem of white youth is rooted in the seductive lure of a black youth, marked by criminality, violent hypermasculinity, welfare fraud, drug abuse, and unchecked misogyny. Smith unapologetically relies upon this analysis of black youth culture to portray poor white youth as dangerous and hip-hop culture as the source of that danger. Within this discourse the representation of youth moves from caricature to that poisonous terrain Toni Morrison calls race talk: "The explicit insertion into everyday life of racial signs and symbols that have no meaning other than pressing African Americans to the lowest level of the racial hierarchy....the rhetorical [and representational] experience renders blacks as noncitizens, already discredited outlaws."[17]

Whatever his intentions, Smith's analysis contributes to the growing assumption in the popular imagination that young people are at best a social nuisance and at worst a danger to social order. Clearly his analysis of working class and black youth bespeak an ideological and political irresponsibility rooted in an overidentification with the recklessness of the young. As such, these representations contribute not only to the ongoing demonization of youth, especially youth of color, but further legitimate the emergence of a state that is radically moving from a politics of social investment to a politics of containment and militarization.[18]

I have spent some time on these articles because I think they reflect and perpetuate in dramatically different ways not only the ongoing demonization of young people, but also the growing refusal within the larger society to understand the problems of youth (and especially youth of color) as symptomatic of the crisis of democratic politics itself. Under the rule of neoconservative and neoliberal ideology, American society increasingly finds it difficult to invest in those ethical and political values that support public spaces in an earnest, if not fully realized, manner where norms are made explicit and debated, institutions are maintained that promote democratic notions of the collective good, and support is given to forms of civic education that provide the foundation for nurturing and sustaining individual and collective agency. As the state is stripped of its power to mediate between capital and human needs, thus losing its capacity to offer social guarantees to youth and other marginalized groups, public life becomes barren, vacuous, and stripped of substance.[19] Of course, the crisis over public schools has been escalating for at least a decade, as forms of civic education that promote individual agency, social responsibility, and noncommercial values have been abandoned for job training and accountability schemes.

As the state is divested of its capacity to regulate social services and limit the power of capital, those public spheres that traditionally served to empower individuals and groups to strike a balance between "the individual's liberty from interference and the citizen's right to interfere"[20] are dismantled. At the same time, it becomes more difficult for citizens to put limits on the power of neoliberalism to shape daily life—particularly as corporate economic power is feverishly consolidated on a transnational level. Nor can they prevent the assault on the state as it is being forced to abandon its already limited social role as the guardian of public interests. The result is a state increasingly reduced to its policing functions, and a public sector reduced to a replica of the market. As neoliberalism increases its grip over all aspects of cultural and economic life, the relative autonomy once afforded to the worlds of cinema, publishing, and media production begins to erode. Public schools are increasingly defined as a source of profit rather than a public good. And, as Pierre Bourdieu points out, a "new kind of moral Darwinism which, with the cult of the 'winner', establishes the struggle of all against all and cynicism as the norm of all practices."[21] Through talk shows, film, music, and cable television, for example, the media promote a growing political apathy and cynicism by providing a steady stream of daily representations and spectacles in which abuse becomes the primary vehicle for registering human interaction. At the same time, dominant media such as the *New York Times* condemn the current cultural landscape—represented in their account through reality television, professional wrestling, gross out blockbuster films, and the beat-driven boasts and retorts of hip-hop—as aggressively evoking a vision of humanity marked by a "pure Darwinism" in which "the messages of popular culture are becoming more brutally competitive."[22]

Unfortunately, for mainstream media commentators in general, the emergence of such representations and values is about the lack of civility and has little to do with considerations of youth bashing, racism, corporate power, and politics. In this sense, witness to degradation now becomes the governing feature of community and social life. Most importantly, what critics take up as a "youth problem" is really a problem about the corruption of politics, the shriveling up of public spaces and resources for young people, the depoliticization of large segments of the population, and the emergence of a corporate and media culture that is defined through an unadulterated "authoritarian form of kinship that is masculinist, intolerant and militaristic."[23] At issue here is how we understand the ways in which youth produce and engage popular culture at a time in history when depravation is read as depravity. How do we comprehend the choices young people are making under circumstances in which they have become the object of policies that signals a shift from investing in their future to assuming they have no future? Certainly not a future in which they can depend on adult society for either compassion or support.

Zero Tolerance and the Politics/Color of Punishment

In what follows, I want to address the social costs and implications of removing youth from the inventory of ethical and political concerns through policies that replace social compassion with containment while increasingly abandoning young people, especially youth of color, to the dictates of a repressive penal state in which government, at all levels, is addressing social problems through the police, courts, and prison system. More specifically, I will address how the policing function of the state bears down on young people by examining, in particular, the emergence of zero tolerance policies in the public schools. While my focus is on the relationship between education and zero tolerance policies, the context for my analysis points to a broader set of repressive conditions that not only targets young people across a wider variety of public spheres, but also undermines the guarantee of rights and institutional structures that a realized democracy represents. I begin with a definition of domestic militarization taken from critical educator and activist Ruth Wilson Gilmore in order to provide the larger political, social, and cultural context for understanding the growing attacks on youth through the emergence of zero tolerance policies.[24] According to Gilmore, expressions of domestic militarization can be found in the deadly violence waged against people of color such as Amadou Diallo, an unarmed black man who was shot 41 times by NYPD policemen, and Tyisha Miller, who was shot a dozen times by California police while she was sitting in her car. Such violence can also be found in the countless acts of humiliation, harassment, and punishment handed out to the poor and people of color by the forces of the repressive state every day in the United States.[25] In this regard, the brutal attacks by police on Rodney King and Abner Louima stand out. Evidence of domestic militarization can also be seen in the rise of the prison-industrial complex, the passing of retrograde legislation that targets immigrants, the appearance of gated communities, the widespread use of racial profiling by the police, and the ongoing attacks on the welfare state. Of course, state repression is not new, but what is unique about contemporary political culture is that:

> The new State is shedding social welfare in favor of domestic militarization. Programs that provide for people's welfare, protect the environment, or regulate corporate behavior have been delegitimized and jettisoned. There is a new consensus among the powers that be that focuses the domestic State on defense against enemies, both foreign and U.S.–born. What's new is the scale of militarism being directed at people inside the U.S., and the scope for what comes into the crosshairs of the prison industrial complex rather than some helping agency.[26]

Critics such as Gilmore and Christian Parenti rightfully argue that as the "War on Poverty" ran out of steam with the social and economic crisis that emerged in the 1970s, it has been replaced with an emphasis on domestic warfare, and that the policies of social investment, at all levels of government, have given way to an emphasis on repression, surveillance, and control.[27] Starting with Reagan's war on drugs[28] and the privatization of the prison industry in the 1980s and escalating to the war on immigrants in the early 1990s, and the rise of the prison-industrial complex by the close of the decade, the criminalization of social policy has now become a part of everyday culture and provides a common referent point that extends from governing prisons and regulating urban culture to running schools. Hence, it comes as no surprise when former New York City Mayor, Rudi Giuliani, "over the opposition of most parents and the schools chancellor, formally assigns the oversight of discipline in the public schools to the police department."[29]

Once it was clear that Giuliani would receive high marks in the press for lowering the crime rate due to zero tolerance policies adopted by the city's police force, it seemed reasonable to him to use the same policies in the public schools. What the popular press ignored, until the killing of Amadou Diallo at the hands of New York City's police, was that zero tolerance policing strategies exacted a heavy price on the poor and people of color, and resulted in more people being stopped and searched as well as larger settlements being paid out to quell charges of police abuse.[30] What was also ignored by the public and popular press nationally was that as the call for more police, prisons, and get tough laws reached fever pitch among politicians and legislators, the investment in domestic militarization began to exceed more than $100 billion a year.[31]

Domestic militarization as a central feature of American life is evident in the ongoing criminalization of social policy, which is probably most visible in the emergence of zero tolerance laws that have swept the nation since the 1980s, and gained full legislative strength with the passage of the Violent Crime Control and Law Enforcement Act of 1994. Following the mandatory sentencing legislation and get tough policies associated with the "war on drugs" declared by the Reagan and Bush administrations, this bill calls for a "three strikes and you're out" policy, which puts repeat offenders, including nonviolent offenders, in jail for life, regardless of the seriousness of the crime. The general idea behind the bill is "to increase the prison sentence for a second offense and require life in custody without parole for a third offense."[32] It also provides 60 new offenses punishable by death, while at the same time limiting the civil rights and appeal process for those inmates sentenced to die. In addition, the largest single allocation in the bill is for prison construction.[33] Since the bill was passed in 1994, the prison industry has become big business with many states spending "more on prison construction than on university construction."[34] Yet, even as the crime rate plummets dramatically, more people, especially people of color, are being arrested, harassed, punished, and put in jail.[35] As it has been widely reported, the United States is now the biggest jailer in the world. Between 1985 and 2000 the prison population grew from 744,206 to 2.0 million (approaching the combined populations of Idaho, Wyoming, and Montana), and prison budgets jumped from $7 billion in 1980 to $40 billion in 2000.[36] Manning Marable points out that the United States is "spending $35,000 a year to maintain a single prisoner, one prisoner, in a minimum security cell. It costs nearly $80,000 a year to confine a prisoner in a maximum security cell. We are building over a hundred new prison cells a day."[37]

The explosion in the prison population has also resulted in the move towards privatizing prisons.[38] As Robin D. G. Kelley points out, by the close of 1997, at least 102 for-profit private prisons existed in the United States, "each receiving some form of federal subsidy with limited federal protection of prisoners' rights or prison conditions."[39] Prisoners, especially the widely disproportionate pool of African American inmates, which has tripled since 1980, provide big business not only "with a new source of consumers but a reservoir of cheap labor."[40] The Report of the National Criminal Justice Commission noted in 1996 that as "spending on crime fighting has risen three times faster than defense spending," the biggest beneficiary appears to be "private businesses [that] reap enormous profits from the fear of crime and the expansion of the criminal justice system."[41] Moreover, many critics of the private prison system have pointed out rightly that it "is particularly disturbing that corporations should be making a profit from policies that are not in the public interest—such as excessive prison sentences and the incarceration of nonviolent offenders."[42] At a time when over 550,000 black males are interned in jails in the United States, "the concept of private companies profiting from prisoners evokes the convict leasing system of the Old South."[43]

As the "prison-industrial complex" becomes a dominant force in the economy of states such as California, competing with land developers, service industries, and unions, it does more than rake in huge profits for corporations; it also contributes to what Mike Davis calls a "permanent prison class."[44] One measure of the power of the prison-industrial complex as a high-powered growth industry can be gauged by the increasing power of prison guard unions to shape legislative policy in many states. For instance, the California Correctional Peace Officers Union has grown in one decade from 4,000 to over 29,000 members. During the 1998 political campaign, the prison guard union was the state's number one "donor to legislative races, setting a record by spending $1.9 million."[45] Yet, the prison-industrial complex does more than fuel profits and shape legislative policies for those eager to invest in high growth industries; it also legitimates a culture of punishment and incarceration, aimed most decisively at "African American males who make up less than 7 percent of the U.S. population, yet they comprise almost half of the prison and jail population."[46] The statistics for a wide range of indices can demonstrate the racist significance of this figure, but the shameful fact is that the number of African Americans in prison far exceeds the number of African American males who commit crime. For instance, law professor David Cole, in his unsparing analysis of the racial disparities that fuel the government's drug war, points out that while "76 percent of illicit drug users were white, 14 percent black, and 8 percent Hispanic—figures which roughly match each group's share of the general population," African Americans constitute "35 percent of all drug arrests, 55 percent of all drug convictions, and 74 percent of all sentences for drug offences."[47] A Justice Department Report points out that on any given day in this country "more than a third of the young African American men aged 18–34 in some of our major cities are either in prison or under some form of criminal justice supervision."[48] The same department reported in April of 2000 that "black youth are forty-eight times more likely than whites to be sentenced to juvenile prison for drug offenses."[49]

Domestic militarization in this instance functions not only to contain "surplus populations" and provide new sources of revenue; it also actively promotes and legitimates retrograde social policies. For example, an increasing number of states such as California and New York are spending more on prison construction than on higher education and hiring more prison guards than teachers. A recent study by the Correctional Association of New York and the Washington, D.C.–based Justice Policy Institute claims that millions of dollars are being diverted from the public university budget in New York and diverted into prison construction. The reports point out that "between fiscal year 1988 and fiscal year 1998, New York's public universities saw their operating budgets plummet by 29 percent while funding for prisons rose 76 percent. In actual dollars, there has been nearly a one-to-one tradeoff, with the Department of Corrections in New York State receiving a $761 million increase during that ten-year period, while state funding for New York City and state university systems, declined by $615 million."[50] In California, the average prison guard now earns $10,000 more than the average public school teacher, and increasingly more than many professors working in the state university system.[51] This is more than a travesty of justice, it is a stern lesson for many students of color and working class white youths—viewed as a generation of suspects by the dominant society—that it is easier for them to go to jail than it is to get a decent education. For the wider public, the lesson to be learned is that there is a greater payoff when society invests more in prisons than in those public institutions that educate young people to become public servants in crucial spheres such as education. In this instance, the culture of punishment and its policies of containment and brutalization become more valued to the dominant social order than any consideration of what it means for a society to expand and strengthen the mechanisms and freedoms central to sustaining a substantive democracy.[52]

Rather than viewing "three strike" policies and mandatory sentencing as part of a racist-inspired expression of domestic militarization and a source of massive injustice, corporate America and conservative politicians embrace it as both a new venue for profit and a legitimate expression of the market driven policies of neoliberalism. Within this discourse, social costs and racial injustice, when compared to corporate profit, are rendered irrelevant.[53] How else to explain a recent *New York Times* article by Guy Trebay that focuses on "jailhouse chic" as the latest in youth fashion.[54] Surrendering any attempt at socially responsible analysis, Trebay reports that the reason so many teens are turning prison garb into a fashion statement is that an unprecedented number of youths are incarcerated in the United States. When they get released, "they take part of that culture with them." The retail market for prison style work clothes is so strong, Trebay points out, that prisons, such as those managed by the Oregon Corrections Department, are gaining a foothold in the fashion market by producing their own prison blues clothing lines (which can be found on their web site: www.prisonblues.com). The market trumps social justice in this account as incarcerated youth are praised for being fashion trendsetters, prisons are celebrated for their market savvy, and cheap prison labor is affirmed for its contribution to cutting edge street culture.

Zero tolerance policies as one manifestation of domestic militarization have been especially cruel in the treatment of juvenile offenders.[55] Rather than attempting to work with youth and make an investment in their psychological, economic, and social well being, a growing number of cities are passing sweep laws—curfews and bans against loitering and cruising—designed not only to keep youth off the streets, but to make it easier to criminalize their behavior. For example, within the last decade, "45 states ... have passed or amended legislation making it easier to prosecute juveniles as adults" and in some states "prosecutors can bump a juvenile case into adult court at their own discretion."[56] A particularly harsh example of these Draconian measures can be seen in the recent passing of Proposition 21 in California. The law makes it easier for prosecutors to try teens fourteen and older in adult court who are convicted of felonies. These youth would automatically be put in adult prison and be given lengthy mandated sentences. As Louise Cooper points out, "It also ... increases the discretionary powers for routine police surveillance, random searches and arrest of young people."[57] The overall consequence of the law is to largely eliminate intervention programs, increase the number of youth in prisons, especially minority youth, and keep them there for longer periods of time. Moreover, the law is at odds with a number of studies that indicate that putting youth in jail with adults both increases recidivism and poses a grave danger to young offenders who, as a recent Columbia University study suggested, are "five times as likely to be raped, twice as likely to be beaten and eight times as likely to commit suicide than adults in the adult prison system."[58]

Paradoxically, the moral panic against crime that increasingly feeds the calls for punishment rather than rehabilitation programs for young people exist in conjunction with the disturbing fact that the United States is currently one of only seven countries (Congo, Iran, Nigeria, Pakistan, Saudi Arabia and Yemen) in the world that permit the death penalty for juveniles, and that in the last decade it has executed more juvenile offenders than all other countries combined that allow such executions.[59] Given the assumption among neoliberal hardliners that market values are more important than values that involve trust, compassion, and solidarity, it is not surprising that

Wall Street's emphasis on profits views the growth in the prison industry and the growing incarceration of young people as good news. For instance, Gary Delgado reports that even though "crime has dropped precipitously," stock analyst Bob Hirschfield notes that "males 15–17 years old are three times as likely to be arrested than the population at large, and the proportion of 15–17 year olds is expanding at twice the overall population." Rather than being alarmed, if not morally repulsed, over these figures, Hirschfield concludes that it is a "great time to purchase shares" in the new prison growth industry.[60]

While the social costs for such policies are cause for grave alarm, they are all the more disturbing since the burden they inflict upon society appears to be far greater for young people of color than for any other group. The National Criminal Justice Commission report claims that while "get tough" policies are likely to be more severe when dealing with children, they are particularly repressive when applied to youth of color, especially as a result of the war on drugs and the more recent eruption of school shootings. Numerous studies have documented that unlike middle-class white youth, minority youth are "more likely to be arrested, referred to court, and placed outside the home when awaiting disposition of their cases....[Moreover] all things being equal, minority youths face criminal charges more often than white youths for the same offenses. Also, African American youths are charged more often than whites with a felony when the offense could be considered a misdemeanor.... Minority youth are also more likely to be waived to adult court, where they will face longer sentences and fewer opportunities for rehabilitative programs."[61] Fed by widespread stereotypical images of black youth as superpredators and black culture as the culture of criminality, minority youth face a criminal justice system that not only harasses and humiliates them but also a larger society that increasingly undercuts their chances for a living wage, quality jobs, essential social services, and decent schools.[62] Within such a context, the possibilities for treating young people of color with respect, dignity, and support vanishes and with it the hope of overcoming a racial abyss that makes a mockery out of justice and a travesty of democracy.

The growing influence of zero tolerance laws in the United States can be seen in the application of such laws in areas as different as airport security, the criminal justice system, immigration policy and drug testing programs for athletes. The widespread use of these policies has received a substantial amount of critical analyses within the last decade. Unfortunately, these analyses rarely make connections between what is going on in the criminal justice system and the public schools.[63] While schools share some proximity to prisons in that they are both about disciplining the body, though for allegedly different purposes, little has been written about how zero tolerance policies in schools resonate powerfully with prison practices that signify a shift away from treating the body as a social investment (i.e., rehabilitation) to viewing it as a threat to security, demanding control, surveillance, and punishment.[64] Little has also been written on how such practices have exceeded the boundaries of the prison-industrial complex, providing models and perpetuating a shift in the very nature of educational leadership and pedagogy. Of course, there are exceptions such as Lewis Lapham's lament that schools do more than teach students to take their place within a highly iniquitous class-based society. In many larger cities, high schools, according to Lapham, now "possess many of the same attributes as minimum security prisons—metal detectors in the corridors, zero tolerance for rowdy behavior, the principal as a warden and the faculty familiar with the syllabus of concealed weapons." According to Lapham, schools resemble prisons in that they both warehouse students to prevent flooding the labor market while "instilling the attitudes of passivity and apprehension, which in turn induce the fear of authority and the habits of obedience."[65] Another notable and far more insightful exception is Manning Marable, who argues that "One of the central battlegrounds for democracy in the U.S. in the twenty-first century will be the effort to halt the dismantling of public education and public institutions in general for the expansion of [the] prison-industrial complex."[66]

As schooling is defined largely as a disciplinary institution that prepares students for the workplace, the discourse of leadership has been supplanted by a pragmatics of classroom management. Similarly, pedagogy often ignores the specificity of contexts that informs students' lives and substitutes issues of accountability (measured through test scores) for a qualitative interest in producing critical citizens; moreover, such pedagogies of transmission are particularly intolerant of notions of difference, critical questioning, or resistance. Pedagogy in this model of control relies heavily on those forms of standardization and values that are consistent with the norms and relations that drive the market economy. Teachers teach for the tests as student behaviors are consistently monitored and knowledge is increasingly quantified.

Made over in the image of corporate culture, schools are no longer valued as a public good but as a private interest; hence, the appeal of such schools is less in their capacity to educate students according to the demands of critical citizenship than it is about enabling students to master the requirements of a market-driven economy. Under these circumstances, many students increasingly find themselves in schools that lack any language for relating the self to public life, social responsibility, or the imperatives of democratic life. In this instance, democratic education with its emphasis on respect for others, critical inquiry, civic courage, and concern for the collective good is suppressed and replaced by an excessive emphasis on the language of privatization, individualism, self-interest, and brutal competitiveness. Lost in this discourse of schooling is any notion of democratic community or models of leadership capable of raising questions about what public schools should accomplish in a democracy and why, under certain circumstances, they fail.

The growth and popularity of zero tolerance policies within the public schools have to be understood as part of a broader educational reform movement in which the market is now seen as the master design for all pedagogical encounters. At the same time, the corporatizing of public schooling cannot be disassociated from the assault on those public spheres within the larger society that provide the conditions for greater democratic participation in shaping society. As the state is downsized and support services dry up, containment policies become the principle means to discipline youth and restrict dissent. Within this context, zero tolerance legislation within the schools simply extend to young people elements of harsh control and administration implemented in other public spheres where inequalities breed the conditions for dissent and resistance. Schools increasingly resemble other enervated public spheres as they cut back on trained psychologists, school nurses, programs such as music, art, athletics, and valuable after school activities. Jesse Jackson argues that under such circumstances, schools do more than fail to provide students with a well-rounded education; they often "bring in the police, [and] the school gets turned into a feeder system for the penal system."[67] In addition, the growing movement to define schools as private interests rather than as public assets not only reinforces the trend to administer them in ways that resemble how prisons are governed, it also points to a disturbing tendency on the part of adult society to direct a great deal of anger and resentment toward youth. In what follows, I analyze zero tolerance policies in schools and address the implications they have for a society that signals a dramatic shift away from civic education—the task and responsibility of which is to prepare students for shaping and actively participating in democratic public life—to models of training and regulation whose purpose opens the door to ultraconservative forms of political culture and authoritarian modes of social regulation.

Schooling and the Pedagogy of Zero Tolerance

Across the nation school districts have embraced zero tolerance policies. Emulating state and federal laws passed in the 1990s based on mandatory sentencing and "three strikes and you're out" policies, many educators first invoked zero tolerance rules against those kids who brought guns to schools. But over time the policy was broadened, and now includes a range of behavioral infractions that include everything from possessing drugs to harboring a weapon to *threatening* other students—all broadly conceived. For instance, "in many districts school administrators won't tolerate even one instance of weapon possession, drug use, or harassment."[68] One of the most publicized cases illustrating the harshness of zero tolerance policies took place in Decatur, Illinois when seven African American students, who participated in a fight at a football game that lasted 17 seconds and was marked by the absence of any weapons, were expelled for two years. Two of the young men were seniors about to graduate. None of the boys at their hearing were allowed counsel or the right to face their accusers; nor were their parents allowed any degree of involvement in the case. When Jesse Jackson brought national attention to the incident, the Decatur school board reduced the expulsions to one year.

Fueled by moral panics about the war on drugs and images of urban youth of color as ultraviolent, drug pushing, gang bangers, a national mood of fear provided legitimacy for zero tolerance policies in the schools as both an ideology of disdain and a policy of punishment. Unfortunately, any sense of perspective seems lost, as school systems across the country clamor for metal detectors, armed guards, see-through knapsacks, and, in some cases, armed teachers. Some school systems are investing in new software in order to "profile" students who might exhibit criminal behavior.[69] Overzealous laws relieve educators of exercising deliberation and critical judgment as more and more young people are either suspended or expelled from school often for ludicrous reasons. For example, two Virginia fifth-graders who allegedly put soap in their teacher's drinking water were charged with a felony.[70] Officials at Rangeview High School in Colorado, after unsuccessfully trying to expel a student because they found three baseball bats on the floor of his car, ended up suspending him.[71] In a similar litany of absurdities, USA Today reported on two Illinois seven-year-olds who were "suspended for having nail clippers with knifelike attachments."[72] Jesse Jackson offers the example of a student who was suspended on a weapons charge because school officials discovered a little rubber hammer as part of his Halloween costume. Jackson provides another equally absurd example of a student accused with a drug charge because he gave another youth two lemon cough drops.[73]

As Boston Globe columnist Ellen Goodman points out, zero tolerance does more than offer a simple solution to a complex problem, it has become a code word for a "quick and dirty way of kicking kids out" of school.[74] This becomes clear as states such as Colorado in their eagerness to appropriate and enforce zero tolerance policies in their districts do less to create a safe environment for students than to simply kick more kids out of the public school system. For example, the Rocky Mountain News reported in June of 1999 that "partly as a result of such rigor in enforcing Colorado's zero tolerance law, the number of kids kicked out of public schools has skyrocketed since 1993—from 437 before the law to nearly 2,000 in the 1996–1997 school year."[75] In Chicago, the widespread adoption of zero tolerance policies in 1994 resulted in a 51 percent increase in student suspensions for the next four years, and a 3,000 percent increase in expulsions, jumping "from 21 in 1994–'95 to 668 in 1997–'98."[76] Within such a climate of disdain and intolerance, expelling students does more than pose a threat to innocent kids, it also suggests that local school boards are refusing to do the hard work of exercising judgment, trying to understand what the conditions are that undermine school safety, and providing reasonable services for all students, and viable alternatives for the troubled ones. But there is more at stake than merely bad judgment behind the use of zero tolerance laws in American public schools. As the criminalization of young people finds its way into the classroom, it becomes easier to punish students rather than listen to them.[77] Even though such policies clog up the courts and put additional pressure on an already overburdened juvenile justice system, educators appear to have few qualms about implementing them. And the results are far from inconsequential for the students themselves.

Zero tolerance laws make it easier to expel students rather than for school administrators to work with parents, community justice programs, religious organizations, and social service agencies. Moreover, automatic expulsion policies do little to either produce a safer school or society since as Clare Kittredge points out "we already know that lack of attachment to the school is one of the prime predictors of delinquency."[78] Most insidiously, zero tolerance laws, while a threat to all youth and any viable notion of democratic public education, reinforce in the public imagination the image of students of color as a source of public fears and a threat to public school safety. Zero tolerance policies and laws appear to be well-tailored to mobilizing racialized codes and racial based moral panics that portray black and brown urban youth as a new and frightening violent threat to the safety of 'decent' Americans. Not only do most of the high profile zero tolerance cases such as the Decatur school incident often involve African American students, but such policies also reinforce the racial inequities that plague school systems across the country. For example, Tamar Lewin, a writer for the *New York Times,* has reported on a number of studies illustrating "that black students in public schools across the country are far more likely than whites to be suspended or expelled, and far less likely to be in gifted or advanced placement classes."[79] Even in a city such as San Francisco, considered a bastion of liberalism, African American students pay a far greater price for zero tolerance policies. Libero Della Piana reports that "According to data collected by Justice Matters, a San Francisco agency advocating equity in education, African Americans make up 52 percent of all suspended students in the district—far in excess of their 16 percent of the general population."[80]

Marilyn Elias reported in a recent issue of *USA Today* that "In 1998, the first year national expulsion figures were gathered, 31 percent of kids expelled were black, but blacks made up only 17 percent of the students in public schools."[81] The tragedy underlying such disparities in treating black and white students appears to be completely lost on those educators defending zero tolerance policies. For instance, Gerald Tirozzi, executive director of the

National Association of Secondary School Principals, argues, without irony, that such policies "make everything very clear" and "promote fair, equitable treatment in discipline."[82]

As compassion and understanding give way to rigidity and intolerance, schools increasingly become more militarized and function as a conduit to the penal system. The measure of such a transformation is not limited to the increasing fortress quality of American schools—which are marked by the foreboding presence of hired armed guards in the corridors, patrolled cafeterias, locked doors, video surveillance cameras, electronic badges, police dogs, and routine drug searches. It is also present in racist culture of fear that exhibits a deep distrust, if not hostility and revulsion towards young people, especially youth of color.[83] For instance, in Louisiana, board member Ray St. Pierre proposed that any student in junior high or high school who is caught fighting "would be handcuffed inside the school by sheriff's deputies and taken to a juvenile facility where he would be charged with disturbing the peace."[84] In case parents miss the point, they would have to pay a cash bond for their child's release. As a result of St. Pierre's notion of getting tough on misbehavior, the school provides not only an opportunity for students to leave with a diploma but also with a police record. The image of kids being handcuffed, pulled out of a school, and dragged away in the back of a police van or patrol car has become so commonplace in the United States that the psychological, political, and social consequences of such brutal practices barely lift an eyebrow and are more routinely met with public approval. In some instances, the zero tolerance policies are not just affecting students in schools. In an attempt to root out pedophiles in the public school system in the state of Maine, the FBI is demanding that teachers submit to fingerprinting and criminal history checks. Many teachers have refused to comply and may lose their certification and jobs.[85] Within the current climate of domestic militarization, it may be just a matter of time before the surveillance cameras, profiling technologies, and other tools of the penal state become a routine part of the climate of teaching in America's schools. Stanley Aronowitz is right in arguing that as the "state's police functions tend to overpower and mediate its diminishing social functions," one consequence is that "[p]olice now routinely patrol urban public high schools and universities as if they were identical with the mean streets of the central cities or, more to the point, tantamount to day prisons."[86]

To be sure, zero tolerance policies turn schools into an adjunct of the criminal justice system, but they also further rationalize misplaced legislative priorities. And that has profound social costs. Instead of investing in early childhood programs, repairing deteriorating school buildings, or hiring more qualified teachers, schools now spend millions of dollars to upgrade security. Moral panic and fear reproduce a fortress mentality in which the logic of domestic militarization produces an authoritarian irrationalism, as in Fremont

High School in Oakland, California, where school administrators decided to build a security fence costing $500,000 "while the heating remained out of commission."[87] Another instance of such irrationality can be found, as I mentioned earlier, in the fact that many states now spend "more on prison than on university construction."[88] Young people are quickly realizing that schools have more in common with military boot camps and prisons than they do with other institutions in American society. In addition, as schools abandon their role as democratic public spheres and are literally "fenced off" from the communities that surround them, they lose their ability to become anything other than spaces of containment and control. As schools become militarized, they lose their ability to provide students with the skills to cope with human differences, uncertainty, and the various symbolic and institutional forces that undermine political agency and democratic public life itself. In this context, discipline and training replace education for all but the privileged as schools increasingly take on an uncanny resemblance to oversized police precincts, tragically disconnected both from the students who inhabit them and the communities that give meaning to their historical experiences and daily lives. Coupled with the corporate emphasis on privatizing schools, the motif of punishment and withdrawal—civic and interpersonal—governs this new form of school regulation and administration.

Zero tolerance policies in schools have been criticized roundly by a number of social and educational critics. William Ayers and Bernadine Dohrn rightly argue that zero tolerance policies do not teach but punish and that students need not less but more tolerance.[89] Ellen Goodman echoes this view by claiming that schools that implement such laws are not paying attention to children's lives, because, as she nicely puts it, it is "harder to talk with troubled teens than to profile them."[90] Daniel Perlstein has argued that zero tolerance programs not only fail to ensure school safety, they also deflect educators from addressing crucial considerations that structure racial, class, and social divisions in schools.[91] Of course, as all of these critics point out, zero tolerance laws do more than turn schools into policing institutions that ignore the problems of tracking, racism, and the exclusionary and hierarchical nature of school culture, they also further reproduce such problems. These critiques are important, and I have addressed them elsewhere.[92] But these criticisms do not go far enough. It is also necessary for educators to place school-based zero tolerance policies within a broader context that makes it possible to see them as part of the ideology of neoconservatism, neoliberalism, and domestic militarization that is ravaging conditions for critical political agency, destroying the deployment of even minimal ethical principles, and undermining the conditions necessary within schools and other public spheres to produce the symbolic and material resources necessary to engage in the struggle for critical citizenship, freedom, democracy, and justice.

Schooling and the Crisis of Public Life

I want to conclude by arguing that zero tolerance policies in both the schools and other domestic spheres cannot be understood outside of a range of broader considerations that constitute a crisis in the very nature of civic agency, ethics, politics, and democracy. As the state disengages from its role as a mediator between capital and human needs, and market forces bear heavily on redefining the meaning of education as a private enterprise, it becomes all the more difficult to imagine public schools as important contested sites in the struggle for civic education and authentic democracy. If neoconservatism provides the ideological ammunition to turn a generation of youth into suspects, neoliberalism works both to produce a deregulated consumer culture and limit the possibilities for noncommodified social domains where young and old alike can experience dissent and difference as part of a multicultural democracy, locate metaphors of hope, respond to those who carry on the legacies of moral witnessing, and imagine relationships outside of the dictates of the market and the authoritarian rule of penal control. Educators and others need to rethink what it would mean to both interrogate and break away from the dangerous and destructive representations and practices of zero tolerance policies as they work to reinforce modes of authoritarian control and social amnesia in a vast and related number of powerful institutional spheres. This suggests a struggle both for public space and a public dialogue about how to imagine reappropriating a notion of politics that is linked to the regime of authentic democracy while articulating a new discourse, set of theoretical tools, and social possibilities for re-visioning civic education as a basis for political agency and social transformation in ways that go beyond its historical limitations. Zero tolerance is not *the* problem as much as it is symptomatic of a much broader set of issues centered around the gulf between the *regime of the political*—everything that concerns modes of power—and the *realm of politics*—the multiple ways in which human beings question established power, transform institutions, and reject "all authority that would fail to render an account and provide reasons ... for the validity of its pronouncements."[93] Neoliberalism offers no intellectual tools or political vocabulary for addressing this gap because it has no stake in defining political culture outside of the interest of the market. Nor does it have any interest in supporting forms of civic education designed to question, challenge, and transform power as part of a political and ethical response to the demise of democratic public life. Neoliberalism has thrown into question the very feasibility of politics and democracy and, in part, has been successful at doing so because it defines citizenship through the narrow logic of consumerism and politics as having no foundation in agency as a form of self-determination and critical strategic action. Hence, there is no room in this discourse for providing the knowledge, skills, and values necessary for young people and adults to define civic education anew as an "essential step towards agency, self-representation, and an effective democracy."[94]

Against the social and economic policies of neoliberalism, educators, youth, parents, and various cultural workers need to rethink the meaning of democracy, ethics, and political agency in an increasingly globalized world in which power is being separated from traditional political forms such as the nation state. But the war against youth must be understood as an attempt to contain, warehouse, control, and even eliminate all those groups and social formations that the market finds expendable (i.e., unable to further the interests of the bottom line or the logic of cost effectiveness). For progressives, this suggests a decisive and important struggle over a notion of politics that refuses the ongoing attempts on the part of huge corporations, conservatives and other "masters of the private economy"[95] to make public life irrelevant, if not dangerous, by replacing an ethic of reciprocity and mutual responsibility with a market-driven ethic of individualism in which "competitiveness is the only human ethic, one that promotes a war against all."[96]

There is more at stake here than recognizing the limits and social costs of a neoliberal philosophy that reduces all relationships to the exchange of goods and money, there is also the responsibility on the part of critical intellectuals and other activists to rethink the nature of the public. It also demands new forms of social citizenship and civic education that have a purchase on people's everyday lives and struggles expressed through a wide range of institutions. Central here is the need to rethink a notion of cultural politics that makes politics more pedagogical and the pedagogical a permanent feature of politics in a wide variety of sites, including schools. In this instance, politics is inextricably connected to pedagogies that effectively mobilize the beliefs, desires, and forms of persuasion that organize and give meaning to particular strategies of social engagement and policy transformation.[97] Education as a form of persuasion, power, and intervention is constitutive of those ongoing struggles that shape the social. Challenging neoliberal hegemony as a form of domination is crucial to reclaiming an alternative notion of the political and rearticulating the relationship between political agency and substantive democracy.

Intellectuals and other cultural workers bear an enormous responsibility in opposing neoliberalism by not only reviving the rhetoric of democratic political culture, but also expanding its social consequences in ways that democratic societies have yet to realize. Part of this challenge suggests creating new locations of struggle, vocabularies, and subject positions that allow people in a wide variety of public spheres to become more than they are now, to question what it is they have become within existing institutional and social formations and "to give some thought to their experiences so that they can transform their relations of subordination and oppression."[98] Cornelius Castoriadis insightfully argues that for any regime of democracy to be vital, it needs to create citizens who are critical thinkers capable of calling existing institutions into question, asserting individual rights, and assuming public responsibility. In this instance, critical pedagogy as an alternative form of civic education and literacy provides oppositional knowledges, skills, and theoretical tools for highlighting the workings of power and reclaiming the possibility of intervening in its operations and effects. But Castoriadis also suggests that civic education must be linked to the task of creating new locations of struggle that offer critical opportunities for experiencing political agency within social domains that provide the concrete conditions in which people can exercise their capacities and skills "as part of the very process of governing."[99] In this context culture becomes a space for hope, and pedagogy becomes a valuable tool in reclaiming the promise of democracy and reabsorbing the political back into a viable notion of politics.

Zero tolerance has become a metaphor for hollowing out the state and expanding the forces of domestic militarization, for reducing democracy to the rule of capital, and replacing an ethic of mutual aid with an appeal to excessive individualism and social indifference.[100] Within this logic, the notion of the political increasingly equates power with domination, and politics with consumerism and passivity. Under this insufferable climate of manufactured indifference, increased repression, and unabated exploitation, young people become the new casualties in an ongoing war against justice, freedom, social citizenship, and democracy. As despairing as these conditions appear at the present moment, they increasingly have become the basis for a surge of political resistance on the part of many youth, intellectuals, labor unions, educators, and other activists and social movements.[101] Under such circumstances, it is time to remind ourselves that collective problems deserve collective solutions and that what is at risk is not only a generation of young people now considered to be a generation of suspects, but the very promise of democracy itself. The issue is no longer whether it is possible to invest in the idea of the political and politics but what are the consequences for not doing so.

Notes

1. One excellent source analyzing the various debates over citizenship can be found in Gershon Shafir, ed., *The Citizenship Debates: A Reader* (Minneapolis: University of Minnesota Press, 1998).

2. Jacques Derrida, "Intellectual Courage: An Interview," trans. Peter Krapp, *Culture Machine,* Vol. 2 (2000), p. 9.

3. In this respect, one can point to the welfare reform bill signed into law by former President Bill Clinton. The bill cut $55 billion from federal antipoverty programs. Peter Edelman, former Under Secretary of Health and Human Services, resigned over Clinton's support of the bill, calling it in an article in the *Atlantic Monthly* the worst thing that Bill Clinton has done. Not only did the bill produce budget cuts

that affect low-income people, but 10 percent of all families will also lose income; moreover, Edelman estimated that the bill would move 2.6 million people, including 1.1 million children, into poverty. The bill also results in drastic cuts in child nutrition programs—$3 billion in six years, and support for social services—$2.5 billion in over six years as well. See Peter Edelman, "The Worst Thing Bill Clinton Has Done," *Atlantic Monthly 279*:3 (March 1997), pp. 43–58. See also the moving analysis by Deborah R. Connolly of the problems experienced daily by a group of poor women trying their best to negotiate a social service system that is under served and overburdened, in Deborah R. Connolly, *Homeless Mothers: Face to Face with Women and Poverty* (Minneapolis: University of Minnesota Press, 2000).

4. Paul Gilroy, "On the State of Cultural Studies: An Interview with Paul Gilroy," *Third Text 49* (Winter 1999–2000): 21. There are too many texts to mention on media control of public spaces, but one good example is Robert W. McChesney, *Corporate Media and the Threat to Democracy* (New York: Seven Stories Press, 1997).

5. Zygmunt Bauman, *Globalization: The Human Consequences* (New York: Columbia University Press, 1998), p. 21.

6. Lisa Belkin, The Backlash Against Children," *New York Times Magazine* (July 23, 2000): 30.

7. Ibid., p. 32.

8. Ibid., p. 34.

9. Ibid., p. 34.

10. R. J. Smith, "Among the Mooks," *New York Times Magazine* (August 6, 2000), p. 38.

11. This refusal of many critics to deal with the social, economic, and cultural conditions that produce gangsta rap is taken up in George Lipsitz, "The Hip Hop Hearings: Censorship, Social Memory, and Intergenerational Tensions Among African Americans," in Joc Austin and Michael Nevin Willard, eds., *Generations of Youth* (New York: New York University Press, 1998), pp. 395–411.

12. I have addressed the right wing attack on youth in great detail in Henry A. Giroux, *Fugitive Cultures: Race, Violence, and Youth* (New York: Routledge Publishing, 1996); Henry A. Giroux, *Channel Surfing: Race Talk and the Destruction of American Youth* (New York: St. Martin's Press, 1997); Henry A. Giroux, *Stealing Innocence: Youth, Corporate Power, and the Politics of Culture* (New York: St. Martin's Press, 2000).

13. Ibid., p. 39.

14. Ibid., p. 39.

15. Robin D. G. Kelley, *Yo' Mama's Disfunktional! Fight the Culture Wars in Urban America*, (Boston: Beacon Press, 1997), p. 17.

16. What writers such as Belkin and Smith leave out of their account of children in America is astonishing. For instance, Marian Wright Edelman reports that "13.5 million children live in poverty, 12 million have no health insurance, and 5 million are home alone every day after school lets out. And more than 4,000 each year pays the ultimate price for adult irresponsibility: they are killed by guns. [Moreover] millions more receive substandard education in crumbling schools without enough books, equipment or teachers. Or they are eligible for Head Start programs or childcare assistance when parents work, but receive neither. Or they are abused or neglected, or are languishing in temporary foster homes, waiting for adoption." Marian Wright Edelman, "There's no Trademark on Concern for Kids," *New York Times,* July 29, 2000, p. A27.

17. Toni Morrison, "On the Backs of Blacks," *Time* (Fall 1993): 57.

18. It is important to stress here that in arguing that the state is being hollowed out, I am not suggesting that the state is homogeneous nor am I suggesting that the state is losing its power. On the contrary, rather than losing its power, the state is simply abdicating power by refusing to both curb the excesses of capital and to guarantee those public goods, provisions, and safety nets that offer people a modicum of basic needs and protection. Peter Marcuse rightly suggests, "that the importance of state action in enabling the capitalist system of the industrialized world to function is increased, not reduced, as that system spreads internationally." On this issue, see Peter Marcuse, "The Language of Globalization," *Monthly Review* (July–August, 2000) http://www.monthlyreview.org/700marc.htm, p. 2.

19. Cornel West, "America's Three-Fold Crisis," *Tikkun 9*, no. 2 (1994): 41–44.

20. Zygmunt Bauman, *In Search of Politics* (Stanford: Stanford University Press, 1999), p. 166.

21. Pierre Bourdieu, *Acts of Resistance* (New York: Free Press, 1998), p. 102. For an insight into the human toll that such ideologies produce at the level of everyday experiences, see Pierre Bourdieu, et al., *The Weight of the World: Social Suffering in Contemporary Society* (Stanford: Stanford University Press, 1999).

22. Stephen Holden, "Can Art and Cinema Survive Cruder Times?" *New York Times*, September 1, 2000, p. B8.

23. Paul Gilroy, *Against Race* (Cambridge, MA: Harvard University Press, 2000), p. 221.

24. *Colorlines* Staff, "Behind the Power: An Interview with Ruth Wilson Gilmore," *Colorlines* (Winter 1999–2000): 16–20.

25. For one compilation of such acts, see Jill Nelson, ed., *Police Brutality* (New York: Norton, 2000). Also see Christian Parenti, *Lockdown America: Police and Prisons in the Age of Crisis* (London: Verso, 1999).

26. *Colorlines* Staff, "Behind the Power: An Interview with Ruth Wilson Gilmore," *Colorlines* (Winter 1999–2000): 17.

27. For an analysis of the rise of the culture of repression, see Ibid.

28. For an insightful commentary on the media and the racial nature of the war on drugs, see Jimmie L. Reeves and Richard Campbell, *Cracked Coverage: Television News, the Anti-Cocaine Crusade, and the Reagan Legacy* (Durham: Duke University Press, 1994).

29. Patricia J. Williams, "An American Litany," *Nation* (October 12, 1998), p. 10.

30. Edward Helmore, "The World: Reverend Al Rises Again: Black Leader Returns to Plague New York's Rudi Giuliani," *Observer* (April 4, 1999), p. 23.

31. Ibid., "Behind the Power," p. 16.

32. Steven R. Donziger, ed., *The Real War on Crime: The Report of the National Criminal Justice Commission* (New York: Harper Perennial, 1996), p. 19.

33. For specifics on this bill, see C. Stone Brown, "Legislating Repression: The Federal Crime Bill and the Anti-Terrorism and Effective Death Penalty Act," in Elihu Rosenblatt, *Criminal Injustice: Confronting the Prison Crisis* (Boston: South End Press, 1996), pp. 100–107.

34. Anthony Lewis, "Punishing the Country, *New York Times*, December 2, 1999, p. A1.

35. For some extensive analyses of the devastating affects the criminal justice system is having on black males, see Michael Tonry, *Malign Neglect: Race, Crime, and Punishment in America* (New York: Oxford University Press, 1995); Jerome Miller, *Search and Destroy: African-American Males in the Criminal Justice System* (Cambridge: Cambridge University Press, 1996); David Cole, *No Equal Justice: Race and Class in the American Criminal Justice System* (New York: The New Press, 1999).

36. These figures are taken from the following sources: Gary Delgado, "'Mo' Prisons Equals Mo' Money," *Colorlines* (Winter 1999–2000): 18; Fox Butterfield, "Number in Prison Grows Despite Crime Reduction," *New York Times*, August 10, 2000, p. A10; Lewis, Op. cit. A1.

37. Manning Marable, "Green Party Politics," Transcript of speech given in Denver, Colorado, on June 24, 2000, p. 3.

38. Prisoners being held in private facilities make up the fastest growing segment of the jail and prison population in the United States. At the same time, only 7 percent of prisons and jails are privately run. It is worth noting that such prisons have bad track records around human rights and providing decent services. Corrections guards unions also actively oppose them. Cited in Lisa Featherstone, "A Common Enemy: Students Fight Private Prisons," *Dissent* (Fall 2000): 78.

39. Robin D. G. Kelley, *Yo' Mama's Disfunktional!* (Boston: Beacon Press, 1997), p. 98.

40. Ibid., p. 98.

41. Donziger, Ibid., p. xii.

42. Lisa Featherstone, "A Common Enemy: Students Fight Private Prisons," *Dissent* (Fall 2000): 78.

43. Ibid., p. 81.

44. Mike Davis, "The Politics of Super Incarceration," in Elihu Rosenblatt, ed., *Criminal Injustice: Confronting the Prison Crisis* (Boston: South End Press, 1996), p. 73.

45. Cited in Jennifer Warren, *Los Angeles Times*, August 21, 2000, p. 2. Available at http://mapinc.org/drugnews/v00/n1213/a05.html.

46. Donziger, Ibid., p. 102.

47. David Cole, *No Equal Justice: Race and Class in the American Criminal Justice System* (New York: The New Press, 1999), p. 144.

48. Donziger, Ibid., p. 101.

49. Cited in Eyal Press, "The Color Test," *Lingua Franca* (October 2000): 55.

50. Cited in Manning Marable, "Green Party Politics," Transcript of speech given in Denver, Colorado, on June 24, 2000, p. 4.

51. Cited from Eric Lotke, "The Prison-Industrial Complex," *Multinational Monitor* (November 1996). Available at http://www.igc.org/ncia/pic.html.

52. Even more shameful is that fact that such discrimination against African Americans is often justified from the Olympian heights of institutions such as Harvard University by apologists such as lawyer/author Randall Kennedy who argue that such laws, criminal policies, and police practices are necessary to protect "good" blacks from "bad" blacks who commit crimes. See Randall Kennedy, *Race, Crime, and the Law* (New York: Pantheon, 1997).

53. In their drive to turn a profit, private prisons often keep their facilities full, "cut costs by trimming prisoner facilities and services [such as training for guards

and programs for inmates], and inasmuch as they are paid on a per capita basis, they have a strong financial incentive to retain prisoners in lockup as long as possible." Corrections Corporation of America, one of the nation's leading private prison conglomerates, has seen its stock go through the roof since the late 1990s. In fact, one of its facilities, Wackenhut Corrections in Florida, was so successful in turning a profit due to its use of cheap prison labor that it was named by *Forbes* magazine as one of the "200 Best Small Companies" in 1996. Cited in Kelley, op.cit., p. 98.

54. Guy Trebay, "Jailhouse Chic, An Anti-Style Turns into a Style Itself," *New York Times,* June 13, 2000, p. A23.

55. For a moving narrative of the devastating effects of the juvenile justice system on teens, see Edward Humes, *No Matter How Loud I Shout: A Year in the Life of Juvenile Court* (New York: Touchstone, 1996).

56. Margaret Talbot, "The Maximum Security Adolescent," *New York Times Magazine* (September 10, 2000): 42.

57. Louise Cooper, Youth Activists Fight Prop 21," *Against the Current 86* (May/June 2000): 12.

58. Cited in Evelyn Nieves, "California Proposal Toughens Penalties for Young Criminals," *New York Times,* March 6, 2000, pp. A1, A15.

59. Cited in Sara Rimer and Raymond Bonner, "Whether to Kill Those Who Killed as Youths," *New York Times,* August 22, 2000, p. A16. For a general critique of the death penalty system in the United States, see Robert Sherrill, "Death Trip: The American Way of Execution," *Nation* (January 8/15 2001): 13–34.

60. Cited in Gary Delgado, "Mo' Prisons Equals Mo' Money," *Colorlines* (Winter 1999–2000), p. 18.

61. Donziger, Ibid., p. 123.

62. When Tom Smith of the National Opinion Research Center at the University of Chicago asked respondents to compare blacks and other minorities "on a variety of personal traits in 1990, he found that 62 percent of nonblack respondents thought that blacks were lazier than other groups, 56 percent felt they were more prone to violence, 53 percent saw them as less intelligent, and 78 percent thought they were less self-supporting and more likely to live off welfare." Cited in Douglas S. Massey and Nancy A. Denton, *American Apartheid* (Cambridge, MA: Harvard University Press, 1993), p. 95. I mention this study as simply one example of the widespread racism that permeates American culture. Of course, while blacks are not the only group victimized by stereotypes, unlike many other groups they often do not have the material resources to fight back and prevent such stereotypes from spreading and influencing individual behavior and social policy. Hence, African Americans, especially black youth, as a group are more likely to suffer the abuse such stereotypes generate. For a more extensive study of the ongoing presence of racism in American society, see: David K. Shipler, *A Country of Strangers: Blacks and Whites in America* (New York: Vintage, 1998); Ronald Walters, "The Criticality of Racism," *Black Scholar* 26:1 (Winter 1996): 2–8. Of course, one could compile an endless list of sources on the latter subject. I only mention three because of limited space.

63. A typical example can be seen in Margaret Talbot, "The Maximum Security Adolescent," *New York Times Magazine* (September 10, 2000): 41–47, 58–60, 88, 96. Talbot takes up the get tough policies that currently characterize the juvenile justice system but makes no connections to wider social, economic, or political considerations

or for that matter to the related assaults on teens taking place in a variety of spheres outside of the criminal justice system. Of course, the right-wingers and reactionary leaning liberals who call for zero tolerance policies have almost nothing to say about the hypocrisy involved in the contradiction between punishing minorities according to get tough policies and either saying nothing or actively supporting a corporate culture that appears addicted to marketing guns and the imagery and culture of gun violence to young children, teens, and adults. The call for zero tolerance laws rather than gun control appears odd in a country in which handguns were used to kill 9,390 people in 1996, while in countries with tough handgun laws, the number of such deaths were drastically reduced. For example, "handguns were used to kill 2 people in New Zealand, 15 in Japan, 30 in Great Britain, 106 in Canada, and 213 in Germany." Cited in Bob Herbert, "Addicted to Guns," *New York Times,* January 1, 2001, p. 1. Available at http://www.nytimes.com/2001/01/01opinion/01Herb.html.

64. A classic example of this type of omission can be found in Gregory Michie, "One Strike and You're Out: Does Zero Tolerance Work? Or Does Kicking Kids Out of School Just Make Things Worse?" *Chicago Reader 29,* no. 49 (September 8, 2000): 1, 18, 22, 24, 26, 28.

65. Lewis Lapham, "School Bells," *Harper's Magazine* (August 2000): 8.

66. Manning Marable, "Green Party Politics," Transcript of speech given in Denver, Colorado, on June 24, 2000, p. 5.

67. An Interview with Jesse Jackson, "First Class Jails, Second-Class Schools," *Rethinking Schools* (Spring 2000): 16.

68. Kate Beem, "Schools Adopting Safety Measures," *Centre Daily Times,* March 3, 2000, p. 3A.

69. See Brian Moore, "Letting Software Make the Call," *Chicago Reader 29,* no. 49 (September 8, 2000): 18.

70. Ellen Goodman, "'Zero Tolerance' Means Zero Chance for Troubled Kids," *Centre Daily Times,* January 4, 2000, p. 8.

71. Editorial, "Zero Tolerance Is the Policy," *Rocky Mountain News,* June 22, 1999, p. 38A.

72. Editorial, "Growing Zeal for Zero Tolerance Ignores Needs of Troubled Youth," *USA Today,* November 22, 1999, p. 27A.

73. An Interview with Jesse Jackson, "First Class Jails, Second-Class Schools," *Rethinking Schools* (Spring 2000): 16.

74. Ellen Goodman, "'Zero Tolerance' Means Zero Chance for Troubled Kids," *Centre Daily Times,* January 4, 2000, p. 8.

75. Editorial, "Zero Tolerance Is the Policy," *Rocky Mountain News,* June 22, 1999, p. 38A.

76. Gregory Michie, "One Strike and You're Out: Does Zero Tolerance Work? Or Does Kicking Kids Out of School Just Make Things Worse?" *Chicago Reader 29,* no. 49 (September 8, 2000): 24.

77. It was recently reported in the *New York Times* that in responding to the spate of recent school shootings, the FBI has provided educators across the country with a list of behaviors that could identify "students likely to commit an act of lethal violence." One such behavior is "resentment over real or perceived injustices." The reach of domestic militarization becomes more evident as the F.B.I. not only takes on the role of monitoring potentially disruptive student behavior, but also to the

degree to which teachers are positioned to become adjuncts of the criminal justice system. The story and quotes appear in Editorial, "F.B.I. Caution Signs for Violence In Classroom," *New York Times,* September 7, 2000, p. A18.

78.   Clare Kittredge, "Penalties no Panacea for Youth Violence, a Specialist Warns; Juvenile Aggression Is Conference Topic," *Boston Globe,* May 16, 1999, New Hampshire Weekly section, p. 1.

79.   Tamar Lewin, "Study Finds Racial Bias in Public Schools," *New York Times,* March 11, 2000, p. A14.

80.   Libero Della Piana, "Crime and Punishment in Schools: Students of Color are Facing More Suspensions Because of Racially Biased Policies," *San Francisco Chronicle,* February 9, 2000, p. A21.

81.   Marilyn Elias, "Disparity in Black and White?" *USA Today,* December 11, 2000, p. 9D.

82.   Tirozzi cited and paraphrased in Elias, op. cit., p. 9D.

83.   One example of the effects of this system of punishment on African American students can be seen in a recent report from the Kids First! Coalition in Oakland, which reported that "local discipline policies resulted in students missing more than 29,000 school days in the 1997–1998 school year alone. Seventy-two percent of these students were African American. Cited in Libero Della Piana, op. cit., p. A21. For a systematic examination of the effects of racial discrimination in U.S. public schools, see Rebecca Gordon, Libero Della Piana, and Terry Keleher, *Facing the Consequences: An Examination of Racial Discrimination in U.S. Public Schools* (Oakland, CA: Applied Research Center, 2000).

84.   Andrea Shaw Jefferson, "Zero-Tolerance by Schools Troubling," *Times-Picayune,* April 18, 1999, Metro section, p. B7.

85.   Bernie Huebner, "I Refuse: Teachers in Main Revolt against Fingerprinting," *Progressive* (August 2000): 23–25.

86.   Stanley Aronowitz, *The Knowledge Factory* (Boston: Beacon Press, 2000), pp. 61–62.

87.   Libero Della Piana, Ibid., p. A21.

88.   Cited in Anthony Lewis, "Punishing the Country," *New York Times,* December 21, 1999, p. A31.

89.   William Ayers and Bernadine Dohrn, "Resisting Zero Tolerance," *Rethinking Schools* (Spring, 2000): 14.

90.   Ellen Goodman, "'Zero Tolerance' Means Zero Chance for Troubled Kids," *Centre Daily Times,* January 4, 2000, p. 8.

91.   Daniel Perlstein, Failing at Kindness: Why Fear of Violence Endangers Children," *Educational Leadership* (March 2000): 76–79.

92.   See for instance, Henry A. Giroux and Stanley Aronowitz, *Education Still under Siege,* 2nd ed. (Westport, CT: Bergin and Garvey Press, 1994); Henry A. Giroux, *Pedagogy and the Politics of Hope: Theory, Culture, and Schooling* (Boulder, CO: Westview Press, 1997); Henry A. Giroux, *Stealing Innocence* (New York: St. Martin's Press, 2000).

93.   Cornelius Castoriadis, "Democracy as Procedure and Democracy as Regime," *Constellations 4,* no. 1 (1997): 4.

94.   Gary Olson and Lynn Worsham "Staging the Politics of Difference: Homi Bhabha's Critical Literacy," *Journal of Advanced Composition 19,* no. 1 (Fall, 1999): 3.

95. Noam Chomsky, *Profit over People* (New York: Seven Stories Press, 1999), p. 20.

96. Len Terry, "Traveling 'The Hard Road to Renewal': A Continuing Conversation with Stuart Hall," *Arena Journal 8* (1997): 56.

97. In this instance, I am not suggesting that education simply be viewed as a way to promote critical consciousness, demystify knowledge, or provide alternative, progressive views of the world. I am also suggesting that pedagogy become performative and be seen as a valuable, if not crucial tool, in linking theory to action and, in particular, in shaping social policy. On the issue of linking cultural politics and public policy, see Tony Bennett, "Putting Policy into Cultural Studies," in Lawrence Grossberg, Cary Nelson, and Paula Treichler, eds., *Cultural Studies* (New York: Routledge, 1992), pp. 23–37; Michael Berube, *The Employment of English* (New York: New York University Press, 1998), especially the chapter, "Cultural Criticism and the Politics of Selling Out," pp. 216–242.

98. Lynn Worsham and Gary A. Olson, "Rethinking Political Community: Chantal Mouffe's Liberal Socialism," *Journal of Composition Theory 19*, no. 2 (1999): 178.

99. Cornelius Castoriadis, "Democracy as Procedure and Democracy as Regime," *Constellations 4*, no. 1 (1997): 11.

100. For a provocative analysis of the relationship between what Norman Geras calls "the contract of mutual indifference," the Holocaust, and neoliberalism's refusal of the social as a condition for contemporary forms of mutual indifference, see Norman Geras, *The Contract of Mutual Indifference* (London: Verso, 1998).

101. For some recent commentaries on the new student movement, see Lisa Featherstone, "The New Student Movement," *Nation* (May 15, 2000): 11–15; David Samuels, "Notes from Underground: Among the Radicals of the Pacific Northwest," *Harper's* (May 2000): 35–47; Katazyna Lyson, Monique Murad, and Trevor Stordahl, "Real Reformers, Real Results," *Mother Jones* (October 2000): 20–22.

IV
From Critical Pedagogy
to Public Pedagogy

7

Is There a Role for Critical Pedagogy in Language/Cultural Studies?

An Interview with Henry A. Giroux

MANUELA GUILHERME

⊸

Henry Giroux became established as a leading figure in radical education theory in the 1980s. Not only did he revive the arguments for civic education proposed by the main educational theorists of the 20th century, namely Dewey, Freire and others such as the reconstructionists Counts, Rugg and Brameld, but he also advanced their theories by expanding them into the idea of a "border pedagogy." His proposal can be viewed as the application of a post-colonial cosmopolitan perspective to the North American notion of democratic civic education. Giroux provides us with a vision for education that addresses the challenges that demographically and politically changing western societies are facing at the beginning of the 21st century. The longer it takes for policy makers in education to take his guidance seriously, the more time and possibilities we will all be wasting and missing. In fact, educators at all levels of the educational system and all over the world are experiencing growing de-motivation and even frustration because they feel they have been forced backwards lately instead of moving forwards in challenging themselves, both as professionals and citizens, to meet the needs of our fast-changing societies. Giroux has urged educators and academics to oppose these paralyzing pressures and to be critical, creative and hopeful about the potential that both they and their students offer, in order to counter the conservative political tendencies which have been imposing a definition of excellence in education that means submission to market pressures rather than educational excellence in terms of innovative intellectual production. Giroux argues for both critique and possibility in education and advocates independence and responsibility for teachers and students, that is, he claims dignity and respect for educational institutions, teachers and students. Giroux has bravely recovered the political nature of the everyday labor of educational researchers and of educators themselves. Furthermore, Giroux has also eloquently theorized a critical pedagogy of Cultural Studies based on what was proposed by cultural and educational theorist Raymond Williams himself. In fact, the field of Cultural Studies has been problematized, and is itself problematic, although very rich and promising, since it has broken down the barriers between disciplines. Therefore, it needs to be fully theorized in order to describe its goals, as well as the bases of its knowledge and processes. Giroux has made important contributions to these processes by mapping the relationships between language, text, society, new technologies and underlying power structures. He has thus responded to its critics and to those academics who have adhered to it in order to follow fashion or find a way out of their now neglected traditional disciplines. In addition, he has indicated new paths that go beyond recuperating Williams' and Hall's politically committed and scientifically founded new field of Cultural Studies and move into examining the implications of new technologies in the exchange and re-creation of new knowledge within new power relationships. It is nonetheless worth mentioning that Giroux has also been successful in identifying new modes of representation and learning.

Giroux has indeed advanced a new school of thought and inspired both educational theorists and practitioners into action with his powerful, vibrant and committed voice. By advocating a pedagogy of responsibility, he has himself taken responsibility for his own political and social role as an academic. He has focused his sights on redefining and strengthening the notion of "the public" with regard to knowledge, education and civic life, mainly by incorporating into the construction of those fields the concepts of "public time" and "public arena." While most educational theorists have focused on the influence of society on the educational context, Giroux, although critically unveiling the political and economic forces that threaten academic and school independence and creativity, is more daring and clearly draws our attention to the transformative potential of the academy and the school within a wider society. In doing so, he recaptures the political in the pedagogical. Finally, even though he focuses his discourse on general education, civic education and cultural studies, Giroux's proposals for educational theory and practice offer language and intercultural communication theorists and practitioners a basis for renewing their visions and practices. Having made these points, in an attempt to contextualize Giroux's statements below, it is now time to let his voice emerge.

In your work, you show a deep and consistent concern for civic life in a globalized world. How do you define a more globalized form of citizenship?

Citizenship invokes a notion of the social in which individuals have duties and responsibilities to others. A globalized notion of citizenship extends that concept of the social contract beyond the boundaries of the nation-state, invoking a broader notion of democracy in which the global becomes the space for exercising civic courage, social responsibility, politics, and compassion for the plight of others. Clearly, for example, citizens' obligations to the environment cannot be seen as merely a national problem. At the same time, a globalized notion of citizenship accentuates matters of responsibility and interdependence, invoking citizenship not just as a political issue of rights and entitlements but also as an ethical challenge to narrow the gap between the promise and the reality of a global democracy. It is also important to recognize that the idea of citizenship cannot be separated from the spaces in which citizenship is developed and nurtured. This suggests that any struggle over a globalized and meaningful notion of citizenship that encourages debate and social responsibility must include fostering and developing democratic public spheres such as schools, media, and other institutions in which critical civic pedagogies can be developed. The notion of global citizenship suggests that politics must catch up with power which today has removed itself from local and state control. New political structures, global institutions, and social movements must develop in ways that can reach and control the flows of uncontrolled power, particularly economic power. Real citizenship in the global sense means enabling people to have a say in the shaping of international laws governing trade, the environment, labor, criminal justice, social protections, and so on. Citizenship as the essence of politics has to catch up with new social formations that the current political and social institutions of the nation-state cannot influence, contain, or control.

What specific capacities does this new cosmopolitan citizen need to develop?

Citizens for a global democracy need to be aware of the interrelated nature of all aspects of physical, spiritual, and cultural life. This means having a deep-rooted understanding of the relational nature of global dependencies, whether we are talking about the ecosphere or the circuits of capital. Second, citizens need to be multi-literate in ways that not only allow them access to new information and media-based technologies, but also enable them to be border crossers capable of engaging, learning from, understanding, and being tolerant of and responsible to matters of difference and otherness. This suggests reclaiming as central to any viable notion of citizenship, the values of mutual worth, dignity, and ethical responsibility. At stake here is the recognition that there is a certain civic virtue and ethical value in extending our exposure to difference and otherness. Citizens need to cultivate loyalties that extend beyond the nation-state, beyond a theoretical distinction in which the division between friend and enemy is mediated exclusively around national boundaries. Clearly, citizenship as a form of empowerment means acquiring the skills that enable one to critically examine history and resuscitate those dangerous memories in which knowledge expands the possibilities for both self-knowledge and critical and social agency. Knowledge cannot be only indigenous to be empowering. Individuals must also have some distance from the knowledge of their birth, origins, and specificity of place. This suggests appropriating those knowledges that emerge through dispersal, travel, border crossings, diaspora, and through global communications. A cosmopolitan notion of citizenship must recognize the importance of dissent and a culture of questioning to any global concept of democracy. The global public sphere must be a place where authority can be questioned, power held accountable, and dissent seen as having a positive value. There is a growing authoritarianism in many parts of the world, particularly the United States. In facing this threat to democracy around the globe, it is crucial for educators, parents, young people, workers, and others to fight the collapse of citizenship into forms of jingoistic nationalism. This means educators and others will have to reinvigorate democracy by assuming the pedagogical project of prioritizing debate, deliberation, dissent, dialogue, and public spaces as central to any viable notion of global citizenship. In addition, if citizenship is to be global, it must develop a sense of radical humanism that comprehends social and environmental justice outside of national boundaries. Human suffering does not stop at the borders of nation-states.

In my view, one of your most inspiring proposals is the claim for a more dignifying and committed role of the educator at all levels of the educational system. Do you confirm this as one of your main goals? How do you summarize the main goals of your writing?

I have always argued that teachers must be treated as a critical public resource, essential not only to the importance of an empowering educational experience for students but also the formation of a democratic society. At the institutional level, this means giving teachers an opportunity to exercise power over the conditions of their work. We cannot separate what teachers do from the economic and political conditions that shape their work, that is, their academic labor. This means they should have both the time and the power to institute structural conditions that allow them to produce curriculum, collaborate with parents, conduct research, and work with communities. Moreover, school buildings must be limited in size to permit teachers and others to construct, maintain, and enhance a democratic community for themselves and their students. We are talking not only about the issue of class size but how space is institutionally constructed as part of a political project compatible with the formation of lived, democratic communities. Secondly, teachers should be given the freedom to shape the school curricula, engage in shared research with other teachers and with others outside of the school, and to play a central role in the governance of the school and their labor. Educational empowerment for teachers cannot be separated from issues of power and governance. Educators should be valued as public intellectuals who connect critical ideas, traditions, disciplines, and values to the public realm of everyday life. But at the same time, educators must assume the responsibility of connecting their work to larger social issues, while raising questions about what it means to provide students with the skills they need to write policy papers, be resilient against defeat, analyze social problems, and learn the tools of democracy, and learning how to make a difference in one's life as a social agent.

You also propose a close link between theory and practice, which have been made separate in our academic systems and in our societies. Can you please expand on the advantages of linking them for the purposes of citizenship education?

Citizenship education must take seriously the connection between theory and practice, reflection and action. All too often, theory in academia slides into a form of theoreticism in which theory either becomes an end in itself, relegated to the heights of an arcane, excessive and utterly ethereal existence, or it degenerates into a form of careerism, offering the fastest train to academic prominence. But theory is hardly a luxury connected to the fantasy of intellectual power. On the contrary, theory is a resource that enables us to both define and respond to problems as they emerge in particular contexts. Its transformative power resides in the possibility of enabling forms of agency not in its ability to solve problems. Its politics is linked to the ability to imagine the world differently and then to act differently and this is its offering to any viable notion of citizenship education. At stake here is not the question does theory matter, which should be as obvious as asking whether critical thought matters, but the issue of what the political and public responsibilities of theory might be, particularly in theorizing a global politics for the twenty-first century. Theory is not just about contemplation or paving a way to academic stardom, it is foremost about intervention in the world, raising ideas to the worldly space of public life, social responsibility, and collective intervention in the world. If learning is a fundamental part of social change, theory is a crucial resource to studying the full range of everyday practices that circulate throughout diverse social formations and to find better forms of knowledge and modes of intervention in the face of the challenge of either a growing authoritarianism or a manufactured cynicism.

You have often been accused of equating education with instilling ideological propaganda in students and you have rejected these accusations by arguing for a particular view of critical pedagogy. How, do you think, does a critical pedagogy promote a free mind?

Far from instilling propaganda in students, I think critical pedagogy begins with the assumption that knowledge and power should always be subject to debate, held accountable, and critically engaged. Central to the very definition of critical pedagogy is a common concern for reforming schools and developing modes of pedagogical practice in which teachers and students become critical agents actively questioning and negotiating the relationship

theory and practice, critical analysis and common sense, and learn-
ocial change. This is hardly a prescription for propaganda. I think
edagogy is often seen as dangerous because it is built around a
hat goes to the very heart of what education is about and is framed
around a series of important and often ignored questions such as: Why
do we [as educators] do what we do the way we do it? Whose interest does
schooling serve? How might it be possible to understand and engage the
diverse context in which education takes place? But critical pedagogy is not
concerned simply with offering students new ways to think critically and act
with authority as agents in the classroom, it is also concerned with providing
teachers and students with the skills and knowledge to expand their capacities to both question deep-seated assumptions and myths that legitimate the
most archaic and disempowering social practices that structure every aspect
of society and to take responsibility for intervening in the world. In other
words, critical pedagogy forges critique and agency through a language of
scepticism and possibility.

*The relevance of humanities departments in universities worldwide is being reconsidered
by the university management, by the labor market and the wider society more generally.
How can, in your opinion, those departments face the challenge not only of survival
but also of countering the "crisis of culture," which you cite from Raymond Williams,
and of reclaiming their relevance?*

In recent years, I have been working out of a series of projects which address a number of interrelated concerns: the substantive role of culture, in
particular popular culture, as the primary site where pedagogy and learning
take place, especially for young people; the role that academics and cultural
workers might assume as public intellectuals mindful of the constitutive
force culture plays in shaping public memory, moral awareness, and political
agency; the significance of the university, specifically the humanities, as a
public sphere essential to sustaining a vibrant democracy yet under assault
by the forces of corporatization; and the centrality of youth as an ethical
register for measuring the changing nature of the social contract since the
1980s and its implications for a broader discourse on hope and the future.
The humanities traditionally have offered both a refuge and a possibility
for thinking about these issues, though under historical conditions which
bear little resemblance to the present. This is particularly evident as the
conditions for the production of knowledge, national identity, and citizenship have changed in a rapidly globalizing, post-9/11 world order marked
by the expansion of new electronic technologies; the consolidation of
global media; Western de-industrialization, deregulation, and downsizing;
the privatization of public goods and services; and the marketization of all
aspects of social life.

The "crisis" in the humanities reflects a crisis within the larger society about the meaning and viability of institutions that define themselves as serving a public rather than private good. The ongoing vocationalization of higher education, the commodification of the curriculum, the increasing role the university plays as part of the national security state, and the transformation of students into consumers have undermined the humanities in its efforts to offer students the knowledge and skills they need for learning how to govern as well as develop the capacities necessary for deliberation, reasoned arguments, and social action. The incursion of corporate and military culture into university life undermines the university's responsibility to provide students with an education that allows them to recognize the dream and promise of a substantive democracy. While it is true that the humanities must keep up with developments in the sciences, the new media, technology, and other fields, its first responsibility is to treat these issues not merely pragmatically as ideas and skills to be learned but as sites of political and ethical intervention, deeply connected to the question of what it means to create students who can imagine a democratic future for all people.

In its best moments, this era of crisis, fear, and insecurity has reinvigorated the debate over the role that the humanities and the university more generally might play in creating a pluralized public culture essential for animating basic precepts of democratic public life. Matters of history, global relations, ethical concerns, creativity and the development of new literacies and modes of communication should be central to any humanities education and the conversation they enable but, at the same time, such conversations have for the most part failed to consider more fundamental issues about the need to revitalize the language of civic education as part of a broader discourse of political agency and critical citizenship in a globalized society. More specifically, a better understanding of why the humanities has avoided the challenge of those critical discourses capable of interrogating how the society represents itself (for example, the gap suggested by the apogee of democracy at the precise moment of its hollowing out) and how and why individuals fail to critically engage such representations is crucial to understand if educators are to intervene in the oppressive social relationships they often legitimate.

Given these contexts, educators in the humanities must ask new kinds of questions beginning with: How do educators respond to value-based questions regarding the "usefulness" of the humanities and the range of purposes it should serve? What knowledges are of most worth? What does it mean to claim authority in a world where borders are constantly shifting? What role does the humanities have in a world in which the "immaterial production" of knowledge becomes the most important form of capital? How might pedagogy be understood as a political and moral practice rather than a technical strategy in the service of corporate culture? And, what relation should the humanities have to young people as they develop a sense of agency, particularly in relation to the obligations of critical citizenship and public life in a radically transformed cultural and global landscape?

As citizenship becomes increasingly privatized and youth are increasingly educated to become consuming subjects rather than critical social subjects, it becomes all the more imperative for educators working within the humanities to rethink the space of the social, and to develop a critical language in which notions of the public good, public issues, and public life become central to overcoming the privatizing and depoliticizing language of the market. Central to this issue for me is the role that higher education might play as a democratic public sphere.

You challenge the traditional understanding of the word "intellectual." How does this notion apply to the contemporary world?

I have always believed that the notion of the intellectual carries with it a number of important political, cultural, and social registers. In contrast to the notion that intellectuals are a specialized group of experts, I have argued that everybody is an intellectual in that we all have the capacity to think, produce ideas, be self-critical, and connect knowledge (wherever it comes from) to forms of self and social development. At the same time, those intellectuals who have the luxury of defining their social function through the production of intellectual ideas have a special responsibility to address how power works through the institutions, individuals, social formations, and everyday life so as to enable or close down democratic values, identities, and relations. More specifically, I believe that the most important obligation that intellectuals have to knowledge is through understanding its relationship to power not as a complementary relation but as one of opposition. I think intellectuals whether in or outside of the academy must connect ideas to the world and engage their skills and knowledge as part of a larger struggle over democratic ideas, values and justice. Intellectuals have a responsibility not only to make truth prevail in the world and fight injustice wherever it appears, but also to organize their collective passions to prevent human suffering, genocide, and diverse forms of unfreedom linked to domination and exploitation. Intellectuals have a responsibility to analyze how language, information, and meaning work to organize, legitimate, and circulate values, structure reality, and offer up particular notions of agency and identity. For public intellectuals, the latter challenge demands a new kind of literacy and critical understanding with respect to the emergence of the new media and electronic technologies, and the new and powerful role they play as instruments of public pedagogy.

Critical reflection is an essential dimension of justice and is central to civic education, and it is precisely with respect to keeping justice and democracy alive in the public domain that intellectuals have a responsibility to the global world. Today, the concept of the intellectual, as Pierre Bourdieu reminds us, has become synonymous with public relations, sycophantic apologists, and fast-talking media types. Educators as public intellectuals need a new vocabulary for linking hope, social citizenship, and education to the demands of substantive democracy. I am suggesting that educators need a new vocabulary for connecting not only how we read critically but also how we engage in movements for social change. I also believe that simply invoking the relationship between theory and practice, critique and social action will not do. Any attempt to give new life to a substantive democratic politics must address both how people learn to be political agents and what kind of educational work is necessary within many kinds of public spaces to enable people to use their full intellectual resources to both provide a profound critique of existing institutions and struggle to work towards fulfilling the promise of a radical global democracy. As public intellectuals, educators and other cultural workers need to understand more fully why the tools we used in the past feel awkward in the present, often failing to respond to problems now facing the United States and other parts of the globe. More specifically, we face the challenge posed by the failure of existing critical discourses to bridge the gap between how the society represents itself and how and why individuals fail to understand and critically engage such representations in order to intervene in the oppressive social relationships they often legitimate. By combining the mutually interdependent roles of critic and active citizen, intellectual work at its best can exercise civic courage as a political practice, a practice that begins when one's life can no longer be taken for granted. Such a stance not only connects intellectual work to making dominant power accountable, it also makes concrete the possibility for transforming hope and politics into an ethical space and public act that confronts the flow of everyday experience and the weight of social suffering with the force of individual and collective resistance and the unending project of democratic social transformation. The road to authoritarianism begins when societies stop questioning themselves and, when such questioning stops, it is often because intellectuals either have become complicit with such silence or they actively produce it. Clearly, critical intellectuals have a responsibility to oppose this deafening quiet in the face of an emerging global barbarism, evidence of which can be seen in a number of growing religious, political, and economic fundamentalisms.

One of your most radical statements is that every educational act is political and that every political act should be pedagogical. In the same way that your work crosses into different disciplinary areas, you have also tried to link different institutional divisions in which pedagogy takes place: education, politics and the media, just to name a few. What are your reasons for and the risks of such an undertaking?

In the last few decades, I have tried to resurrect the profound insights of theorists such as Antonio Gramsci, Raymond Williams, Edward Said, and others who have argued that the educational force of the broader culture has become one of the most important political sites in the struggle over ideas, values, and agency. Permanent education is a fundamental part of what it means to create those identities and values that constitute the narrative of the political. In the past, education was limited to schooling, but it has become clear that most of the education that takes place today, which is so vital to any democracy, takes place in a broader number of sites including screen culture, popular culture, the Internet, and in the all-encompassing old and new media. I have stressed that these new sites of education, which I call the realm of public pedagogy, are crucial to any notion of politics because they are the sites in which people often learn, unlearn, or simply do not get the knowledge and skills that prepare them to become critical agents, capable of not merely understanding the society and world in which they live but also being able to assume the mantle of governance.

You have dedicated a great amount of your recent work to what you consider an unfair treatment of the youth in contemporary societies by both public and private institutions (e.g., the government, the educational system, the press and society in general). What specific role can educators play in countering this trend?

Well, the first thing they can do is to recognize the obligation that adults have to youth if in fact we are going to take seriously not only the social contract but the very possibility of a democratic future. The second thing that can be done is to try to understand those forces, especially neoliberalism, neoconservatism, militarism and religious fundamentalism, that view youth either as a commodity or as utterly expendable, especially poor youth and youth of color, and how they can be challenged in every social institution and addressed through policies that truly view youth as a social investment rather than a threat, fodder for the military, or a commodity.

How do you view the introduction of a new academic interdisciplinary subject that aims to develop intercultural competencies, that is, to improve the students' capacity to communicate and interact effectively across cultures, both nationally and internationally? How can educators implement this interdisciplinary and intercultural subject within a critical pedagogy approach? Does this project relate to your claims for a "new language for expressing global solidarity"?

I think that the question of intercultural competencies has to be understood within a broader notion of literacy linked to both the acquisition of agency and the ability to recognize that matters of difference are inextricably tied to issues of respect, tolerance, dialogue, and our responsibility to others. Multicultural literacy as a discursive intervention is an essential step toward not only a broader notion of self-representation, but also a more global notion of agency and democracy. Literacy in this sense not only is pluralized and expanded, it is also the site in which new dialogical practices and social relations become possible. Literacy, as I am using it here, does a kind of bridging work necessary to democracy while also offering up modes of translation that challenge strategies of common sense and domination. At the same time, intercultural competencies must be connected to the central dynamics of power as a way of engaging differences and exclusions so as to understand their formations as part of a historical process of struggle and negotiation. In this instance, such competencies further more than understanding and awareness; they also serve as modes of critical understanding in which dialogue and interpretation are connected to modes of intervention in which cultural differences can be viewed as an asset rather than a threat to democracy.

Your writing style is very powerful and idiosyncratic, and you have been both criticized and praised for it. Some of your readers find it too obscure and impregnated with ideology and others find it vibrant, stimulating, and very inspiring. I belong to the latter and I would like to ask you to what extent its use is purposeful and what purposes it serves?

I have tried in the last decade to make my writing accessible to a broader public while not compromising its theoretical rigor. This seems to present a lot of problems for those academics whose discourse is largely impenetrable, highly specialized, and plugged into narrow definitions of careerism. Academics, especially on the Left in the United States, are generally very bad writers, a problem connected less to matters of skill than to an arcane notion of professionalism. Many live in "theory world" and generally address very specialized audiences. On the one hand, much of their work is indebted to a kind of postmodern irony or cleverness, or it is so pedantic that it lacks either any political integrity or passion. On the other hand, the bar has been set so low in the United States around matters of clarity and style that it is always difficult to reach a broader public if conventional matters of style and language are challenged, as they are in my work. Of course, the grumbling about my work is not merely about style, it is also because I often make the political primary to my work in a way that makes the project I am working out of quite clear. The backlash against committed writing, if not engaged politics, is so strong in universities, the media and other established sites of public pedagogy that asserting the importance of politics as a crucial aspect of everyday life and learning is an incredibly difficult but absolutely necessary fight to wage.

You have been very critical about what the contemporary developed world is providing to the youth, namely more surveillance in schools, the so-called excellence in education translated into more standardized assessment, a commercialized culture, etc. I have no doubts that you are very aware that it is difficult for critical educators, as individual professionals burdened themselves by the demands of the government, the school management, students and parents, and society as a whole, to counter these tendencies on their own. Your writings have undoubtedly inspired and supported their efforts. Do you have any special message for them?

Yes, these are very difficult times, but the stakes are very high, and if we value democracy and have any hope whatsoever for the future, we must continue the struggle for connecting education to democracy, learning social change, and excellence to equity. The only other option is either cynicism or complicity and no educator deserves that. I also think it is important to recognize that these struggles are going on all over the world, and that we are not alone and shouldn't be alone in taking on these crucial battles, battles that will determine the fate of global democracy in the twenty-first century.

How do you account for the increasing interest of foreign language/culture educators in your work, despite their traditional little interest in the critical theories of schooling and pedagogy?

Of course, one has to recognize that historically there have been a number of foreign language/culture educators who have addressed the connection between language and critical pedagogy, particularly people working in TE-SOL. I think much of that work was produced far ahead of its time and only now are the conditions emerging that enable educators to recognize its importance to the current discursive/pedagogical/educational global context. As it becomes clear that you cannot decouple issues concerning language usage from issues of dialogue, communication, culture, and power, matters of politics and pedagogy become crucial to how one understands pedagogy as a political issue and the politics of language as a deeply pedagogical consideration. I have argued for a number of years that language as both an object and subject of mastery, understanding, and engagement is the site in which people negotiate the most fundamental elements of their identities, the relationship between themselves and others, and their relationship to the larger world. I have also made clear that it has become very difficult in light of this understanding to treat language as simply a technical issue. Clearly, its importance lies in recognizing that it is a moral and political practice deeply connected to both matters of critical agency and the unending struggle to expand and deepen democracy itself. Matters of language and culture are crucial to how one is shaped and what one does as an intellectual. Hence, language is the cultural foundation for how educators both address and define the meaning and purpose of pedagogy in the formation and acquisition of particular modes of individual and social agency. This is a question that I have been addressing in my work for over thirty years but also one that I have taken up as part of a larger concern with what it means to make the pedagogical more political in its ongoing task of expanding democratic values, relationships, identities, and public spheres. This is where I think my work seems to resonate in the current historical conjuncture. Learning a foreign language is a largely humanistic endeavor rather than an elite or strictly methodological task, and the force of its importance has to be tied to its relevance as an empowering, emancipatory, and democratic function.

My work understands language as a mode of learning and dissent, one that is both crucial to configuring and translating the boundaries between the public and the private, and attending to questions of politics, power, public consciousness, and civic courage. More than ever language needs to be revitalized as part of a public pedagogy that energizes the imagination, expands the autonomy of the individual, and deepens a viable notion of political agency. Language is part of what Edward Said called a politics of worldliness inextricably tied up to matters of history, power, and a culture of questioning and democratic struggles. Critical pedagogy in my work has always taken the latter concerns seriously and it just might be that this work is now being rediscovered and used by foreign language/culture educators. I think many people are desperate for a discourse that links critique to hope, knowledge to passion, and pedagogy to justice. I would like to believe my work offers them some hope in dark times.

Henry Giroux moved to Canada in 2004 and currently holds the Global Television Network Chair in Communication Studies at McMaster University. Although his parents were originally from Canada, he was born and lived in the United States until this recent move. Having started his career in education as a high school teacher of history, he achieved a distinguished academic career for which he has been recognized internationally. Giroux is a member of various editorial boards of relevant national and international journals in the fields of education and cultural studies, and several of his books received awards by the American Educational Studies Association as the most significant volumes of the respective year of publication. The list of his publications is immense, including several books, chapters in many volumes, and articles in the leading journals focusing on different areas connected with education and cultural studies. Many can be found in his website (www.henryagiroux.com).

Manuela Guilherme is a senior researcher at the Center for Social Studies, University of Coimbra in Portugal, where she coordinates two European projects focusing on Intercultural Education (www.ces.uc.pt/researchers; www.ces.uc.pt/icopromo; www.ces.uc.pt/interact). She is the author of *Critical Citizens for an Intercultural World: Foreign Language Education as Cultural Politics* (Multilingual Matters, 2002), where she draws on Giroux's theories, and co-editor of *Critical Pedagogy: Political Approaches to Language and Intercultural Communication* (Multilingual Matters, 2004) which includes Giroux's chapter entitled "Betraying the Intellectual Tradition: Public Intellectuals and the Crisis of Youth."

This interview was first published in the *Language and Intercultural Communication Journal,* 6:2. We are grateful to its editors for allowing the publication of this interview in this volume.

8
Cultural Studies, Critical Pedagogy, and the Responsibility of Intellectuals

⊷

> If you accept my definition that this is really what Cultural Studies has been about, of taking the best we can in intellectual work and going with it in this very open way to confront people for whom it is not a way of life, for whom it is not in any probability a job, but for whom it is a matter of their own intellectual interest, their own understanding of the pressures on them, pressures of every kind, from the most personal to the most broadly political—if we are prepared to take that kind of work and to revise the syllabus and discipline as best we can, on this site which allows that kind of interchange, then Cultural Studies has a very remarkable future indeed.
>
> —Raymond Williams[1]

Within the last few decades, a number of critical and cultural studies theorists such as Stuart Hall, Lawrence Grossberg, Douglas Kellner, Meghan Morris, Toby Miller, and Tony Bennett have provided valuable contributions to our understanding of how culture deploys power and is shaped and organized within diverse systems of representation, production, consumption, and distribution. Particularly important to such work is an ongoing critical analysis of how symbolic and institutional forms of culture and power are mutually entangled in constructing diverse identities, modes of political agency, and the social world itself. Within this approach, material relations of power and the production of social meaning do not cancel each other out but constitute the precondition for all meaningful practices. Culture is recognized as the social field where goods and social practices are not only produced, distributed, and consumed, but also invested with various meanings and ideologies that are implicated in the generation of political effects. Culture is partly defined as a circuit of power, ideologies, and values in which diverse images and sounds are produced and circulate, identities are constructed, inhabited and discarded, agency is manifested in both individualized and social forms, institutions produce and constrain social practices, and discourses are created which make culture itself the object of inquiry and critical analyses. Rather than being viewed as a static force, the substance of culture and everyday life—knowledge, goods, social practices, and contexts—repeatedly mutates and is subject to ongoing changes and interpretations.

Following the work of Antonio Gramsci, Raymond Williams, and Stuart Hall, many cultural theorists acknowledge the primacy of culture's role as an educational site where identities are being continually transformed, power is enacted, and learning assumes a political dynamic as it becomes not only the condition for the acquisition of agency but also the sphere for imagining oppositional social change. As both a space for the production of meaning and social interaction, culture is viewed by many contemporary theorists as an important terrain in which various modes of agency, identity, and values are neither prefigured nor always in place but subject to negotiation and struggle and open for creating new democratic transformations, though always within various degrees of iniquitous power relations. Rather than dismissed as a reflection of larger economic forces or as simply the "common ground" of everyday life, culture is recognized by many advocates of cultural studies as both a site of contestation and as a site of utopian possibility, a space in which an emancipatory politics can be fashioned which "consists in making seem possible precisely that which, from within the situation, is declared to be impossible."[2]

Cultural studies theorists have greatly expanded our theoretical understanding of the ideological, institutional, and performative workings of culture, but as important as this work might be, it does not go far enough—though there are some exceptions as in the work of Stanley Aronowitz, bell hooks, and Nick Couldry—in connecting the most critical insights of cultural studies with an understanding of the importance of critical pedagogy, particularly as part of a larger project for expanding the possibilities of a democratic politics, the dynamics of resistance, and the capacities for social agency. For too many theorists, pedagogy often occupies a limited role theoretically and politically in configuring cultural studies as a form of cultural politics.[3] While many cultural studies advocates recognize the political importance of pedagogy, it is often acknowledged in a very limited and narrow way. For instance, when invoked as an important political practice, pedagogy is either limited to the role that oppositional intellectuals might play within academia or it is reduced almost entirely to forms of learning that take place in schools. Even when pedagogy is related to issues of democracy, citizenship, and the struggle over the shaping of identities and identifications, it is rarely taken up as part of a broader public politics—as part of a larger attempt to explain how learning takes place outside of schools or what it means to assess the political significance of understanding the broader educational force of culture in the new age of media technology, multimedia, and computer-based information and communication networks. Put differently, pedagogy is limited to what goes on in schools, and the role of cultural studies theorists who address pedagogical concerns is largely reduced to doing or teaching cultural studies within the classroom.

Within this discourse, cultural studies becomes available as a resource to educators who can then teach students how to look at the media (industry and texts), analyze audience reception, challenge rigid disciplinary boundaries, critically engage popular culture, produce critical knowledge, or use cultural studies to reform the curricula and challenge disciplinary formations within public schools and higher education. For instance, Shane Gunster has argued that the main contribution that cultural studies makes to pedagogy "is the insistence that any kind of critical education must be rooted in the culture, experience, and knowledge that students bring to the classroom."[4] While this is an important insight, it has been argued in enormously sophisticated ways for over fifty years by a host of progressive educators that include John Dewey, Maxine Greene, and Paulo Freire. But the problem lies not in Gunster's unfamiliarity with such scholarship, but in his willingness to repeat the presupposition that the exclusive site in which pedagogy becomes a relevant object of analysis is the classroom. If he had crossed the disciplinary boundaries that he decries in his celebration of cultural studies, he would have found that educational theorists such as Roger Simon, David Trend, and others have expanded the meaning of pedagogy as a political and moral practice and extended its application far beyond the classroom while also attempting to combine the cultural and the pedagogical as part of a broader notion of political education and cultural studies.

Many cultural studies theorists, such as Lawrence Grossberg, have rightly suggested that cultural studies has an important role to play in helping educators rethink, among other things, the nature of pedagogy, knowledge, the purpose of schooling, and how schools are impacted by larger social forces.[5] And, surely, Gunster takes such advice seriously, but fails to understand its limits and in doing so repeats a now familiar refrain among critical educational theorists about connecting pedagogy to the histories, lived experiences, and discourses that students bring to the classroom. In spite of the importance of bringing matters of culture and power to the schools, I think that too many cultural studies theorists are remiss in suggesting that pedagogy is primarily about schools and by implication that the intersection of cultural studies and pedagogy has little to do with theorizing the role that pedagogy might play in linking learning to social change outside of traditional sites of schooling.[6] Pedagogy is not simply about the social construction of knowledge, values, and experiences, it is also a performative practice embodied in the lived interactions among educators, audiences, texts, and institutional formations. Pedagogy, at its best, implies that learning takes place across a spectrum of social practices and settings in society. As Roger Simon observes, pedagogy points to the multiplicity of sites in which education takes place and offers the possibility for a variety of cultural workers

> to comprehend the full range of multiple, shifting and overlapping of sites of learning that exist within the organized social relations of everyday life. This

means being able to grasp, for example, how workplaces, families, community and institutional health provision, film and television, the arts, groups organized for spiritual expression and worship, organized sport, the law and the provision of legal services, the prison system, voluntary social service organizations, and community based literacy programs all designate sets of organized practices within which learning is one central feature and outcome.[7]

In what follows, I want to argue that pedagogy is central to any viable notion of cultural politics and that cultural studies is crucial to any viable notion of pedagogy. Moreover, it is precisely at the intersection at which diverse traditions in cultural studies and pedagogy mutually inform each other that the possibility exists of making the pedagogical more political for cultural studies theorists and the political more pedagogical for educators. I am particularly concerned about how the intersection of cultural studies, pedagogy, and politics can be read as an effort to redefine the role of academics as public intellectuals, higher education as a crucial public sphere for educating students to address matters vital to a democratic society, and pedagogy as enabling both a culture of questioning as well as strategic interventions into those practices, structures and struggles that connect learning to public life.

Rethinking the Importance of Cultural Studies for Educators

My own interest in cultural studies emerges out of an ongoing project to theorize the regulatory and emancipatory relationship among culture, power, and politics as expressed through the dynamics of what I call public pedagogy. Such a project concerns, in part, the diverse ways in which culture functions as a contested sphere over the production, distribution, and regulation of power and how and where it operates both symbolically and institutionally as an educational, political, and economic force. Drawing upon a long tradition in cultural studies work, I take up culture as constitutive and political, not only reflecting larger forces but also constructing them; in this instance, culture not only mediates history, it shapes it. I want to argue that culture is the primary terrain for realizing the political as an articulation and intervention into the social, a space in which politics is pluralized, recognized as contingent, and open to many formations.[8] I also argue that it is a crucial terrain in order to render visible both the global circuits that now frame material relations of power and a cultural politics in which matters of representation and meaning shape and offer concrete examples of how politics is expressed, lived, and experienced. Culture, in this instance, is the ground of both contestation and accommodation, and it is increasingly characterized by the rise of mega corporations and new technologies which are transforming the traditional spheres of the economy, industry, society, and everyday life. Culture now plays a central role in producing narratives, metaphors, and images that exercise a powerful pedagogical force over how people think of themselves and their relationship to others. From my perspective, culture is the primary sphere in which individuals, groups, and institutions engage in the art of translating the diverse and multiple relations that mediate between private life and public concerns. It is also the sphere in which the translating possibilities of culture are under assault, particularly as the forces of neoliberalism dissolve public issues into utterly privatized and individualistic concerns.

Central to my work in cultural studies is the assumption that the primacy of culture and power be organized through an understanding of how the political becomes pedagogical, particularly in terms of how private issues are connected to larger social conditions and collective forces; that is, how the very processes of learning constitute the political mechanisms through which identities are shaped, desires mobilized, and experiences take on form and meaning within and through collective sets of conditions and those larger forces that constitute the realm of the social. In this context, pedagogy is no longer restricted to what goes on in schools, but becomes a defining principle of a wide ranging set of cultural apparatuses engaged in what Raymond Williams has called "permanent education." Williams rightfully believed that education in the broadest sense plays a central role in any viable form of cultural politics. He writes

> What [permanent education] valuably stresses is the educational force of our whole social and cultural experience. It is therefore concerned, not only with continuing education, of a formal or informal kind, but with what the whole environment, its institutions and relationships, actively and profoundly teaches.... [Permanent education also refers to] the field in which our ideas of the world, of ourselves and of our possibilities, are most widely and often most powerfully formed and disseminated. To work for the recovery of control in this field is then, under any pressures, a priority. [9]

Williams argued that any viable notion of critical politics would have to pay closer "attention to the complex ways in which individuals are formed by the institutions to which they belong, and in which, by reaction, the institutions took on the color of individuals thus formed."[10] Williams also foregrounded the crucial political question of how agency unfolds within a variety of cultural spaces structured within unequal relations of power.[11] He was particularly concerned about the connections between pedagogy and political agency, especially in light of the emergence of a range of new technologies that greatly proliferated the amount of information available to people while at the same time constricting the substance and ways in which such meanings entered the public domain. The realm of culture for Williams had taken on a new role in the latter part of the twentieth century because the actuality of economic power and its attendant networks of control now exercised more influence than ever before in shaping how identities are produced, desires mobilized, and everyday social relations take on the force and meaning of common sense.[12] Williams clearly understood that making the political more pedagogical meant recognizing that where and how the psyche locates itself in public discourse, visions, and passions provides the groundwork for agents to enunciate, act, and reflect on themselves and their relations to others and the wider social order.

Following Williams, I want to reaffirm the importance of pedagogy in any viable understanding of cultural politics. In doing so, I want to comment on some very schematic and incomplete elements of cultural studies that I think are useful for thinking about not only the interface between cultural studies and critical pedagogy, but also for deepening and expanding the theoretical and political horizons of critical pedagogical work. I believe that pedagogy represents both a mode of cultural production and a type of cultural criticism that is essential for questioning the conditions under which knowledge is produced, values affirmed, affective investments engaged, and subject positions are put into place, negotiated, taken up, or refused. Pedagogy is a referent for understanding the conditions for critical learning and the often hidden dynamics of social and cultural reproduction. As a critical practice, pedagogy's role lies in not only changing how people think about themselves, their relationship to others and the world, but also in energizing students and others to engage in those struggles that further possibilities for living in a more just and fairer society. But like any other body of knowledge which is constantly struggled over, pedagogy must constantly enter into dialogue with other fields, theoretical domains, and emerging theoretical discourses. As diverse as cultural studies is as a field, there are a number of insights it provides that are crucial to educators who use critical pedagogy both in and outside of their classrooms.

First, in the face of contemporary forms of political and epistemological relativism a more politicized version of cultural studies makes a claim for the use of highly disciplined, rigorous theoretical work. Not only does such a position reject the notion that intellectual authority can only be grounded in particular forms of social identity, it also refuses an increasing anti-intellectualism that posits theory as too academic and complex to be of any use in addressing important political issues. While many cultural studies advocates refuse to either separate culture studies from politics or reject theory as too complex and abstract, they also reject theory as a sterile form of theoreticism and an academicized vocabulary that is as self-consciously pedantic as it is politically irrelevant. Matters of language, experience, power, ideology, and representation cannot make a detour around theory, but that is no excuse for elevating theory to an ethereal realm that has no referent outside of its own obtuseness or rhetorical cleverness. While offering no guarantees, theory in a more critical perspective is seen as crucial to attending to questions of politics, power, and public considerations. Moreover, theory in this view is called upon as a resource to do the important bridging work in which cultural studies is connected to those sites and spheres of contestation in which it becomes possible to open up rhetorical and pedagogical spaces between the actual conditions of dominant power and the promise of future space informed by a range of democratic alternatives.[13] Theory in this instance does not merely reference itself but is valued by both its ability to open up new horizons of possibilities and offer strategic interventions into shaping everyday life. Lawrence Grossberg clearly articulates this position in his comment on the role of theory within cultural studies. He writes:

> Theory in cultural studies is measured by its relation to, its enablement of, strategic interventions into the specific practices, structures, and struggles characterizing its place in the contemporary world. Cultural studies is propelled by its desire to construct possibilities, both immediate and imaginary, out of its historical circumstances. It has no pretensions to totality or universality; it seeks only to give us a better understanding of where we are so that we can get somewhere else (some place, we hope, that is better—based on more just principles of equality and the distribution of wealth and power), so that we can have a little more control over the history that we are already making ... A theory's ability to "cut into the real," to use Benjamin's metaphor, is measured by the political positions and trajectories theory enables in response to the concrete contexts of power it confronts. Just like people in everyday life, cultural studies begins to grapple with and analyze difficult experiences at hand; it draws upon and extends theories to enable it to break into experience in new ways.[14]

Underlying such a public project is a firm commitment to intellectual rigor and a deep regard for matters of compassion and social responsibility aimed at deepening and extending the possibilities for critical agency, racial justice, economic democracy, and the just distribution of political power. Hence, cultural studies theorists often reject the anti-intellectualism, specialization, and methodological reification often found in other disciplines. Similarly, such theorists also reject both the universalizing dogmatism found in some strands of radical theory as well as a postmodern epistemology that enshrines difference, identity, and plurality at the expense of developing more inclusive notions of the social that bring together historically and politically differentiated forms of struggles. The more progressive strains of cultural studies do not define or value theory and knowledge strictly within particular interests as much as they define their political currency and promise as part of a more generalized notion of freedom that combines democratic principles, values, and experiences with the rights and discourses that build on the histories and struggles of those excluded others. For instance, cultural studies theorist Imre Szeman has looked at the ways in which globalization opens up not only a new space for pedagogy but "constitutes a problem of and for pedagogy."[15] Szeman looks at the various forms of public pedagogy at work in the rhetoric of newspapers, TV news shows, financial service companies, advertising industries, and the mass media, and how such rhetoric fashions a triumphalist view of globalization. He then offers an analysis of how alternative pedagogies are produced within various globalization protest movements that have taken place in cities such as Seattle, Toronto, and Genoa—movements that have attempted to open up new modes and sites of learning while enabling new forms of collective resistance. What is particularly important about Szeman's analysis is how new pedagogical practices of resistance are being fashioned through the use of new media such as the Internet and digital video to challenge official pedagogies of globalization.

Second, cultural studies is radically contextual in that the very questions that it asks change in every context. Theory and criticism do not become an end in themselves but are always engaged as a resource and method in response to problems raised in particular contexts, social relations, and institutional formations. This suggests that how we respond as educators and critics to the spheres in which we work is conditioned by the interrelationship between the theoretical resources we bring to a specific context and the worldly space of publicness that produces distinct problems and conditions particular responses to them. Politics as an intervention into public life is expressed, in this instance, as part of a broader attempt to provide a better understanding of how power works in and through historical and institutional contexts and particular relations of power while simultaneously opening up imagined possibilities for changing them. Lawrence Grossberg puts it well in arguing that cultural studies must be grounded in an act of doing, which in this case means "intervening into contexts and power ... in order to enable people to act more strategically in ways that may change their context for the better."[16] For educators, this suggests that pedagogy *is not* an a priori set of methods that simply needs to be uncovered and then applied regardless of the contexts in which one teaches but is the outcome of numerous deliberations and struggles between different groups over how contexts are made and remade, often within unequal relations of power. At the same time, it is crucial for educators to recognize that while educators need to be attentive to the particular context in which they work, they cannot separate such contexts from larger matters and configurations of power, culture, ideology, politics, and domination. As Doug Kellner and Meenakshi Gigi Durham observe, "pedagogy does not elide or occlude issues of power....Thus, while the distinctive situation and interests of the teachers, students, or critics help decide what precise artifacts are engaged, what methods will be employed, and what pedagogy will be deployed, the sociocultural environment in which cultural production, reception, and education occurs must be scrutinized as well."[17]

The notion that pedagogy is always contextual rightly points to linking the knowledge that is taught to the experiences that students bring to their classroom encounters. One implication for such work is that future and existing teachers be educated about the viability of developing context-dependent learning that takes account of student experiences and their relationships to popular culture and its terrain of pleasure, including those cultural industries that are often dismissed as producing mere entertainment. Despite the growing diversity of students in both public schools and higher education, there are few examples of curriculum sensitivity to the multiplicity of economic, social, and cultural factors bearing on students' lives. Even where there is a proliferation of programs such as ethnic and black studies in higher education, these are often marginalized in small programs far removed from the high status prestige associated with courses organized around business, computer science, and Western history. Cultural studies at least provides the theoretical tools for allowing teachers to recognize the important, though not unproblematic, cultural resources that students bring to school and the willingness to affirm and engage them critically as forms of knowledge crucial to the production of the students' sense of identity, place, and history. Equally important, the knowledge produced by students offers educators opportunities to learn from young people and to incorporate such knowledge as an integral part of their own teaching. Yet, there is an important caveat that cannot be stated too strongly.

I am not endorsing a romantic celebration of the notion of relevance or the knowledge and experience that students bring to the classroom. Nor am I arguing that larger contexts that frame both the culture and political economy of the schools and the experiences of students be ignored. I am also not suggesting that teaching be limited to the resources that students already have as much as I am arguing that educators need to find ways to make knowledge meaningful in order to make it critical and transformative. Moreover, by locating students within differentiated sets of histories, experiences, literacies, and values, pedagogical practices can be employed that not only raise questions about the strengths and limitations of what students know, but also grapple with the issue of what conditions must be engaged to expand the capacities and skills needed by students to become engaged global citizens and responsible social agents. This is not a matter of making a narrow notion of relevance the determining factor in the curriculum. But it is an issue of connecting knowledge to everyday life, meaning to the act of persuasion, schools and universities to broader public spheres, and rigorous theoretical work to affective investments and pleasures that students use in mediating their relationship to others and the larger world.

Third, the cultural studies emphasis on transdisciplinary work is important because it provides a rationale for challenging how knowledge has been historically produced, *hierarchically ordered,* and used within disciplines to sanction particular forms of authority and exclusion. By challenging the established academic division of labor, a transdisciplinary approach raises important questions about the politics of representation and its deeply entrenched entanglement with specialization, professionalism, and dominant power relations. The commitment to a transdisciplinary approach is also important because such work often operates at the frontiers of knowledge, and prompts teachers and students to raise new questions and develop models of analysis outside of the officially sanctioned boundaries of knowledge and the established disciplines that sanction them. Transdisciplinarity in this discourse serves a dual function. On the one hand, it firmly posits the arbitrary conditions under which knowledge is produced and encoded, stressing its historically and socially constructed nature and deeply entrenched connection to power and ideological interests. On the other hand, it endorses the relational nature of knowledge, inveighing against any presupposition that knowledge, events, and issues are either fixed or should be studied in isolation. Transdisciplinary approaches stress both historical relations and broader social formations, always attentive to new linkages, meanings, and possibilities. Strategically and pedagogically, these modes of analyses suggest that while educators may be forced to work within academic disciplines, they can develop transdisciplinary tools to make established disciplines the object of critique while simultaneously contesting the broader economic, political, and cultural conditions that reproduce the academic division of labor. This is a crucial turn theoretically and politically because transdisciplinary approaches foreground the necessity of bridging the work educators do within the academy to other academic fields as well as other public spheres. Such approaches also suggest that educators function as public intellectuals by engaging in ongoing public conversations that cut across particular disciplines while attempting to get their ideas out to more than one type of audience. Under such circumstances, educators must address the task of learning the forms of knowledge and skills that enable them to speak critically and broadly on a number of issues to a vast array of publics.

Fourth, in a somewhat related way, the emphasis on the part of many cultural studies theorists to study the full range of cultural practices that circulate in society opens the possibility for understanding a wide variety of new cultural forms that have become the primary educational forces in advanced industrial societies. This seems especially important at a time when new electronic technologies and the emergence of visual culture as a primary educational force offer new opportunities to inhabit knowledge and ways of knowing that simply do not correspond to the long standing traditions and officially sanctioned rules of disciplinary knowledge or of the one-sided academic emphasis on print culture. The scope and power of these new informational technologies, multimedia, and visual culture warrant that educators become more reflective about engaging both the production, reception, and situated use of new technologies, popular texts, and diverse forms of visual culture and how they structure social relations, values, particular notions of community, the future, and varied definitions of the self and others. Texts in this sense do not merely refer to the culture of print or the technology of the book, but to all those audio, visual, and electronically mediated forms of knowledge that have prompted a radical shift in the construction of knowledge and the ways in which knowledge is produced, received, and consumed. Recently, my own work has focused on the ways in which Disney's corporate culture—its animated films, radio programs, theme parks, and Hollywood blockbusters—functions as an expansive teaching machine which appropriates media and popular culture in order to rewrite public memory and offer young people an increasingly privatized and commercialized notion of citizenship.[18]

Contemporary youth do not simply rely on the culture of the book to construct and affirm their identities; instead, they are faced with the daunting task of negotiating their way through a decentered media-based cultural landscape no longer caught in the grip of either a technology of print or closed narrative structures.[19] I don't believe that educators and other cultural workers can critically understand and engage the shifting attitudes, representations, and desires of new generations of youth strictly within the dominant disciplinary configurations of knowledge and practice and traditional forms of pedagogy. Educators need a more expansive view of knowledge and pedagogy that provides the conditions for young people and adults to engage popular media and mass culture as serious objects of social analysis and to learn how to read them critically through specific strategies of understanding, engagement, and transformation. Informing this notion of knowledge and pedagogy is a view of literacy that is multiple and dynamic rather than singular and fixed. The modernist emphasis on literacy must be reconfigured in order for students to learn multiple literacies rooted in a mastery of diverse symbolic domains. At the same time, it is not enough to educate students to be critical readers across a variety of cultural domains, they must also become cultural producers, especially if they are going to create new alternative public spheres in which official knowledge and its one-dimensional configurations can be challenged. That is, students must also learn how to utilize the new electronic technologies, how to think about the dynamics of cultural power and how it works on and through them so that they can build alternative cultural spheres in which such power is shared and used to promote noncommodified values rather than simply mimic corporate culture and its underlying transactions.

Fifth, cultural studies provocatively stresses analyzing public memory not as a totalizing narrative, but as a series of ruptures and displacements. Historical learning in this sense is not about constructing a linear narrative but about blasting history open, rupturing its silences, highlighting its detours, acknowledging the events of its transmission, and organizing its limits within an open and honest concern with human suffering, values, and the legacy of the often unrepresentable or misrepresented. History is not an artifact to be merely transmitted, but an ongoing dialogue and struggle over the relationship between representation and agency, material relations of power and maps of meaning. The emphasis on struggle not only makes clear the discursive nature of historical narrative, but also situates history within a notion of contingency that removes it from offering any guarantees. This is not meant to imply that some histories are not more truthful and accurate than others. Such a position is undeniable and warrants important concerns about matters of argument, evidence, logic, and methodology. What is being suggested is that history is addressed through narratives that cannot free themselves from their own social conditioning and that while some historical accounts may offer important lessons, they offer no guarantees. James Clifford is insightful in arguing that history should "force a sense of location on those who engage with it."[20] This means challenging official narratives of conservative educators such as William Bennett, Lynne Cheney, Diane Ravitch, and Chester Finn for whom history is primarily about recovering and legitimating selective facts, dates, and events. A pedagogy of public memory is about making connections that are often hidden, forgotten, or willfully ignored. Public memory in this sense becomes not an object of reverence but an ongoing subject of debate, dialogue, and critical engagement. Public memory is also about critically examining one's own historical location amid relations of power, privilege, or subordination. More specifically, this suggests engaging history, as has been done repeatedly by radical intellectuals such as Howard Zinn and Noam Chomsky, by analyzing how knowledge is constructed through its absences. Public memory as a pedagogical practice functions, in part, as a form of critique that addresses the fundamental inadequacy of official knowledge in representing marginalized and oppressed groups along with, as John Beverly points out, the deep-seated injustices perpetrated by institutions that contain such knowledge and the need to transform such institutions in the "direction of a more radically democratic nonhierarchical social order."[21]

Sixth, cultural studies theorists are increasingly paying attention to their own institutional practices and pedagogies.[22] They have come to recognize that pedagogy is deeply implicated in how power and authority are employed in the construction and organization of knowledge, desires, values, and identities. Such a recognition has produced a new self-consciousness about how particular forms of teacher authority, classroom knowledge, and social practices are used to legitimate particular values and interests within unequal relations of power. Questions concerning how pedagogy works to articulate knowledge, meaning, desire, and values to effects not only provides the conditions for a pedagogical self-consciousness among teachers and students, but also foregrounds the recognition that pedagogy is a moral and political practice and cannot be reduced to an a priori set of skills or techniques. Rather, pedagogy in this instance is defined as a cultural practice that must be accountable ethically and politically for the stories it produces, the claims it makes on public memories, and the images of the future it deems legitimate. As both an object of critique and a method of cultural production, critical pedagogical practices cannot hide behind claims of objectivity, and should work, in part, to link theory and practice in the service of organizing, struggling over, and deepening democratic political, economic, and social freedoms. In the broadest sense, critical pedagogy should offer students and others—outside of officially sanctioned scripts—the historically and contextually specific knowledge, skills, and tools they need to both participate in, govern, and change when necessary those political and economic structures of power that shape their everyday lives. Needless to say, such tools are not pregiven but are the outcome of struggles, debate, dialogue, and engagement across a variety of public spheres.

While this list is both schematic and incomplete, it points to some important theoretical considerations that can be appropriated from the field of cultural studies as a resource for advancing a more public and democratic vision for higher education. Hopefully, it suggests theoretical tools for constructing new forms of collaboration among faculty, a broadening of the terms of teaching and learning, and new approaches toward interdisciplinary research that address local, national, and international concerns. The potential that cultural studies has for developing forms of collaboration that cut across national boundaries is worth taking up.

Where Is the Project(s) in Cultural Studies

Like any other academic field, cultural studies is marked by a number of weaknesses that need to be addressed by educators drawn to some of its more critical assumptions. First, there is a tendency in some cultural studies work to be simply deconstructive, that is, there is a refusal to ask questions about the insertion of symbolic processes into societal contexts and their imbrication with the political economy of power. Any viable form of cultural studies cannot insist exclusively on the primacy of signification over power, and in doing so reduce its purview to questions of meaning and texts. An obsession in some cases with cultural texts results in privileging literature and popular culture over history and politics. Within this discourse, material organizations and economic power disappear into some of the most irrelevant aspects of culture. Matters of fashion, cultural trivia, isolated notions of performance, and just plain cultural nonsense take on the aura of cultural analyses that yield to the most privatized forms of inquiry while simultaneously "obstructing the formulation of a publically informed politics."[23] In opposition to this position, cultural studies needs to foreground the ways in which culture and power are related through what Stuart Hall calls "combining the study of symbolic forms and meanings with the study of power," or more specifically the "insertion of symbolic processes into societal contexts and their imbrication with power."[24] Douglas Kellner for years has also argued that any viable approach to cultural studies has to overcome the divide between political economy and text-based analyses of culture.[25] But recognizing such a divide is not the same thing as overcoming it. Part of this task necessitates that cultural studies theorists anchor their own work, however diverse, in a radical project that seriously engages the promise of an unrealized democracy against its really existing forms. Of crucial importance to such a project is rejecting the assumption that theory can understand social problems without contesting their appearance in public life. At the same time, it is crucial to any viable notion of cultural studies that it reclaim politics as an ongoing critique of domination and society as part of a larger search for justice. Any viable cultural politics needs a socially committed notion of injustice if we are to take seriously what it means to fight for the idea of the good society. I think Zygmunt Bauman is right in arguing that "If there is no room for the idea of *wrong* society, there is hardly much chance for the idea of good society to be born, let alone make waves."[26] Cultural studies advocates need to be more forceful, if not committed, to linking their overall politics to modes of critique and collective action that address the presupposition that democratic societies are never too just or just enough, and such a recognition means that a society must constantly nurture the possibilities for self-critique, collective agency, and forms of citizenship in which people play a fundamental role in critically discussing, administrating and shaping the material relations of power and ideological forces that shape their everyday lives. Moreover, the struggle over creating an inclusive and just democracy can take many forms, offers no political guarantees, and provides an important normative dimension to politics as an ongoing process of democratization that never ends. Such a project is based on the realization that a democracy that is open to exchange, question, and self-criticism never reaches the limits of justice, that is, it is never just enough, and is never finished. It is precisely the open-ended and normative nature of such a project that provides a common ground for cultural studies theorists to share their differences and diverse range of intellectual pursuits.

Second, cultural studies is still largely an academic discourse and as such is often too far removed from other cultural and political sites where the work of public pedagogy takes place. In order to become a public discourse of any importance, cultural studies theorists will have to focus their work on the immediacy of problems that are more public and that are relevant to important social issues. Such issues might include the destruction of the ecological biosphere, the current war against youth, the hegemony of neoliberal globalization, the widespread attack by corporate culture on public schools, the ongoing attack on the welfare system, the increasing rates of incarceration of people of color, the increasing gap between the rich and the poor, or the dangerous growth of the prison-industrial complex. Moreover, cultural studies theorists need to write for a variety of public audiences, rather than for simply a narrow group of specialized intellectuals. Such writing needs to become public by crossing over into sites and avenues of expression that speak to more general audiences in a language that is clear but not theoretically simplistic. Intellectuals must combine their scholarship with commitment in a discourse that is not dull or obtuse and expands the reach of their audience. This suggests using opportunities offered by a host of public means of expression including the lecture circuit, radio, Internet, interview, alternative magazines, and the church pulpit, to name only a few.

Third, cultural studies theorists need to be more specific about what it would mean to be both self-critical as well as attentive to learning how to work collectively through a vast array of networks across a number of public spheres. This might mean sharing resources with cultural workers both within and outside of the university such as the various groups working for global justice or those activists battling the ongoing destruction of state provisions both within and outside of the United States. This suggests that cultural studies become more active in addressing the ethical and political challenges of globalization. As capital, finance, trade, and culture become extraterritorial, removed from traditional political constraints, it becomes all the more pressing that global networks and political organizations be put into play to provide an effective response to the reach and power of neoliberal globalization. Engaging in intellectual practices that offer the possibility of alliances and new forms of solidarity among cultural workers such as artists, writers, journalists, academics, and others who engage in forms of public pedagogy grounded in a democratic project represents a small, but important, step in addressing the massive and unprecedented reach of global capitalism.

Critical educators also need to register and make visible their own subjective involvement in what they teach, interact in the classroom and other cultural sites, and locate, mediate, and defend the political nature of their work as teachers and cultural workers, but not exclusively in individualized terms, which refuse to link commitment, scholarship, and pedagogy. Such a task points to the necessity for educators and cultural theorists to define intellectual practice "as part of an intricate web of morality, rigor and responsibility"[27] that enables them to speak with conviction, enter the public sphere in order to address important social problems, and demonstrate alternative models for what it means to bridge the gap between higher education and the broader society. One useful approach is for educators to think through the distinction between a politicizing pedagogy, which insists wrongly that students think as we do, and a political pedagogy that teaches students by example the importance of taking a stand without standing still while rigorously engaging with the full range of ideas about an issue. Political pedagogy connects understanding and critical engagement with the issue of social responsibility and what it would mean to educate students to not only critically engage the world but also be responsible enough to fight for those political and economic conditions that make its democratic possibilities viable. Such a pedagogy affirms the experience of the social and the obligations it evokes regarding questions of responsibility and social transformation by opening up for students important questions about power, knowledge, and what it might mean for them to critically engage the conditions under which life is presented to them and simultaneously work to overcome those social relations of oppression that make living unbearable for those who are poor, hungry, unemployed, refused adequate social services, and under the aegis of neoliberalism, viewed largely as disposable. What is important about this type of critical pedagogy is the issue of responsibility and what it would mean for cultural studies educators to encourage students to reflect on what it would mean to connect knowledge and criticism to becoming an actor, buttressed by a profound desire to overcome injustice and a spirited commitment to social agency. Political education teaches students to take risks, challenge those with power, and encourage them to be reflexive about how power is used in the classroom. Political education proposes that the role of the public intellectual is not to consolidate authority, but to question and interrogate it and that teachers and students should temper any reference for authority with a sense of critical awareness and an acute willingness to hold it accountable for its consequences. Moreover, political education foregrounds education not within the imperatives of specialization and professionalization, but within a project designed to expand the possibilities of democracy by linking education to modes of political agency that promote critical citizenship and engage the ethical imperative to alleviate human suffering. On the other hand, politicizing education silences in the name of orthodoxy and imposes itself on students while undermining dialogue, deliberation, and critical engagement. Politicizing education is often grounded in a combination of self-righteousness and ideological purity that silences students as it imposes "correct" positions. Authority in this perspective rarely opens itself to self-criticism or for that matter to any criticism, especially from students. Politicizing education cannot decipher the distinction between critical teaching and pedagogical terrorism because its advocates have no sense of the difference between encouraging human agency and social responsibility and molding students according to the imperatives of an unquestioned ideological position. Politicizing education is more religious than secular, more about training than educating, and it harbors a great dislike for complicating issues, promoting critical dialogue, and generating a culture of questioning.

Finally, if cultural studies theorists are truly concerned about how culture operates as a crucial site of power in the modern world, they will have to take more seriously how pedagogy functions on local and global levels to secure and challenge the ways in which power is deployed, affirmed, and resisted within and outside traditional discourses and cultural spheres. In this instance, pedagogy becomes an important theoretical tool for understanding the institutional conditions that place constraints on the production of knowledge, learning, and academic labor itself. Pedagogy also provides a discourse for engaging and challenging the production of social hierarchies, identities, and ideologies as they traverse local and national borders. In addition, pedagogy as a form of production and critique offers a discourse of possibility, a way of providing students with the opportunity to link meaning to commitment, and understanding to social transformation—and to do so in the interest of the greatest possible justice. Unlike traditional vanguardists or elitist notions of the intellectual, cultural studies should embrace the notion that the vocation of intellectuals be rooted in pedagogical and political work tempered by humility, a moral focus on suffering, and the need to produce alternative visions and policies that go beyond a language of critique. I now want to shift my frame a bit in order to focus on the implications of the concerns I have addressed thus far and how they might be connected to developing an academic agenda for teachers as public intellectuals in higher education, particularly at a time when neoliberal agendas increasingly guide social policy.

The Responsibility of Intellectuals and the Politics of Education

In opposition to the corporatizing of everything educational, educators need to define higher education as a resource vital to the democratic and civic life of the nation. At the heart of such a task is the challenge for academics, cultural workers, and labor organizers to join together and oppose the transformation of higher education into commercial spheres, to resist what Bill Readings has called a consumer oriented corporation more concerned about accounting than accountability.[28] As Zygmunt Bauman reminds us, schools are one of the few public spaces left where students can learn the "skills for citizen participation and effective political action. And where there is no [such] institution, there is no "citizenship" either."[29] Public and higher education may be one of the few sites available in which students can learn about the limits of commercial values, address what it means to learn the skills of social citizenship, and learn how to deepen and expand the possibilities of collective agency and democratic life. Defending education at all levels of learning as a vital public sphere and public good rather than merely a private good is necessary to develop and nourish the proper balance between democratic public spheres and commercial power, between identities founded on democratic principles and identities steeped in forms of competitive, self-interested individualism that celebrate selfishness, profit making, and greed. This view suggests that public and higher education be defended through intellectual work that self-consciously recalls the tension between the democratic imperatives and possibilities of public institutions and their everyday realization within a society dominated by market principles. If public and higher education are to remain sites of critical thinking, collective work, and social struggle, public intellectuals need to expand their meaning and purpose. As I have stressed repeatedly, academics, teachers, students, parents, community activists, and other socially concerned groups must provide the first line of defense in defending public and higher education as a resource vital to the moral life of the nation, open to people and communities whose resources, knowledge, and skills have often been viewed as marginal. Such a project suggests that educators and cultural studies theorists develop a more inclusive vocabulary for aligning politics with the tasks of leadership. In part, this means providing the language, knowledge, and social relations for students to engage in the "art of translating individual problems into public issues, and common interests into individual rights and duties."[30] Leadership demands a politics and pedagogy that refuses to separate individual problems and experience from public issues and social considerations. Within such a perspective, leadership displaces cynicism with hope, challenges the neoliberal notion that there are no alternatives with visions of a better society, and develops a pedagogy of commitment that puts into place modes of literacy in which competency and interpretation provide the basis for actually intervening in the world. Leadership invokes the demand to make the pedagogical more political by linking critical thought to collective action, human agency to social responsibility, and knowledge and power to a profound impatience with a status quo founded upon deep inequalities and injustices.

One of the most crucial challenges that educators and cultural studies advocates face is rejecting the neoliberal collapse of the public into the private, the rendering of all social problems as biographical in nature. The neoliberal obsession with the private not only furthers a market-based politics that reduces all relationships to the exchange of money and the accumulation of capital, it also depoliticizes politics itself and reduces public activity to the realm of utterly privatized practices and utopias, underscored by the reduction of citizenship to the act of buying and purchasing goods. Within this discourse all forms of political solidarity, social agency, and collective resistance disappear into the murky waters of a biopolitics in which the pursuit of privatized pleasures and ready-made individual choices are organized on the basis of marketplace pursuits and desires that cancel out all modes of social responsibility, commitment, and action. The current challenge intellectuals face is to reclaim the language of the social, agency, solidarity, democracy, and public life as the basis for rethinking how to name, theorize, and strategize a new kind of politics, notions of political agency, and collective struggle.

This challenge suggests, in part, positing new forms of social citizenship and civic education that have a purchase on people's everyday lives and struggles. Academics bear an enormous responsibility in opposing neoliberalism—the most dangerous ideology of our time—by bringing democratic political culture back to life. Part of this effort demands creating new locations of struggle, vocabularies, and subject positions that allow people in a wide variety of public spheres to become more than they are now, to question what it is they have become within existing institutional and social formations, and "to give some thought to their experiences so that they can transform their relations of subordination and oppression."[31] One element of this struggle could take the form of resisting attacks on existing public spheres such as the schools while creating new spaces in clubs, neighborhoods, bookstores, trade unions, alternative media sites, and other places where dialogue and critical exchanges become possible. At the same time, challenging neoliberalism means fighting against the ongoing reconfiguration of the state into the role of an enlarged police precinct designed to repress dissent, regulate immigrant populations, incarcerate youth who are considered disposable, and safeguard the interests of global investors. As governments globally give up their role of providing social safety nets, social provisions, and regulating the excesses of corporate greed, capital escapes beyond the reach of democratic control and marginalized individuals and groups are left to their own meager resources to survive. Under such circumstances, it becomes difficult to create alternative public spheres that enable people to become effective agents of change. Under neoliberalism's reign of terror, public issues collapse into privatized discourses and a culture of personal confessions, greed, and celebrities emerges that sets the stage for depoliticizing public life and providing the grounds for turning citizenship and governance into a form of consumerism.

The growing attack on public and higher education in American society may say less about the reputed apathy of the populace than it might about the bankruptcy of old political languages and orthodoxies and the need for new vocabularies and visions for clarifying our intellectual, ethical and political projects, especially as they work to reabsorb questions of agency, ethics, and meaning back into politics and public life. In the absence of such a language and the social formations and public spheres that make democracy and justice operative, politics becomes narcissistic and caters to the mood of widespread pessimism and the cathartic allure of the spectacle. In addition, public service and government intervention is sneered upon as either bureaucratic or a constraint upon individual freedom. Any attempt to give new life to a substantive democratic politics must address the issue of both how people learn to be political agents and what kind of educational work is necessary within what kind of public spaces to enable people to use their full intellectual resources to provide a profound critique of existing institutions and struggle to make the operation of freedom and autonomy possible for as many people as possible in a wide variety of spheres. As critical educators, we are required to understand more fully why the tools we used in the past feel awkward in the present, often failing to respond to problems now facing the United States and other parts of the globe. More specifically, educators face the challenge posed by the failure of existing critical discourses to bridge the gap between how society represents itself and how and why individuals fail to understand and critically engage such representations in order to intervene in the oppressive social relationships they often legitimate.

Against neoliberalism, educators, cultural studies theorists, students, and activists face the task of providing a language of resistance and possibility, a language that embraces a militant utopianism while constantly being attentive to those forces that seek to turn such hope into a new slogan or punish and dismiss those who dare to look beyond the horizon of the given. Hope is the affective and intellectual precondition for individual and social struggle, the mark of courage on the part of intellectuals in and out of the academy who use the resources of theory to address pressing social problems. But hope is also a referent for civic courage which translates as a political practice and begins when one's life can no longer be taken for granted, making concrete the possibility for transforming politics into an ethical space and public act that confronts the flow of everyday experience and the weight of social suffering with the force of individual and collective resistance and the unending project of democratic social transformation.

There is a lot of talk among social theorists about the death of politics and the inability of human beings to imagine a more equitable and just world in order to make it better. I would hope that of all groups, educators would be the most vocal and militant in challenging this assumption by making it clear that at the heart of any form of inclusive democracy is the assumption that learning should be used to expand the public good, create a culture of questioning, and promote democratic social change. Individual and social agency become meaningful as part of the willingness to imagine otherwise "in order to help us find our way to a more human future."[32] Under such circumstances, knowledge can be used for amplifying human freedom and promoting social justice, and not for simply creating profits. The diverse but connected fields of cultural studies and critical pedagogy offer some insights for addressing these issues, and we would do well to learn as much as possible from them in order to expand the meaning of the political and revitalize the pedagogical possibilities of cultural politics and democratic struggles. The late Pierre Bourdieu has argued that intellectuals need to create new ways for doing politics by investing in political struggles through a permanent critique of the abuses of authority and power, especially under the reign of neoliberalism. Bourdieu wanted scholars to use their skills and knowledge to break out of the microcosm of academia, combine scholarship with commitment, and "enter into sustained and vigorous exchange with the outside world (especially with unions, grassroots organizations, and issue-oriented activist groups) instead of being content with waging the 'political' battles, at once intimate and ultimately, and always a bit unreal, of the scholastic universe."[33]

At a time when our civil liberties are being destroyed and public institutions and goods all over the globe are under assault by the forces of a rapacious global capitalism, there is a sense of concrete urgency that demands not only the most militant forms of political opposition on the part of academics, but new modes of resistance and collective struggle buttressed by rigorous intellectual work, social responsibility, and political courage. The time has come for intellectuals to distinguish caution from cowardice and recognize the ever fashionable display of rhetorical cleverness as a form of "disguised decadence."[34] As Derrida reminds us, democracy "demands the most concrete urgency ... because as a concept it makes visible the promise of democracy, that which is to come."[35] We have seen glimpses of such a promise among those brave students and workers who have demonstrated in Seattle, Genoa, Prague, New York, and Toronto. As public intellectuals, academics can learn from such struggles by turning the university and public schools into vibrant critical sites of learning and unconditional sites of pedagogical and political resistance. The power of the existing dominant order does not merely reside in the economic or in material relations of power, but also in the realm of ideas and culture. This is why intellectuals must take sides, speak out, and engage in the hard work of debunking corporate culture's assault on teaching and learning, orient their teaching for social change, connect learning to public life, link knowledge to the operations of power, and allow issues of human rights and crimes against humanity in their diverse forms to occupy a space of critical and open discussion in the classroom. It also means stepping out of the classroom and working with others to create public spaces where it becomes possible to not only "shift the way people think about the moment, but potentially to energize them to do something differently in that moment," to link one's critical imagination with the possibility of activism in the public sphere.[36] This is, of course, a small step, but if we do not want to repeat the present as the future or, even worse, become complicit in the dominant exercise of power, it is time for educators to mobilize collectively their energies by breaking down the illusion of unanimity that dominant power propagates while working diligently, tirelessly, and collectively to reclaim the promises of a truly global, democratic future.

Notes

1. Raymond Williams, "The Future of Cultural Studies," *The Politics of Modernism* (London: Verso, 1989), pp. 161–162.

2. Alain Badiou, *Ethics: An Essay on the Understanding of Evil* (London: Verso, 2001), p. 121.

3. For instance in a number of readers on cultural studies, the issue of critical pedagogy is left out altogether. Typical examples include: Toby Miller, ed., *A Companion to Cultural Studies* (Malden, MA: Blackwell, 2001); Simon During, ed., *The Cultural Studies Reader*, 2nd ed. (New York: Routledge, 1999); and John Storey, ed., *What Is Cultural Studies? A Reader* (New York: Arnold Press, 1996).

4. Shane Gunster, "Gramsci, Organic Intellectuals, and Cultural Studies," in Jason, Frank and John Tambornino, eds., *Vocations of Political Theory* (Minneapolis: University of Minnesota Press, 2000), p. 253.

5. For instance, see the brilliant, early essay by Lawrence Grossberg on education and cultural studies in "Introduction: Bringin' It All Back Home—Pedagogy and Cultural Studies," in Henry A. Giroux and Peter McLaren, eds., *Border Crossings: Pedagogy and the Politics of Cultural Studies* (New York: Routledge, 1994), pp. 1–25.

6. I take this issue up in greater detail in Henry A. Giroux, *Impure Acts: The Practical Politics of Cultural Studies* (New York: Routledge, 2000); *Stealing Innocence: Corporate Culture's War on Children* (New York: Palgrave, 2000).

7. Roger Simon, "Broadening the Vision of University-Based Study of Education: The Contribution of Cultural Studies" *Review of Education, Pedagogy, and Cultural Studies 12*, no. 1 (1995): 109.

8. On the importance of problematizing and pluralizing the political, see Jodi Dean, "The Interface of Political Theory and Cultural Studies," in Jodi Dean, ed., *Cultural Studies and Political Theory* (Ithaca: Cornell University Press, 2000), pp. 1–19.

9. Raymond Williams, "Preface to Second Edition," *Communications* (New York: Barnes and Noble, 1967), pp. 15, 16.

10. Raymond Williams, "Preface to Second Edition," *Communications* (New York: Barnes and Noble, 1967), p. 14.

11. See especially Raymond Williams, *Marxism and Literature* (New York: Oxford University Press, 1977) and Raymond Williams, *The Year 2000* (New York: Pantheon, 1983).

12. Williams, *Marxism and Literature*.

13. Matthias Fritsch, "Derrida's Democracy to Come," *Constellations 9*, no. 4 (December 2002): 579.

14. Lawrence Grossberg, "The Circulation of Cultural Studies," in John Storey, ed., *What Is Cultural Studies? A Reader* (New York: Arnold, 1996), pp. 179–180.

15. Imre Szeman, "Learning to Learn from Seattle," *Review of Education, Pedagogy, and Cultural Studies 24*, no. 1–2 (2002): 4.

16. Lawrence Grossberg, "Toward a Genealogy of the State of Cultural Studies," in Cary Nelson and Dilip Parameshwar Gaonkar, eds., *Disciplinarity and Dissent in Cultural Studies* (New York: Routledge, 1996), p. 143.

17. Douglas M. Kellner and Meenakshi Gigi Durham, "Adventures in Media and Cultural Studies: Introducing Key Works," in Douglas M. Kellner and Meenakshi Gigi Durham, eds., *Media and Cultural Studies: Key Works* (Malden, MA: Blackwell, 2001), p. 29.

18. Henry A. Giroux, *The Mouse that Roared: Disney and the End of Innocence* (Lanham, MD: Rowman and Littlefield, 2000); also see Henry A. Giroux, *Impure Acts* (New York:

Routledge, 2000) and Henry A. Giroux, *Breaking into the Movies: Film and the Politics of Culture* (Malden, MA: Blackwell, 2002).

19. See, for instance, Meenakshi Gigi Durham and Douglas M. Kellner, eds., *Media and Cultural Studies: Key Works* (Malden, MA: Blackwell, 2001).

20. James Clifford, "Museums in the Borderlands," Carol Becker, et al., eds., *Different Voices* (New York: Association of Art Museum Directors, 1992), p. 129.

21. John Beverly, "Pedagogy and Subalternity: Mapping the Limits of Academic Knowledge," in Rolland G. Paulston, ed., *Social Cartography* (New York: Garland, 1996), p. 354.

22. See Henry A. Giroux and Peter McLaren, eds., *Between Borders: Pedagogy and the Politics of Cultural Studies* (New York: Routledge, 1993).

23. Arif Dirlik, "Literature/Identity: Transnationalism, Narrative, and Representation," *Review of Education, Pedagogy,* and *Cultural Studies 24,* no. 3 (July–September 2002): 218. One example of such work can be found in Marjorie Garber, *Sex and Real Estate: Why We Love Houses* (New York: Anchor Books, 2000) or even better Marjorie Garber, *Dog Love* (New York: Touchstone Press, 1997).

24. Stuart Hall cited in Peter Osborne and Lynne Segal, "Culture and Power: Stuart Hall Interviewed," *Radical Philosophy 86* (November–December 1997): 24.

25. See, for example, Douglas Kellner, *Media Culture: Cultural Studies, Identity, and Politics* (New York: Routledge, 1995).

26. Zygmunt Bauman, *Society under Siege* (Malden, MA: Blackwell: 2002), p. 170.

27. Arundhati Roy, *Power Politics* (Cambridge, MA: South End Press, 2001), p. 6.

28. Bill Readings, *The University in Ruins* (Cambridge, MA: Harvard University Press, pp. 11, 18.

29. Zygmunt Bauman, *In Search of Politics* (Stanford: Stanford University Press, 1999), p. 170.

30. Zygmunt Bauman, *Society under Siege* (Malden, MA: Blackwell: 2002), p. 70.

31. Lynn Worsham and Gary A. Olson, "Rethinking Political Community: Chantal Mouffe's Liberal Socialism," *Journal of Composition Theory 19,* no. 2 (1999): 178.

32. Noam Chomsky, "Paths Taken, Tasks Ahead," *Profession* (2000): 34.

33. Pierre Bourdieu, "For a Scholarship of Commitment," *Profession* (2000): 44.

34. Arundhati Roy, *Power Politics* (Boston: South End Press, 2001), p. 12.

35. Jacques Derrida, "Intellectual Courage: An Interview," Trans. Peter Krapp, *Culture Machine,* Vol. 2 (2000), p. 9.

36. A Conversation between Lani Guinier and Anna Deavere Smith, "Rethinking Power, Rethinking Theater," *Theater 31,* no. 3 (Winter 2002): 34–35.

9
Mouse Power

Public Pedagogy, Cultural Studies, and the Challenge of Disney

֎

> The Disney stores promote the consumer products, which promote the theme parks, which promote the TV shows. The TV shows promote the company. Roger Rabbit promotes Christmas at Disneyland.
> —Michael Eisner, Chairman, CEO, and President of Walt Disney Company[1]

> There is nothing innocuous left. The little pleasures, expressions of life that seemed exempt from the responsibility of thought, not only have an element of deviant silliness, of callous refusal to see, but directly serve their diametrical opposite.
> —Theodor Adorno[2]

Adorno's insights seem particularly appropriate at a time when multinational corporations have become the driving force behind media culture, making it increasingly difficult to maintain what has always been a problematic position—that the entertainment industry provides people with the moments of pleasure and escape they request. That corporate culture is rewriting the nature of children's culture becomes clear as the boundaries once maintained between spheres of formal education and that of entertainment collapse into each other. To be convinced of this, one only has to consider a few telling events from the growing corporate interest in schools as profit-making ventures, the production of curricular materials by toy and food companies, or the increasing use of school space and time for the advertising and sale of consumer goods.

The organization and regulation of culture by large corporations such as Disney profoundly influence children's culture and their everyday life. The concentration of control over the means of producing, circulating, and exchanging information has been matched by the emergence of new technologies which have transformed culture, especially popular culture, into the primary educational site in which youth learn about themselves, their relationship to others, and the larger world. The Hollywood film industry, television, satellite broadcasting technologies, the internet, posters, magazines, billboards, newspapers, videos, and other media forms and technologies have transformed culture into a pivotal force in "shaping human meaning and behavior and regulat[ing] our social practices at every turn."[3] Although the endlessly proliferating sites of media production promise unlimited access to vast stores of information, such sites are increasingly controlled by a handful of multinationals. Consider the Disney corporation's share of the communication industry. Disney's numerous holdings include: a controlling interest in 20 television stations that reach 25 percent of all U.S. households; ownership of over 21 radio stations and the largest radio network in the United States—serving 3,400 stations and covering 24 percent of all households in the country. In addition, Disney owns three music studios, ABC primetime Network News, and five motion picture studios. Other holdings include, but are not limited to, television and cable channels, book publishing, sports teams, theme parks, insurance companies, magazines, and multimedia productions.[4] Mass produced images fill our daily lives and condition our most intimate perceptions and desires. At issue for parents, educators, and others is how culture, particularly media culture, has become a substantive, if not the primary, educational force in regulating the meanings, values, and tastes that set the norms and conventions that offer up and legitimate particular subject positions—what it means to claim an identity as a male, female, white, black, citizen, or noncitizen as well as to define the meaning of childhood, the national past, beauty, truth, and social agency.[5] The scope and impact of new electronic technologies as teaching machines can be seen in some rather astounding statistics. It is estimated that "the average American spends more than four hours a day watching television. Four hours a day, 28 hours a week, 1456 hours a year."[6] The American Medical Association reports that the "number of hours spent in front of a television or video screen is the single biggest chunk of time in the waking life of an American child."[7]

Such statistics warrant grave concern given that the pedagogical messages often provided through such programming are shaped largely by a $130 billion dollar a year advertising industry, which sells not only its products but also values, images, and identities that are largely aimed at teaching young people to be consumers. It would be reductionistic not to recognize that there is also some excellent programming that is provided to audiences, but by and large much of what is produced on television and in the big Hollywood studios panders to the lowest common denominator, defines freedom as consumer choice, and debases public discourse by reducing it to a spectacle.[8]

Nothing appears to be out of bounds for the mega corporations and their counterparts in the advertising industry when it comes to transforming childhood dreams into potential profits. For example, within two days after Mark

McGwire belted out his sixty-second homerun, breaking Roger Maris's record, a television ad ran on all the major networks in which McGwire appeared hitting the home run, jogging around the bases, and picking up his son in celebration of his record breaking event. With his son in his arms, a camera zooms in on McGwire—hero to millions of kids—and a voice in the background asks: "What are you going to do now?" McGwire smiles, looks directly at the camera, and replies "I am going to take my son to Disneyland."

The McGwire ad was followed up with the announcement in the dominant media, including the three major television network news programs, that the grounds keeper who had picked up McGwire's record setting baseball would give it back to him, and that this generous deed would be rewarded with a free round trip ticket to Disneyland. Once again, Disney managed to appropriate a high profile American image and turn it into an advertisement for corporate America.

But such commercialism is not limited to appropriating events deeply associated in the national imagination with the efforts of heroic sports figures such as Mark McGwire and Michael Jordan, among others. No identity, desire, or need appears to escape the advertiser's grip. For instance, *The Disney Magazine* recently ran an ad for "The 'Baby Mickey' Porcelain Doll." The ad features a baby wearing a cap with the logo "Disney babies" on it. The baby's pajama top also had a Mickey Mouse logo on it and just in case the reader missed the point, the baby is holding a Baby Mickey doll, with "Baby Mickey" emblazoned on its bib. The caption for the ad reads: "He drifts off to dreamland with Baby Mickey to cuddle nearby!"[9] The doll is part of the Ashton-Drake Galleries collection offered to adults who can both rewrite their own memories of being a child in Disney's terms while simultaneously indulging a commodified view of innocence that they can use to introduce their own infants into Disney's version of childhood. The ad appeals to innocence as it appropriates it at one of its most seductive and vulnerable moments.

The Disney commercial fantasy machine uses innocence as a representational image to infantilize the very adults at whom it is aimed. Of course, the larger issue is that the commercialization of the media and the culture, in general, limits the choices that children and adults can make in extending their sense of agency beyond a commercial culture that enshrines an intensely myopic and conservative sense of self and society. Under these circumstances, one has to ask what price the public pays by simply focusing on merely the pleasure and fun that culture industries such as Disney provide while excluding the growing influence they have in shaping so many other facets of national and global life. Consider the enormous control that a handful of transnational corporations have over the diverse properties that shape popular and media culture: "51 of the largest 100 economies in the world are corporations."[10] Moreover, fewer than 10 conglomerates, whose annual sales range from $10 to $27 billion dollars, dominate the media in the United States. These include major corporations such as Time Warner, General Electric, Disney, Viacom, TCI, and Westinghouse. Not only are these firms major producers of much of the entertainment, news, culture, and information that permeates our daily lives, they also produce "media software and have distribution networks like television networks, cable channels and retail stores."[11] Of course, the notion that corporations are involved in every aspect of cultural production—ranging from the production of identities, representations, and texts to control over the production, circulation, and distribution of cultural goods—is not a new insight to theorists of cultural studies. But what has been missing from such work is an analysis of the educational role that such corporations play in promoting a public pedagogy that uses, as Raymond Williams has pointed out, the educational force of all of its institutions, resources, and relationships to actively and profoundly teach an utterly privatized notion of citizenship and democracy. All too often within the parameters of such a public democracy, consumption is the only form of citizenship being offered to children, and democracy is privatized through an emphasis on egoistic individualism, low levels of participation in political life, and a diminishing of the importance of noncommodified public spheres. In what follows, I want to point to some theoretical and political implications for focusing on corporations as "teaching machines" engaged in a particular form of public pedagogy. In doing so, I will focus specifically on the Disney Corporation and what I will call its discourse of innocence as a defining principle in structuring its public pedagogy of commercialism within children's culture.

Disney and the Politics of Innocence

Since the 1990s, the rise of corporate power and its expansion into all aspects of everyday life has grown by leaps and bounds.[12] One of the most visible examples of such growth can be seen in the expanding role that The Walt Disney Company plays in shaping popular culture and daily life in the United States and abroad. The Disney Company is an exemplary model of the new face of corporate power at the beginning of the twenty-first century. Like many other megacorporations, its focus is on popular culture, and it continually expands its reach to include not only theme parks but also television networks, motion pictures, cruise lines, baseball and hockey teams, Broadway theater, and a children's radio program. What is unique about Disney is that, unlike Time Warner or Westinghouse, its brand name is almost synonymous with the notion of childhood innocence. As an icon of American culture and middle-class family values, Disney actively appeals to both parental concerns and children's fantasies as it works hard to transform every child into a lifetime consumer of Disney products and ideas. In this scenario, a contradiction emerges between Disney's cutthroat commercial ethos and a Disney culture that presents itself as the paragon of virtue and childlike innocence. Disney has built its reputation on both profitability and wholesome entertainment. Largely removing itself from issues of power, politics, and ideology, it embraces a pristine, self-image associated with the magic of pixie dust and Mainstreet, USA. Yet, this is merely the calculating rhetoric of a corporate giant, whose annual revenues in 1997 exceeded $22 billion as a result of its ability to manufacture, sell, and distribute culture on a global scale, making it the world's most powerful leisure icon.[13] Michael Ovitz, a former Disney executive, touches on the enormous power Disney wields in claiming "Disney isn't a company as much as it is a nation-state with its own ideas and attitudes, and you have to adjust to them."[14]

The image of Disney as a political and economic power promoting a specific culture and ideology appears at odds with a public relations image that portrays the company as one that offers young people the promise of making their dreams come true through the pleasures of wholesome entertainment. The contradiction between the politics at work in shaping Disney culture and the appeal the company puts forth in order to construct and influence children's culture is disturbing and problematic. But making Disney accountable for the ways in which it shapes children's desires and identities becomes all the more important as the Disney corporation increasingly presents itself not only as a purveyor of entertainment and fun, but also as a political force in developing models of education that influence how young people are educated in public schools, spheres traditionally understood to offer children the space for critical and intellectual development uninhibited by the relentless fascinations of consumer culture.

Disney has given new meaning to the politics of innocence as a narrative for shaping public memory and for producing a "general body of identifications" that promote a sanitized version of American history.[15] Innocence also serves as a rhetorical device that cleanses the Disney image of the messy influence of commerce, ideology, and power. In other words, Disney's strategic association with childhood, a world cleansed of contradictions and free of politics, represents not just the basic appeal of its theme parks and movies, but also provides a model for defining corporate culture separate from the influence of corporate power. Hence, Michael Eisner, President and CEO of Walt Disney Company, is caught in a contradiction when he repeats the company line that Disney only gives children what they want, or when he panders to the rhetoric of innocence by arguing that his own role as CEO is comparable to being in charge of a giant toy store.[16] Such comments are more than simple disingenuousness. Eisner willfully refuses to acknowledge responsibility for the role that Disney plays in harnessing children's identities and desires to an ever-expanding sphere of consumption; for editing public memory to reconstruct an American past in its own image; or for setting limits on democratic public life by virtue of its controlling influence on the media and its increasing presence in the schools. Education is never innocent, because it always presupposes a particular view of citizenship, culture, and society, and yet it is this very appeal to innocence, bleached of any semblance of politics, that has become a defining feature of Disney culture and pedagogy.

The Walt Disney Company's attachment to the appeal of innocence provides both a rationale for Disney to reaffirm its commitment to children's pleasure and to downplay any critical assessments of the role Disney plays as a benevolent corporate power in sentimentalizing childhood innocence as it simultaneously commodifies it. Stripped of the historical and social constructions that give it meaning, innocence in the Disney universe becomes an atemporal, ahistorical, apolitical, and atheoretical space where children share a common bond free of the problems and conflicts of adult society. Disney both markets this ideal and presents itself as a corporate parent who safeguards this protective space for children by magically supplying the fantasies that nourish it and keep it alive. Michael Eisner not only recognizes the primacy of innocence for Disney's success, he reaffirms the company's longstanding public relations position that innocence somehow exists outside of the reach of adult society, and that Disney alone provides the psychic economy through which kids can express their childlike fantasies. He comments: "The specific appeal of Disneyland, Disney films and products—family entertainment—comes from the contagious appeal of innocence.... Obviously, Disney characters strike a universal chord with children, all of whom share an innocence and openness *before* they become completely molded by their respective societies" (emphasis added).[17] Eisner's claim is important because it now suggests that Disney culture reflects rather than shapes a particular version of childhood innocence and subjectivity. There is little to insinuate in Eisner's comments that Disney has always viewed children as an enormously productive market to fuel company profits, and that old Walt Disney clearly understood the appeal to innocence as a universal mechanism for exploiting the realm of childhood fantasies in its "relentless quest for new images to sell."[18] Old Walt may have had the best of intentions when it comes to making kids happy—and he had few doubts about the enormous commercial potential of youth.

Innocence plays a complex role in the Disney Company's attempt to market its self-image to the American public. Not only does it register Disney's association with a sentimentalized notion of childhood fantasy, innocence also functions as the principle concept of moral regulation and as part of a politics of historical erasure. Further elaborating this dual strategy reveals that in Disney's moral order innocence is "presented as the deepest truth,"[19] which when unproblematized can be used with great force and influence to legitimate the spectacle of entertainment as escapist fantasy. In addition, innocence becomes the ideological and educational yardstick through which Disney promotes a conservative set of ideas and values as the normative and taken-for-granted "premises of a particular and historical form of social order."[20] Recognizing that Disney has a political stake in creating a particular moral order favorable to its commercial interests raises fundamental questions about what it teaches to produce the meanings, desires, and dreams through which it attempts to inscribe both young people and adults within the Disney worldview.

Making the Political More Pedagogical

Although my focus is on Disney because of its particular attempt to mystify its corporate agenda with appeals to fun, innocence, and purity, the seriousness of the threat that Disney and other corporations present to a vibrant democracy in their control over information cannot be underestimated. I don't mean to suggest that Disney is engaged in a conspiracy to undermine American youth or democracy around the world. Nor do I want to suggest that Disney is part of an evil empire incapable of providing joy and pleasure to the millions of kids and adults who visit its theme parks, watch its videos and movies, or buy products from its toy stores. On the contrary, the main issue here is that such entertainment now takes place under conditions "in which the media becomes a critical site for the articulation of a major intellectual shift in the ground of public discourse ... in which pricing systems are now brought to bear on any problem, anytime, anywhere."[21] In other words, media conglomerates such as Disney are not merely producing harmless entertainment, disinterested news stories, or unlimited access to the information age; nor are they removed from the realm of power, politics, and ideology. Recognizing the pleasure Disney provides on a global scale does not mean that it is only about the production of entertainment and enjoyment.

I also want to avoid at the outset suggesting that Disney will have the same impact through its films, radio stations, theme parks, magazines, and other products on all those children and adults who are exposed to and experience Disney culture. Disney does not represent a self-contained system of formal conventions that is unchanging or static. Disney culture, like all cultural formations, is riddled with contradictions; rather than viewing the Disney empire as monolithic, it is important to emphasize that within Disney culture there are potentially subversive moments and pleasures. There are no passive dupes in this script, and many of Disney's texts offer opportunities for oppositional readings. But at the same time, the potential for subversive readings, the recognition of the complex interplay of agency, or the mixture of alienation and pleasure that the culture industry promotes does not cancel out the power of a corporation like Disney to monopolize the media and saturate everyday life with its own ideologies. Although it is true that people mediate what they see, buy, wear, and consume, and bring different meanings to the texts and products that companies like Disney produce, it is crucial that any attempt to deal with the relationship between culture and politics not stop with such a recognition but investigate both its limits and its strengths, particularly in dealing with the three- to eight-year-old crowd.[22] Hence, it is crucial that any rendering and interpretation of Disney culture not be seen as either static or universal but be addressed as a pedagogical attempt to challenge the diverse meanings and commonsense renderings that students and others bring to their encounter with Disney culture in its various manifestations.

Engaging Disney's public pedagogy as a cultural studies strategy, one that combines the political and the pedagogical, is meant to offer readers a set of problematics that enables them to inquire into what Disney represents in a way that they might not have thought about and to shatter commonsense assumptions regarding Disney's claim to both promoting fun and games and protecting childhood innocence. In short, the aim of such a project is to both challenge and go beyond the charge that cultural critics who take a critical stand on Disney or argue for a particular interpretation of what Disney culture represents fail to consider other possible readings of Disney texts or "simply offer self-righteous tirades against an endless litany of 'isms'."[23] In fact, the real issue may not be one of ideological rigidity on the part of progressive cultural critics or their failure to assign multiple interpretations to Disney's texts, but how to read cultural forms as they articulate with a whole assemblage of other texts, ideologies, and practices. How audiences interpret Disney's texts may not be as significant as how some ideas, meanings, and messages under certain political conditions become more highly rated as representations of reality than others, and how these representations assume the force of ideology by making an appeal to common sense while at the same time shaping political policies and programs that serve very specific interests—such as the passing of the 1996 Telecommunications Act, or the forging of school-business partnerships.

For some cultural theorists, the strength of Disney's texts lies in the potential they have for pleasure and for the multiple readings—outside of the realm of ideology—they provide for diverse audiences. Granted, recognizing that reception is itself constitutive of how meaning is produced and that the work of conferring meaning cannot be specified in advance is an important insight, but not one that by default eliminates the inordinate power of mega-corporations such as Disney to control the range of meanings that circulate within society. There is a difference between political formations, which involve a mix of institutional and ideological forces, and reading methods that remind us that the relationship between determinations and effects are problematic. Similarly, Edward Said makes an important point about the relationship between method and politics when he insists that some theorists "have fallen into the trap of believing that method is sovereign and can be systematic without also acknowledging that method is always part of some larger ensemble of relationships headed and moved by authority and power."[24] For Said, the forces of cultural production and reception are not equal; and this suggests dealing very differently with how we actually think about the relationship among politics, power, and pedagogy in linking these two modes of intervention. Focusing on how subjects interpret, mediate, or resist different messages, products, and social practices does not cancel out the concentrated assemblage of power that produces them, nor does it address the broader historical, cultural, and institutional affiliations that often privilege texts with specific intentions and meanings. Nor does such a method suggest that one is actually working out of a project that takes a stand against particular forms of domination while struggling to expand democratic relations and pluralize democratic public spheres. What is the celebration of any method, including audience research (in its various manifestations) actually against? What is the project that gives it meaning? And how does this appeal to method actually address the growing concentration of political and economic power and the broad spectrum of texts, institutions, and social practices that corporations such as Disney effectively reproduce?

Yet, how people mediate texts, produce different readings of various cultural forms, and allow themselves to experience the pleasure of various aspects of Disney culture cannot be ignored. However, the ways in which such messages, products, and conventions "work" on audiences is one that must be left open to the investigation of particular ethnographic interventions and/or pedagogical practices. There is no virtue, ideologically or politically, in simply pronouncing what Disney means—as if that is all there is to do. I am suggesting a very different approach to Disney, one that highlights the pedagogical and the contextual by raising questions about Disney—such as what role it plays in shaping childhood identity, public memory, national identity, gender roles, or in suggesting who qualifies as an American or what the role of consumerism is in American life—that expand the scope of inquiry in order to allow people to enter into such a discussion in a way that they ordinarily might not have. Disney needs to be engaged as a public discourse, and doing so means offering an analysis that forces civic discourse and popular culture to rub up against each other. Such an engagement represents both a pedagogical intervention and a way of recognizing the changing contexts in which any text must be understood and engaged.

Questioning what Disney teaches is part of a much broader inquiry regarding what it is that parents, children, educators and other cultural workers need to know in order to critique and challenge, when necessary, those institutional and cultural forces that have a direct impact on public life. Such inquiry is all the more important at a time when corporations hold such an inordinate amount of power in shaping children's culture into a largely commercial endeavor, using their various cultural technologies as teaching machines to relentlessly commodify and homogenize all aspects of everyday life, and in this sense posing a potential threat to the real freedoms associated with a substantive democracy. But questioning what megacorporations such as Disney teach also means appropriating the most resistant and potentially subversive ideas, practices, and images at work in their various cultural productions.

What Disney teaches cannot be abstracted from a number of important larger issues: What does it mean to make corporations accountable to the public? How might cultural studies theorists link public pedagogy to a critical democratic view of citizenship? How might diverse cultural workers develop forms of critical education that enable young people and adults to become aware of and interrogate the media as a major political, pedagogical, and social force? At the very least, such a project suggests that cultural studies theorists might give more thought to the importance of public pedagogy as a vital political project. More specifically, how might such a project be incorporated as a defining principle of cultural studies in order to offer students and others the opportunity for learning how to use and critically read the new media technologies and their various cultural productions as pedagogical practices designed to secure particular identifications and desires in the service of a privatized notion of citizenship and democracy? Organizing to democratize the media and make it accountable to a participating citizenry also demands engaging in the hard political and pedagogical task of opening up corporations such as Disney to public interrogation and critical dialogue.[25]

Disney's overwhelming presence in the United States and abroad reminds us that the battle over culture is central to the struggle over meaning and institutional power, and that for learning to become meaningful, critical, and emancipatory, it must not be surrendered to the dictates of consumer choice or to a prohibition on critically engaging how ideologies work within various social formations and cultural discourses. On the contrary, critical learning must be linked to the empowering demands of social responsibility, public accountability, and critical citizenship precisely as a form of cultural politics.

How we educate our youth is related to the collective future embodied in the stories that are told in the noncommodified spheres of our public culture. As noncommodified public culture comes under assault, we are faced with a growing commercial sphere that profoundly limits the vocabulary and imagery available to youth and others for defining, defending, and reforming the state, civil society, and public culture as centers for critical learning and citizenship. None of us stand outside of the cultures of pleasure and entertainment that now hold such sway over American society. The test of such cultures may not lie in whether they are capable of producing joy and merriment, but in their capacity to offer narratives of pleasure without undermining the basic institutions of a substantive democracy. What we don't need is a culture industry that increasingly moves towards producing stories that turn children's desires and dreams into fodder for the Disney Imagineers and profits for the Disney stores.

Notes

1. Eisner quoted in Don Hazen and Julie Winokur, eds., *We the Media* (New York: The New Press, 1997), p. 46.
2. Theodor Adorno, *Minima Moralia* (London: New Left Books, 1974), p. 25.
3. Stuart Hall, "The Centrality of Culture: Notes on the Cultural Revolutions of Our Time," in Kenneth Thompson, ed., *Media and Cultural Regulation* (Thousand Oaks, CA: Sage, 1997), p. 232.
4. Cited in a list of Disney's holdings in "The National Entertainment State Media Map," *Nation* (June 3, 1996): 23–26.
5. The concentrated power of the media market by corporations is evident in the following figures:

In cable, Time Warner and TCI control 47.4 percent of all subscribers; in radio, Westinghouse, in addition to owning the CBS Television network, now owns 82 radio stations; in books, Barnes and Noble and Borders sell 45 percent of all books in the United States; ... three studies share 57 percent of the overall market. In newspapers, only 24 cities compared to 400 fifty years ago support two or more daily newspapers. Cited in Robert W. McChesney, "Global Media for the Global Economy," in Don Hazen and Julie Winokur, eds. *We the Media* (New York: The New Press, 1997), p. 27.

6. Don Hazen and Julie Winokur, eds., *We the Media* (New York: The New Press, 1997), p. 64.
7. Cited in Hazen and Winokur, eds., *We the Media* op. cit., p. 64.
8. Pierre Bourdieu's analysis of the systemic corruption of television in France is equally informative when applied to the United States. See Pierre Bourdieu, *On Television*, translated by Priscilla Parkhust Ferguson (New York: The New Press, 1998).
9. The ad appears in *Disney Magazine* (Fall 1998): 61.
10. Cited in Joshua Karliner, "Earth Predators," *Dollars and Sense* (July/August 1998), p. 7.
11. Cited in Robert W. McChesney, *Corporate Media and the Threat to Democracy* (New York: Seven Stories Press, 1997), p. 18. There is an enormous amount of detailed information about the new global conglomerates and their effects on matters of democracy, censorship, free speech, social policy, national identity, and foreign policy. For example, see such classics as Herbert I. Schiller, *Culture Inc.: The Corporate Takeover of Public Expression* (New York: Oxford University Press, 1989); Edward S. Herman and Noam Chomsky, *Manufacturing Consent* (New York: Pantheon, 1988); Ben H. Bagdikian, *The Media Monopoly*, 4th ed. (Boston: Beacon Press, 1992); George Gerbner and Herbert I. Schiller, eds. *Triumph of the Image* (Boulder, CO: Westview Press, 1992); Douglas Kellner, *Television and the Crisis of Democracy* (Boulder: Westview Press, 1990); Philip Schlesinger, *Media, State, and Nation* (London: Sage, 1991); John Fiske,

Media Matters (Minneapolis: University of Minnesota Press, 1994); Jeff Cohen and Norman Solomon, *Through the Media Looking Glass* (Monroe, ME: Common Courage Press, 1995); Erik Barnouw, *Conglomerates and the Media* (New York: The New Press, 1997).

12. Two recent critical commentaries can be found in Robert W. McChesney, *Corporate Media and the Threat to Democracy* (New York: Seven Stories Press, 1997) and Erik Barnouw, et al., *Conglomerates and the Media* (New York: The New Press, 1997).

13. Figures taken from Michael D. Eisner, "Letter to Shareholders," *The Walt Disney Company 1997 Annual Report* (Burbank, CA: The Walt Disney Company, 1997), p. 2.

14. Michael Ovitz cited in Peter Bart, "Disney's Ovitz Problem Raises Issues for Showbiz Giants," *Daily Variety* (December 16, 1996): 1.

15. Kenneth Burke, *A Rhetoric of Motives*, (Berkeley, CA: University of California Press, 1962), p. 26.

16. Michael D. Eisner, "Letter to Shareholders," *The Walt Disney Company 1997 Annual Report* (Burbank, CA: The Walt Disney Company, 1997), p. 5.

17. Michael Eisner, "Planetized Entertainment," *New Perspectives Quarterly 12*:4 (Fall 1995): 9.

18. Mike Wallace, *Mickey Mouse History* (Philadelphia: Temple University Press, 1996), p. 170.

19. Chris Rojeck, "Disney Culture," *Leisure Studies 12* (1993), p. 121.

20. Philip Corrigan and Derek Sayer, *The Great Arch* (London: Basil Blackwell, 1985), p. 4.

21. Toby Miller, *Technologies of Truth* (University of Minnesota Press), p. 90.

22. I am invoking Meghan Morris's argument where she identifies the chief error of cultural studies to be the narcissistic identity that is made "between the knowing subject of cultural studies, and a collective subject, the 'people'." The people in this discourse "have no necessary defining characteristics—except an indomitable capacity to 'negotiate' readings, generate new interpretations, and remake the materials of culture.... So against the hegemonic force of the dominant classes, 'the people' in fact represent the most creative energies and functions of critical reading. In the end they are not simply the cultural student's objects of study, [but] his native informants. The people are also the textually delegated, allegorical emblem of the critic's own activity." See Meaghan Morris, "Banality in Cultural Studies," *Discourse 10*, no. 2 (Spring–Summer, 1988): 17.

23. A classic example of this type of critique can be found in David Buckingham, "Dissin' Disney: Critical Perspectives on Children's Media Culture," *Media, Culture, and Society 19* (1997): 290.

24. Edward W. Said, *The World, the Text, and the Critic* (Cambridge, MA: Harvard University Press, 1983), p. 169.

25. On another political register expanding democratic public culture means working hard to get organized labor and progressive social movements to join together to forge new partnerships willing to pool some of their intellectual and material resources in order to create alternative public spheres in which democratic identities, relations, and values can flourish and offer multiple sites of resistance to a culture industry such as Disney in which the call for innocence, happiness, and unity appears to be "transformed into a prohibition on thinking itself. Theodor W. Adorno, *Critical Models* (New York: Columbia University Press, 1998), p. 290.

V
The Politics of Higher Education

10
Racial Politics, Pedagogy, and the Crisis of Representation in Academic Multiculturalism

⊸

> Normative theoretical conceptions not tested against the worst calamities of our time might be thought to be taking life more easily than they should. Theories of rights and justice which do not seriously measure themselves against the realities of violation—violation of the norms about which they theorize, violation of the lives of human beings—and do not seriously measure themselves against the factors conducive to such violation, might be reckoned by this failure to be lacking in an important way.
>
> —Norman Geras[1]

The Politics of Academic Multiculturalism

Within the last decade a number of critical theorists have made a strong case for rethinking the political and pedagogical possibilities of multiculturalism within higher education.[2] Signaling a new understanding of how the mechanisms of domination and exclusion work to reproduce and legitimate the entrenched dynamics of class, race, gender, and sexual hierarchies in higher education, critical multiculturalists often combine the study of symbolic forms and signifying practices with a reinvigorated and necessary study of the relations between culture and politics.[3] For many critical multiculturalists the process of schooling is viewed as a terrain of struggle over the meaning and purpose of the humanities, the value of disciplinarity, the regulatory function of culture, the relationship between knowledge and authority, and who has ownership over the conditions for the production of knowledge.[4] Critical multiculturalists have also called into question the foundational categories that establish the canons of great works, the "high" and "low" culture divide, and the allegedly "objective" scholarship that marks the exclusions within and between various disciplines.[5] Similarly, they have fought bitter battles to establish academic programs that address the interests of various groups, including women's studies, Latino studies, and gay and lesbian programs.[6] In addition to challenging the content of curricula, they have successfully confronted the institutional distribution of power in higher education, in part, by expanding through affirmative action and other programs the opportunities for minority students to gain access to colleges and universities.

Critical academic multiculturalism has scored some of its greatest successes by significantly adding to the sum of public discourses available within the university that provide students with a range of pedagogical options in which they can invest, act, and speak in order to affirm their capacities for critical, social agency. Within progressive notions of multiculturalism, old disciplinary and cultural boundaries have given way to new ones, and the grip of monoculturalism has been significantly eased through a sustained emphasis on pluralized cultures in which various groups can now lay claim to the particularized identities and histories that inform and shape diverse cultural experiences.[7]

Arguing that cultural texts are inextricably related to broader social processes and material relations of power, critical academic multiculturalists have enhanced our understanding of how culture functions within higher education to construct knowledge, produce different social identities, and legitimate particular maps of meaning. Such insights have furthered our notion of cultural politics and the opportunity to make the pedagogical more political by linking the reading and writing of cultural texts to the acquisition of those skills and knowledges necessary to become critical readers and social actors. Drawing upon various theories of deconstruction, poststructuralism, and postmodernism, academic multiculturalists have appropriated the critical turn toward language, particularly the emphasis on strategies of indeterminacy, uncertainty, and polyvocal meanings, in order to challenge Western logocentrism and reveal the racial codes that discursively construct "whiteness" as a mode of oppression and domination. Texts are now seen not only as objects of struggle in challenging dominant modes of racial and colonial authority but also as pedagogical resources to rewrite the possibilities for new narratives, identities, and cultural spaces. Focusing on the politics of representation to call attention to the ways in which texts mobilize meanings in order to suppress, silence, and contain marginalized histories, voices, and experiences, academic multiculturalists have reasserted the power of the symbolic as a pedagogical force in securing authority and as a pedagogical strategy for producing particular forms of contestation and resistance.

Subjectivity and representation constitute the core determinants in shaping cultural politics in the liberal and radical discourses of academic multiculturalism and serve to foreground pedagogical strategies that privilege the reading of texts and the related struggle over the control and production of identities.[8] Although academic multiculturalists have been attentive to the relationship between culture and systemic relations of power within the university, they have largely focused their efforts pedagogically on matters of language, negotiation, and cultural identity. Within these discourses, the political as a form of ideology critique defines literacy largely as the pedagogical imperative to read texts differently, "draw attention to discursive ambivalence," recognize different logics of signification, and unsettle the consensus of common sense that constitutes dominant public values, national identity, and the meaning of citizenship.[9] Academic multiculturalism in its more radical strains has emphasized more than simply opening texts to a multiplicity of interpretations, an in-between space of translation where subaltern knowledge can be represented and heard. It has also insisted on the need for dominant intellectuals to work against the grain of their own embedded interests and privileges while "undoing the authority of the academy and knowledge centers at the same time that [they] continue to participate fully in them and to deploy their authority as teachers, researchers, planners and theorists."[10]

At its best, academic multiculturalism has reinvigorated the debate over the role the humanities and the university might play in creating a pluralized public culture essential for animating basic precepts of democratic public life. It has also worked to provide an institutionalized space for generating new bodies of knowledge, critical methods, and social relationships along side of the old, traditional, and familiar.[11] Academic multiculturalism has provided new discourses for contesting oppressive power within the university in order to produce the formation of new publics of difference. In pluralizing literacy, critical multiculturalists have redefined the pedagogical possibilities for teachers and students to engage their own historical locations and hybridized identities as formative rather than static, as part of a process of border crossing and mode of becoming in which the production of cultural differences is both ongoing and an invaluable asset to democratic public life.[12]

Beyond the Textualization of Politics

As important as these developments have been within higher education, they have not gone far enough in taking seriously the role that academics might play as engaged intellectuals willing to link the imperatives of a radical multiculturalism or a politics of difference with struggles outside of the university. If the academy is to assume a meaningful role in contesting racial injustice, class hierarchies, and the politics of exclusion, progressive academics will have to do more than challenge right wing assaults on the curriculum or the attempt by corporate centrists to reduce multiculturalism to a market strategy; they will also have to challenge those poststructuralist and postmodern versions of multicultural textualism that reduce culture to the logic of signification. This suggests that critical multiculturalism must overcome its insularity and reliance on textual strategies and address a cultural politics of difference that takes seriously the relationship between culture and power, and the implications the latter has for connecting work within the university to broader struggles in the larger society. As Lawrence Grossberg points out, culture must not be equated with the domain of meaning and representation, but rather addressed as "both a form of discursive practice and an analysis of institutional conditions."[13]

Although it is widely recognized that academic multiculturalism's emphasis on textuality has provided an important theoretical service in opening up institutional spaces that enable teachers and students to interrogate different readings of cultural texts and address critically the signifying power of such texts to create and affirm particular social identities, such work has often resulted in reductive pedagogical and political practices. Removed from broader public discourses and analyzed outside of a whole assemblage of other cultural formations, texts either become the reified markers of a narrow version of identity politics or pedagogical resources for uncovering the attributes of specific identities.

Critical multiculturalists, especially those that inhabit literary theory programs, often focus inordinate attention on texts, signs, and disciplinary turfs. Herman Gray, in response to the textualization of politics within the academy, rightfully insists that "By privileging cultural texts over practice as the site of the social and political, the social and historical contexts that shape, situate, and structure cultural texts/products are largely ignored."[14] David Theo Goldberg reinforces Gray's criticism by arguing that cultural politics is not simply a signifying scheme through which identities are produced, but also a "mobilization around material resources regarding education, employment conditions, and political power."[15] Both of these theorists are correct in assuming that the textualization of multiculturalism, with its emphasis on expanding the curricula, its uncritical endorsement of multiple readings, and its use of texts to recover and affirm marginalized identities offers a narrow version of cultural politics. The politics of textuality has little to say about the underlying political and economic forces that keep various social groups marginalized or how to address the often subtle ways in which cultural practices both deploy power and are deployed in material relations of power.[16]

Within many liberal and critical approaches to academic multiculturalism, the politics of meaning becomes relevant only to the degree that it is separated from a broader politics of engagement. Reading texts becomes a hermetic process, once removed from larger social and political contexts, and engages questions of power exclusively within a politics of representation. Such readings largely function to celebrate a textuality that has been diminished to a bloodless formalism and the nonthreatening, if not accommodating, affirmation of indeterminacy as a transgressive aesthetic. Lost here is any semblance of a radical political project that "grounds itself in the study of concrete cultural practices and ... understands that struggles over meaning are inevitably struggles over resources."[17] By failing to connect the study of texts, identity politics, and the politics of difference to the interests of a project that expands the goals of the civil rights movement, human rights campaigns against international tyranny, radical democratic feminist visions, and the opposition to antiwelfare and immigration policies, many critical multiculturalists conceive politics as largely representational or abstractly theoretical.[18]

Equally important to politically viable academic work is the recognition that the struggle over culture is not a substitute for some kind of "real" or "concrete" form of politics, but a crucial "site of the production and struggle over power—where power is understood not necessarily in the form of domination,"[19] but as a productive and mediating force for the making and remaking of diverse and interconnected social, political, and economic contexts that make up daily life. As citizenship becomes increasingly privatized and students are increasingly educated to become consuming subjects rather than critical social subjects, it becomes all the more imperative for critical educators to rethink how the educational force of the culture works to both secure and resist particular identities and values. In opposition to born again multiculturalists, such as Nathan Glazer, who declare that "we are all multiculturalists now," critical educators can foreground the importance of progressive work in higher education as part of a broader radical democratic project to recover and rethink the ways in which culture is related to power and how and where it functions both symbolically and institutionally as an educational, political, and economic force that refuses to live with difference or simply manage it as part of the deadly logic of assimilation and control.

Linking Culture and Power

As more and more young people face a world of increasing poverty, unemployment, and diminished social opportunities, those of us in education can struggle to vindicate the crucial connection between culture and politics in defending higher education as an essential democratic public sphere dedicated to providing students with the knowledge, skills, and values they will need to address some of the most urgent questions of our time. But if addressing multiculturalism as a form of cultural politics within the university is to become a meaningful pedagogical practice, critical academics will have to reevaluate the relationship between culture and power as a starting point for bearing witness to the ethical and political dilemmas that connect the university to other spheres within the broader social landscape. In doing so, we need to become more attentive to how multicultural politics gets worked out in urban spaces and public spheres that are currently experiencing the full force of the right-wing attack on culture and racial difference. It is no longer possible for academics to make a claim to a radical politics of multiculturalism by defining it merely as a set of intellectual options and curriculum imperatives. Critical multiculturalism must also examine actual struggles taking place in the name of cultural difference within institutional sites and cultural formations that bear the brunt of dominant machineries of power designed to exclude, contain, or disadvantage the oppressed. The institutional and cultural spheres bearing the brunt of the racialization of the social order are increasingly located in the public schools, in the criminal justice system, in retrograde anti-immigrant policy legislation, and in the state's ongoing attempts to force welfare recipients into workfare programs.[20]

I am not suggesting that we redefine multiculturalism by moving away from issues of representation or that we shift our pedagogical efforts in the interests of a democratic politics of difference away from the university. On the contrary, we need to vitalize our efforts within the university by connecting the intellectual work we do there with a greater effort to pressing public problems and social responsibilities. A radical approach to multiculturalism must address how material relations of power work to sustain structures of inequality and exploitation in the current racialization of the social order. It must ask specific questions about the forms racial domination and subordination take within the broader public culture and how their organization, operation, and effects both implicate and affect the meaning and purpose of higher education. At stake here is the need for critical educators to give meaning to the belief that academic work matters in its relationship to broader public practices and policies; and that such work holds the possibility for understanding not just how power operates in particular contexts, but also how such knowledge "will better enable people to change the context and hence the relations of power"[21] that inform the inequalities that undermine any viable notion of multiculturalism within spheres as crucial to democracy as the public schools and higher education.

In short, I want to insist that multiculturalism is not simply an educational problem. At its roots, it is about the relationship between politics and power; it's about a historical past and a living present where racist exclusions appear "calculated, brutally rational, and profitable." Embedded within a systemic history of black restriction, subjugation, and white privilege, the politics of multiculturalism is still, as Supreme Court Justice Ruth Bader Ginsburg puts it, "evident in our workplaces, markets and neighborhoods."[22] David Shipler argues powerfully that race and class are the two most powerful determinants shaping American society. After interviewing hundreds of people over a five year period, Shipler's book, *A Country of Strangers,* bears witness to a racism that "is a bit subtler in expression, more cleverly coded in public, but essentially unchanged as one of the 'deep abiding currents' in every day life, in both the simplest and the most complex interactions of whites and blacks."[23]

Although there can be little doubt that racial progress has been achieved in many areas in the last fifty years,[24] it is also true that such progress has not been sustained. This is particularly evident in the dramatic increase in black prisoners and the growth of the prison-industrial complex, crumbling city infrastructures, segregated housing, soaring black and Latino unemployment, exorbitant school dropout rates among black and Latino youth coupled with the realities of failing schools more generally, and deepening inequalities of incomes and wealth between blacks and whites.[25] Pushing against the grain of civil rights reform and racial justice are reactionary and moderate positions ranging from the extremism of right wing skinheads and Jesse Helms–like conservatives to the moderate "color-blind" positions of liberals such as Randall Kennedy.[26]

Crucial to the reemergence of this "new" racism is a cultural politics that plays a determining role in how race shapes our popular unconscious. This is evident in the widespread articles, reviews, and commentaries in the dominant media that give inordinate amounts of time and space to mainstream conservative authors, film makers, and critics who rail against affirmative action, black welfare mothers, and the alleged threats black youth and rap artists pose to middle-class existence. Rather than dismiss such rampant conservatism as either indifferent to the realities of racism or deconstruct its racialized codes to see where such language falls in on itself, educators can engage these commentaries more constructively by analyzing how they function as public discourses, how their privileged meanings work intertextually to resonate with ideologies produced in other sites, and how they serve largely to construct and legitimate racially exclusive practices, policies, and social relations. Central to such a project is the need to engage a multicultural politics that offers students and teachers opportunities to critically engage how certain racialized meanings carried in cultural texts gain the force of common sense in light of how racialized discourses are articulated in other public spheres and institutionalized sites.

In order to deepen the cultural politics of multiculturalism, educators can address questions of culture, power, identity, and representation as part of a broader discourse about public pedagogy and social policy. In this pedagogical approach, power becomes central to the study of cultural texts and practices, and socially relevant problems can be explored through theoretical engagements with wider institutional contexts and public spaces in which multicultural discourses gain their political and economic force. If teaching students to interrogate, challenge, and transform those cultural practices that sustain racism is a central objective of multicultural education, such a pedagogy must be addressed in ways that link cultural texts to the major social problems that animate public life. Texts in this instance would be analyzed as part of a "social vocabulary of culture" that points to how power names, shapes, defines, and constrains relationships between the self and the other, constructs and disseminates what counts as knowledge, and produces representations that provide the context for identity formation.[27]

Within this type of pedagogical approach, multiculturalism must find ways to acknowledge the political character of culture through strategies of understanding and engagement that link an antiracist and radically democratic rhetoric with strategies to transform racist institutionalized structures within and outside of the university.

At its best, critical multiculturalism should forge a connection between reading texts and reading public discourses in order to link the struggle for inclusion with relations of power in the broader society. It is precisely within the realm of a cultural politics that teachers and students develop pedagogical practices that close the gap between intellectual debate and public life not simply as a matter of relevance, but as a process through which students can learn the skills and knowledge to develop informed opinions, make critical choices, and function as citizen activists. Robin D. G. Kelley provides one direction such a project might take. He insightfully argues:

> [Multiculturalism cannot ignore] how segregation strips communities of resources and reproduces inequality. The decline of decent-paying jobs and city services, erosion of public space, deterioration of housing stock and property values, and stark inequalities in education and health care are manifestations of investment strategies under de facto segregation.... [Progressives must address] dismantling racism, bringing oppressed populations into power and moving beyond a black/white binary that renders invisible the struggles of Latino, Asian Americans, Native Americans and other survivors of racist exclusion and exploitation.[28]

Implicit in Kelley's call for action is the recognition that any viable pedagogy and politics of representation needs to address the realities of historical processes, the actuality of economic power, and the range of public spaces and institutions that constitute the embattled terrain of racial difference and struggle. This suggests developing a critical vocabulary for viewing texts not only in relation to other modes of discourse "but also in relationship to contemporaneous social institutions and nondiscursive practices."[29] Within this approach, cultural texts cannot be isolated from the social and political conditions of their production. Nor can the final explanation of such texts be found within the texts themselves. On the contrary, such texts become meaningful when viewed both in relation to other discursive practices and in terms of "the objective social field from which [they] derive."[30] Pedagogically, this suggests addressing how cultural texts in the classroom construct themselves in response to broader institutional arrangements, contexts of power, and the social relations that they both legitimate and help to sustain.

In what follows, I demonstrate the theoretical relevance for developing a multicultural pedagogical practice in which issues of representation and social transformation mutually inform each other. In doing so, I want to focus on a recent Hollywood blockbuster, *187*, that illustrates how pedagogy might be taken up as a public project designed to integrate representations of cultural and racial difference with material relations of power that animate the dynamics of racially exclusive practices and policies in sites that often appear too far removed from the privileged security of the university to be included in the discourse of an academicized multiculturalism.

Racial Coding in the Hollywood Text

In the late 1990s, a number of Hollywood films such as *Dangerous Minds* (1995), *The Substitute I* (1996), and *High School High* (1996) capitalized on the prevailing racially coded popular "wisdom" that public schools are out of control, largely inhabited by illiterate, unmotivated, and violent urban youth who are economically and racially marginalized. The increasingly familiar script suggests a correlation between urban public space and rampant drug use, daily assaults, broken teachers, and schools that do nothing more than contain deviants who are a threat to themselves and everybody else. *187* was a recent addition to this genre, but takes the pathologizing of poor, urban students of color to extremes that go so far beyond existing cinematic conventions that it stands out as a public testimony to broader social and cultural formations within American society that makes the very existence of this blatantly racist film possible.

Directed by Kevin Reynolds and written by Scott Yagemann, a former school teacher, *187* narrates the story of Trevor Garfield (Samuel L. Jackson), a science teacher who rides to school on a bike in order to teach at a high school in Bedford-Stuyvesant. Garfield is portrayed as an idealistic teacher who against all odds is trying to make his classes interesting and do his best to battle daily against the ignorance, chaos, and indifference that characterizes the urban public school in the Hollywood imagination. But the film quickly turns away from a call for educational reform and a defense of those teachers who face a Sisyphean task in trying to improve the lives of urban youth and quickly degenerates into a rationale for abandoning urban public schools and the black and brown students who inhabit their hallways and classrooms.

In the film's opening scenes, students move through metal detectors under the watchful eyes of security guards—props that have become all too familiar to urban high school settings. Clearly, the students in *187* are far removed from the squeaky clean, high-tech classrooms of white suburbia. On the contrary, the school looks more like a prison, and the students, with their rap music blaring in the background, look more like inmates being herded into their cells. The threat of violence is palpable in this school and Garfield confronts it as soon as he enters his classroom and picks up his textbook, which has the figure "187" scrawled all over it. Recognizing that the number is the police code for homicide, Garfield goes to the principal to report what he believes is a threat on his life. The principal tells Garfield he is overreacting, dismissing him with "You know what your problem is? On the one hand, you think someone is going to kill you, and on the other hand, you actually think kids are paying attention in your class." But Garfield hasn't left before the principal confirms his worst fears by revealing that he has told a student in Garfield's class that he has flunked the course. Not only has the principal violated Garfield's privacy, but also the student who he has flunked is on probation and, as a result of the failing grade, will now be sent back to prison. The threat of violence and administrative ineptitude set the stage for a hazardous series of confrontations between Garfield and the public school system. Garfield leaves the principal's office terrified and walks back to his classroom. Each black male student he now sees appears menacing and poised to attack. Shot in slow motion, the scene is genuinely disturbing. And before Garfield reaches his classroom, he is viciously and repeatedly stabbed with a nine-inch nail in the hallway by the black male student he has flunked.

Fifteen months later Garfield has relocated and finds a job as a substitute teacher at John Quincy Adams High School in Los Angeles. The students in this school are mostly Latino, wear oversized pants and torn shirts, carry boom boxes blaring rap music, and appear as menacing as the African American students Garfield taught in Brooklyn. As the camera pans their bodies and expressions, it becomes clear that what unites these inner-city students of color is a culture that is dangerous, crime-ridden, and violent. Assigned to teach his class in a bungalow, Garfield's first day is a nightmare as students taunt him, throw paper wads at him, and call him "bitch." Garfield has moved from New York to California only to find himself in a public high school setting that has the look and feel of hell. Images of heat rising from the pavement, pulsating rap music, shots of graffiti, and oversized shadows of gang members playing basketball filtering through the classroom window paint an ominous picture of what Garfield is about to experience.

But Garfield has to face more than dangerous students. His new principal prides himself on never having been a teacher, refers to students as clients, and makes it clear that his primary concern is to avoid potential lawsuits. Hollywood's message in this case is clear: public schools are filled with administrators who would rather cater to a liberal discourse about the civil rights of students—who clearly don't deserve any—than protect the welfare of teachers who face the threat of daily violence.

Garfield's fellow teachers are no better. The first teacher he meets, Dave Childress (John Heard), is an alcoholic burnout who stashes a .357 magnum in his desk drawer, thoroughly hates his students, and, we later learn, has had sexual relations with a very young, emotionally shaken, Latina student. Hanging on for the paycheck, Childress serves as a reminder of what such schools do to teachers. Robbed of his passion, Childress regards every kid as a social menace or macho punk, waiting to kill or be killed.

Garfield does strike up a friendship and romance with Ellen Henry (Kelly Rowan), a perky, blond computer science teacher but it soon turns sour as the bleak and dangerous environment in which they find themselves eventually pushes Garfield over the edge. Ellen tries to draw close to Garfield, but he is too battered and isolated, telling Ellen at one point that when he was assaulted in New York, it robbed him of his "passion, my spark, my unguarded self—I miss them."

Garfield's descent into madness begins when his bungalow is completely trashed by the gang members in his class. He becomes edgy, living life in a shadow of fear heightened by his past. Ellen then tells Garfield that Benny, a particularly vicious gang member in his class, has threatened to hurt her, and indicates to Garfield that she doesn't know what to do. Soon afterwards Benny disappears, but her troubles are not over as Benny's sidekick, Cesar, and his friends kill her dog. As a result, Cesar becomes the object of vigilante justice. Roaming drunk near the LA freeway, he is stalked, shot with a spiked arrow, and while unconscious his finger is cut off. The tension mounts as Ellen finds Benny's rosary beads in Garfield's apartment and confronts him with the evidence that he might be the killer. Garfield is immune to their reproach, arguing that someone has to take responsibility since the system will not protect "us" from "them." Ellen tells Garfield she doesn't know him anymore, and Garfield replies, "I am a teacher just like you." As the word circulates that Garfield may be the vigilante killer and assailant, the principal moves fast to protect the school from a lawsuit and fires him. Garfield, now completely broken, goes home and is soon visited by Cesar and his gang who, inspired by the film, *The Deer Hunter,* force Garfield into a game of Russian roulette. With little to lose, Garfield tells Cesar he is not really a man, and ups the stakes of the game by taking Cesar's turn. Garfield pulls the trigger and kills himself. Forced into questioning his own manhood, Cesar decides to take his turn, puts the gun to his head, and fatally shoots himself as well. In the final scene of the film, as a student is reading a graduation speech about how teachers rarely get any respect, the shot switches to Ellen who is in her classroom. Ellen takes her framed teaching certificate off the wall, throws it into the wastebasket, and walks out of the school.

Accessing a Pedagogy of the Cultural Object

Pedagogically, films such as *187* can be interrogated initially by analyzing both the common sense assumptions that inform them as well as the absences and exclusions that limit the range of meanings and information available to audiences. Analyzing such films as public discourses also provides pedagogical opportunities to engage complex institutional frameworks that provide the conditions for the construction, legitimation, and meaning of such cultural texts. As public discourses, these cultural texts can be addressed in terms of how they are constituted as objects that gain their relevance through their relationship to other social institutions, resources, and nondiscursive practices. In this instance, *187* would be taken up as a discursive practice whose effects might be addressed in relation to struggles over race in related contexts where struggles over meaning and representation are connected to struggles over power, social agency, and material resources. Some of these issues are illustrated below.

187 provides ample representations of students of color as the pathological other, and public schools as not only dysfunctional but also as an imminent threat to the dominant society. Represented as a criminalized underclass, black and brown students in *187* are viewed as dangerous and public schools as holding centers that contain such students through the heavy-handed use of high-tech monitoring systems and military-style authority. Reinforcing such stereotypes is a decontextualized and depoliticized cinematic narrative that erases the conditions that produce such denigrating images of inner-city public schools—poverty, family turmoil, violent neighborhoods, unemployment, crumbling school buildings, lack of material resources, or iniquitous tax structures. In this instance, *187* represents more than a text that portrays a particularly offensive image of urban schools and minority students, it also participates as a public pedagogy in enabling, legitimizing, and reinforcing discursive practices whose effect is to condemn the children of the urban poor to public schools increasingly subject to electronic surveillance, private police forces, padlocks, and alarms suggestive of prisons or "war zones."[31]

Clearly, if the dominant codes at work in such a film are to be questioned, it is imperative for students to address how the absences in such a film tie it to prevailing discourses about public education, multiculturalism, and the ongoing assault on minorities of class and color in and outside of public schooling. Marking such absences is crucial to understanding such a film— the refusal to point to the need for smaller class sizes, inspiring teachers, visionary administrators, and ample learning resources—but such absences become meaningful when understood within a broader struggle over issues of racial identity, power, representation, and everyday life.

Films like *187* carry the logic of racial stereotyping to a new level and represent one of the most egregious examples of how popular cultural texts can be used to demonize black and Latino youth while reproducing a consensus of common sense that legitimates racist policies of either containment or abandonment in the inner cities. But such instances of racial coding cannot reside merely within the boundaries of the text to be fully understood as part of the broader landscape of racial injustice. Depictions of urban youth as dangerous, pathological, and violent, in turn, must be located in terms of where different possibilities of uses and effects of such representations may ultimately reside in contexts of everyday life that are at the forefront of multicultural struggles. For example, the depictions of youth in *187* resonate powerfully with the growth of a highly visible criminal justice system whose get-tough policies fall disproportionately on poor black and brown youth. What is the potential effect of a film such as *187* in addressing the political, racial, and economic conditions that promote a specious, yet celebrated, "war on drugs," whose policies threaten to wipe out a whole generation of young black males who are increasingly incarcerated in prisons and jails, and whose populations are growing at the rate of about seven percent a year and costs more than 30 billion annually to operate?[32] The figures are disturbing:

> Between 1983 and 1998 the number of prisoners in the U.S. increased from 650,000 to more than 1.7 million. About 60 percent of that number are African Americans and Latinos. More than one-third of all young black men in their 20s are currently in jail, on probation or parole, or awaiting trial. We are now adding 1,200 new inmates to US jails and prisons each week, and adding about 260 new prison beds each day.[33]

This state of affairs is compounded by the disturbing fact that as a result of serving time nearly half of the next generation of black males will forfeit their rights to vote in several states. How might a cultural text such as *187* be used to address the relationship between the increase in prison growth and the plight caused by industrial downscaling and rising unemployment among young black men across America's inner cities in the 1990s? What might it mean for students to address their own responses to the moral panics concerning crime and race that have swept across the middle classes in the last decade, made manifest in strong electoral support for harsh crime laws and massive increases in prison growth?[34] At the very least, educators can address *187* not merely in terms of what such a text might mean but how it functions within a set of complex social reactions that create the conditions of which it is a part and from which it stems. Larry Grossberg insightfully argues that such a pedagogy would:

> involve the broader exploration of the way in which discursive practices construct and participate in the machinery by which the ways people live their lives are themselves produced and controlled. Rather than looking for the "said" or trying to derive the saying from the said, rather than asking what texts mean or what people do with texts, [a critical pedagogy] would be concerned with what discursive practices do in the world.[35]

Engaging the potential discursive effects of films such as *187* might mean discussing the implication of this Hollywood film in appropriating the name of the controversial California proposition to deny mostly nonwhite students access to public schools. Or engaging how *187* contributes to a public discourse that rationalizes both the demonization of minority youth and the defunding of public and higher education at a time when in states such as California, "approximately 22,555 African Americans attend a four-year public university ... while 44,792 (almost twice as many) African Americans are in prison [and] this figure does not include all the African Americans who are in county jails or the California Youth authority or those on probation or parole."[36]

Hollywood films such as *187* must be addressed and understood within a broader set of policy debates about education and crime that often serve to legitimate policies that disempower poor and racially marginalized youth. For example, nationwide state spending for corrections has increased 95 percent over the last decade, while spending on higher education decreased 6 percent. Similarly, "over a ten year period, the number of correctional officers increased four times the rate of public higher education faculty." Again, it is not surprising that the chosen setting for *187* is primarily California, a state that now "spends more on corrections (9.4 percent of the General Fund) than on higher education."[37] While it would be absurd to suggest to students that films such as *187* are responsible for recent government spending allocations, they do take part in a public pedagogy and representational politics that cannot be separated from a growing racial panic and fear over minorities, the urban poor, and immigrants.

As public discourses, films such as *187, The Substitute I* and *II, Dangerous Minds,* and *Belly* fail to rupture the racial stereotypes that support harsh, discriminatory crime policies and growing incidents of police brutality, such as the highly publicized torture of Abner Louima by Brooklyn patrolmen or the recent shooting of Amadou Diallo by four New York City policemen, who riddled his body and an apartment building vestibule with forty-one bullets, in spite of the fact that Diallo was unarmed. Such films also have little to say about police assaults on poor black neighborhoods such as those conducted by former LA police Chief Daryl Gates against south central Los Angeles. Exploiting the race-based moral panics that fuels popular antagonism to affirmative action, immigrants, bilingual education, the inner city, and the unmarried "welfare queen," films such as *187* capitalize on modes of exclusion through what Jimmie Reeves and Richard Campbell call the "discourse of discrimination" and the "spectacle of stigmatization." Within this discourse, urban black and brown youth are depicted as "the pathological Other—a delinquent beyond rehabilitation."[38] What is unique about *187* is that it explores cinematically what the logical conclusion might be in dealing with urban youth for whom reform is no longer on the national agenda, for which containment or the militarization of school space seem both inadequate and too compromising. Carried to the extreme, *187* flirts with the ultimate white supremacist logic, that is, extermination and genocide of those others deemed beyond the pale of social reform, inhuman, and despicable. *187* capitalizes on the popular conception reported endlessly in the media that public education is not safe for white, middle-class children, that racial violence is rampant in the public schools, that minority students have turned classroom discipline into a joke, that administrators are paralyzed by insensitive bureaucracies, and the only thing that teachers and students share is the desire to survive the day. But the implications of cultural texts such as *187* become meaningful not just as strategies of understanding and critical engagement that raise questions about related discourses, texts, and social issues, they also become meaningful in probing what it might mean to move beyond the sutured institutional space of the classroom to address social issues in related spheres marked by racial injustices and unequal relations of power.

The popularity of such films as *187* in the heyday of academic multiculturalism points to the need, in light of such representations, for educators to expand their understanding of politics as part of a broader project designed to address major social issues in the name of a multiracial democracy. This suggests getting beyond reducing multiculturalism to simply the study of texts or discourse, and addressing multicultural politics as part of the struggle over power and resources in a variety of public spheres. This might mean engaging and fighting to change how the "economics of school funding and school policy [work to] sustain segregation in American public education [through] inhuman fiscal policies that have ensured the continuous impoverishment of schools attended wholly by black or Hispanic schoolchildren."[39] Or what it might mean for students to engage in a politics of multiculturalism aimed at reforming a criminal justice system that disproportionately incarcerates and punishes minorities of class and color. Issues of representation and identity in this case offer the opportunity for multicultural educators to explore and challenge both the strengths and limits of cultural texts. This suggests developing a pedagogy that promotes a social vocabulary of cultural difference that links strategies of understanding to strategies of engagement, that recognizes the limits of the university as a site for social engagement, and refuses to reduce politics to matters of language and meaning that erase broader issues of systemic political power, institutional control, economic ownership, and the distribution of cultural and intellectual resources in a wide variety of public spaces.

I recognize academics cannot become public intellectuals by the mere force of will, given the professional and institutional constraints under which they operate. But at the same time, if multiculturalism is not going to abandon the world of public politics and take seriously the link between culture and power, progressive educators will have to rethink collectively what it means to link the struggle for change within the university to struggles for change in the broader society. Combining theoretical rigor with social relevance may be risky politically and pedagogically, but the promise of a multicultural democracy far outweighs the security and benefits that accompany a retreat into academic irrelevance and color-blind professionalism.

Notes

1. Norman Geras, *The Contract of Mutual Indifference: Political Philosophy after the Holocaust* (New York: Verso, 1998), p. 26.

2. Multiculturalism covers an extraordinary range of views about the central issues of culture, diversity, identity, nationalism, and politics. Moreover, the theoretical and political slipperiness of the term immediately makes suspect any analysis that moves from the specific to the general in engaging a topic as diverse as multiculturalism. And yet the arbitrary nature of such an analysis seems necessary if certain general tendencies that characterize a field are to be addressed and critically engaged, in spite of the presence of marginal discourses that are sometimes at odds with such tendencies. Some important recent books that address the multiple meanings of multiculturalism include Henry A. Giroux, *Living Dangerously: Multiculturalism and the Politics of Culture* (New York: Peter Lang, 1993); Henry A. Giroux, *Border Crossings* (New York: Routledge, 1992); David Theo Goldberg, ed., *Multiculturalism: A Critical Reader* (Cambridge, MA: Basil Blackwell, 1994); Avery Gordon and Christopher Newfield, eds. *Mapping Multiculturalism* (Minneapolis: University of Minnesota Press, 1996); David Bennett, ed., *Multicultural States* (New York: Routledge, 1998).

3. For an extensive topography and critical analysis of diverse positions in multicultural education, see Joe L. Kincheloe and Shirley R. Steinberg, *Changing Multiculturalism* (New York: Open University Press, 1997).

4. A classic example of this type of work is Becky W. Thompson and Sangeeta Tyagi, eds., *Beyond a Dream Deferred: Multicultural Education and Politics* (Minneapolis: University of Minnesota Press, 1993).

5. A classic example of this work can be found in Lawrence Levine, *The Opening of the American Mind* (Boston: Beacon Press, 1996).

6. On the reforms in general education that have been enacted under the banner of multiculturalism, see Michael Geyer, "Multiculturalism and the Politics of General Education," *Critical Inquiry 19* (Spring 1993): 499–533.

7. One important text in this genre is Gloria Ansaldua, ed., *Making Face, Making Soul: Haciendo Caras: Creative and Critical Perspectives by Women of Color* (San Francisco: Aunt Lute Foundation, 1990). I would include here the emergence of critical scholarship on whiteness studies. The literature is too extensive to cite but some recent work includes: Richard Delgado and Jean Stefanic, eds., *Critical Whiteness Studies* (Philadelphia: Temple University Press, 1997); Ruth Frankenberg, ed., *Displacing Whiteness* (Durham: Duke University Press, 1997); Mike Hill, ed., *Whiteness: A Critical Reader* (New York: New York University Press, 1997); Annalee Newitz and Matthew Wray, eds., *White Trash* (New York: Routledge, 1997); David R. Roediger, ed., *Black on White: Black Writers on What It Means to Be White* (New York: Schocken Books, 1998); Abby L. Ferber, *White Man Falling* (Boulder: Rowman and Littlefield, 1998). For an interesting essay on white studies, see Mike Hill, " 'Souls Undressed': The Rise and Fall of New Whiteness Studies," *Review of Education, Pedagogy, and Cultural Studies 20,* no. 3 (1998): 229–239.

8. See, for example, Michael Awkward, *Negotiating Difference* (Chicago: University of Chicago Press, 1995).

9. This notion of breaking into common sense is taken from Homi Bhabha in Gary Olson and Lynn Worsham, "Staging the Politics of Difference: Homi Bhabha's Critical Literacy—An Interview," *Journal of Composition Theory 18,* no. 3 (1998): 367.

10. John Beverly, "Pedagogy and Subalternity: Mapping the Limits of Academic Knowledge," in Rolland G. Paulston, ed., *Social Cartography* (New York: Garland, 1996), p. 351–352.

11. For a selection of articles that address these issues, see David Theo Goldberg, ed., *Multiculturalism: A Critical Reader* (Boston: Basil Blackwell, 1994).

12. On the issue of multiculturalism and border crossing, see Henry A. Giroux, *Border Crossings* (New York: Routledge, 1992).

13. Lawrence Grossberg, "Cultural Studies: What's in a Name?" *Bringing It All Back Home: Essays on Cultural Studies* (Durham: Duke University Press, 1997), p. 268.

14. Herman Gray, "Is Cultural Studies Inflated?" in Cary Nelson and Dilip Parameshwar Goankar, eds., *Disciplinarity and Dissent in Cultural Studies* (New York: Routledge, 1996), p. 211.

15. David Theo Goldberg, "Introduction-Multicultural Conditions," in David Theo Goldberg, ed., *Multiculturalism: A Critical Reader* (Cambridge, MA: Basil Blackwell, 1994), p. 13–14.

16. Of course, there are many exceptions to this rule, but they are marginal to the multiculturalist discourses within the university. See, for example, many of the essays in Cameron McCarthy and Warren Crichlow, eds., *Race, Identity, and Representation in Education* (New York: Routledge, 1993) as well as: William V. Flores and Rina Benmayor, *Latino Cultural Citizenship* (Boston: Beacon Press, 1997); E. San Juan, Jr., *Articulations of Power in Ethnic and Racial Studies in the United States* (New Jersey: Humanities Press, 1992); Peter McLaren, *Revolutionary Multiculturalism* (Boulder: Westview Press, 1997); Slavoj Zizek, "Multiculturalism, or, the Cultural Logic of Multinational Capitalism," *New Left Review* 225 (September/October 1997): 28–51.

17. George Lipsitz, "Listening to Learn and Learning to Listen: Popular Culture, Cultural Theory, and American Studies," *American Quarterly 42,* no. 4 (December 1990): 621.

18. Larry Grossberg argues that Edward Said's *Orientalism* is a classic example of a text that focuses on questions of difference almost entirely in terms of identity and subjectivity while ignoring the related issues of materialism and power. See Lawrence Grossberg, "Identity and Cultural Studies. Is That All There Is?" in Stuart Hall and Paul Du Gay, ed., *Questions of Cultural Identity* (Thousand Oaks: Sage, 1996), pp. 87–107.

19. Grossberg, "Cultural Studies: What's in a Name?" Op cit., p. 248.

20. Manning Marable, "Beyond Color-Blindness," *Nation* (December 14, 1998): 31.

21. Lawrence Grossberg, "Cultural Studies: What's in a Name?" Op cit., pp. 252–253.

22. Ginsburg cited in Editorial, "Race On Screen and Off," *Nation* (December 29, 1997): 6.

23. Shipler summarized in Jack H. Geiger, "The Real World of Race," *Nation* (December 1, 1998): 27. See also, David Shipler, "Reflections on Race," *Tikkun 13,* no. 1 (1998): 59, 78; David Shipler, *A Country of Strangers: Blacks and Whites in America* (New York: Vintage, 1998).

24. Ellen Willis argues that the two major upheavals to America's racial hierarchy have been the destruction of the Southern caste system of and the subversion of whiteness as an unquestioned norm. She also argues rightly that to dismiss these

achievements as having done little to change racist power relations insults people who have engaged in these struggles. See Ellen Willis, "The Up and Up: On the Limits of Optimism," *Transition 7,* no. 2 (1998): 44–61.

25. For a compilation of figures suggesting the ongoing presence of racism in American society, see Ronald Walters, "The Criticality of Racism," *Black Scholar 26,* no. 1 (Winter 1996): 2–8; Children's Defense Fund, *The State of America's Children* (Boston: Beacon Press, 1998).

26. For a devastating critique of Randall Kennedy's move to the right, see Derrick Bell, "The Strange Career of Randall Kennedy," *New Politics 7,* no. 1 (Summer 1998): 55–69.

27. Katya Gibel Azoulay, "Experience, Empathy and Strategic Essentialism," *Cultural Studies 11,* no. 1 (1997): 91.

28. Robin D. G. Kelley, "Integration: What's Left?" *Nation* (December 14, 1998): 18.

29. Cited in Randall Johnson, "Editor's Introduction: Pierre Bourdieu onto make learning part of the process of social change itself." Art, Literature and Culture," in Pierre Bourdieu, *The Field of Cultural Production* (New York: Columbia University Press, 1993), p. 19.

30. Randall Johnson, "Editor's Introduction: Pierre Bourdieu onto make learning part of the process of social change itself." Art, Literature and Culture," in Pierre Bourdieu, *The Field of Cultural Production* (New York: Columbia University Press, 1993), p. 17.

31. This issue is taken up in John Devine, *Maximum Security: The Culture of Violence in Inner-City Schools* (Chicago: University of Chicago Press, 1996). Unfortunately, Devine's remedy for the militarization of school space is to blame students for not being civil enough. Hence, Devine undermines an interesting analysis of the culture of violence in schools by framing his solutions within a paradigm that is utterly privatized and trapped within the discourse of the genteel brigade led by ultra self-righteous moralizers such as William Bennett.

32. These figures are cited in Fox Butterfield, "Crime Keeps on Falling, But Prisons Keep on Filling," *New York Times,* September 28, 1997, p. 1. Jimmie Reeves and Richard Campbell provide a more extensive picture prison growth in the United States: "During the Reagan era, in fact, the U.S. prison population nearly doubled (from 329,821 in 1980 to 627,402 in 1989) as the number of drug arrests nationwide increased from 471,000 in 1980 to 1,247,000 in 1989. By 1990 the United States had the highest incarceration rate in the world: 9,426 per 100,000 compared to 333 per 100,000 in South Africa, its closest competitor). In that same year—when about half the inmates in federal prisons were there on drug offenses—African Americans made up almost half of the U.S. prison population, and about one in four young black males in their twenties were either in jail, on parole, or on probation (compared to only 6 percent for white males)." Cited in Jimmie L. Reeves and Richard Campbell, *Cracked Coverage: Television News, the Anti-cocaine Crusade, and the Reagan Legacy* (Durham: Duke University Press, 1994), p. 41.

33. Manning Marable, "Beyond Color-Blindness," *Nation* (December 14, 1998): 31.

34. These issues are taken up in David Theo Goldberg, "Surplus Value: The Political Economy of Prisons," in Joy James, ed., *Police, Detention, Prisons* (New York: St. Martin's Press, forthcoming), pp. 3–25.

35. Cited in Lawrence Grossberg, "The Victory of Culture, Part I," University of North Carolina at Chapel Hill, unpublished manuscript, February 1998, p. 27.

36. Figures cited in "From Classrooms to Cell Blocks: How Prison Building Affects Higher Education and African American Enrollment in California" (San Francisco, CA: Justice Policy Institute, 1996), p. 2.

37. Cited in "From Classrooms to Cell Blocks," Justice Policy Institute (1996), p. 2.

38. These quotes come from Jimmie L. Reeves and Richard Campbell, *Cracked Coverage: Television News, the Anti-cocaine Crusade, and the Reagan Legacy* (Durham: Duke University Press, 1994), pp. 40–41.

39. Both quotes are from Michael Berube, "Disuniting America Again," *Journal of the Midwest Modern Language Association 26,* no. 1 (Spring 1993): 41.

11
Youth, Higher Education, and the Crisis of Public Time
Educated Hope and the Possibility of a Democratic Future

‹ℰ›

Children are the future of any society. If you want to know the future of a society look at the eyes of the children. If you want to maim the future of any society, you simply maim the children. The struggle for the survival of our children is the struggle for the survival of our future. The quantity and quality of that survival is the measurement of the development of our society.
—Ngugi Wa Thiong'O[1]

Youth and the Crisis of the Future

Any discourse about the future has to begin with the issue of youth because more than any other group, youth embody the projected dreams, desires, and commitment of a society's obligations to the future. This echoes a classical principle of modernity in which youth both symbolized society's responsibility to the future and offered a measure of its progress. For most of the 20th century, Americans embraced as a defining feature of politics that all levels of government would assume a large measure of responsibility for providing the resources, social provisions, security, and modes of education that simultaneously offered young people a future as it expanded the meaning and depth of a substantive democracy. In many respects, youth not only registered symbolically the importance of modernity's claim to progress, they also affirmed the importance of the liberal, democratic tradition of the social contract in which adult responsibility was mediated through a willingness to fight for the rights of children, enact reforms that invested in their future, and provide the educational conditions necessary for them to make use of the freedoms they have while learning how to be critical citizens. Within such a modernist project, democracy was linked to the well being of youth, while the status of how a society imagined democracy and its future was contingent on how it viewed its responsibility towards future generations.

253

But the category of youth did more than affirm modernity's social contract rooted in a conception of the future in which adult commitment and intergenerational solidarity were articulated as a vital public service, it also affirmed those vocabularies, values and social relations central to a politics capable of both defending vital institutions as a public good, and contributing to the quality of public life. Such a vocabulary was particularly important for higher education, which often defined and addressed its highest ideals through the recognition that how it educated youth was connected to both the democratic future it hoped for and its claim as an important public sphere.

Yet, at the dawn of the new millennium, it is not at all clear that we believe any longer in youth, the future, or the social contract, even in its minimalist version. Since the Reagan/Thatcher revolution of the 1980s, we have been told that there is no such thing as society and, indeed, following that nefarious pronouncement, institutions committed to public welfare have been disappearing ever since. Those of us who, against the prevailing common sense, insist on the relationship between higher education and the future of democracy have to face a disturbing reversal in priorities with regard to youth and education, which now defines the United States and other regions under the reign of neoliberalism.[2] Rather than being cherished as a symbol of the future, youth are now seen as a threat to be feared and a problem to be contained. A seismic change has taken place in which youth are now being framed as both a generation of suspects and a threat to public life. If youth once symbolized the moral necessity to address a range of social and economic ills, they are now largely portrayed as the source of most of society's problems. Hence, youth now constitute a crisis that has less to do with improving the future than with denying it. A concern for children is the defining absence in almost any discourse about the future and the obligations this implies for adult society. To witness the abdication of adult responsibility to children we need look no further than the current state of children in America who once served as a "kind of symbolic guarantee that America still had a future, which it still believed in a future, and that it was crucial to America to invest in that future."[3]

No longer "viewed as a privileged sign and embodiment of the future,"[4] youth are now demonized by the popular media and derided by politicians looking for quick-fix solutions to crime, joblessness, and poverty. In a society deeply troubled by their presence, youth prompt a public rhetoric of fear, control, and surveillance, which translates into social policies that signal the shrinking of democratic public spheres, the highjacking of civic culture, and the increasing militarization of public space. Equipped with police and drug sniffing dogs, though not necessarily teachers or textbooks, public schools increasingly resemble prisons. Students begin to look more like criminal suspects who need to be searched, tested, and observed under the watchful eye of administrators who appear to be less concerned with educating them than with containing their every move. Nurturance, trust, and respect now give way to fear, disdain, and suspicion. In many suburban malls, young people, especially urban youth of color, cannot shop or walk around without having appropriate identification cards or being in the company of a parent. Children have fewer rights than almost any other group and fewer institutions protecting these rights. Consequently, their voices and needs are almost completely absent from the debates, policies, and legislative practices that are constructed in terms of their needs.

Instead of providing a decent education to poor young people, American society offers them the growing potential of being incarcerated, buttressed by the fact that the U.S. is one of the few countries in the world that sentences minors to death and spends "three times more on each incarcerated citizen than on each public school pupil."[5] Instead of guaranteeing them food, decent health care, and shelter, we serve them more standardized tests; instead of providing them with vibrant public spheres, we offer them a commercialized culture in which consumerism is the only obligation of citizenship. But in the hard currency of human suffering, children pay a heavy price in one of the richest democracies in the world: 20 percent of children are poor during the first three years of life and more than 13.3 million live in poverty; 9.2 million children lack health insurance; millions lack affordable child care and decent early childhood education; in many states more money is being spent on prison construction than on education; the infant mortality rate in the United States is the highest of any other industrialized nations. When broken down along racial categories, the figures become even more despairing. For example, "In 1998, 36 percent of black and 34 percent of Hispanic children lived in poverty, compared with 14 percent of white children."[6] In some cities, such as the District of Columbia, the child poverty rate is as high as 45 percent.[7] While the United States ranks first in military technology, military exports, defense expenditures and the number of millionaires and billionaires, it is ranked 18th among the advanced industrial nations in the gap between rich and poor children, 12th in the percent of children in poverty, 17th in the efforts to lift children out of poverty, and 23rd in infant mortality.[8] One of the most shameful figures on youth as reported by Jennifer Egan, a writer for the *New York Times,* indicates that "1.4 million children are homeless in America for a time in any given year ... and these children make up 40 percent of the nation's homeless population."[9] In short, economically, politically and culturally, the situation of youth in the United States is intolerable and obscene. It is all the more unforgivable since President Bush insisted during the 2000 campaign that "the biggest percentage of our budget should go to children's education." He then passed a 2002 budget in which 40 times more money went for tax cuts for the wealthiest 1 percent of the population rather than for education.[10] But

Bush's insensitivity to American children represents more than a paean to the rich since he also passed a punitive welfare reform bill that requires poor, young mothers to work a 40-hour week while at the same time cutting low-income childcare programs.

Youth have become the central site onto which class and racial anxieties are projected. Their very presence in an age where there is no such thing as society represents the broken promises of democracy. Corporate deregulation and downsizing and a collective fear of the consequences wrought by systemic class inequalities, racism, and a culture of "infectious greed" have created a generation of displaced and unskilled youth who have been expelled from the "universe of moral obligations."[11] Youth within the economic, political, and cultural geography of neoliberal capitalism occupy a degraded borderland in which the spectacle of commodification exists side by side with the imposing threat of the prison-industrial complex and the elimination of basic civil liberties. As neoliberalism disassociates economics from its social costs, "the political state has become the corporate state."[12] Under such circumstances, the state does not disappear, but, as Pierre Bourdieu has brilliantly reminded us, is refigured as its role in providing social provisions, intervening on behalf of public welfare, and regulating corporate plunder is weakened.[13] The neoliberal state no longer invests in solving social problems, it now punishes those who are caught in the downward spiral of its economic policies. Punishment, incarceration, and surveillance represent the face of the new state. One consequence is that the implied contract between the state and citizens is broken and social guarantees for youth as well as civic obligations to the future vanish from the agenda of public concern. Similarly, as market values supplant civic values, it becomes increasingly difficult "to translate private worries into public issues and, conversely, to discern public issues in private troubles."[14] Alcoholism, homelessness, poverty, and illiteracy, among other issues, are not seen as social but as individual problems—matters of character, individual fortitude, and personal responsibility. In light of the increased antiterrorism campaign waged by the Bush administration, it becomes easier to militarize domestic space, criminalize social problems, and escape from the responsibilities of the present while destroying all possibilities of a truly democratic future. Moreover, the social costs of the complex cultural and economic operations of this assault can no longer be ignored by educators, parents, and other concerned citizens.

The war against youth, in part, can be understood within those fundamental values and practices that characterize a rapacious, neoliberal capitalism. For many young people and adults today, the private sphere has become the only space in which to imagine any sense of hope, pleasure, or possibility. Culture as an activity in which people actually produce the conditions of their own agency through dialogue, community participation, resistance and political struggle is being replaced by a "climate of cultural and linguistic privatization" in which culture becomes something you consume and the only kind of speech that is acceptable is that of the savvy shopper.[15] Neoliberalism, with its emphasis on market forces and profit margins, narrows the legitimacy of the public sphere by redefining it around the related issues of privatization, deregulation, consumption, and safety. Big government, recalled from exile after September 11th, is now popularly presented as a guardian of security—security not in terms of providing adequate social provisions or a social safety net, but with increasing the state's role as a policing force. The new emphasis on national security has resulted in the ongoing abridgement of basic freedoms and dissent, the criminalization of social problems, and the prioritizing of penal methods over social investments. Ardent consumers and disengaged citizens provide fodder for a growing cynicism and depoliticization of public life at a time when there is an increasing awareness not just of corporate corruption, financial mismanagement, and systemic greed, but also of the recognition that a democracy of critical citizens is being replaced quickly by an ersatz democracy of consumers. The desire to protect market freedoms and wage a war against terrorism, ironically, has not only ushered in a culture of fear but has also dealt a lethal blow to civil freedoms. Resting in the balance of this contradiction is both the fate of democracy and the civic health and future of a generation of children and young people.

Under this insufferable climate of increased repression and unabated exploitation, young people become the new casualties in an ongoing war against justice, freedom, citizenship, and democracy. What is happening to children in America and what are its implications for addressing the future of higher education? Lawrence Grossberg argues that "the current rejection of childhood as the core of our social identity is, at the same time, a rejection of the future as an affective investment."[16] But the crisis of youth not only signals a dangerous state of affairs for the future, it also portends a crisis in the very idea of the political and ethical constitution of the social and the possibility of articulating the relevance of democracy itself; it is in reference to the crisis of youth, the social, and democracy that I want to address the relationship between higher education and the future.

Higher Education and the Crisis of the Social

There is a prominent educational tradition in the United States extending from Thomas Jefferson and W. E. B. Dubois to John Dewey and C. Wright Mills in which the future of the university is premised on the recognition that in order for freedom to flourish in the worldly space of the public realm, citizens had to be educated for the task of self-government. John Dewey, for example, argued that higher education should provide the conditions for people to involve themselves in the deepest problems of society, to acquire the knowledge, skills, and ethical responsibility necessary for "reasoned participation in democratically organized publics."[17] C. Wright Mills challenged schooling as a form of corporate training and called for fashioning higher education within a public philosophy committed to a radical conception of citizenship, civic engagement, and public wisdom.[18] Education in this context was linked to public life through democratic values such as equality, justice, and freedom, rather than as an adjunct of the corporation whose knowledge and values were defined largely through the prism of commercial interests. Education was crucial to a notion of individual agency and public citizenship, integral to defending the relationship between an autonomous society—rooted in an ever-expanding process of self-examination, critique, and reform—and autonomous individuals, for whom critical inquiry is propelled by the need to engage in an ongoing pursuit of ethics and justice as a matter of public good. In many ways, higher education has been faithful, at least in theory, to a project of modern politics, the purpose of which was to create citizens capable of defining and implementing universal goals such as freedom, equality, and justice as part of a broader attempt to deepen the relationship between an expanded notion of the social and the enabling ground of a vibrant democracy.

Within the last two decades a widespread pessimism about public life and politics has developed in the United States. Individual interests now outweigh collective concerns as market ideals have taken precedence over democratic values. Moreover, the ethos of citizenship has been stripped of its political dimensions and is now reduced to the obligations of consumerism. In the vocabulary of neoliberalism, the public collapses into the personal, and the personal becomes "the only politics there is, the only politics with a tangible referent or emotional valence,"[19] and it is within such an utterly personal discourse that human actions are shaped and agency is privatized. Under neoliberalism, hope becomes dystopian as the public sphere disappears and, as Peter Beilharz argues, "politics becomes banal, for there is not only an absence of citizenship but a striking absence of agency."[20] As power is increasingly separated from the specificity of traditional politics and public obligations, corporations are less subject to the control of the state and "there is a strong impulse to displace political sovereignty with the sovereignty of the market, as if the latter has a mind and morality of its own."[21] Under the auspices of neoliberalism, the language of the social is either devalued or ignored altogether as the idea of the public sphere is equated with a predatory space, rife with danger and disease—as in reference to public restrooms, public transportation, and urban public schools. Dreams of the future are now modeled on the narcissistic, privatized, and self-indulgent needs of consumer culture and the dictates of the alleged free market. Mark Taylor, a social critic turned apologist for the alleged free market, both embodies and captures the sentiment well with his comment: "Insofar as you want to engage in practice responsibly, you have to play with the hand you're dealt. And the hand we're dealt seems to me to be one in which the market has certainly won out over other kinds of systems."[22] There is more at stake here than another dominant media story about a left academic who finally sees the entrepreneurial light. The narrative points to something much larger. Samuel Weber has suggested that what seems to be involved in this transformation is "a fundamental and political redefinition of the social value of public services in general, and of universities and education in particular."[23]

Within this impoverished sense of politics and public life, the university is gradually being transformed into a training ground for the corporate workforce, rendering obsolete any notion of higher education as a crucial public sphere in which critical citizens and democratic agents are formed. As universities become increasingly strapped for money, corporations provide the needed resources for research and funds for endowed chairs, exerting a powerful influence on both the hiring of faculty, and how research is conducted and for what purposes. In addition, universities now offer up buildings and stadiums as billboards for brand name corporations in order to procure additional sources of revenue while also adopting the values, management styles, cost-cutting procedures, and the language of excellence that has been the hallmark of corporate culture. Under the reign of neoliberalism and corporate culture, the boundaries between commercial culture and public culture become blurred as universities rush to embrace the logic of industrial management while simultaneously forfeiting those broader values both central to a democracy and capable of limiting the excesses of corporate power. Although the university has always had ties to industry, there is a new intimacy between higher education and corporate culture, characterized by what Larry Hanley calls a "new, quickened symbiosis."[24] As Masao Miyoshi points out, the result is "not a fundamental or abrupt change perhaps, but still an unmistakable radical reduction of its public and critical role."[25] What was once the hidden curriculum of many universities—the subordination of higher education to capital—has now become an open and much celebrated policy of both public and private higher education.[26] How do we understand the university in light of both the crisis of youth and the related crisis of the social that have emerged under the controlling hand of neoliberalism? How can the future be grasped given the erosion of the social and public life over the last twenty years? What are the implications for the simultaneous corporatization of higher education in light of these dramatic changes? Any concern about the future of the university has to both engage and challenge this transformation while reclaiming the role of the university as a democratic public sphere. In what follows, I want to analyze the university as a corporate entity within the context of a crisis of the social. In particular, I will focus on how this crisis is played out not only through the erosion of public space, but through the less explained issues of public versus corporate time, on the one hand, and the related issues of agency, pedagogy, and public mission on the other.

Public Time versus Corporate Time

Questions of time are crucial to how a university structures its public mission, the role of faculty, the use of space, student access, and the legitimation of particular forms of knowledge, research, and pedagogy. Time is not simply a question of how to invoke the future, but is also used to legitimate particular social relations and make claims on human behavior, representing one of the most important battlefields for determining how the future of higher education is played out in political and ethical terms. Time refers not only to the way in which it is mediated differently by institutions, administrators, faculty, and students but also how it shapes and allocates power, identities, and space through a particular set of codes and interests. But more importantly time is a central feature of politics and orders not merely the pace of the economic, but the time available for consideration, contemplation, and critical thinking. When reduced to a commodity, time often becomes the enemy of deliberation and thoughtfulness and undermines the ability of political culture to function critically.

For the past twenty years, time as a value and the value of time have been redefined through the dictates of neoliberal economics, which has largely undermined any notion of public time guided by non-commodified values central to a political and social democracy. As Peter Beilharz observes,

> [T]ime has become our enemy. The active society demands of us that we keep moving, keep consuming, experience everything, travel, work as good tourists more than act as good citizens, work, shop and die. To keep moving is the only way left in our cultural repertoire to push away ... meaning....[and consequently] the prospects, and forms of social solidarity available to us shrink before our eyes.[27]

Without question, the future of the university will largely rest on the outcome of the current struggle between the university as a public space with the capacity to slow time down in order to question what Jacques Derrida calls the powers that limit "a democracy to come" and a corporate university culture wedded to a notion of accelerated time in which the principle of self-interest replaces politics and consumerism replaces a broader notion of social agency.[28] A meaningful and inclusive democracy is indebted to a notion of public time, while neoliberalism celebrates what I call corporate time. In what follows, I want to briefly comment on some of the theoretical and political work performed by each of these notions of time and the implications they have for addressing the future of higher education.

Public time as a condition and critical referent makes visible how politics is played out through the unequal access different groups have to "institutions, goods, services, resources, and power and knowledge."[29] That is, it offers a critical category for understanding how the ideological and institutional mechanisms of higher education work to grant time to some faculty and students and to withhold it from others, how time is mediated differently within different disciplines and among diverse faculty and students, how time can work across the canvas of power and space to create new identities and social formations capable of "intervening in public debate for the purpose of affecting positive change in the overall position and location in society."[30] When linked to issues of power, identity, ideology, and politics, public time can be an important social construct for orientating the university towards a vision of the future in which critical learning becomes central to increasing the scope of human rights, individual freedom, and the operations of a substantive democracy. In this instance, public time resonates with a project of leadership, teaching, and learning in which higher education seems an important site for investing democratic public life with substance and vibrancy.

Public time rejects the fever-pitch appeals of "just in time" or "speed time," demands often made within the context of "ever faster technological transformation and exchange,"[31] and buttressed by corporate capital's golden rule: "time is money." Public time slows time down, not as a simple refusal of technological change or a rejection of all calls for efficiency but as an attempt to create the institutional and ideological conditions that promote long-term analyses, historical reflection, and deliberations over what our collective actions might mean for shaping the future. Rejecting an instrumentality that evacuates questions of history, ethics, and justice, public time fosters dialogue, thoughtfulness, and critical exchange. Public time offers room for knowledge that contributes to society's self-understanding, that enables it to question itself, and seeks to legitimate intellectual practices that are not only collective and non-instrumental but deepen democratic values while encouraging pedagogical relations that question the future in terms that are political, ethical, and social. As Cornelius Castoriadis observes, public time puts into question established institutions and dominant authority, rejecting any notion of the social that either eliminates the question of judgment or "conceals ... the question of responsibility." Rather than maintaining a passive attitude towards power, public time demands and encourages forms of political agency based on a passion for self-governing, actions informed by critical judgment, and a commitment to linking social responsibility and social transformation. Public time legitimates those pedagogical practices that provide the basis for a culture of questioning, one that enables the knowledge, skills, and social practices necessary for resistance, a space of translation, and a proliferation of discourses. Public time unsettles common sense and disturbs authority while encouraging critical and responsible leadership. As Roger Simon observes, public time "presents the question of the social—not as a space for the articulation of pre-formed visions through which to mobilize action, but as the movement in which the very question of the possibility of democracy becomes the frame within which a necessary radical learning (and questioning) is enabled."[32] Put differently, public time affirms a politics without guarantees and a notion of the social that is open and contingent. Public time also provides a conception of democracy that is never complete and determinate but constantly open to different understandings of the contingency of its decisions, mechanisms of exclusions, and operations of power.[33] Public time challenges neoliberalism's willingness to separate the economic from the social as well as its failure to address human needs and social costs.

At its best, public time renders governmental power explicit and, in doing so, it rejects the language of religious rituals and the abrogation of the conditions necessary for the assumption of basic freedoms and rights. Moreover, public time considers civic education the basis, if not essential dimension, of justice because it provides individuals with the skills, knowledge, and passions to talk back to power while simultaneously emphasizing both the necessity to question that accompanies viable forms of political agency and the assumption of public responsibility through active participation in the very process of governing. Expressions of public time in higher education can be found in shared notions of governance between faculty and administration, in modes of academic labor that encourage forms of collegiality tied to vibrant communities of exchange and democratic values, and in pedagogical relations in which students do not just learn about democracy but experience it through a sense of active participation, critical engagement, and social responsibility. The notion of public time has a long history in higher education and has played a formative role in shaping some of the most important principles of academic life. Public time, in this instance, registers the importance of pedagogical practices that provide the conditions for a culture of questioning in which teachers and students engage in critical dialogue and unrestricted discussion in order to affirm their role as social agents, inspect their own past, and engage the consequences of *their own actions in shaping the future.*

As higher education becomes increasingly corporatized, public time is replaced by *corporate time.* In corporate time, the "market is viewed as a 'master design for all affairs',"[34] profit making becomes the defining measure of responsibility, and consumption is the privileged site for determining value between the self and the larger social order. Corporate time fosters a narrow sense of leadership, agency, and public values and is largely indifferent to those concerns that are critical to a just society, but are not commercial in nature. The values of hierarchy, materialism, competition, and excessive individualism are enshrined under corporate time and play a defining role in how it allocates space, manages the production of particular forms of knowledge, and regulates pedagogical relations. Hence, it is not surprising that corporate time accentuates privatized and competitive modes of intellectual activity, largely removed from public obligations and social responsibilities. Divested of any viable democratic notion of the social, corporate time measures relationships, productivity, space, and knowledge according to the dictates of cost efficiency, profit, and a market-based rationality. Time, within this framework, is accelerated rather than slowed down and reconfigures academic labor increasingly through, though not limited to, new computer generated technologies that are making greater demands on faculty time, creating larger teaching loads, and producing bigger classes. Under corporate time, speed controls and organizes place, space, and communication as a matter of quantifiable calculation. And as Peter Euben observes under such circumstances, a particular form of rationality emerges as common sense: "When speed rules so does efficient communication. Calculation and logic are in, moral imagination and reasoned emotions are out. With speed at a premium, shorthand, quantification and measurements become dominant modes of thought. Soon we will talk in clichés and call it common sense and wisdom."[35]

Corporate time maps faculty relationships through self-promoting market agendas and narrow definitions of self-interest. Caught on the treadmill of getting more grants, teaching larger classes, and producing more revenue for the university, faculty become another casualty of a business ideology that attempts to "extract labor from campus workers at the lowest possible cost, one willing to sacrifice research independence and integrity for profit."[36] Under corporatization, time is accelerated and fragmented. Overworked and largely isolated, faculty are now rewarded for intellectual activities privileged as entrepreneurial, "measured largely in the capacity to transact and consume."[37] Faculty are asked to spend more time in larger classrooms while they are simultaneously expected to learn and use new instructional technologies such as power point, the Web, and various multimedia pedagogical activities. Faculty now interact with students not only in their classes and offices, but also in chat rooms and through e-mail.

Grounded in the culture of competitiveness and self-interest, corporate time reworks faculty loyalties. Faculty interaction is structured less around collective solidarities built upon practices which offer a particular relationship to public life than through corporate imposed rituals of competition and production that conform to the "narrowly focused ideas of the university as a support to the economy."[38] For instance, many universities are now instituting post-tenure review as an alleged measure of faculty accountability and an efficient way to eliminate "deadwood" professors. As Ben Agger points out, what is "especially pernicious is the fact that faculty are supposed to axe their own colleagues, thus pitting them against each other and destroying whatever remains of the fabric of academic community and mutuality."[39]

Corporate time also fragments time by redefining academic labor "as part-time labor versus academic work as full-time commitment and career."[40]

Under such conditions, faculty solidarities are weakened ever more as corporate time evokes cost-efficient measures by outsourcing instruction to part-time faculty who are underpaid, overworked, lack health benefits, and deprived of any power to shape the conditions under which they work. Powerlessness breeds resentment and anger between part-time faculty, and fear and insecurity among full-time faculty, who no longer believe that their tenure is secure. Hence, the heavy hand of universities reproduces the divide between part- and full-time faculty as they downsize and outsource under the rubric of fiscal responsibility and accountability, especially in a post 9-11 era that demands increasing amounts of public resources be devoted to the War on Terror. But more is reproduced than structural dislocations among faculty; there is also a large pool of crippling fear, insecurity, and resentment that makes it difficult for faculty to take risks, forge bonds of solidarity, engage in social criticism, and perform as public intellectuals rather than as technicians in the service of corporate largesse.

Leadership under the reign of corporate culture and corporate time has been rewritten as a form of homage to business models of governance. As Stanley Aronowitz points out, "Today ... leaders of higher education wear the badge of corporate servants proudly."[41] Gone are the days when university presidents were hired for intellectual status and public roles. College presidents are now labeled as Chief Executive Officers, and are employed primarily because of their fundraising abilities. Deans of various colleges are often pulled from the ranks of the business world and pride themselves on the managerial logic and cost-cutting plans they adopt from the corporate culture of Microsoft, Disney, and IBM. Bill Gates and Michael Eisner replace John Dewey and Robert Hutchins as models of educational leadership. Rather than defend the public role of the university, academic freedom, and worthy social causes, the new corporate heroes of higher education now focus their time selling off university services to private contractors, forming partnerships with local corporations, searching for new patent and licensing agreements, and urging faculty to engage in research and grants that generate external funds. Under this model of leadership the university is being transformed from a place to think to a place to imagine stock options and profit windfalls.

Corporate time provides a new framing mechanism for faculty relations and modes of production and suggests a basic shift in the role of the intellectual. Academics now become less important as a resource to provide students with the knowledge and skills they need to engage the future as a condition of democratic possibilities. In the "new economy," they are entrepreneurs who view the future as an investment opportunity and research as a private career opportunity rather than as a civic and collective effort to improve the public good. Increasingly academics find themselves being deskilled as they are pressured to teach more service oriented and market based courses and devote less time to their roles either as well-informed, public intellectuals or as "cosmopolitan intellectuals situated in the public sphere."[42]

Corporate time not only transforms the university as a democratic public sphere into a space for training while defining faculty as market oriented producers, it also views students as merely customers and potential workers, or simply as sources of revenue. As customers, students "are conceptualized in terms of their ability to pay.... and the more valued customers are those who can afford to pay more."[43] One consequence, as Gary Rhoades points out, is that student access to higher education is "now shaped less by considerations of social justice than of revenue potential."[44] Consequently, those students who are poor and under-serviced are increasingly denied access to the benefits of higher education. Of course, the real problem, as Cary Nelson observes, is not merely one of potential decline, but "long term and continuing failure to offer all citizens, especially minorities of class and color, equal educational opportunities,"[45] a failure that has been intensified under the authority of the corporate university. As a source of revenue, students are now subjected to higher fees and tuition costs, and are bombarded by brand name corporations who either lease space on the university commons to advertise their goods or run any one of a number of student services from the dining halls to the university bookstore. Almost every aspect of public space in higher education is now designed to attract students as consumers and shoppers, constantly subjecting them to forms of advertisements mediated by the rhythms of corporate time which keeps students moving through a marketplace of brand name products rather than ideas. Such hyper-commercialized spaces increasingly resemble malls, transforming all available university space into advertising billboards, and bringing home the message that the most important identity available to students is that of a consuming subject. As the line between public and commercial space disappears, the gravitational pull of Taco Bell, McDonald's, Starbucks, Barnes and Noble, American Express, and Nike, among others, creates a "geography of nowhere,"[46] a consumer placelessness in which all barriers between a culture of critical ideas and branded products simply disappear.[47] Education is no longer merely a monetary exchange in which students buy an upscale, lucrative career, it is also an experience designed to evacuate any broader, more democratic notions of citizenship, the social, and the future that students may wish to imagine, struggle over, and enter. In corporate time, students are disenfranchised "as future citizens and reconstitute[d] ... as no more than consumers and potential workers."[48]

Corporate time not only translates faculty into multinational operatives and students into sources of revenue and captive consumers, it also makes a claim on how knowledge is valued, how the classroom is to be organized, and how pedagogy is defined. Knowledge under corporate time is valued as a form of capital. As Michael Peters observes, entire disciplines and bodies of knowledge are now either valued or devalued on the basis of their "ability to attract global capital and....potential for serving transnational corporations. Knowledge is valued for its strict utility rather than as an end in itself or for its emancipatory effects."[49] Good value for students means taking courses labeled as "relevant" in market terms, which are often counterposed to courses in the social sciences, humanities, and the fine arts, which are concerned with forms of learning that do not readily translate into either private gain or commercial value. Under the rule of corporate time, the classroom is no longer a public sphere concerned with issues of justice, critical learning, or the knowledge and skills necessary for civic engagement. As training replaces education, the classroom, along with pedagogy itself, is transformed as a result of the corporate restructuring of the university.

As the structure and content of education change, intellectual and pedagogical practices are less identified with providing the conditions for students to learn how to think critically, hold institutional authority accountable for its actions, and act in ways that further democratic ideals. Rather than providing the knowledge and skills for asserting the primacy of the political, social responsibility, and the ethical as central to preparing students for the demands of an inclusive democracy, intellectual practice is subordinated to managerial, technological, and commercial considerations. Not only is classroom knowledge and intellectual practice bought and traded as a marketable commodity, but they are also defined largely within what Zygmunt Bauman calls "the culture of consumer society, which is more about forgetting, [than] learning."[50] That is, forgetting that knowledge can be emancipatory, that citizenship is not merely about being a consumer, and that the future cannot be sacrificed to ephemeral pleasures and values of the market. When education is reduced to training, the meaning of self-government is devalued and democracy is rendered meaningless.

What is crucial to recognize in the rise of corporate time is that while it acknowledges that higher education should play a crucial role in offering the narratives that frame society, it presupposes that faculty, in particular, will play a different role and assume a "different relation to the framing of cultural reality."[51] Many critics have pointed to the changing nature of governance and management structures in the university as a central force in redefining the relationship of the university to the larger society, but little has been said about how the changing direction of the university impacts on the nature of academic activity and intellectual relations.[52] While on one level, the changing nature of the institution suggests greater control of academic life by administrators and an emerging class of managerial professionals, it also points to the privileging of those intellectuals in the techno-sciences whose services are indispensable to corporate power, while recognizing information as the reigning commodity of the new economy. Academic labor is now prized for how it fuses with capital, rather than how it contributes to what Geoff Sharp calls "society's self-understanding."[53] The changing institutional and social forms of the university reject the elitist and reclusive models of intellectual practice that traditionally have refused to bridge the gap between higher education and the larger social order, theory and practice, the academic and the public. Within the corporate university, transformation rather than contemplation is now a fundamental principle for judging and rewarding intellectual practice. Removed from matters of either social justice or democratic possibilities, transformation is defined through a notion of the social that is entirely rooted in privileging the material interests of the market. Higher education's need for new sources of funding neatly dovetails with the inexhaustible need on the part of corporations for new products. Within this symbiotic relationship, knowledge is directly linked to its application in the market, mediated by a collapse of the distinction between knowledge and the commodity. Knowledge has become capital to invest in the market but has little to do with the power of self-definition, civic commitments, or ethical responsibilities that "require an engagement with the claims of others"[54] and with questions of justice. At the same time, the conditions for scholarly work are being transformed through technologies that eliminate face to face contact, speed up the labor process, and define social exchange in terms that are more competitive, instrumental, and removed from face to face interactions.

Electronic, digital, and image-based technologies shape notions of the social in ways that were unimaginable a decade ago. Social exchanges can now proceed without the presence of "real" bodies. Contacts among faculty and between teachers and students are increasingly virtual, yet these practices profoundly delineate the nature of the social in instrumental, abstract, and commodified terms. As John Hinkson and Geoff Sharp have pointed out, these new intellectual practices and technological forms are redefining the nature of the social in higher education in ways in which the free sharing of ideas and cooperativeness as democratic and supportive forms of collegiality seem to be disappearing among faculty.[55] This is not just an issue that can be taken up strictly as an assault on academic labor, it also raises fundamental questions about where those values that support democratic forms of solidarity, sharing, dialogue, and mutual understanding are to be found in university life. This is an especially important issue since such values serve as a "condition for the development of intellectual practices devoted to public service."[56] Within these new forms of instrumental framing and intellectual practice, the ethic of public service that once received some support in higher education is being eliminated and with it those intellectual relations, scholarly practices, and forms of collegiality that leave some room for addressing a less commodified and more democratic notion of the social.

In opposition to this notion of corporate time, instrumentalized intellectual practices, and a deracinated view of the social, I want to reassert the importance of academic social formations that view the university as a site of struggle and resistance. A primary facet of this challenge is the necessity to define intellectual practice "as part of an intricate web of morality, rigor and responsibility"[57] that enables academics to speak with conviction, enter the public sphere in order to address the most pressing social problems, and demonstrate alternative models for what it means to bridge the gap between higher education and the broader society. This is a notion of intellectual practice that refuses to be instrumentalized or protected by the privileged isolation of academia. It is also a type of intellectual practice that affirms a broader vision of learning that links knowledge to the power of self-definition and the capacities of administrators, academics, and students to expand the scope of democratic freedoms, particularly as they address the crisis of the social as part and parcel of the crisis of both youth and democracy itself. Implicit in this notion of social and intellectual practice is a view of academics as public intellectuals. Following Edward Said, I am referring to those academics engaged in intellectual practices that interpret and question power rather than merely consolidate it, enter into the public sphere in order to alleviate human suffering, make the connections of power visible, and work individually and collectively to create the pedagogical and social conditions necessary for what the late Pierre Bourdieu has called "realist utopias."[58] I want to conclude this essay by taking up how the role of both the university as a democratic public sphere and the function of academics as public intellectuals can be further enabled through what I call a politics of educated hope.

Toward a Politics of Educated Hope

If the rise of the corporate university is to be challenged, educators and others need to reclaim the meaning and purpose of higher education as an ethical and political response to the demise of democratic public life. At stake here is the need to insist on the role of the university as a public sphere committed to deepening and expanding the possibilities of democratic identities, values, and relations. This approach suggests new models of leadership based on the understanding that the real purpose of higher education means encouraging people to think beyond the task of simply getting a lucrative job. Beyond this ever narrowing instrumental justification there is the more relevant goal of opening higher education up to all groups, creating a critical citizenry, providing specialized work skills for jobs that really require them, democratizing relations of governance among administrators, faculty, and students, and taking seriously the imperative to disseminate an intellectual and artistic culture. Higher education may be one of the few sites left in which students learn how to mediate critically between democratic values and the demands of corporate power, between identities founded on democratic principles and identities steeped in forms of competitive, atomistic individualism that celebrate self-interest, profit making, and greed. This view suggests that higher education be defended through intellectual work that self-consciously recalls the tension between the democratic imperatives and possibilities of public institutions and their everyday realization within a society dominated by market principles. Toni Morrison is right in arguing that "If the university does not take seriously and rigorously its role as a guardian of wider civic freedoms, as interrogator of more and more complex ethical problems, as servant and preserver of deeper democratic practices, then some other regime or ménage of regimes will do it for us, in spite of us, and without us."[59] Only if educators and others take this struggle seriously can the university be reclaimed as a space of debate, discussion, and at times dissidence. Within such a pedagogical space, time can be unconditionally apportioned to what Cornelius Castoriadis calls "an unlimited interrogation in all domains" of society, especially with regards to the operations of dominant authority and power and the important issues that shape public life, practices ultimately valued for their contribution to the unending process of democratization.[60]

Higher education should be defended as a form of civic education where teachers and students have the chance to resist and rewrite those modes of pedagogy, time, and rationality that refuse to include questions of judgment and issues of responsibility. Understood as such, higher education is viewed neither as a consumer driven product nor as a form of training and career preparation but a mode of critical education that renders all individuals fit "to participate in power.... to the greatest extent possible, to participate in a common government," to be capable, as Aristotle reminds us, of both governing and being governed.[61] If higher education is to bring democratic public culture and critical pedagogy back to life, educators need to provide students with the knowledge and skills that enable them not only to judge and choose between different institutions but also to create those institutions they deem necessary for living lives of decency and dignity. In this instance, education provides not only the tools for citizen participation in public life, but also for exercising leadership. As Castoriadis insists, "People should have not just the typical right to participate; they should also be educated in every aspect (of leadership and politics) in order to be able to participate" in governing society.[62]

Reclaiming higher education as a public sphere begins with the crucial project of challenging corporate ideology and its attendant notions of time, which covers over the crisis of the social by dissociating all discussions about the goals of higher education from the realm of democracy. This project points to the important task of redefining higher education as a democratic public sphere not only to assert the importance of the social, but also to reconfigure it so that "economic interests cease to be the dominant factor in shaping attitudes" about the social as a realm devoid of politics and democratic possibilities.[63] Education is not only about issues of work and economics, but also about questions of justice, social freedom, and the capacity for democratic agency, action, and change as well as the related issues of power, exclusion, and citizenship. These are educational and political issues and should be addressed as part of a broader concern for renewing the struggle for social justice and democracy. Such a struggle demands, as the writer Arundhati Roy points out, that as intellectuals we ask ourselves some very "uncomfortable questions about our values and traditions, our vision for the future, our responsibilities as citizens, the legitimacy of our 'democratic institutions,' the role of the state, the police, the army, the judiciary, and the intellectual community."[64]

While it is crucial for educators and others to defend higher education as a public good, it is also important to recognize that the crisis of higher education cannot be understood outside of the overall restructuring of the social and civic life. The death of the social, the devaluing of political agency, the waning of non-commercial values, and the disappearance of non-commercialized public spaces have to be understood as part of a much broader attack on public entitlements such as healthcare, welfare, and social security, which are being turned over to market forces and privatized so that "economic transactions can subordinate and in many cases replace political democracy."[65]

Against the increasing corporatization of the university and the advance of global capitalism, educators need to resurrect a language of resistance and possibility, a language that embraces a militant utopianism while constantly being attentive to those forces that seek to turn such hope into a new slogan or punish and dismiss those who dare look beyond the horizon of the given. Hope as a form of militant utopianism, in this instance, is one of the preconditions for individual and social struggle, the ongoing practice of critical education in a wide variety of sites—the attempt to make a difference by being able to imagine otherwise in order to act in other ways. Educated hope is utopian, as Ruth Levitas observes, in that it is understood "more broadly as the desire for a better way of living expressed in the description of a different kind of society that makes possible that alternative way of life."[66] Educated hope also demands a certain amount of courage on the part of intellectuals in that it demands from them the necessity to articulate social possibilities, mediate the experience of injustice as part of a broader attempt to contest the workings of oppressive power, undermine various forms of domination, and fight for alternative ways to imagine the future. This is no small challenge at a time in American history when, next to shopping, jingoistic patriotism is the only obligation of citizenship and dissent is viewed increasingly as the refuge of those who support terrorists.

Educated hope as a utopian longing becomes all the more urgent given the bleakness of the times, but also because it opens horizons of comparison by evoking not just different histories but different futures; at the same time, it substantiates the importance of ambivalence while problematizing certainty, or as Paul Ricoeur has suggested, it is "a major resource as the weapon against closure."[67] As a form of utopian thinking, educated hope provides a theoretical service in that it pluralizes politics by generating dissent against the claims of a false harmony, and it provides an activating presence in promoting social transformation. Jacques Derrida has observed in another context that if higher education is going to have a future that makes a difference in promoting democracy, it is crucial for educators to take up the "necessity to rethink the concepts of the possible and the impossible."[68] What Derrida is suggesting is that educated hope provides a vocabulary for challenging the presupposition that there are no alternatives to the existing social order, while simultaneously stressing the dynamic, still unfinished elements of a democracy to be realized.[69]

Educated hope—as a form of oppositional utopianism—accentuates the ways in which the political can become more pedagogical and the pedagogical more political. In the first instance, pedagogy merges politics and ethics with revitalized forms of civic education that provide the knowledge, skills, and experiences enabling individual freedom and social agency. Making the pedagogical more political demands that educators become more attentive to the ways in which institutional forces and cultural power are tangled up with everyday experience. It means understanding how higher education in the information age now interfaces with the larger culture, how it has become the most important site for framing public pedagogies and authorizing specific relations between the self, the other, and the larger society that often shut down democratic visions. Any viable politics of educated hope must tap into individual experiences while at the same time linking individual responsibility with a progressive sense of social agency. Politics and pedagogy both spring "from real situations and from what we can say and do in these situations."[70] As an empowering practice, educated hope translates into civic courage as a political and pedagogical practice and begins when one's life can no longer be taken for granted. In doing so, it makes concrete the possibility for transforming higher education into an ethical practice and public event that confronts the flow of everyday experience and the weight of social suffering with the force of individual and collective resistance and the promise of an ongoing project of democratic social transformation.

Emphasizing politics as a pedagogical practice and performative act, educated hope accentuates that notion that politics is played out not only on the terrain of imagination and desire, but is also grounded in material relations of power and concrete social formations through which people live out their daily lives. Freedom and justice, in this instance, have to be mediated through the connection between civic education and political agency, which presupposes that the goal of educated hope is not to liberate the individual from the social—a central tenet of neoliberalism—but to take seriously the notion that the individual can only be liberated through the social. Educated hope, if it is to be meaningful, should provide a link, however transient, provisional, and contextual between vision and critique, on the one hand, and engagement and transformation on the other. But for such a notion of hope to be meaningful it has to be grounded in a vision and notion of pedagogy that has some hold on the present.

The limits of the utopian imagination are related, in part, to the failure of academics and intellectuals in a variety of public spheres not only to conceive of life beyond profit margins, but also to imagine what pedagogical conditions might be necessary to bring into being forms of political agency that might expand the operations of individual rights, social provisions, and democratic freedoms. Against such failures and dystopian notions, it is crucial for educators to address utopian longings as anticipatory rather than messianic, as temporal rather than merely spatial, forward looking rather than backwards. Utopian thinking in this view is neither a blue print for the future nor a form of social engineering, but a belief that different futures are possible. Utopian thinking rejects a politics of certainty and holds open matters of contingency, context, and indeterminacy as central to any notion of agency and the future. This suggests a view of hope based on the recognition that it is only through education that human beings can learn about the limits of the present and the conditions necessary for them to "combine a gritty sense of limits with a lofty vision of possibility."[71] Educated hope poses the important challenge of how to reclaim social agency within a broader discourse of ethical advocacy while addressing those essential pedagogical and political elements necessary for envisioning alternatives to global neoliberalism and its attendant forms of corporate time and its assaults on public time and space.

Educated hope takes as a political and ethical necessity the need to address what modes of education are required for a democratic future and further requires that we ask such questions as: What pedagogical projects, resources, and practices can be put into place that would convey to students the vital importance of public time and its attendant culture of questioning as an essential step toward self-representation, agency, and a substantive democracy? How might public time with its imperative to "take more time," compel respect rather than reverence, critique rather than silence, while challenging the narrow and commercial nature of corporate time? What kinds of social relations necessarily provide students with time for deliberation as well as spaces of translation in which they can critically engage those forms of power and authority that speak directly to them both within and outside of the academy? How might public time, with its unsettling refusal to be fixed or to collapse in the face of corporate time, be used to create pedagogical conditions that foster forms of self- and social critique as part of a broader project of constructing alternative desires and critical modes of thinking, on the one hand, and democratic agents of change on the other? How to deal with these issues is a major question for intellectuals in the academy today and their importance resides not just in how they might provide teachers and students with the tools to fight corporatization in higher education, but also how they address the need for fundamental institutional change in the ongoing struggles for freedom and justice in a revitalized democracy.

There is a long-standing tradition among critical theorists that pedagogy as a moral and political practice plays a crucial role in constituting the social. Far from innocent, pedagogical practices operate within institutional contexts that carry great power in determining what knowledge is of most worth, what it means for students to know something, and how such knowledge relates to a particular understanding of the self and its relationship to both others and the future. Connecting teaching as knowledge production to teaching as a form of self production, pedagogy presupposes not only a political and ethical project that offers up a variety of human capacities, it also propagates diverse meanings of the social. Moreover, as an articulation of and intervention in the social, pedagogical practices always sanction particular versions of what knowledge is of most worth, what it means to know something, how to be attentive to the operations of power, and how we might construct representations of ourselves, others, and our physical environment. In the broadest sense, pedagogy is a principle feature of politics because it provides the capacities, knowledge, skills, and social relations through which individuals recognize themselves as social and political agents. As Roger Simon points out, "talk about pedagogy is simultaneously talk about the details of what students and others might do together and the cultural politics such practices support."[72]

While many critical educators and social theorists recognize that education, in general, and pedagogy, more specifically, cannot be separated from the dual crisis of representation and political agency, the primary emphasis in many of these approaches to critical pedagogy suggests that its foremost responsibility is to provide a space where the complexity of knowledge, culture, values, and social issues can be explored in open and critical dialogue within a vibrant culture of questioning. This position is echoed by Judith Butler who argues, "For me there is more hope in the world when we can question what is taken for granted, especially about what it is to be human."[73] Zygmunt Bauman goes further, arguing that the resurrection of any viable notion of political and social agency is dependent upon a culture of questioning, whose purpose, as he puts it, is to "keep the forever unexhausted and unfulfilled human potential open, fighting back all attempts to foreclose and pre-empt the further unraveling of human possibilities, prodding human society to go on questioning itself and preventing that questioning from ever stalling or being declared finished."[74]

Central to any viable notion of critical pedagogy is its willingness to take seriously those academic projects, intellectual practices, and social relations in which students have the basic right to raise, if not define, questions both within and outside of disciplinary boundaries. Such a pedagogy also must bear the responsibility of being self-conscious about those forces that sometimes prevent people from speaking openly and critically, whether they are part of a hidden curriculum of either racism, class oppression, or gender discrimination or part of those institutional and ideological mechanisms that silence students under the pretext of a claim to professionalism, objectivity, or unaccountable authority. Crucial here is the recognition that a pedagogical culture of questioning is not merely about the dynamics of communication but also about the effects of power and the mechanisms through which it either constrains, denies, or excludes particular forms of agency—preventing some individuals from speaking in specific ways, in particular spaces, under specific circumstances. Clearly such a pedagogy might include a questioning of the corporatization of the educational context itself, the role of foreign policy, the purpose and meaning of the burgeoning prison-industrial complex, and the declining nature of the welfare state. Pedagogy makes visible the operations of power and authority as part of its processes of disruption and unsettlement—an attempt, as Larry Grossberg points out, "to win an already positioned, already invested individual or group to a different set of places, a different organization of the space of possibilities."[75]

At its best, such a pedagogy is self-reflective, and views its own practices and effects not as pregiven but as the outcome of previous struggles. Rather than defined as either a technique, method, or "as a kind of physics which leaves its own history behind and never looks back," critical pedagogy is grounded in a sense of history, politics, and ethics which uses theory as a resource to respond to particular contexts, problems, and issues. I want to suggest that as educators we need to extend this approach to critical pedagogy beyond the project of simply providing students with the critical knowledge and analytic tools that enable them to use them in any way they wish. While this pedagogical approach rightly focuses on the primacy of dialogue, understanding, and critique, it does not adequately affirm the experience of the social and the obligations it evokes regarding questions of responsibility and social transformation. Such a pedagogy attempts to open up for students important questions about power, knowledge, and what it might mean for students to critically engage the conditions under which life is presented to them, but it does not directly address what it would mean for them to work to overcome those social relations of oppression that make living unbearable for those youths and adults who are poor, hungry, unemployed, refused adequate social services, and under the aegis of neoliberalism, viewed largely as disposable.

Some educators such as Jeffrey C. Goldfarb have argued that education should primarily be used to engage students in "the great conversation," enable them to "pay attention to their critical faculties," and provoke informed discussion.[76] But Goldfarb also believes that education should be free from politics, providing students ultimately with the tools for civic discussion without the baggage of what he calls debilitating ideology. But by denying the relationship between politics and education, Goldfarb has no language for recognizing how pedagogy itself is shot through with issues of politics, power, and ideology. In opposition to Goldfarb, I believe that teaching and learning are profoundly political practices, as is evident in the most basic pedagogical and educational concerns, such as: How does one draw attention to the different ways in which knowledge, power, and experience are produced under specific conditions of learning? How are authority and power individually and institutionally distributed in both the university and the classroom? Who produces classroom knowledge and for whom? Who determines what knowledge is included or excluded? What is the agenda that informs the production and teaching of knowledge? What are the social and ideological horizons that determine student access to classrooms, privilege particular forms of cultural capital—ways of talking, writing, acting, dressing, and embodying specific racial, gendered, and class histories? How does one determine how politics is connected to everyday questions of identity, beliefs, subjectivity, dreams, and desires? How does one acknowledge, mediate, or refuse dominant academic values, pressures, and social relations? Goldfarb confuses politics with indoctrination and in doing so has no way of critically analyzing how his own intellectual practices are implicated in relations of power that structure the very knowledge, values, and desires that mediates his relations to students and the outside world. Consequently, his willingness to separate education from matters of power and politics runs the risk of reproducing the latter's worse effects. Goldfarb wants to deny the symbiotic relationship between politics and education, but the real issue is to recognize how such a relationship might be used to produce pedagogical practices that condition but do not determine outcomes, that recognize that "the educator's task is to encourage human agency, not mold it in the manner of Pygmalion."[77] A critical education should enable students to question existing institutions as well as to view politics as "a labor aimed at transforming desirable institutions in a democratic direction."[78] But to acknowledge that critical pedagogy is directed and interventionist is not the same as turning it into a religious ritual. Critical approaches to pedagogy do not guarantee certainty or impose a particular ideology, nor should they. But they should make a distinction between a rigorous ethical and scholarly approach to learning implicated in diverse relations of power and those forms of pedagogy that belie questions of responsibility, while allowing dialogue to degenerate into opinion and academic methods into unreflective and damaging ideological approaches to teaching. Rather than deny the relationship between education and politics, it seems far more crucial to engage it openly and critically so as to prevent pedagogical relations from degenerating into forms of abuse, terrorism, or contempt immune from any viable form of self-reflection and analysis.

A pedagogy that simply promotes a culture of questioning says nothing about what kind of future is or should be implied by how and what educators teach; nor does it address the necessity of recognizing the value of a future in which matters of liberty, freedom, and justice play a constitutive role. While it is crucial for education to be attentive to those practices in which forms of social and political agency are denied, it is also imperative to create the conditions in which forms of agency are available for students to learn how to not only think critically but to act differently. People need to be educated for democracy not only by expanding their capacities to think critically, but also for assuming public responsibility through active participation in the very process of governing and engaging important social problems. This suggests connecting a pedagogy of understanding with pedagogical practices that are empowering and oppositional, practices that offer students the knowledge and skills needed to believe that a substantive democracy is not only possible but is worth both taking responsibility for and struggling over. Any notion of critical pedagogy has to foreground issues not only of understanding but also social responsibility and address the implications the latter has for a democratic society. As Vaclav Havel has noted, "Democracy requires a certain type of citizen who feels responsible for something other than his own well feathered little corner; citizens who want to participate in society's affairs, who insist on it; citizens with backbones; citizens who hold their ideas about democracy at the deepest level, at the level that religion is held, where beliefs and identity are the same."[79]

Pedagogy plays a crucial role in nurturing this type of responsibility and suggests that students should learn about the relevance of translating critique and understanding to civic courage, of translating what they know as a matter of private privilege into a concern for public life. Responsibility breathes politics into educational practices and suggests both a different future and the possibility of politics itself. Responsibility makes politics and agency possible, because it does not end with matters of understanding since it recognizes the importance of students becoming accountable to others through their ideas, language, and actions. Being aware of the conditions that cause human suffering and the deep inequalities that generate dreadfully undemocratic and unethical contradictions for many people is not the same as resolving them. If pedagogy is to be linked to critical citizenship and public life, it needs to provide the conditions for students to learn in diverse ways how to take responsibility for moving society in the direction of a more realizable democracy. In this case, the burden of pedagogy is linked to the possibilities of understanding and acting, engaging knowledge and theory as a resource to enhance the capacity for civic action and democratic change.

The future of higher education is inextricably connected to the future that we make available to the next generation of young people. Finding our way to a more human future means educating a new generation of scholars who not only defend higher education as a democratic public sphere, but who also frame their own agency as both scholars and citizen activists willing to connect their research, teaching and service with broader democratic concerns over equality, justice, and an alternative vision of what the university might be and what society might become.

Notes

A much shorter version of this paper was delivered as the Herbert Spencer Lecture at Oxford University on November 15, 2002.

1. Ngugi Wa Thiong'O, *Moving the Centre: The Struggle for Cultural Freedoms* (Portsmouth, NH: Heinemann, 1993), p. 76.

2. For some excellent critical commentaries on various aspects of neoliberalism and its consequences, see Noam Chomsky, *Profit over People: Neoliberalism and the Global Order* (New York: Seven Stories Press, 1999); Pierre Bourdieu, *Acts of Resistance; Against the Tyranny of the Market* (New York: The New Press, 1998); Pierre Bourdieu, et al., *The Weight of the World: Social Suffering in Contemporary Society* (Stanford: Stanford University Press, 1999); Robert W. McChesney, *Rich Media, Poor Democracy: Communication Politics in Dubious Times* (New York: The New Press, 1999); Zygmunt Bauman, *Work, Consumerism, and the New Poor* (Philadelphia: Open University Press, 1998); Zygmunt Bauman, *Society under Siege* (Cambridge, UK: Polity Press, 2002).

3. Lawrence Grossberg, "Why Does Neo-Liberalism Hate Kids? The War on Youth and the Culture of Politics," *Review of Education, Pedagogy, and Cultural Studies 23*, no. 2 (2001): 133.

4. Ibid., p. 133.

5. Heather Wokusch, "Leaving Our Children Behind," *Common Dreams News Center* (July 8, 2002), p. 1. Available at www.commondreams.org/views02/0708–08.htm.

6. These figures are taken from Child Research Briefs, "Poverty, Welfare, and Children: A Summary of the Data." Available at www.childtrends.org.

7. These figures are taken from Childhood Poverty Research Brief 2, "Child Poverty in the States: Levels and Trends from 1979 to 1998." Available at http://www.nccp.org.

8. These figures largely come from Children's Defense Fund, *The State of Children in America's Union: A 2002 Action Guide to Leave No Child Behind* (Washington, DC: Children's Defense Fund Publication, 2002), pp, iv–v, 13.

9. Jennifer Egan, "To Be Young and Homeless," *New York Times Magazine* (March 24, 2002): 35.

10. Heather Wokusch, Op cit., p. 1.

11. Zygmunt Bauman, *Work, Consumerism, and the New Poor* (Philadelphia: Open University Press, 1999), p. 77.

12. Noreena Hertz, *The Silent Takeover: Global Capitalism and the Death of Democracy* (New York: The Free Press, 2001), p. 11.

13. Pierre Bourdieu, *Acts of Resistance: Against the Tyranny of the Market* (New York: The New Press, 1998); Pierre Bourdieu, et al., *The Weight of the World: Social Suffering in Contemporary Society* (Stanford: Stanford University Press, 1999).

14. Zygmunt Bauman, *In Search of Politics* (Stanford, CA: Stanford University Press, 1999), p. 2.

15. Naomi Klein, *No Logo* (New York: Picador, 1999), p. 177.

16. Lawrence Grossberg, "Why Does Neo-Liberalism Hate Kids? The War on Youth and the Culture of Politics," *Review of Education, Pedagogy, and Cultural Studies 23,* no. 2 (2001): 133.

17. Cited in Frank Hearn, *Reason and Freedom in Sociological Thought* (Boston: Unwin Hyman, 1985), p. 175. The classic statements by Dewey on this subject can be found in John Dewey, *Democracy and Education* (New York: The Free Press, 1997 [1916]). See also John Dewey, *The Public and Its Problems* (Columbus: Ohio University Press, 1954).

18. C. Wright Mills, *Power, Politics, and People,* edited by Irving Louis Horowitz (New York: Oxford University Press, 1963).

19. Jean Comaroff and John L. Comaroff, "Millennial Capitalism: First Thoughts on a Second Coming," *Public Culture 12,* no. 2 (2000): 305–306.

20. Peter Beilharz, *Zygmunt Bauman: Dialectic of Modernity* (London: Sage, 2000), p. 160.

21. Jean Comaroff and John L. Comaroff, "Millennial Capitalism: First Thoughts on a Second Coming," p. 332.

22. James Traub, "This Campus Is Being Simulated," *New York Times Magazine* (November 19, 2000): 93.

23. Cited in Roger Simon, "The University: A Place to Think?" in Henry A. Giroux and Kostas Myrsiades, eds., *Beyond the Corporate University* (Lanham, MD: Rowman and Littlefield, 2001), pp. 47–48.

24. Larry Hanley, "Conference Roundtable," *Found Object 10* (Spring 2001): 103.

25. Masao Miyoshi, "'Globalization,' Culture, and the University," in Fredric Jameson and Masao Miyoshi, eds., *The Cultures of Globalization* (Durham, NC: Duke University Press, 1998), p. 263.

26. Stanley Aronowitz, "The New Corporate University," *Dollars and Sense* (March–April 1998): 32.

27. Peter Beilharz, *Zygmunt Bauman: Dialectic of Modernity* (London: Sage, 2000), p.161.

28. Jacques Derrida, "Intellectual Courage: An Interview," *Culture Machine* Vol. 2 (2000), p. 9.

29. Michael Hanchard, "Afro-Modernity: Temporality, Politics, and the African Diaspora," *Public Culture 11,* no. 1 (Winter 1999): 253.

30. Michael Hanchard, "Afro-Modernity: Temporality, Politics, and the African Diaspora," *Public Culture 11,* no. 1 (Winter 1999): 256.

31. Jerome Bind, "Toward an Ethic of the Future," *Public Culture 12,* no. 1 (2000): 52.

32. Roger I. Simon, "On Public Time," Ontario Institute for Studies in Education. Unpublished paper, April 1, 2002, p. 4.

33. Simon Critchley, "Ethics, Politics, and Radical Democracy—The History of a Disagreement," *Culture Machine,* available at www.culturemachine.tees.ac.uk/frm_fl.htm.

34. James Rule, "Markets in Their Place," *Dissent* (Winter 1998): 30.

35. Peter Euben, "Reforming the Liberal Arts," *Civic Arts Review 2* (Summer–Fall, 2000): 8.

36. Cary Nelson, "Between Anonymity and Celebrity: The Zero Degrees of Professional Identity," *College English 64,* no. 6 (July 2002): 717.

37. Jean Comaroff and John L. Comaroff, "Millennial Capitalism: First Thoughts on a Second Coming," p. 306.

38. Geoff Sharp, "The Idea of the Intellectual and After," in Simon Cooper, John Hinkson, and Geoff Sharp, eds., *Scholars and Entrepreneurs* (Melbourne: Arena Publications, 2002), p. 280.

39. Ben Agger, "Sociological Writing in the Wake of Postmodernism," *Cultural Studies/Critical Methodologies 2,* no. 4 (November 4, 2002): 444.

40. Gary Rhoades, "Corporate, Techno Challenges, and Academic Space," *Found Object 10* (Spring 2001): 143.

41. Stanley Aronowitz, "The New Corporate University," *Dollars and Sense* (March–April 1998): 32.

42. Agger, "Sociological Writing," p. 444.

43. Gary Rhoades, "Corporate, Techno Challenges, and Academic Space," p. 122.

44. Ibid.

45. Cary Nelson, "Between Anonymity and Celebrity: The Zero Degrees of Professional Identity," *College English 64,* no. 6 (July 2002): 713.

46. Taken from James Howard Kunstler, *The Geography of Nowhere* (New York: Touchstone, 1993).

47. The most extensive analysis of the branding of culture by corporations can be found in Naomi Klein, *No Logo* (New York: Picador, 1999).

48. Jeffrey L. Williams, "Franchising the University," in Henry A. Giroux and Kostas Myrsiades, eds., *Beyond the Corporate University: Culture and Pedagogy in the New Millennium* (Lanham, MD: Rowman and Littlefield, 2001), p. 23.

49. Michael Peters, "The University in the Knowledge Economy," in Simon Cooper, John Hinkson, and Geoff Sharp, eds., *Scholars and Entrepreneurs: The University in Crisis* (Melbourne: Arena Publications, 2002) p. 148.

50. Zygmunt Bauman, *Globalization: The Human Consequences* (New York: Columbia University Press, 1998), p. 81.

51. Geoff Sharp, "The Idea of the Intellectual and After," in Simon Cooper, John Hinkson, and Geoff Sharp, eds., *Scholars and Entrepreneurs* (Melbourne: Arena Publications, 2002), p. 275.

52. See Sharp and Hinkson, "Perspectives on the Crisis of the University," in John Hinkson and Geoff Sharp, eds. *Scholars and Entrepreneurs* (Melbourne: Arena Publications, 2002), pp. 233–267.

53. Geoff Sharp, "The Idea of the Intellectual and After," in John Hinkson and Geoff Sharp, eds. *Scholars and Entrepreneurs* (Melbourne: Arena Publications, 2002), pp. 284–285.

54. Nick Couldry, "Dialogue in an Age of Enclosure: Exploring the Values of Cultural Studies," *Review of Education, Pedagogy, and Cultural Studies 23,* no. 1 (2001): 17.

55. John Hinkson, "Perspectives on the Crisis of the University," in John Hinkson and Geoff Sharp, eds., *Scholars and Entrepreneurs* (Melbourne: Arena Publications, 2002), pp. 233–267.

56. Ibid., p. 259.

57. Arundhati Roy, *Power Politics* (Cambridge, MA: South End Press, 2001), p. 6.

58. The ideas on public intellectuals are taken directly from Edward Said, *Reflections on Exile and Other Essays* (Cambridge, MA: Harvard University Press, 2001), pp. 502–503. For the reference to realist utopias, see Pierre Bourdieu, "For a Scholarship with Commitment," *Profession* (2000): 42.

59. Toni Morrison, "How Can Values Be Taught in the University?" *Michigan Quarterly Review* (Spring 2001): 278.

60. Cornelius Castoriadis, "Culture in a Democratic Society," in David Ames Curtis, ed., *The Castoriadis Reader* (Malden, MA: Blackwell, 1997), p. 343.

61. Cornelius Castoriadis, "The Nature and Value of Equity," *Philosophy, Politics, Autonomy: Essays in Political Philosophy* (New York: Oxford University Press, 1991), p. 140.

62. Cornelius Castoriadis, "The Problem of Democracy Today," *Democracy and Nature 8* (April 1996): 24.

63. Cornelius Castoriadis, "The Greek Polis and the Creation of Democracy," *Philosophy, Politics, Autonomy: Essays in Political Philosophy* (New York: Oxford University Press, 1991), p. 112.

64. Arundhati Roy, *Power Politics* (Cambridge, MA: South End Press, 2001), p. 3.

65. Christopher Newfield, "Democratic Passions: Reconstructing Individual Agency," in Russ Castronovo and Dana Nelson, eds., *Materializing Democracy* (Durham: Duke University Press, 2002), p. 314.

66. Ruth Levitas, "The Future of Thinking about the Future," in Jon Bird, et al., *Mapping the Futures* (New York: Routledge, 1993), p. 257.

67. Cited in Zygmunt Bauman, *Work, Consumerism, and the New Poor* (Philadelphia: Open University Press, 1998), p. 98.

68. Jacques Derrida, "The Future of the Profession or the Unconditional University," in Laurence Simmons and Heather Worth, eds., *Derrida Downunder* (Auckland, NZ: Dunmore Press, 2001), p. 7.

69. Samir Amin has captured this sentiment in his comment: "Neither modernity nor democracy has reached the end of its potential development. That is why I prefer the term 'democratization,' which stresses the dynamic aspect of a still-unfinished process, to the term 'democracy,' which reinforces the illusion that we can give a definitive formula for it." See Samir Amin, "Imperialization and Globalization," *Monthly Review* (June 2001): 12.

70. Alain Badiou, *Ethics: An Essay on the Understanding of Evil* (London: Verso, 2001), p. 96.

71. Ron Aronson, "Hope after Hope?" *Social Research 66*, no. 2 (Summer 1999): 489.

72. Roger Simon, "Empowerment as a Pedagogy of Possibility," *Language Arts 64*, no. 4 (April 1987): 371.

73. Cited in Gary A. Olson and Lynn Worsham, "Changing the Subject: Judith Butler's Politics of Radical Resignification," *JAC 20*, no. 4 (2000): 765.

74. Zygmunt Bauman and Keith Tester, *Conversations with Zygmunt Bauman* (Malden, MA: Polity Press, 2001), p. 4.

75. Lawrence Grossberg, "Introduction: Bringin' It All Back Home—Pedagogy and Cultural Studies," in Henry A. Giroux and Peter McLaren, eds., *Between Borders: Pedagogy and the Politics of Cultural Studies* (New York: Routledge, 1994), p. 14.

76. Jeffrey C. Goldfarb, "Anti-Ideology: Education and Politics as Democratic Practices" in Russ Castronovo and Dana Nelson, eds., *Materializing Democracy* (Durham: Duke University Press, 2002), pp. 345–367.

77. Stanley Aronowitz, "Introduction," in Paulo Freire, *Pedagogy of Freedom* (Lanham: Rowman and Littlefield, 1998), p. 10–11.

78. Cornelius Castoriadis, "Democracy as Procedure and Democracy as Regime," *Constellations 4,* no. 1 (1997): 4–5.

79. Cited in Paul Berman, "The Philosopher-King Is Mortal," *New York Times Magazine* (May 11, 1997): 36.

VI
Public Intellectuals and Their Work

12
Paulo Freire and the Politics of Postcolonialism

⊕

> Yet we have different privileges and different compensations for our posi-
> tions in the field of power relations. My caution is against a form of theoreti-
> cal tourism on the part of the first world critic, where the margin becomes
> a linguistic or critical vacation, a new poetics of the exotic.
>
> —Caren Kaplan[1]

The work of Paulo Freire continues to exercise a strong influence on a variety of liberal and radical educators. In some quarters his name has become
synonymous with the very concept and practice of critical pedagogy. Increasingly, Freire's work has become the standard reference for engaging in what
is often referred to as teaching for critical thinking, dialogical pedagogy, or
critical literacy. As Freire's work has passed from the origins of its production in Brazil, through Latin America and Africa to the hybrid borderlands
of North America, academics, adult educators, and others who inhabit the
ideology of the West have often appropriated it in ways that often reduce it
to a pedagogical technique or method. Of course, the requisite descriptions
generally invoke terms like "politically charged," "problem-posing," or the
mandatory "education for critical consciousness," and they often contradict
the use of Freire's work as a revolutionary pedagogical practice.[2] But in such
a context, these are terms that speak less to a political project constructed
amidst concrete struggles than they do to the insipid and dreary demands
for pedagogical recipes dressed up in the jargon of abstracted progressive
labels. What has been increasingly lost in the North American and Western
appropriation of Freire's work is the profound and radical nature of its theory
and practice as an anticolonial and postcolonial discourse. More specifically,
Freire's work is often appropriated and taught "without any consideration
of imperialism and its cultural representation. This lacuna itself suggests the
continuing ideological dissimulation of imperialism today."[3] This suggests
that Freire's work has been appropriated in ways that denude it of some of
its most important political insights. Similarly, it testifies to how a politics
of location works in the interest of privilege and power to cross cultural,
political, and textual borders so as to deny the specificity of the other and to

reimpose the discourse and practice of colonial hegemony. I want to argue that Paulo Freire's work must be read as a postcolonial text and that North Americans, in particular, must engage in a radical form of border crossing in order to reconstruct Freire's work in the specificity of its historical and political construction. More specifically, this means making problematic a politics of location situated in the privilege and power of the West and how engaging the question of the ideological weight of such a position constructs one's specific reading of Freire's work. At the same time, becoming a border-crosser engaged in a productive dialogue with others means producing a space in which those dominant social relations, ideologies, and practices that erase the specificity of the voice of the other must be challenged and overcome.

Homelessness and the Border Intellectual

In order to understand the work of Paulo Freire in terms of its historical and political importance, cultural workers have to become border-crossers. This means that teachers and other intellectuals have to take leave of the cultural, theoretical, and ideological borders that enclose them within the safety of "those places and spaces we inherit and occupy, which frame our lives in very specific and concrete ways."[4] Being a border-crosser suggests that one has to reinvent traditions not within the discourse of submission, reverence, and repetition, but "as transformation and critique. [That is] ... one must construct one's discourse as difference in relation to that tradition and this implies at the same time continuities and discontinuities."[5] At the same time, border crossing engages intellectual work not only in its specificity and partiality, but also in terms of the intellectual function itself as part of the discourse of invention and construction, rather than a discourse of recognition whose aim is reduced to revealing and transmitting universal truths. In this case, it is important to highlight intellectual work as being forged in the intersection of contingency and history arising not from the "exclusive hunting grounds of an elite [but] from all points of the social fabric."[6]

This task becomes all the more difficult with Paulo Freire because the borders that defined his work shifted over time in ways that paralleled his own exile and movement from Brazil to Chile, Mexico, the United States, Geneva, and back to Brazil. Freire's work not only drew heavily upon European discourses, but also upon the thought and language of theorists in Latin America, Africa, and North America. Freire's political project still raises enormous difficulties for educators who situate Freire's work in the reified language of methodologies and in empty calls that enshrine the practical at the expense of the theoretical and political.

Freire was an exile for whom being home was often tantamount to being "homeless" and for whom his own identity and the identities of Others were viewed as sites of struggle over the politics of representation, the exercise of power, and the function of social memory.[7] It is important to note that the concept of "home" being used here does not refer exclusively to those places in which one sleeps, eats, raises children, and sustains a certain level of comfort. For some, this particular notion of "home" is too mythic, especially for those who literally have no home in this sense; it also becomes a reification when it signifies a place of safety which excludes the lives, identities, and experiences of the Other, that is, when it becomes synonymous with the cultural capital of white, middle-class subjects.

"Home," in the sense I am using it, refers to the cultural, social, and political boundaries that demarcate varying spaces of comfort, suffering, abuse, and security that define an individual or group's location and positionality. To move away from "home" is to question in historical, semiotic, and structural terms how the boundaries and meanings of "home" are constructed in self-evident ways often outside of criticism. "Home" is about those cultural spaces and social formations that work hegemonically and as sites of resistance. In the first instance, "home" is safe by virtue of its repressive exclusions and hegemonic location of individuals and groups outside of history. In the second case, home becomes a form of "homelessness," a shifting site of identity, resistance, and opposition that enables conditions of self- and social formation. JanMohammed captures this distinction quite lucidly:

> "Home" comes to be associated with "culture" as an environment, process, and hegemony that determine individuals through complicated mechanisms. Culture is productive of the necessary sense of belonging, of "home"; it attempts to suture ... collective and individual subjectivity. But culture is also divisive, producing boundaries that distinguish the collectivity and what lies outside it and that define hierarchic organizations with in the collectivity. "Homelessness", on the other hand, is....an enabling concept ... associated with ... the civil and political space that hegemony cannot suture, a space in which "alternative acts and alternative intentions which are not yet articulated as a social institution or even project can survive. "Homelessness," then, is a situation wherein utopian potentiality can endure.[8]

For Freire, the task of being an intellectual was always forged within the trope of homelessness: between different zones of theoretical and cultural difference; between the borders of non-European and European cultures. In effect, Freire was a border intellectual,[9] whose allegiance was not tied to a specific class and culture as in Gramsci's notion of the organic intellectual; instead, Freire's writings embody a mode of discursive struggle and opposition that not only challenges the oppressive machinery of the State but is also sympathetic to the formation of new cultural subjects and movements engaged in the struggle over the modernist values of freedom, equality, and justice. In part, this explains Freire's interest for educators, feminists, and revolutionaries in Africa, Latin America, and South Africa.

As a border intellectual, Freire ruptured the relationship between individual identity and collective subjectivity. His work makes visible a politics that links human suffering with a project of possibility, not as a static plunge into a textuality disembodied from human struggles, but as a politics of literacy forged in the political and material dislocations of regimes that exploit, oppress, expel, maim, and ruin human life. As a border intellectual, Freire occupied a terrain of "homelessness" in the postmodern sense that suggests there is little possibility of ideological and hegemonic closure, no relief from the incessant tensions and contradictions that inform one's own identity, ideological struggles, and project of possibility. It is this sense of "homelessness," this constant crossing over into terrains of Otherness, which characterized both Freire's life and work. It was as an exile, a border being, an intellectual posed between different cultural, epistemological, and spatial borders that Freire undertook the challenge to situate his own politics of location as a border-crosser.

It is to Freire's credit as a critical educator and cultural worker that he was extremely conscious about the intentions, goals, and effects of crossing borders and how such movements offer the opportunity for new subject positions, identities, and social relations that can produce resistance to and relief from the structures of domination and oppression. While such an insight continuously invested his work with a healthy "restlessness," it has not meant that Freire's work has developed unproblematically. For example, in his earlier work, Freire attempted to reconcile an emancipatory politics of literacy and a struggle over identity and difference, with certain problematic elements of modernism. Freire's incessant attempts to construct a new language, produce new spaces of resistance, imagine new ends and opportunities to reach them were sometimes constrained in totalizing narratives and binary oppositions that deemphasized the mutually contradictory and multiple character of domination and struggle. In this sense, Freire's earlier reliance on emancipation as one and the same with class struggle sometimes erased how women were subjected differently to patriarchal structures; similarly, his call for members of the dominating groups to commit class suicide downplayed the complex, multiple, and contradictory nature of human subjectivity. Finally, Freire's reference to the "masses" or oppressed as being inscribed in a culture of silence appeared to be at odds with both the varied forms of domination these groups labored under and Freire's own belief in the diverse ways in which the oppressed struggle and manifest elements of practical and political agency. While it is crucial to acknowledge the theoretical and political brilliance that informed much of this work, it is also necessary to recognize that it bore slight traces of vanguardism. This is evident not only in the binaries that inform *Pedagogy of the Oppressed* but also in *Pedagogy in Process: The Letters to Guinea-Bissau,* particularly in those sections where Freire argues that the culture of the masses must develop on the basis of science and that emancipatory pedagogy must be aligned with the struggle for national reconstruction.

Without adequately addressing the contradictions these issues raise between the objectives of the state, the discourses of everyday life, and the potential for pedagogical violence being done in the name of political correctness, Freire's work is open to the charge made by some leftist theorists of being overly totalizing. But this can be read less as a reductive critique of Freire's work than as an indication of the need to subject it and all forms of social criticism to analyses that engage its strengths and limitations as part of a wider dialogue in the service of an emancipatory politics. The contradictions raised in Freire's work offer a number of questions that need to be addressed by critical educators about not only Freire's earlier work but also about their own. For instance, what happens when the language of the educator is not the same as that of the oppressed? How is it possible to be vigilant against taking up a notion of language, politics, and rationality that undermines recognizing one's own partiality and the voices and experiences of Others? How does one explore the contradiction between validating certain forms of "correct" thinking and the pedagogical task of helping students assume rather than simply follow the dictates of authority, regardless of how radical the project informed by such authority. Of course, it cannot be forgotten that the strength of Freire's early discourse rests, in part, with its making visible not merely the ideological struggle against domination and colonialism but also the material substance of human suffering, pain, and imperialism. Forged in the heat of life and death struggles, Freire recourse to binary oppositions such as the oppressed versus the oppressor, problem-solving versus problem-posing, science versus magic, raged bravely against dominant languages and configurations of power that refused to address their own politics by appealing to the imperatives of politeness, objectivity, and neutrality. Here Freire straddled the boundary between modernist and anticolonialist discourse; he struggled against colonialism, but in doing so he often reversed rather than ruptured its basic problematic. Benita Parry locates a similar problem in the work of Frantz Fanon: "What happens is that heterogeneity is repressed in the monolithic figures and stereotypes of colonialist representations. ...[But] the founding concepts of the problematic must be refused."[10]

In his later work, particularly in his work with Donaldo Macedo, in his numerous interviews, and in his talking books with authors such as Ira Shor, Antonio Faundez, and Myles Horton, Freire undertook a form of social criticism and cultural politics that pushed against those boundaries that invoke the discourse of the unified, humanist subject, universal historical agents, and Enlightenment rationality.[11] Having refused the privilege of home as a border intellectual situated in the shifting and ever-changing universe of struggle, Freire invoked and constructed elements of a social criticism that shared an affinity with emancipatory strands of postmodern discourse. That is, in his refusal of a transcendent ethics, epistemological foundationalism, and political teleology, he further developed a provisional ethical and political discourse subject to the play of history, culture, and power. As a border intellectual, he constantly reexamined and raised questions about what kind of borders are being crossed and revisited, what kind of identities are being remade and refigured within new historical, social, and political borderlands, and what effects such crossings have for redefining pedagogical practice. In Freire's work, it can be observed that pedagogy is a cultural practice and politics that takes place not simply in schools, but in all cultural spheres. In this instance, all cultural work is pedagogical, and cultural workers inhabit a number of sites that include but are not limited to schools. In a dialogue with Antonio Faundez, Freire talked about his own self-formation as an exile and border-crosser. He states:

> It was by travelling all over the world, it was by travelling through Africa, it was by travelling through Asia, through Australia and New Zealand, and through the islands of the South Pacific, it was by travelling through the whole of Latin America, the Caribbean, North America and Europe—it was by passing through all these different parts of the world as an exile that I came to understand my own country better. It was by seeing it from a distance, it was by standing back from it, that I came to understand myself better. It was by being confronted with another self that I discovered more easily my own identity. And thus I overcame the risk which exiles sometimes run of being too remote in their work as intellectuals from the most real, most concrete experiences, and of being somewhat lost, and even somewhat contented, because they are lost in a game of words, what I usually rather humorously call "specializing in the ballet of concepts."[12]

It is here that we get further indications of some of the principles that informed Freire as a revolutionary. It is in this work and his work with Donaldo Macedo, Ira Shor, and others that we see traces, images, and representations of a political project that are inextricably linked to Freire's own self-formation. It is here that Freire was at his most prescient in unraveling and dismantling ideologies and structures of domination as they emerged in his confrontation with the ongoing exigencies of daily life as manifested differently in the tensions, suffering, and hope between the diverse margins and centers of power that have come to characterize a postmodern/postcolonial world.

Reading Freire's work for the last fifteen years has drawn me closer to Adorno's insight that, "It is part of morality not to be at home in one's home."[13] Adorno was also an exile, raging against the horror and evil of another era, but he was also insistent that it was the role of intellectuals, in part, to challenge those places bounded by terror, exploitation, and human suffering. He also called for intellectuals to refuse and transgress those systems of standardization, commodification, and administration pressed into the service of an ideology and language of "home" that occupied or were complicit with oppressive centers of power. Freire differed from Adorno in that a more profound sense of rupture, transgression, and hope, intellectually and politically, can be witnessed in his work. This is evident in his repeated calls for educators, social critics, and cultural workers to fashion a notion of politics and pedagogy outside of established disciplinary borders; outside of the division between high and popular culture; outside of "stable notions of self and identity ... based on exclusion and secured by terror";[14] outside of homogeneous public spheres; and outside of boundaries that separate desire from rationality, the body from the mind.

Of course, this is not to suggest that intellectuals have to go into exile to take up Freire's work, but it does suggest that in becoming border-crossers, it is not uncommon for many of them to engage his work as an act of bad faith. Refusing to negotiate or deconstruct the borders that define their own politics of location, they have little sense of moving into an "imagined space," a positionality, from which they can unsettle, disrupt, and "illuminate that which is no longer home-like, *heimlich*, about one's home."[15] From the comforting perspective of the colonizing gaze, such theorists often appropriate Freire's work without engaging its historical specificity and ongoing political project. The gaze in this case becomes self-serving and self-referential, its principles shaped by technical and methodological considerations. Its perspective, in spite of itself, is largely "panoptic and thus dominating."[16] To be sure, such intellectuals cross borders less as exiles than as colonialists. Hence, they often refuse to hold up to critical scrutiny their own complicity in producing and maintaining specific injustices, practices, and forms of oppression that deeply inscribe the legacy and heritage of colonialism. Edward Said captured the tension between exile and critic, home and "homelessness" in his comment on Adorno, though it is just as applicable to Paulo Freire:

> To follow Adorno is to stand away from "home" in order to look at it with the exile's detachment. For there is considerable merit in the practice of noting the discrepancies between various concepts and ideas and what they actually produce. We take home and language for granted; they become nature and their underlying assumptions recede into dogma and orthodoxy. The exile knows that in a secular and contingent world, homes are always provisional. Borders and barriers, which enclose us within the safety of familiar territory can also become prisons, and are often defended beyond reason or necessity. Exiles cross borders, break barriers of thought and experience.[17]

Of course, intellectuals from the First World, especially white academics, run the risk of acting in bad faith when they appropriate the work of a Third World intellectual such as Paulo Freire without "mapping the politics of their forays into other cultures,"[18] theoretical discourses, and historical experiences. It is truly disconcerting that First World educators rarely articulate the politics and privileges of their own location, in this case, so at the very least to be self-conscious about not repeating the type of appropriations that inform the legacy of what Said called "Orientialist" scholarship.[19]

I want to conclude by raising some issues regarding what it might mean for cultural workers to resist the recuperation of Freire's work as an academic commodity, a recipe for all times and places. Similarly, I want to offer some broad considerations for reinventing the radicality of Freire's work within the emergence of a postcolonial discourse informed by what Cornel West terms the "decolonization of the Third World, [and characterized by] the exercise of ... agency and the [production of] new ... subjectivities and identities put forward by those persons who had been degraded, devalued, hunted, and harassed, exploited and oppressed by the European maritime empires."[20] The challenge presented by Freire and other postcolonial critics offers new theoretical possibilities to address the authority and discourses of those practices wedded to the legacy of a colonialism that either directly constructs or is implicated in social relations that keep privilege and oppression alive as active constituting forces of daily life within the centers and margins of power.

Postcolonial discourses have made clear that the old legacies of the political left, center, and right can no longer be so easily defined. Indeed, postcolonial critics have gone further and provided important theoretical insights into how such discourses either actively construct colonial relations or are implicated in their construction. From this perspective, Robert Young argues that postcolonialism is a dislocating discourse that raises theoretical questions regarding how dominant and radical theories "have themselves been implicated in the long history of European colonialism—and, above all, the extent to which [they] continue to determine both the institutional conditions of knowledge as well as the terms of contemporary institutional practices—practices which extend beyond the limits of the academic institution."[21] This is especially true for many of the theorists in a variety of social movements who have taken up the language of difference and a concern for the politics of the Other. In many instances, theorists within these new social movements have addressed political and pedagogical issues through the construction of binary oppositions that not only contain traces of racism and theoretical vanguardism but also fall into the trap of simply reversing the old colonial legacy and problematic of oppressed versus oppressor. In doing so, they have often unwittingly imitated the colonial model of erasing the complexity, complicity, diverse agents, and multiple situations that constitute the enclaves of colonial/hegemonic discourse and practice.[22]

Postcolonial discourses have both extended and moved beyond the parameters of this debate in a number of ways. First, postcolonial critics have argued that the history and politics of difference is often informed by a legacy of colonialism that warrants analyzing the exclusions and repressions that allow specific forms of privilege to remain unacknowledged in the language of Western educators and cultural workers. At stake here is the task of demystifying and deconstructing forms of privilege that benefit maleness, whiteness, and property as well as those conditions that have disabled others to speak in places where those who are privileged by virtue of the legacy of colonial power assume authority and the conditions for human agency. This suggests, as Gayatri Spivak has pointed out, that more is at stake than problematizing discourse. More importantly, educators and cultural workers must be engaged in "the unlearning of one's own privilege. So that, not only does one become able to listen to that other constituency, but one learns to speak in such a way that one will be taken seriously by that other constituency."[23] In this instance, postcolonial discourse extends the radical implications of difference and location by making such concepts attentive to providing the grounds for forms of self-representation and collective knowledge in which the subject *and* object of European culture are problematized.[24]

Second, postcolonial discourse rewrites the relationship between the margin and the center by deconstructing the colonialist and imperialist ideologies that structure Western knowledge, texts, and social practices. In this case, there is an attempt to demonstrate how European culture and colonialism "are deeply implicated in each other."[25] This suggests more than rewriting or recovering the repressed stories and social memories of the Other; it means understanding and rendering visible how Western knowledge is encased in historical and institutional structures that both privilege and exclude particular readings, particular voices, certain aesthetics, forms of authority, specific representations, and modes of sociality. The West and Otherness relate not as polarities or binary oppositions in postcolonial discourse but in ways in which both are complicit and resistant, victim and accomplice. In this instance, criticism of the dominating Other returns as a form of self-criticism. Linda Hutcheon captures the importance of this issue with her question: "How do we construct a discourse which displaces the effects of the colonizing gaze while we are still under its influence?"[26] While it cannot be forgotten that the legacy of colonialism has meant large-scale death and destruction as well as cultural imperialism for the Other, the Other is not merely the opposite of Western colonialism, nor is the West a homogeneous trope of imperialism.

This suggests a third rupture provided by postcolonial discourses. The postmodern concern with the "death of the subject" cannot be confused with the necessity of affirming the complex and contradictory character of human agency. Postcolonial discourse reminds us that it is ideologically convenient and politically suspect for Western intellectuals to talk about the disappearance of the speaking subject from within institutions of privilege and power. This is not to suggest that postcolonial theorists accept the humanist notion of the subject as a unified and static identity. On the contrary, postcolonial discourse agrees that the speaking subject must be decentered, but this does not mean that all notions of human agency and social change must be dismissed. Understood in these terms, the postmodernist notion of the subject must be accepted and modified in order to extend rather than erase the possibility for creating the enabling conditions for human agency. At the very least, this would mean coming to understand the strengths and limits of practical reason, the importance of affective investments, the discourse of ethics as a resource for social vision, and the availability of multiple discourses and cultural resources that provide the very grounds and necessity for agency.[27]

Of course, while the burden of engaging these postcolonial concerns must be taken up by those who appropriate Freire's work, it was also necessary for Freire to be more specific about the politics of his own location and what the emerging discourses of postmodernism and postcolonialism meant for self-reflectively engaging both his own work and his location as an intellectual aligned with the State (Brazil). If Freire had the right to draw upon his own experiences, how do these get reinvented so as to prevent their incorporation by First World theorists within colonialist rather than decolonizing terms and practices? But in raising that question, I want to emphasize that what made Freire's work important is that it did not, and still does not, stand still. It is not a text *for* but *against* cultural monumentalism, one that offers itself up to different readings, audiences, and contexts. Moreover, Freire's work has to be read in its totality to gain a sense of how it engaged the postcolonial age. Freire's work cannot be separated from either its history or its author, but it also cannot be reduced to the specificity of intentions or historical location. Maybe the power and forcefulness of Freire's works are to be found here in the tension, poetry, and politics that make it a project for border crossers, those who read history as a way of reclaiming power and identity by rewriting the space and practice of cultural and political resistance. Freire's work represents a textual borderland where poetry slips into politics, and solidarity becomes a song for the present begun in the past while waiting to be heard in the future.

Notes

1. Caren Kaplan, "Deterritorializations: The Rewriting of Home and Exile in Western Feminist Discourse," *Cultural Critique 6* (Spring 1987): 191.
2. An excellent analysis of this problem among Freire's followers can be found in Gail Stygall, "Teaching Freire in North America," *Journal of Teaching Writing* (1988): 113–125.
3. Robert Young, *White Mythologies: Writing History and the West* (New York: Routledge, 1990), p. 158.
4. Joan Borsa, "Towards a Politics of Location," *Canadian Women Studies* (Spring, 1990): 36.
5. Ernesto Laclau quoted in "Building a New Left: An Interview with Ernesto Laclau," *Strategies 1* (1988): 12.

6. Ibid., p. 27.

7. My use of the terms "exile" and "homelessness" have been deeply influenced by the following essays: Carol Becker, "Imaginative Geography," School of the Art Institute of Chicago, unpublished paper, 1991, 12 pp.; Abdul JanMohamed, "Worldliness-Without World, Homelessness-as-Home: Toward a Definition of Border Intellectual," University of California, Berkeley, unpublished paper, 34pp.; Edward Said, "Reflections on Exile." In Russell Ferguson, Martha Gever, Trinh T. Minh-ha, and Cornel West, eds., *Out There: Marginalization and Contemporary Cultures* (New York: New Museum of Contemporary Art and MIT Press, 1990); Biddy Martin and Chandra Talpade Mohanty, "Feminist Politics: What's Home Got to Do With It?" In Teresa de Lauretis, ed., *Feminist Studies/Critical Studies* (Bloomington: Indiana University Press, 1986); Caren Kaplan, "Deterritorializations: The Rewriting of Home and Exile in Western Feminist Discourse," *Cultural Critique 6* (Spring, 1987): 187–198; see also selected essays in bell hooks, *Talking Back* (Boston: South End Press,1989) and *Yearning* (South End Press, 1990).

8. JanMohamed, Ibid. p. 27.

9. I have taken this term from JanMohamed, "Worldliness-Without World, Homelessness-as-Home," Ibid.

10. Benita Parry, "Problems in Current Theories of Colonial Discourse," *Oxford Literary Review 9* (1987): 28.

11. See for example, Paulo Freire, *The Politics of Education* (New York: Bergin and Garvey, 1985); Paulo Freire and Donaldo Macedo, *Literacy: Reading the Word and the World* (New York: Bergin and Garvey, 1987); Paulo Freire and Ira Shor, *A Pedagogy for Liberation* (London: Macmillan, 1987); Myles Horton and Paulo Freire, *We Make the Road by Walking: Conversations on Education and Social Change,* Brenda Bell, John Gaventa, and John Peters, eds. (Philadelphia: Temple University Press, 1990).

12. Paulo Freire quoted in Paulo Freire and Antonio Faundez, *Learning to Question: A Pedagogy of Liberation* (New York: Continuum, 1989), p. 13.

13. Adorno cited in Edward W. Said, "Reflections on Exile," in Russell Ferguson, Martha Gever, Trinh T. Minh-ha, and Cornel West, eds., *Out There: Marginalization and Contemporary Cultures* (New York: New Museum of Contemporary Art and MIT Press, 1990), p. 365.

14. Biddy Martin and Chandra Talpade Mohanty, Ibid., p. 197.

15. Carol Becker, "Imaginative Geography," School of the Art Institute of Chicago, unpublished paper, 1991, p. 1.

16. JanMohamed, Op cit., p. 10.

17. Edward W. Said, "Reflections on Exile," Op cit., p. 365.

18. JanMohamed, Op cit., p. 3.

19. Edward W. Said, *Orientalism* (New York: Vantage Books, 1979).

20. Cornel West, "Decentering Europe: A Memorial Lecture for James Snead," *Critical Inquiry 33,* no. 1 (1991): 4.

21. Robert Young, *White Mythologies: Writing History and the West* (New York: Routledge, 1990), viii.

22. For an excellent discussion of these issues as they specifically relate to postcolonial theory, see Benita Parry, "Problems in Current Theories of Colonial Discourse," *Oxford Literary Review 9* (1987): 27–58; Abdul JanMohamed, *Manichean Aesthetics: The Politics of Literature in Colonial Africa* (Amherst: University of Massachusetts Press,

1983); Gayatri C. Spivak, *The Post-Colonial Critic: Interviews, Strategies, Dialogues* (New York: Routledge, 1990); Robert Young, *White Mythologies: Writing History and the West* (New York: Routledge, 1990); Homi K. Bhabha, ed., *Nation and Narration* (New York: Routledge, 1990). The ways in which binary oppositions can trap a particular author into the most essentialist arguments can be seen in a work by Patti Lather. What is so unusual about this text is that its call for openness, partiality, and multiple perspectives is badly undermined by the binary oppositions which structure around a simple gendered relation of truth to illusion. See Patti Lather, *Getting Smart* (New York: Routledge, 1991).

23. Gayatri C. Spivak, *The Post-Colonial Critic,* op. cit., 42.

24. This position is explored in Helen Tiffin, "Post-Colonialism, Post-Modernism, and the Rehabilitation of Post-Colonial History," *Journal of Commonwealth Literature 23,* no. 1 (1988): 169–181; Helen Tiffin, "Post-Colonial Literatures and Counter-Discourse," *Kunapipi 9,* no. 1 (1987): 17–34.

25. Robert Young, *White Mythologies,* op. cit., 119.

26. Linda Hutcheon, "Circling the Downspout of Empire," in Ian Adam and Helen Tiffin, eds., *Past the Last Post* (Calgary: University of Calgary Press, 1990), 176.

27. I explored this issue in Henry A. Giroux, *Border Crossings: Cultural Workers and the Politics of Education* (New York: Routledge, 1992).

13
The Promise of Democracy and
Edward Said's Politics of Worldliness
Implications for Academics as Public Intellectuals

⊷

It has become commonplace to acknowledge that post–civil rights America is characterized by a declining interest in and cynicism about mainstream national politics. What is much less discussed is the way this crisis in American democracy has been heralded and exacerbated by the nation's increasing skepticism—or even overt hostility—toward the educational system at all levels. Cynicism about politics and skepticism about education have become mutually reinforcing tendencies that to be understood must be analyzed in tandem. Emptied of any substantial content, democracy is imperiled, as individuals are unable to translate their privately suffered misery into broadly shared public concerns and collective action. Civic engagement appears impotent, and public values are rendered invisible, in light of the growing power of multinational corporations not only to shape the content of most mainstream media, but also increasingly to privatize and commercialize remaining public spaces. For many people today, citizenship has become reduced to the act of buying and selling commodities rather than increasing the scope of their freedoms and rights in order to expand the operations of a substantive democracy. An incessant assault on critical thinking itself and a rising bigotry have undercut the possibility for providing a language in which vital social institutions can be defended as a public good. Moreover, as social visions of equity recede from public memory, unfettered brutal self-interest and greed combine with retrograde social polices to make security and safety a top domestic priority. Unfortunately, the university offers no escape and little resistance. Instead, the humanistic knowledge and values of the university are being excised as higher education becomes increasingly corporatized and stripped of its democratic functions. In the corporate university, academics are now expected to be "academic entrepreneurs," valuable only for the money and prestige they bring, and not for the education they can offer. Scholarshit, as Marcuse once put it, now replaces critical scholarship just as the private intellectual now replaces the public intellectual and as the public relations intellectual supplants the engaged intellectual in the wider culture. In addition, faculty are increasingly downsized, turned into an army of part-time workers who are overworked and underpaid, just as graduate students are reduced to wage slavery as they take over many undergraduate teaching functions.

It is important to note that such attacks on higher education in the U.S. come not only from a market-based ideology that would reduce education to training and redefine schools as investment opportunities, they also come from right wingers such as Lynne Cheney, conservative Christian organizations such as the American Family Association, and right-wing politicians who have launched an insidious attack on postcolonial theory, Middle Eastern Studies, critical pedagogy, and any field "which generates critical inquiry and thought often in opposition to the aims of the U.S. State" and the Bush regime.[1] This is the same group who believes that gay married couples are terrorists, while it says nothing about U.S. involvement in the torture and abuse at Abu Ghraib prison or the U.S. policy of Extraordinary Rendition that allows the CIA to kidnap people and send them to authoritarian countries to be tortured.

The nature of the attack on higher education can be seen in attempts by conservative legislators in Ohio and a number of other states to pass bills such as the Academic Bill of Rights which argues that academics should be hired on the basis of their conservative ideology in order not only to balance out faculties dominated by left-wing professors, but also to control what conservative students are taught, allegedly immunizing them against ideas that might challenge or offend their ideological comfort zones. It gets worse. The governor of Colorado recently called for the firing of Ward Churchill because of an essay he wrote shortly after 9/11 in which he condemned U.S. foreign policy. Additionally, U.S. congressman Anthony Weiner from New York has called for the firing of Joseph Massad, a Columbia University professor, who has been critical of Israeli policies against Palestinians. Under the guise of patriotic correctness, conservatives want to fire prominent academics such as Churchill and Massad because of their opposition to U.S. foreign policy, while completely ignoring the quality of their intellectual scholarship. Challenging the current conservative wisdom—that is, holding views at odds with conservative orthodoxy—has now become the grounds for either being labeled as un-American or being dismissed from one's job. For instance, David Horowitz, a favorite benefactor of the conservative Olin Foundation, has insisted that the "250 peace studies programs in America teach students to identify with America's terrorist enemies and to identify America as a Great Satan."[2] Sacrificed in this discourse about higher education is the notion that a vibrant democracy cannot exist without educated citizens, and that for a "robust democracy[,] we need more than rational deliberation[;] we need public realms that remind us that [democratically informed] politics matter."[3] Clearly more is at stake here than the absence of public intellectuals as subjects to theorize and teach about the promise of a radical and inclusive democracy. The real crisis is the devaluation of the university as a democratic public sphere and the ongoing corporatization of intellectual work and academic labor.

In spite of their present embattled status and the inroads made by corporate power and the neoconservative Right, universities and colleges remain uniquely placed to prepare students to both understand and influence the larger educational forces that shape their lives. Such institutions by virtue of their privileged position, division of labor, and alleged dedication to freedom and democracy also have an obligation to draw upon those traditions and resources capable of providing a critical, liberal, and humanistic education to all students in order to prepare them not only for a society in which information and power have taken on new and potent dimensions, but also for confronting the rise of a disturbing number of antidemocratic tendencies in the most powerful country in the world and elsewhere across the globe.

Part of such a challenge means that educators need to rethink the important presupposition that higher education cannot be separated from the imperatives of an inclusive democracy and that the crisis of higher education must be understood as part of the wider crisis of politics, power, and culture. Jacques Derrida argued that democracy contains a promise of what is to come and that it is precisely in the tension between the dream and the reality of democracy that a space of agency, critique, and education opens up and signals both the normative and political character of democracy. But, as Derrida was well aware, democracy also demands a pedagogical intervention organized around the need to create the conditions for educating citizens who have the knowledge and skills to participate in public life, question institutional authority, and engage the contradiction between the reality and promise of a global democracy. For Derrida, democracy must not only contain the structure of a promise, it must also be nurtured in those public spaces in which "the unconditional freedom to question" becomes central to any viable definition of individual and social agency.[4] At stake here is the recognition that if democracy is to become vital, it needs to create citizens who are critical, interrogate authority, hold existing institutions accountable for their actions, and are able to assume public responsibility through the very process of governing.[5] Hence, for Derrida, higher education is one of the few public spaces left where unconditional resistance can be both produced and subjected to critical analysis. In Derrida's perspective, the university "should thus be a place in which nothing is beyond question, not even the current and determined figure of democracy, and not even the traditional idea of critique."[6] The role of the university in this instance, and particularly the humanities, should be to create a culture of questioning and resistance aimed at those ideologies, institutions, social practices, and "powers that limit democracy to come."[7] Derrida's views on higher education and democracy raise important questions about not only the purpose of higher education but also what it means for academics to address what the sociologist Zygmunt Bauman calls "taking responsibility for our responsibility."[8]

Part of the struggle for viewing the university as a democratic public sphere and a site of struggle against the growing forces of militarism, corporatism, neo conservatism, and the religious fundamentalism of the Christian right demands a new understanding of what it means to be a public intellectual which, in turn, suggests a new language for politics itself. Central to such a challenge is the necessity to define intellectual practice in moral and ethical terms that encourage academics to speak with conviction, enter the public sphere in order to take responsibility for and address important social, po-litical and economic issues, and construct alternative models for bridging the gap between higher education and the broader society. This is a notion of intellectual practice that refuses both the instrumentality and privileged isolation of the academy, while affirming a broader vision of learning that links knowledge to the power of self-definition. This type of intellectual practice also conceives of the roles of administrators, academics, and stu-dents in terms of their abilities to expand the scope of democratic freedoms, particularly as they address the crisis of the social as part and parcel of the crisis of democracy itself.

Crisis and criticism are two concepts that are pivotal to defining both the nature of domination and the forms of opposition that often emerge in re-sponse to it. Within the last decade, the urgency associated with the notion of crisis and its implied call to connect matters of knowledge and scholarship to the worldly space of politics has largely given way to a concept of criti-cism among many academics, which implies a narrowing of the definition of politics and an inattentiveness to the public spaces of struggle, politics, and power. As Sheldon Wolin points out, crisis invokes a particular notion of worldliness in which politics embodies a connection between theory and public life.[9] In contrast, criticism signifies a more disembodied, less tactical version of politics. Such a politics downplays or disregards worldliness and is generally more contemplative, spectatorial, and in "search of distance rather than intervention driven by urgency."[10]

Those in the academy who support the professional act of criticism often argue that the close reading of texts has important educational value, espe-cially for students learning how to read critically.[11] Of course, Wolin's notion of criticism as "unworldly" neither denies the pedagogical value of a critical attentiveness to texts nor provides any support for a fashionable anti-intel-lectualism among some die-hard activists. Wolin argues, instead, against the insularity of such a pedagogical task, one that has a tendency to ignore questions of intervention and degenerate into scholasticism, formalism, or career opportunism. We can get a glimpse of how this discourse plays out politically in a recent *New York Times* op ed article in which Stanley Fish urged academics "to just do their jobs, to keep their intellectual work within the ivory tower, and to avoid crossing," as he put it, "the boundary between academic work and partisan advocacy" so that outsiders would be less tempted to interfere. Oddly reversing one of Marx's most important ideas, Fish argues, "Our job is not to change the world, but to interpret it."[12] This is also a far cry from John Dewey's call to link education to the creation of an articulate public. In opposition to Fish's retreat from understanding education as a moral and political practice, rather than a merely contemplative one, a politics of crisis often links knowledge and learning to the performative and worldly space of action and engagement, energizing people to not only think critically about the world around them but to also use their capacities as social agents to intervene in the larger social order and confront the myriad forms of symbolic, institutional, and material relations of power that shape their lives. In my view, it is precisely this connection between pedagogy and agency, knowledge and power, thought and action that must be mobilized in order to confront the current crisis of authoritarianism looming so large in the United States today.

In taking up this crisis, I want to examine Edward Said's notion of worldliness and analyze its implication for both the nature of what it means to be a public intellectual and what it would mean to make the pedagogical more political. Edward Said is particularly relevant here because his work embodied both a particular kind of politics and a specific notion of how intellectuals should engage public life.

Few intellectuals have done more within the last four decades to offer a politics of worldliness designed to confront the crisis of democracy under the reign of neoliberalism and the emerging authoritarianism in the United States and other nations throughout the world than Edward Said, one of the most widely known, influential, and controversial public intellectuals of the latter part of the twentieth century. While known primarily as a critic of Western imperialism and a fierce advocate for the liberation of the Palestinian people, he is also widely recognized for his important contributions as a scholar whose work has had an enormous impact on a variety of individuals, groups, and social movements. His importance as a cultural theorist and engaged intellectual is evident in his pathbreaking work on culture, power, history, literary theory, and imperialism. Not only is Said allegedly responsible for the founding of such academic genres as postcolonial studies and colonial discourse analysis, his work has also had an enormous influence on a wide range of other disciplines as well as on an array of academics and cultural workers, including visual artists, museum curators, filmmakers, anthropologists, and historians. He is one of the few academics whose voice and work addressed with equal ease a variety of specialized and general audiences within a global public sphere. While he was always clear, he was never simplistic, and he managed throughout the course of his forty-year career to provide theoretical discourses and critical vocabularies that enabled a range of academics and activists within a variety of disciplines and public spaces not only to speak truth to power and write against the historical narratives fashioned by ruling classes and groups, but also to reclaim a politics in which matters of power, agency, resistance, and collective struggle became paramount.

A controversial and courageous public intellectual, Said provided an important model for what it meant to combine scholarship and commitment. And in doing so, he did not shy away from the difficult theoretical and political task of trying to understand how the current elements of authoritarianism in changing historical contexts could be addressed and resisted. Said recognized that the newer models of authoritarianism, with their drive towards absolute power and the relentless repression of dissent, were taking different forms from those twentieth century regimes of terror that marked the former Soviet Union, Nazi Germany, and fascist Italy. Protofascism in the new millennium was now emerging under the banner of free-market fundamentalism, a reckless unilateralism in foreign affairs, an embrace of right-wing Christian evangelicism, a neoliberal assault on the welfare state, and the corporate control of a mass media reduced largely to a benign, if not sometimes cranky, adjunct of corporate and government interests. The war on terrorism, Said rightly recognized, had become a rationale for a war on democracy, unleashing both material and symbolic violence at home and abroad on any movement fighting for the right to justice, liberty, and equality, and especially for the rights of the Palestinians to an independent state.

Attentive to how the university and other dominant sites of power constructed historical narratives, Said urged generations of students to take seriously the narrativizing of political culture as a central feature of modern politics. His now legendary works *Orientalism* (1978) and *Culture and Imperialism* (1993) probed deeply into questions concerning who controls the economic, political, and pedagogical conditions for telling historical narratives, which agents produce such stories, how such stories become part of the fabric of commonsense, and what it might mean for scholars/activists to seriously engage the recognition that struggles over culture are also struggles over meaning, identity, power, inclusion, and the future.[13] Of course, such interventions reap no rewards from established powers and his own work was constantly policed and dismissed as either anti-American or anti-Semitic.

One example of such a hostile dismissal can be found in how one of the most powerful newspapers in the world, the *New York Times,* framed his obituary in 2003. Richard Bernstein, the author and a noted conservative, constantly invoked Said's critics who claimed that his work was "drenched in jargon," "ignored vast bodies of scholarship," and that his critiques of Israel were tantamount to "supporting terrorism."[14] Bernstein even went so far as to bring up a story that appeared in 2000 about a photograph that pictured Said at the Lebanese border about to throw a rock allegedly at an Israeli guardhouse. What makes Bernstein's commentary all the more shocking is when it is juxtaposed with Alan Riding's obituary in the *New York Times* of Leni Reifenstahl, the filmmaker for the Third Reich, who had died a few weeks before Said. Considered one of Hitler's most brilliant propagandists, Reifenstahl was treated to a memorial in the *New York Times* that is far more generous and forgiving than the one accorded later to Said.[15] This display of crassly distorted reporting may say less about Bernstein's own ideological prejudices than about the mainstream media's general propensity to be more supportive and comfortable with authoritarian ideologies than with those intellectuals who critique and resist what they perceive as both the escalation of human suffering and the increasing slide of the United States into a new and dangerous form of authoritarianism.[16]

While it is a daunting task to try to assess the contributions of Edward Said's overall work in these dire times in order to resist the increasing move towards what I have called elsewhere a new authoritarianism in the U.S., I think it might be useful to commence such a project by providing a critical commentary on the relevance of Said's notion of wakefulness, and how it both shapes his important consideration of academics as oppositional public intellectuals and his related emphasis on cultural pedagogy and cultural politics. I want to begin with a passage that I think offers a key to the ethical and political force of much of his writing. This selection is taken from his 1999 memoir, *Out of Place*, which describes the last few months of his mother's life in a New York hospital and the difficult time she had falling to sleep because of the cancer that was ravaging her body. Recalling this traumatic and pivotal life experience, Said's meditation moves between the existential and the insurgent, between private suffering and worldly commitment, between the seductions of a "solid self" and the reality of a contradictory, questioning, restless, and at times, uneasy sense of identity. He writes:

"Help me to sleep, Edward," she once said to me with a piteous trembling in her voice that I can still hear as I write. But then the disease spread into her brain— and for the last six weeks she slept all the time—my own inability to sleep may be her last legacy to me, a counter to her struggle for sleep. For me sleep is something to be gotten over as quickly as possible. I can only go to bed very late, but I am literally up at dawn. Like her I don't possess the secret of long sleep, though unlike her I have reached the point where I do not want it. For me, sleep is death, as is any diminishment in awareness.... Sleeplessness for me is a cherished state to be desired at almost any cost; there is nothing for me as invigorating as immediately shedding the shadowy half-consciousness of a night's loss, than the early morning, reacquainting myself with or resuming what I might have lost completely a few hours earlier. I occasionally experience myself as a cluster of flowing currents. I prefer this to the idea of a solid self, the identity to which so many attach so much significance. These currents like the themes of one's life, flow along during the waking hours, and at their best, they require no reconciling, no harmonizing. They are "off" and may be out of place, but at least they are always in motion, in time, in place, in the form of all kinds of strange combinations moving about, not necessarily forward, sometimes against each other, contrapuntally yet without one central theme. A form of freedom, I like to think, even if I am far from being totally convinced that it is. That skepticism too is one of the themes I particularly want to hold on to. With so many dissonances in my life I have learned actually to prefer being not quite right and out of place.[17]

It is this sense of being awake, displaced, caught in a combination of diverse circumstances that suggest a particular notion of worldliness—a critical and engaged interaction with the world we live in mediated by a responsibility for challenging structures of domination and for alleviating human suffering. As an ethical and political stance, worldliness rejects modes of education removed from political or social concerns, divorced from history and matters of injury and injustice. In commenting on his own investment in worldliness, Said writes: "I guess what moves me mostly is anger at injustice, an intolerance of oppression, and some fairly unoriginal ideas about freedom and knowledge."[18] For Said, being awake becomes a central metaphor for defining the role of academics as oppositional public intellectuals, defending the university as a crucial public sphere, engaging how culture deploys power, and taking seriously the idea of human interdependence while at the same time always living on the border—one foot in and one foot out, an exile and an insider for whom home was always a form of homelessness. As a relentless border crosser, Said embraced the idea of the "traveler" as an important metaphor for engaged intellectuals. As Stephen Howe, referencing Said, points out, "It was an image which depended not on power, but on motion, on daring to go into different worlds, use different languages, and 'understand a multiplicity of disguises, masks, and rhetorics. Travelers must suspend the claim of customary routine in order to live in new rhythms and rituals ... the traveler crosses over, traverses territory, and abandons fixed positions all the time.'"[19] And as a border intellectual and traveler, Said embodied the notion of always "being quite not right," evident by his principled critique of all forms of certainties and dogmas and his refusal to be silent in the face of human suffering at home and abroad.

Being awake meant accepting the demands of worldliness, which implied giving voice to complex and controversial ideas in the public sphere, recognizing human injury beyond the privileged space of the academy, and using theory as a form of criticism to redress injustice.[20] Worldliness required not being afraid of controversy, making connections that are otherwise hidden, deflating the claims of triumphalism, bridging intellectual work and the operation of politics. Worldliness meant refusing the now popular sport of academic bashing or embracing a crude call for action at the expense of rigorous intellectual and theoretical work. On the contrary, it meant combining rigor and clarity, on the one hand, and civic courage and political commitment, on the other. Worldliness as a pedagogical construct meant using theory as a resource, recognizing the worldly space of criticism as the democratic underpinning of publicness, defining critical literacy not merely as a competency, but as an act of interpretation linked to the possibility of intervention in the world. Worldliness pointed to a kind of border literacy in the plural in which people learned to read and write from multiple positions of agency; it also was indebted to the recognition forcibly stated by Hannah Arendt that "Without a politically guaranteed public realm, freedom lacks the worldly space to make its appearance."[21]

From the time of his own political awakening after the 1967 Arab-Israeli war, Said increasingly became a border crosser, moving between his Arab past and his New York present, mediating his fierce defense of Palestinian rights and the demands of a university position that gave him the freedom to write and teach but at the same time used its institutional power to depoliticize the politics of knowledge or, to use Said's terms, "impose silence and the normalized quiet of unseen power."[22]

A number of us writing in the fields of critical pedagogy and cultural studies in the 1970s and early 1980s who had been reared on the political courage and critical insights of Herbert Marcuse, Antonio Gramsci, Paulo Freire, and others were particularly taken with Said's view of the engaged public intellectual, particularly his admonition to intellectuals to function within institutions, in part, as exiles, "whose place it is publicly to raise embarrassing questions, to confront orthodoxy and dogma (rather than to produce them), to refuse to be easily co-opted by governments or corporations."[23] This politically charged notion of the oppositional intellectual as homeless—in exile, and living on the border, occupying an unsutured, shifting, and fractured social space in which critique, difference, and a utopian potentiality can endure—provided the conceptual framework for generations of educators fighting against the deadly instrumentalism and reactionary ideologies that shaped dominant educational models at the time and which still do at the beginning of the twenty-first century.[24]

Said provided many of us in the academy with a critical vocabulary for extending the meaning of politics and critical awareness. In part, he did this by illuminating the seductions of what he called the cult of professionalism with its specialized languages, its neutralizing of ideology and politics through a bogus claim to objectivism, and its sham elitism and expertise rooted in all the obvious gendered, racial, and class specific hierarchies. He was almost ruthless in his critique of a narrow ethic of professionalism with its "quasi religious quietism" and its self-inflicted amnesia about serious sociopolitical issues.[25] For Said, the cult of professionalism separated culture, language, and knowledge from power and in doing so avoided the vocabulary for understanding and questioning how dominant authority worked through and on institutions, social relations, and individuals. Rooted in narrow specialisms and thoroughly secure in their professed status as experts, many full-time academics retreated into narrow modes of scholarship that displayed little interest in how power was used in institutions and social life to include and exclude, provide the narratives of the past and present, and secure the authority to define the future.[26]

Said was especially critical of those intellectuals who slipped into a kind of professional somnambulism in which matters of theory have less to do with a conscious challenge to politics, power, and injustice than with either a deadening scholasticism or a kind of arcane cleverness—a sort of narcotic performance in fashionable irony—that as he put it, neither threatens anyone nor opposes anything. He was extremely disheartened by the academic turn in literary theory and cultural studies towards a depoliticized postmodernism in the 1980s, and he viewed such a turn as an unacceptable retreat from one of the primary obligations of politics and intellectuals: "to reduce the violence and hatred that have so often marked human social interaction."[27] But he did more than supply a language of critique; he also illustrated what it meant to link text to context, knowledge to social change, culture to power, and commitment to courage. He gave us a language for politicizing culture, theorizing politics, thinking about what it meant to lead a "nonfascist" life, and recognizing what it meant to make the pedagogical more political. Not only did his pioneering work give us a deeper understanding of how power is deployed through culture, but he laid the foundation for making culture a central notion of politics and politics a crucial feature of pedagogy, thus providing an invaluable connection between pedagogy and cultural politics. More specifically, Said made it clear that pedagogy resided not merely in schools but in the force of the wider culture and in doing so he not only expanded the sites of pedagogy but the possible terrains of struggle within a vast number of public spheres.

Refusing to separate learning from social change, he constantly insisted that we fail theory when we do not firmly grasp what we mean by the political, and that theorizing a politics of and for the twenty-first century was one of the most challenging issues facing the academy. He urged us to enter into a dialogue with colleagues and students about politics and the knowledge we seek to produce together, and to connect such knowledge to broader public spheres and issues. He argued that the role of engaged intellectuals was not to consolidate authority but to understand, interpret, and question it.[28] According to Said, social criticism had to be coupled with a vibrant self-criticism, the rejection "of the seductive persuasions of certainty," and the willingness to take up critical positions without becoming dogmatic or intractable.[29] While he recognized the importance of identity politics, he was equally concerned with how to connect particularized notions of justice with more generalized notions of freedom. What is particularly important about Said's work is his recognition that intellectuals have a special responsibility to promote a state of wakefulness by moving beyond the language of pointless denunciations. As such, he refused to view the oppressed as doomed actors or power as simply a crushing form of oppression. For Said, individuals and collectivities had to be regarded as potential agents and not simply as victims or ineffectual dreamers. It is this legacy of critique and possibility, of resistance and agency that infuses his work with concrete hope, and offers a wealth of resources to people in and out of the academy who struggle on multiple fronts against the rising forces of authoritarianism both at home and abroad.

At a time when domination comes not only from the New Right and neoliberals, but also from the religious right, Said's emphasis on secularism—"the observation that human beings make their own history"—not only reminds us of the need to fight against all those forces that relegate reason to the dustbin of history, but also to recognize the multiple sites in which a mindless appeal to scripture, divine authority, and other extrasocial forms of dogmatism undermines the possibility of human agency.[30] For Said, new sites of pedagogy had to be developed and old ones used to educate existing and future generations to the value of critical thought and social engagement. Said believed that discourses of critique and crisis were always intertwined with public life and that rather than lift the activity of the contemporary critic out of the world it firmly placed him or her in the material and political concerns of the global public sphere, one that could never be removed from the considerations of history, power, politics, and justice. And it is this linking of a healthy skepticism for what authorities say and Said's insistence on the need for human beings to make their own history that gives his notion of secular criticism such force. Of course, Said was against all fundamentalisms, religious and political, and he believed that secular criticism should always come before solidarity. Priestly fundamentalists occupy churches, mosques, synagogues, and the university and their quasireligious quietism—with its appeal to either extra social forces (such as the hidden hand of history or the market) or to complex, theoretical discourses that drown out the worldliness of the text, language, and public life—must be rejected at all costs. Both Said's view of the public intellectual and secular criticism informed each other and is clear in his claim that "even in the very midst of a battle in which one is unmistakably on one side against another, there should be criticism, because there must be critical consciousness if there are to be issues, problems, values, even lives to be fought for."[31]

Near the end of his life, Said argued that the United States government was in the hands of a cabal, a junta "dominated by a group of military-minded neoconservatives" who pose a grave threat to world peace and global democracy.[32] Seymour Hersh, the Pulitzer prize–winning journalist, recently repeated this criticism when he claimed that the United States "has been taken over by a cult of eight or nine neo conservatives who have somehow grabbed the government."[33] For Said, the battle over democracy was in part a struggle over the very status of politics as a critical engagement, agency as an act of intervention geared at shaping public life, and resistance as the ability to think critically and act with civic courage. He believed that every vestige of culture as a site of political struggle and civic courage was being effaced from the American landscape. He argued that such acts of symbolic violence could be seen in Laura Bush's attempt to organize a national conference of poets in ways that gave art "a decorative rather than engaged status;" it was also obvious in former Attorney General John Ashcroft's ordering that the "Spirit of Justice" statue be covered up so as to hide the view of her naked breasts, or the United Nations' willingness to cover up a reproduction of Picasso's famous antiwar painting *Guernica* during former Secretary of Defense Colin Powell's visit to the Security Council.[34] Said believed such acts of censorship provided further evidence of the fact that Americans live in a culture increasingly ruled by fear and repression, a society that has stopped questioning itself, a culture where the gap between the rich and the poor has become obscene, and where the stranglehold of the far right on government does not bode well for the environment, youth, labor, people of color, gays, or the reproductive rights of women.

So much of what Said wrote and did with his life offers both a model and inspiration for what it means to take back politics, social agency, collective struggle, and the ability to define the future. Said recognized with great insight that academics, students, and other cultural workers had important roles to play in arousing and educating the public to think and act as active citizens in an inclusive democratic society. Most importantly, he called upon such groups to put aside their petty squabbling over identities and differences and to join together collectively in order to become part of what he called a "rendezvous of victory," a fully awakened, worldly coalition that directs its energies to opposing those forces at home and abroad that are pushing us into the age of totalitarianism lite, without anyone complaining or, for that matter, even noticing.[35]

There is considerable cynicism among social theorists about the death of politics, and thus, the prospects for a more equitable and just social order in which the most important social and political problems are not reduced to matters of efficiency or profit. I would hope that, of all groups, educators and students would be the most vocal and militant in challenging this assumption by making it clear that at the heart of any form of critical education is the assumption that learning should be used to address major social issues, fully engage matters of power and inequality in all aspects of daily life, and foster in every way possible the imperatives of economic, cultural, and social justice. Public and higher education may be one of the few spheres left for adults to provide the conditions for young people to become not only critically engaged social agents, but also symbols of a future in which democracy creates the conditions for each generation of youth to struggle anew to sustain the promise of a democracy that has no endpoint but must be continuously expanded into a world of new possibilities and opportunities for keeping justice and hope alive and, to echo a current slogan of the global justice movement, to imagine that a new world is possible.

Notes

1. A. Naomi Paik, "Education and Empire, Old and New," unpublished paper. (January 8, 2005). 38pp.

2. Robert Ivie, "Academic Freedom and Political Heresy," unpublished manuscript.

3. Margaret Kohn, "The Mauling of Public Space," *Dissent* (Spring 2001), p. 77.

4. Jacques Derrida, "The Future of the Profession or the Unconditional University," in Laurence Simmons and Heather Worth, eds., *Derrida Downunder* (Auckland, NZ: Dunmore Press, 2001), p. 233.

5. Cornelius Castoriadis, "Democracy as Procedure and Democracy as Regime," *Constellations 4*, no. 1 (1997): 10.

6. Derrida, "The Future of the Profession or the Unconditional University," p. 253.

7. Ibid.

8. Cited in Madeline Bunting, "Passion and Pessimism," *Guardian*, April 5, 2003. Available online: http:/books.guardian.co.uk/print/0,3858,4640858,00.html.

9. Sheldon Wolin, "Political Theory: From Vocation to Invocation," in Jason Frank and John Tambornino, eds., *Vocations of Political Theory* (Minneapolis: University of Minnesota Press, 2000), pp. 3–22.

10. Ibid.

11. See Gerald Graff, *Beyond the Culture Wars: How Teaching the Conflicts Can Revitalize American Education* (New York: W.W. Norton, 1992); Stanley Fish, *Professional Correctness: Literary Studies and Political Change* (New York: Clarendon Press, 1995).

12. Stanley Fish, "Why We Built the Ivory Tower," *New York Times*, May 21, 2004, p. A23. See also Robert Ivie, "A Presumption of Academic Freedom," *Review of Education, Pedagogy, and Cultural Studies 27* (2005): 4.

13. Edward Said, *Orientalism* (New York: Vintage Press, 1979); Edward Said, *Culture and Imperialism* (New York: Knopf, 1992).

14. Richard Bernstein, "Edward W. Said, Literary Critic and Advocate for Palestinian Independence, Dies at 67," *New York Times*, September 26, 2003, p. C23.

15. Alan Riding, "Leni Riefenstahl, 101, Dies; Film Innovator Tied to Hitler," *New York Times*, September 10, 2003, p. C14.

16. A classic example of this can be seen in the November 2, 2003 *New York Times Sunday Magazine*, in which Deborah Solomon interviews Noam Chomsky. Solomon ends the interview by suggesting Chomsky is a self-hating Jew because he criticizes Israeli policies, needs to be psychoanalyzed, and is driven by ambition. She ends the interview

by asking Chomsky if he feels guilty about "living a bourgeois life and driving a nice car" and if he has "considered leaving the United States permanently?" Clearly these questions reveal much more about Solomon, her editors, and the *New York Times* than they might about Chomsky, though he answers all of her questions in ways that reveal how foolish she is. Two of the questions and answers are worth repeating:

How would you explain your large ambition?

[Chomsky:] I am driven by many things. I know what some of them are. The misery that people suffer and the misery for which I share responsibility. That is agonizing. We live in a free society, and privilege confers responsibility.

If you feel so guilty, how can you justify living a bourgeois life and driving a nice car?

If I gave away my car, I would feel even more guilty. When I go to visit peasants in Southern Columbia, they don't want me to give up my car. They want me to help them. Suppose I gave up material things—my computer, my car and so on—and went to live on a hill in Montana where I grew my own food. Would that help anyone? No.

17. Edward Said, *Out of Place: A Memoir* (New York: Knopf, 1999), pp. 294–295.

18. See Stephen Howe, "Edward Said: The Traveller and the Exile," *Open Democracy* (October 2, 2003). Available at http://www.opendemocracy.net/articles/ViewPop UpArticle.jsp?id=10&articleId=1561.

19. Ibid.

20. Elaine Scarry, "Beauty and the Scholar's Duty to Justice," *Profession* (2000): 21–31.

21. Hannah Arendt, *Between Past and Future: Eight Exercises in Political Thought* (New York: Penguin, 1977), p. 149.

22. Edward Said, "The Public Role of Writers and Intellectuals," *Nation* (October 1, 2001): 31.

23. Edward Said, *Representations of the Intellectual: The 1993 Reith Lectures* (New York: Pantheon Books, 1994), pp. 8–9.

24. See Henry A. Giroux, *Border Crossings: Cultural Workers and the Politics of Education* (New York: Routledge, 1992).

25. Abdirahman Hussein, *Edward Said: Criticism and Society* (New York: Verso, 2004), p. 302).

26. Stanley Aronowitz, *How Class Works: Power and Social Movement* (New Haven, CT: Yale University Press, 2003), p. 53.

27. Grant Kester, *Conversation Pieces* (Berkeley: University of California Press, 2004), p. 152).

28. Said, *Representations of the Intellectual*, pp. 8–9.

29. Hussein, Op Cit., p. 297.

30. Edward Said, *Reflections on Exile and Other Essays* (Cambridge, MA: Harvard University Press, 2000), p. 501.

31. Edward Said, *The World, the Text and the Critic* (Cambridge, MA: Harvard University Press, 1983), p. 28.

32. Edward Said, *Culture and Resistance: Interviews with David Barsamian* (Cambridge, MA: South End Press, 2003), p. 167.

33. Seymour Hersh, "We've Been Taken over by a Cult," *Democracy Now* (January 26, 2005). Available at http://www.democracynow.org/article.pl?sid=05/01/26/1450204.

34. Said, *Culture and Resistance*, p. 166.

35. Ibid.

Index

⊶

Abu Ghraib, 298
Academic agenda, 211
Academic Bill of Rights, 298
Academic elitism, 94
Academic labor, 299; corporate time and, 263–264
Accommodation, xix, 28, 36
Accountability, 154, 162, 223, 263, 264; public, 228
Accumulation, 10, 22, 23, 24; negative outcomes in, 25
Action: civic, 276; collective, 37, 212; responsible, 35; self-reflection and, 49; social, 187; state, 172n18; structure and, 15; understanding and, 34
Adorno, Theodor W., 291; on citizenship/democracy, 141; on expressions of life, 219; on home, 290
Adult Education, 94, 119n21
Advertising, xiv, 70–75, 110, 112, 221; children and, 130, 143n14; commerce and, 73, 85; communications and, 75; consumption and, 85; controversial, 81–84, 87n11, 139; corporate time and, 265; cultural signs and, 76; media and, 80; mega corporations and, 220–221; pageants and, 134, 138–139; pedagogy and, 220; politics and, 85; school space, 219
Adweek, on Benetton campaign, 74
Aesthetics, 138, 141; pageant, 134; postmodern, 70, 102; transgressive, 140, 236
Affirmative action, 234, 239, 246
African Americans: discrimination against, 173n52; education and, 246;

imprisonment of, 245, 246; personal traits of, 174n62; punishment for, 176n83
Agency, 6, 174, 186, 213, 256, 259, 272, 294, 302; absence of, 258; acquisition of, 196; civic, xvi, 168; collective, 154; critical, 190, 192, 201; cultural spaces and, 199; education and, 169; forms of, 185; historical, 17; individual, 154, 192, 195, 258, 299; legacy of, 307; notion of, 103, 188, 190; pedagogy and, 301, 307; politics and, 69, 258; responsibility and, 276; social, 195; structure and, 7, *See also* Human agency; Political agency; Social agency
Agger, Ben, 263
AIDS, 80, 142n4; advertisement about, 82, 83
Alcoff, Linda, 56–57
Althusser, Louis, 11, 20; on ideology/consciousness, 10; on school knowledge/reproductive process, 9; on theory of ideology, 9
American Educational Studies Association, 193
American Express, 74, 265
American Family Association, 298
American Medical Association, 220
Amin, Samir: on modernity/democracy, 280n69
"Among the Mooks" (Smith), 152
Anderson, Pamela, 131
"Angelus Novus" (Klee), 64
Anti-intellectualism, 90, 201
Anti–welfare policies, 237, 238
Apple, Michael, 20, 25
Arab-Israeli conflict (1967), 305

Arendt, Hannah, 305
Aristotle, 269
Aronowitz, Stanley, xxv, 196; on counter-logic, 45n87; cultural studies/pedagogy and, 93; on higher education/corporate servants, 264; on human praxis, 6; on labor market, 97; on state's police/social functions, 166
Art, xiii, xiv, 119n21; commerce and, 74; politics and, 75
Ashcroft, John, 308
Atlantic Monthly, on Clinton, 170–171n3
Authoritarianism, xviii, 184, 185, 302, 307; threat of, 301, 303
Authority, 275; critical view of, 51, 174; ethics and, 94; knowledge and, 111, 233; power and, 227; production of, 115
Ayers, William, 167

Babette's Pageant and Talent Gazette, 134
Baby Boon: How Family-Friendly America Cheats the Childless, The (Burkett), 150
"Backlash against Children, The" (Belkin), 149
Barnes and Noble, 229n5, 265
Barthes, Roland, 81–82
Baudelot, Christian, 10–11
Bauman, Zygmunt, 208; on consumer society, 266; on political/social agency, 273; on responsibility, 300; on schools/citizenship, 211
Behavior: ethical, 137; nondiscursive, 36; oppositional, 31, 32, 35–36, 37, 38; school, 12; stereotypes and, 174n62; teacher, 90; unprofessional/unethical, 37
Beilharz, Peter, 258, 260
Belkin, Lisa, 149, 171n16; child free worldview and, 150, 151
Belly (film), 246
Benetton, 110; advertising by, 70–75, 80–84, 87n11; controversy and, 74, 82; corporate image of, 73, 79, 81, 82; criticism of, 75–76; difference and, 77, 79; logo of, 75, 76, 83; representational politics of, 71, 78; social justice and, 78; success for, 71–72, 77
Benetton, Fratelli, 71
Benetton, Luciano, 71, 74, 78
Benetton Youth, 73
Bennett, Tony, 83, 195
Bennett, William, 98, 142n4, 206, 250n31
Bernstein, Richard, 302, 303
Beverly, John, 206

Binary oppositions, 288, 289, 292, 296n22
Birmingham Center for Cultural Studies, 94
Black Velvet, 133
Black youth, 104–105; crime and, 120n29, 153, 161; death of, 96, 109; media and, 96; rite of passage for, 108; stereotypes of, 161; violence and, 96, 104–111; zero tolerance and, 165
Black youth film, 104, 105; coming-of-age, 107; not-coming-of-age, 109; violence of, 106–107, 108
Book of Virtues: A Treasury of Great Moral Stories (Bennett), 98
Border-crossers, 249n12, 286, 290, 291, 305
Border intellectual, homelessness and, 286–294
Border pedagogy, 181; as counter-memory, 54–59; as counter-text, 50–54; notion of, 50, 59, 61; politics of difference and, 59–64
Boston Globe, 164
Boundaries: cultural, 51, 234, 287; social, 287
Bourdieu, Pierre, 155; on authority/power, 214; change and, 17; culture and, 13, 17; cultural reproduction and, 12–13, 14; on domination, 15, 18, 19; on hegemonic curriculum, 14, 42n30; on intellectuals, 188–189; realist utopias and, 268; on schooling, 12, 16, 17; on social provisions, 256; on television, 229n8; working-class failure and, 19
Bourgeois life, 11, 310n16
Bowles, Samuel, 7, 9, 10, 11
Boys N' the Hood (film), 105, 107
Brats! (website), 150
Burkett, Elinor, 150, 151
Bush, George H. W., 102
Bush, George W., 255–256
Bush, Laura, 308
Butler, Judith, 273

Cabrini Green Housing Project, 129
Cagney, James, 105, 106
Caillouet, Linda, 143n24
California Correctional Peace Officers Union, 158
California Youth Authority, 246
Calvin Klein, 139
Campbell, Richard, 246
Capital, 170; accumulation of, 10, 22, 23, 24; cultural, 13, 14, 27, 47, 275; cultural

difference and, 76–77; flight, 97; global, 209, 266; social, 47; State and, 20

Capitalism: class interaction and, 8; class power and, 21; dead-end, 104; economic/ideological structures of, 22; global, 270; hyper, 151; neoliberal, 256; State and, 20; youth and, 256

Careerism, 185, 191, 301

Castoriadis, Cornelius, 269; on civic education, 170; on democracy, 169–170; on public time, 261

Censorship, 142n4, 229n11, 308

Center for Social Studies (University of Coimbra), 193

Centre for Contemporary Cultural Studies, 119n20

Change, xxii; democratic, xxviin4, 276; democratic agents of, 273; educational, 19; theory of, 17. *See also* Social change

Cheney, Lynne, 206, 298

Child abuse, 127, 132, 142n4; pageants and, 130, 138; politics of, 138–141; poverty and, 129; race and, 129; social factors of, 129, 143n10; survivors of, 125

Child care, 150, 171n16, 255, 256

Childhood: commodification of, 224; Disney and, 223; shaping, 227; threats to, 125

Children: adultifying, 126; adults and, 131; advertising and, 130, 143n14; as burden, 151; as commodity, 141; as consumers, 128, 132; cultural elite and, 128; criminal justice and, 126; entitlements for, 127; ethical behavior and, 137; future and, 253; marginalization of, 128, 130, 142n9, 143n16; media and, 127; poverty and, 171nn3, 16, 255; rich-poor gap and, 255; rights of, 255

Childress, Dave, 242–243

Chomsky, Noam, 206, 309–310n16

Christian right, 142n4, 300, 302

Chronicle of Higher Education, 89

Churchill, Ward, 298

CIA, kidnapping by, 298

Citizenship, 167, 186, 196, 224, 257, 266; civic, 141; consumerism and, 148, 168, 255; critical, xxiv, 162, 188, 210, 228, 268; demands of, xxi, 270; democracy and, 85, 115, 141, 183, 265; economic, 141; education and, xix, 169, 185, 211, 270; empowerment and, 183–184; globalized, 182, 183, 184; literacy and, 126; notion of, 138, 183, 184, 208, 222, 235; politics and, 141, 147, 168, 183, 258;

privatization of, 148, 188, 228, 237; public, 258, 276; reduction of, 184, 212, 258; social, 147, 148, 169, 170, 189, 213

Civic courage, xxiii, xxvi, 162, 189, 193, 214, 271, 305, 308

Civic education, 154, 182, 188, 213; alternative form of, 170; arguments for, 181; defining, 169; freedom and, 271–272; higher education and, 269; justice and, 262, 271–272; language of, 187; public time and, 262; revisioning, 168, 271

Civic engagement, 258, 266, 297

Civic life, restructuring, 270

Civil rights, 215, 237, 239, 242, 256

Civil society, 21, 228

Class, 4, 47, 92, 114, 147; control, 13; cultural capital and, 14; dynamics of, 84, 233; exploitation, 59; formations, 11; gender and, 109; inequalities, 8; interaction, 8; interests, 22; mobility, 97; oppression, 64, 174; power, 21; reproduction, 13; social, 11, 33, 39, 77; society, 4, 12; struggle, 22, 24, 28; subordination, 5, 235

Clifford, James, 206

Clinton, Bill, 126, 170–171n3

Coca-Cola, 74, 110

Codes: cultural, xxi, 50, 51, 52, 53, 54; dominant, 244; gender, 135; racial, 84, 97–98, 104–111, 241–243, 244; social, 53

Cohen, Ted, 132–33

Cole, David, 158

Collective good, 154

Collective work, 212

College Literature, 117–118n16

Colonialism, 85, 91, 121n54, 286, 289; legacy of, 84, 292, 293

Colors (magazine), 79–80

Columbia University, study by, 160

Commerce, 71; advertising and, 73, 85; aesthetic of, 83; art and, 74; consumption and, 85; culture and, 79, 84; moral responsibility of, 76; politics and, 70, 86

Commercialism, 77, 87n11, 148; national imagination and, 221

Commercialization, 76, 128; culture of, 79, 109, 191, 221; media and, 221; youth and, 152

Commodification, xi, xxii, 75, 79, 81, 83, 84, 85, 100, 228, 290; curriculum, 187; dynamics of, 77, 128; innocence and, 129; youth and, 104, 131, 132, 139, 141, 149–155, 224

Common sense, 36, 42n21, 191, 249n9
Communication, 89, 112, 192; advertising
and, 75; corporate time and, 263; cultural,
95; dynamics of, 76, 174; global, 184;
intercultural, 182; mass, 79, 95
Community, 59, 71, 113; cultural, 91;
degradation and, 155; democratic, 59, 70;
discourse of, 69, 128; participation, 256;
standards, 144n45
Competitiveness, 148, 162, 262, 263
Composition studies, xiv, 93–94
Connell, Robert, 17–18
Conniff, Ruth, 96
Connolly, Deborah R., 171n3
Consciousness, 11, 16, 42n21; education
and, 177n97, 285; ideology and, 10, 12,
34; individual, 49; public, 193; raising, 37;
self-, 49, 103, 206; structuring of, 21
Consumer culture, 258, 266; Disney and,
223; neoliberalism and, 168; pageants
and, 137–138
Consumerism, 70, 170, 213, 227; citizenship
and, 148, 168, 255; ethic of, 86; justice
and, 71; pedagogy and, 86, 140; social
agency and, 260
Consumption, 80, 195, 223, 257; advertising
and, 85; commerce and, 85; pedagogy of,
110; politics and, 85
Containment, 80, 154, 159, 163
Contestation, xxiii, 22, 38, 234
Convict leasing system, 158
Cooper, Louise, 160
Corporate culture, xxiii, 162, 205, 219, 261,
279n47; assault by, xxv, 215; democracy
and, xxv; Disney and, 225; higher
education and, 259; leadership and, 264;
military culture and, 187; minorities and,
175n63; neoliberalism and, 259; pedagogy
and, 187; privatization by, 148
Corporate power, xxiv, 110, 155, 268;
excesses of, 259; intellectuals and, 266;
rise of, 222; universities and, 299
Corporate time: faculty relationships and,
263, 264–265; knowledge under, 265–266;
neoconservatism and, 260; public time
and, 260–268, 272
Corporations, xxi; culture and, 75,
279n47; public space and, 138. *See
also* Megacorporations; Multinational
corporations
Corporatization, 186, 300; higher education
and, 273

Correctional Association of New York, 159
Corrections Corporation of America,
174n53
Corrigan, Philip, 23
Couldry, Nick, 196
Counterculture, 27, 29
Counter-logic, 29, 40, 45n87
Counter-memory, 49, 62; border pedagogy
as, 54–59; critique/transformation and,
58; identities and, 54; pluralism/diversity
and, 58; politics of solidarity and, 58;
public life and, 59; remembrance as, 57,
58–59
Country of Strangers, A (Shipler), 238
Coupland, Douglas, 73
Crime, xxii, 158; media culture and,
120n29; moral panic about, 160, 245, 246;
rate, 157, 161; youth and, 97, 164; zero
tolerance and, 157
Criminal justice system, xxi, 159, 161,
176n77, 245; black males and, 173n35;
children and, 126; expansion of, 158;
reform of, 247; youth and, 175n63
Crimp, Douglas, 82
*Critical Citizens for an Intellectual World: Foreign
Language Education as Cultural Politics*
(Guilherme), 193
Critical citizenship, xxiv, 162, 210, 268;
obligations of, 188, 228
Critical engagement, 60, 262, 308
Critical learning, 60, 162, 197, 228, 266;
human rights and, 261
Critical pedagogy, xiv, xviii, xx, 35, 89, 93,
96, 100, 170, 182, 190, 193, 207, 210, 275,
285, 298, 305; cultural politics and, xxi,
94; cultural studies and, xxi, 114, 116,
196, 200, 214, 216n3; fear of, 186; as form
of educational criticism, 49; history/
politics/ethics and, 174; importance
of, 91; knowledge/power and, 185;
language and, 192; notion of, 50, 174;
politicizing by, 114–115; public culture
and, 269; public pedagogy and, xxiii–xxiv;
reconstitution of, xxiii, 49
*Critical Pedagogy: Political Approaches to
Language and Intercultural Communication*
(Guilherme), 193
Critical psychology, theory of, 35
Critical theory, xv, xix, 28, 195
Critical thinking, 191, 273, 285; collective
action and, 212; engaging in, 126; justice
and, 188; responsible action and, 35

Criticism, xxvi, 51, 186, 307; counter-memory and, 58; pedagogical value of, 300

Cultural capital, 27, 47, 275; class/power and, 14; culture and, 13; legitimizing, 14

Cultural criticism, 47, 93, 101, 200

Cultural difference, 73, 78, 79, 235, 241, 247; capital and, 76–77; democracy and, 191

Cultural forms, 112, 114, 129, 204, 222, 225, 236, 241

Cultural identity, 86, 112, 234

Cultural landscape, 114, 152, 155, 188

Cultural life, 78, 98, 155

Cultural objects, 75, 243–247

Cultural politics, xx–xxi, xxiii, 30, 71, 199, 200, 228, 236, 240, 303; children and, 138; critical pedagogy and, xxi, 94; cultural studies and, 196; material relations of, 198; oppositional, 51; pedagogy and, 169, 198, 200, 214, 273, 306; public policy and, 177n97; racism and, 239

Cultural practice, 91, 96, 129, 132, 204, 206, 236; children and, 130; cultural theories and, 94; pedagogy as, 95; shaping, 88n37

Cultural production, xxiv, xxviiin17, 30, 48, 112, 115, 202, 207, 222; image and, 103; public spheres and, 141; working-class, 17

Cultural reproduction, xix, 27, 200; model of, 7, 12–19

Cultural space, 234; agency and, 199; home and, 287

Cultural studies, xiii, xiv, xx–xxi, 91, 98, 101, 115, 182, 203, 205, 207, 211, 305, 306; as academic discourse, 208; challenges of, 89–90; critical pedagogy and, xxi, 114, 116, 196, 200, 214; cultural politics and, 196; education and, 193, 216n5; framework for, 89; future of, 195; globalization and, 209; intellectual/academic life and, 113; media and, 197; pedagogy and, 92–96, 109, 110, 116–117n5, 197, 198; popular culture and, 923; power and, 92, 199; progressive strains of, 201; project in, 207–211; resistance to, 90; social change and, 94; teachers and, 113, 198–207; transdisciplinary work and, 203; youth and, 111–115

Cultural studies theorists, 117n15, 195, 196, 201, 208, 212, 214, 222, 228; pedagogy and, 210–211; public audiences of, 209

Cultural texts, 236, 240, 243

Cultural workers, 85, 197, 211, 288, 290, 293,

301, 308; as border-crossers, 286, 291, 292; challenge for, 85, 86, 91

Culture, ix, xiii, xv, xx, 91, 109, 192, 202, 215, 239, 301; attack on, 237; black urban, 104, 120n29, 153; black youth, 119n28, 153, 154; civic, 148, 254; class societies and, 4, 12; commercial, 259; commercialization of, 84, 191, 221, 222, 255; crisis of, 17, 186, 299; democratic, 85, 149, 213; education and, xx, xxi, 196; high, 13, 291; home and, 287; importance of, 28, 30; intellectual/artistic, 268; investigation of, 48, 195; levels/relations of, 53; literary, 9; media/technology and, 220; middle-class, 39; military, xxii, 187; moral guardians of, 132; organization/regulation of, 219; pedagogy and, 95, 121n54, 197, 198–199; political, ix, 156, 163, 168, 260, 302; politics and, 226, 233, 237, 240, 291, 306; popular culture and, 126; postmodern, 99; power and, 95, 111, 112, 115, 116, 195, 234–241, 247, 304, 306; print, 204, 205; private life and, 199; promotional, 73, 83, 87n8; role of, 186, 195, 196; scientific, 9; school, 27, 29, 167; social position and, 53; social vocabulary of, 239; State and, 21; transformation of, 220; Western models of, 138; working-class, 13, 14, 39; youth, 96, 99, 109, 152, 153, 219. See also Corporate culture; Popular culture; Public culture

Culture and Imperialism (Said), 302

Culture industries, 139, 230n25

Curriculum, xix, 91, 203; commodification of, 187; development of, 25, 26, 90, 184; hegemonic, 14, 42n30; hidden, 8, 9, 259; ideology and, 16; popular culture and, 53

Dale, Roger, 17, 25

Dangerous Minds (film), 241, 246

Darwinism, 155

Dash, Julie, 105, 108

Daughters of the Dust (film), 108

Davies, David, 17

Davis, Mike, 158

Decatur school board, Jackson and, 163–164

Decolonization, 292, 294

Decontextualization, 81, 82

Deer Hunter, The (film), 243

Deindustrialization, 128, 137, 186

De Lauretis, Teresa, 59–60

Delgado, Gary, 161

Della Piana, Libero, 165

Democracy, xviii, 161, 167, 169–170, 257, 308; citizenship and, 85, 115, 141, 183, 265; common sense/domination and, 191; crisis of, 141, 266, 297, 300, 301; critical, 59; dedication to, 299; discourse of, 55, 56, 151; economic, 201; education and, 169, 189, 190, 192, 269–270; expanding/deepening, 187, 192; global, 183, 184, 189, 192, 229n112, 308; higher education and, 188, 254, 269, 298, 299; inclusive, xviii, 208, 214, 299; liberal, 147–148; multicultural, 86, 247; multiracial, 86, 247; notion of, 183, 190, 222, 228; pedagogy and, 89, 196; political, 260, 270, 299; politics and, 26, 168, 196; promise of, 183, 187, 215; radical, 55, 56, 57, 64, 91, 147, 148, 149, 189, 262; rethinking, 169, 184; social, 260; struggle for, 57, 168, 309; substantive, 109, 159, 169, 187, 189, 229, 261, 272, 297; tools of, 185; war on, xxv, 170, 302; youth and, 253, 257, 268, 309

Democratic citizens, formation of, 59

Democratic rights, 23, 26

Deregulation, 186, 256, 257

Derrida, Jacques: on democracy, 148, 215, 260, 299, 300; on higher education, 271, 299, 300; radical literature and, 118n19; on universities, 299

Desire, 53, 69, 130

Despair, politics of, 101–104

Dewey, John, xvii–xviii, 181, 197, 257, 264, 278n17; on education/articulate public, 301

Diallo, Amadou, 156, 157, 246

Dialogue, 192, 285; critical, 228; cultural studies and, 113; history as, 48

Dickerson, Ernest, 105, 106

Dickerson, Michael, 107

Difference, 51, 58, 110; articulation of, 55; border pedagogy and, 59–64; capital and, 77; colonization of, 59; critical politics of, 55; cultural, 73, 76–77, 78, 79, 191, 235, 241, 247; democracy and, 56, 191; discourse of, 56, 85; ethnic, 77; human agency and, 69–70; identity and, 71, 308; locating, 55; marketplace and, 70; multiculturalism and, 238; pedagogy of, 61, 86; politics of, 59–64, 76–80, 86, 237, 238; publics of, 235; racial, 73, 77, 237, 240, 241; social, 73; social forms and, 55

Disappearing child, 125–128

Discourse, 54, 55, 56, 85, 151; academic, 208; anticolonial, 285, 289; civil rights, 242; community, 69, 128; critical, 93, 187, 189; ethical, 290, 294; hegemonic, 60, 292; liberal, 242; minority, 58, 63; postcolonial, 285, 292, 293–294; public, ix, xxii–xxiv, 149, 200, 225, 234, 240, 243, 245, 261

Discrimination, 86, 128, 150, 173n52; class-race-gender modes of, 3; effects of, 176n83; gender, 174; stigmatization and, 246

Disney, Walt, 224

Disney Corporation, xxiv, 222; accountability for, 223; advertising by, 221; boycotting, 132; childhood and, 221, 223; communication industry and, 220; corporate culture of, 205, 225, 264; culture and, 219, 223–229, 230n25; education and, 223; innocence and, 222–225; pedagogy and, 224, 226; popular culture and, 222; power of, 223, 226, 228; promotion by, 219; public life and, 227–228

Disneyland, 221

Disney Magazine, The, 221

Diversity, 58, 69, 109, 248n2

Division of labor, xxvi, 9, 77–78, 203, 204, 299; intellectual, 90; sexual, 33; social, 3, 10, 33

Dohrn, Bernadine, 167

Domestic militarization, 156, 167, 175n77, 256; expression of, 159; growth of, 166; investment in, 157; zero tolerance and, 160, 170

Dominant class, 5, 6, 10, 20, 28, 306; capitalist production relations and, 22; dominated classes and, 23; economic/political interests of, 13, 24

Dominant culture, 4, 12, 31, 115, 129; criticism of, 60; cultural politics and, 30; pageants and, 139; resisting, 145n47

Dominant ideology: consciousness and, 12; internalization of, 19; production of, 3, 25

Domination, xiii, 28, 34, 62, 85, 202, 208, 227, 270, 289; democracy and, 191; dialectical model of, 29; dynamics of, 15, 22, 36; human agency and, 11, 12; ideological modes of, 5; learning and, 15; logic of, 19, 26, 37; materiality and, 18; power and, 8; schooling and, 5, 18–19, 32; social, 31; State and, 19

Drugs, 128, 153, 161, 250n32

Du Bois, W. E. B., 257

Durham, Meenakshi Gigi, 202
Dylan, Bob, xvi, xxviiin11
Dyson, Michael, 106–107

Earhart, Amelia, 130
Early childhood programs, 166, 255
Economic growth, 97, 121n53
Economic issues, 24, 78, 86, 98, 111,
112, 148, 156, 184; addressing, 300;
neoliberalism and, 155, 256; political,
xiii, 7, 8; schooling and, 8; State and, 23;
working-class students and, 19
Economic-reproductive model, 7–12
Edelman, Marian Wright, 171n16
Edelman, Peter, 170–171n3
Educated hope, xxv, xxvi, 268–277
Education, ix, xxiii, 148, 159, 182, 202,
219, 224; articulate public and, 301;
citizenship and, xix, 169, 185, 211, 270;
corporatization of, 174; critical, 7, 209,
214, 228, 270, 308; cultural studies and,
193, 216n5; culture and, xx, xxi, 196;
democracy and, 169, 189, 190, 192,
269–270; dynamics of, 112; fear of, 186;
incarceration and, 255; intercultural, 193;
lack of opportunity for, 97; liberal, 3–4,
6, 285; modes of, 253; pedagogy and, 50,
118n18, 189, 273, 275; permanent, 95–96,
190, 199; political, xvii, 44n54, 115, 197,
210; politics and, xvii, 115, 210, 211–215,
274–275, 276; public, 3, 121n53, 162,
244, 309; reproductive functions of, 19;
sociology of, x, xiv, xix–xxi; State and,
20; structure/content of, 266; tax cuts
and, 255; youth and, 254. *See also* Civic
education; Higher education
Educational policy, xxi, xxiv, 8, 13, 24
Educational reform, xxiv, 89, 90, 114
Educational theory, xiii, xix, xxi, 7, 28, 32,
52, 91; cultural studies and, 89–90
Education under Siege (Giroux and
Aronowitz), xxv
Educators: as border-crossers, 291; cultural
studies and, 198–207; foreign language/
culture, 192, 193; as public intellectuals,
184, 189; radical, 3, 27–28, 39, 181, 285;
responsibility of, 213. *See also* Teachers
Egan, Jennifer, 255
Eisner, Michael, 219, 223, 224
Elias, Marilyn, 165
Elkind, David, 137
Ellsworth, Elizabeth, 55, 62, 63

Environmental issues, 148, 183, 184
Epps, Omar, 105
Equality, 147, 258, 287, 302; democracy and,
109; racial, 84; social, 110; struggle for,
109
Establet, Roger, 10–11
Ethics, 90, 91, 105, 154, 213, 290; authority
and, 94; critical pedagogy and, 174;
language of, 70; pedagogy and, 116;
pursuit of, 258; rethinking, 169; zero
tolerance and, 168
Ethnicity, 47, 91, 92
Ethnic studies, 203
Ethnocentrism, 59
Ethnographic studies, 8, 28
Euben, Peter, 115, 263
Ewen, Stewart, 81, 83

Fall/Winter 1992 Advertising Campaign
(Benetton), 76
Fanon, Frantz, 289
Fashion industry, pageants and, 137
Faundez, Antonio, 289, 290
FBI, 166, 175n77
Femininity, 135, 138
Feminism, xx, 93; pageants and, 145nn47,
49
Fine, Michelle, 29–30
Finn, Chester, 206
Fish, Stanley, 301
Forbes magazine, on prison labor, 174n53
Foreign languages, 192–193
Foreign policy, 174, 229n11, 302
Foucault, Michel, 18, 56
Foundationalism, 54, 55, 290
Frankfurt School, xix, xx, 100
Freedom, 55, 110, 147, 167, 214, 257,
258, 287; academic, 264; aesthetic,
76; civic, 269, 271–272; dedication to,
299; democratic, 300; economic, 207;
individual, 271; political, 207, 272–272;
social, 36, 207, 270; struggles for, 273; war
against, 170
Freire, Paulo, xvi, 42n25, 181, 197, 294;
Adorno and, 291; as border-crosser,
290; as border intellectual, 287, 288;
colonialism and, 289; critical pedagogy
and, 285; cultural workers and, 288, 292;
homelessness and, 288; politics/pedagogy
and, 290, 291; Said and, 305; work of, 286,
289, 290
Fressola, Peter, 74, 75

Fundamentalism, 189, 190, 300, 302, 307
Future, 101, 253–257

Gangsta rap, 119n28
Garfield, Trevor, 241, 242, 243
Gates, Bill, 264
Gates, Daryl, 246
Gender, xxiii, 4, 92, 114, 147; anatomy and,
    135; children and, 132; class and, 109;
    dynamics of, 91, 233; inequalities, xx, 8;
    politics of, 91; race and, 109; resistance
    theory and, 33; roles, 138, 227
General Electric, 222
Genocide, 188, 246
Geras, Norman, 177n100, 233
Gill, Jason, 150
Gilmore, Ruth Wilson, 156
Gilroy, Paul, 148
Ginsburg, Ruth Bader, 238
Gintis, Herbert, 7, 9, 10, 11
Girl X, 129
Giroux, Henry: background of, xi, xii;
    learning, x–xviii; as mentor, x–xii; reading,
    xviii–xxvi; representation/learning and,
    182; research of, ix, x, xii–xvi, xix, xxi,
    xxv; as teacher, xvi–xviii
Giuliani, Rudi, 157
Glazer, Nathan, 237
Globalization, 47, 48, 78, 208; ethical/
    political challenges of, 209; pedagogy and,
    201, 202
Goldberg, David Theo, 236
Goldfarb, Jeffrey C., 274–275
Goldstein, Richard, 132
Goodman, Ellen, 164, 167
Government, xiv; repressive/ideological
    apparatuses of, 21
Graff, Gerald, 118n18
Gramsci, Antonio, 189, 196; capitalism and,
    20; on hegemony, 20; organic intellectual
    and, 287; Said and, 305; on State, 20, 21
Gray, Herman, 236
Greene, Maxine, 197
Griffin, Pam, 134
Grossberg, Lawrence, 174, 195, 197, 202,
    245; on cultural studies, 119n24, 201,
    216n5; on culture, 236; on Said, 249n18;
    on social identity, 257
Guernica (Picasso), 308
Guilherme, Manuela, 193
Gunster, Shane, 197
Gun violence, 175n63

Habitus, 15, 16
Hall, Stuart, 77, 112, 119n20, 182, 195, 196;
    on symbolic forms/power, 207–208
Hanley, Larry, 259
Harris, Leslie, 108
Harris, Marly, 137
Haug, Frigga, 62
Hawaiian Tropics, 133, 134
Health, 150, 270; public, xiv, 257; insurance,
    150, 171n16, 255
Heard, John, 242
Hebdige, Dick, 92
Hegemonic-state reproductive model, 19–27
Hegemony, 11, 20–21, 28, 30, 42n21; as
    active process, 43n54; capitalist, 39; force/
    ideology and, 20; ideological, 31; political
    education and, 44n54
Helms, Jesse, 239
Hersh, Seymour, 308
Hewlett, Sylvia Ann, 151
Higher education, xxiv, 93, 203, 207, 268,
    309; access to, 265; attack on, 117n8,
    121n53, 298; civic education and, 269;
    corporatization of, 259, 262, 273; crisis of
    the social and, 257–259; democracy and,
    188, 254, 269, 298, 299; developments in,
    235; distribution of power in, 233–234;
    future of, 260–261, 277; institutions
    of, 89; meaning/purpose of, 238, 268;
    mechanisms of, 261; political/ethical
    terms for, 260; as public good, 270;
    public/private, 259; public time in, 262;
    social identity and, 257–259; spending on,
    246; vocationalization of, 187
High School High (film), 241
Hinkson, John, 267
Hirschfield, Bob, 161
History, xii, 16, 51, 62, 70, 307; critical
    pedagogy and, 174; as dialogue, 48;
    modernist images of, 47; sense of, 203
Hitchcock, Peter, 113
Hitler, Adolf, 303
Hoggart, Richard, 94, 119n20
Hollywood text, racial coding and, 241–243
Home, 291; boundaries/meaning of, 287;
    cultural spaces/social formations and,
    287; culture and, 287; homelessness and,
    287, 291; ideology/language of, 290–291;
    perils of, 128–130
Homelessness, 99, 255, 256, 295n7, 304, 305;
    border intellectual and, 286–294; home
    and, 287, 291

hooks, bell, 196
Hopelessness, 80–84
Hopkins, Jermaine, 105
Horowitz, David, 298
Horton, Myles, 289
Howe, Stephen, 304
Hughes, Albert, 105
Hughes, Allen, 105
Human agency, 16, 27, 293, 294; difference
and, 69–70; domination and, 11, 12;
importance of, 5, 28, 31, 36, 39, 210;
pedagogy and, 40, 307; power of, 110;
social responsibility and, 212; social
structures and, 7, 28
Human rights, 147, 173n38, 237, 261
Hutcheon, Linda, 293
Hutchins, Robert, 264
Hypermasculinity, 153

IBM, corporate culture of, 264
Identities, 51, 60, 109, 110, 192, 195, 196,
223, 286–287, 302; border-crossers and,
290; challenging, 211; counter-memory
and, 54; cultural, 86, 112, 234; democracy
and, 190; democratic, 230n25, 269;
difference and, 71, 308; displacement
of, 54; fragile, 131; hybridized, 235;
individual, 92, 288; lifestyles/ethnicity/
fashion and, 85; plural, 69, 79; political,
59; sense of, 188, 203; shaping, 56, 71,
141, 199, 222, 227, 239, 261; social, 45n77,
61, 92, 96, 234, 236, 257; struggle over,
138; youth and, 99
Identity politics, 56, 91, 236, 237, 275, 307
Ideology, xx, 42n21, 140, 191, 202, 261,
290–291; challenging, 211; consciousness
and, 10, 34; corporate, 79, 269;
curriculum and, 16; dominant, 3, 12, 19,
25, 31; hegemony and, 20; legitimating,
10; market-based, 298; oppositional, 11,
12, 21; school, 17, 34; theory of, 9, 18
Ideology, Culture, and the Process of Schooling
(Giroux), xv, xxv
Image, xxi, 69, 85; cultural production and,
103; power of, 103; reality and, 48
Immigration policy, 161, 237, 238, 246
Imperialism, 84, 285, 301; cultural, 293;
gender/racial/class-specific, 63
Individualism, 162, 170, 222, 269;
celebration of, 148; excessive, 262;
marketplace and, 70, 169; public
education and, 3; self-interested, 211

Individual rights, 26, 170
Inequality, 3, 223; economic/cultural, 28;
education and, 4; fairness/objectivity and,
13; institutional/cultural, 115; power and,
238; racial, 8, 147; structural determinants
of, 19; systemic, 107; of wealth, 239
Information, 48, 77, 103, 115
Injustice, 210, 306; racial, xx, 159, 235;
redressing, 304
Innocence, 136; adults and, 125,
128; commercial profit and, 140;
commodification and, 129; dark quality
of, 139; disappearing child and, 125–128;
discourse of, xxii, 127, 222; impurity and,
130; myth of, 125, 128; notion of, 132,
222; pageants and, 131, 139; politics of,
125–128, 222–225; powerlessness and,
128; protecting, 126, 226; sexualization
and, 129; social analysis and, 139–140;
social investment in, 127–128
Institutions, meaning/viability of, 187
Intellectuals, xxv–xxvi, 20, 188–189;
commitment by, 209; corporate
power and, 266; cultural studies and,
113; location of, xxvi; politics and,
211–215, 306; public relations and, 298;
responsibility of, xxiii, xxvi, 188, 189, 307.
See also Public intellectuals
Intellectual work, 267–268; corporatization
of, 299; public culture and, 113
Interdisciplinary issues, 90, 92, 207
Intervention, 19, 160, 185, 201; political/
ethical, 187

Jackson, Jesse, 163–164
Jackson, Samuel L., 241
Jailhouse chic, 159–160
JanMohammed, Abdul, 58, 63, 287
Jefferson, Thomas, 257
Johnson, Rebecca, 145n49
Johnson, Richard, 119n20
Jordan, Michael, 221
Juice (film), 100, 105–106, 107
Just Another Girl on the IRT (film), 108
Justice, 110, 116, 147, 161, 167, 211,
257, 266, 270, 277, 287, 302, 307;
civic education and, 262, 271–272;
consumerism and, 71; critical reflection
and, 188; cultural, 59; democracy and,
55, 188; pedagogy of, 109, 193; political
agency and, 271–272; racial, 201, 239, 247;
social, 40, 59, 70, 74, 78, 109, 151, 160,

Justice *(continued)*
    184, 214, 265, 267, 309; struggles for, 59,
    258, 273; theory of, 233; war against, 170
Justice Department, 158
Justice Matters, 165
Justice Policy Institute, 159

Kain, Kahalil, 105
Kanka, Megan, 130
Kaplan, Caren, 60, 285
Kaus, Micky, 98, 120n34
Kelley, Robin D. G., 157–158, 240
Kellner, Douglas, 195, 202, 208
Kennedy, Edward, 126
Kennedy, Randall, 173n52, 239
Kid Rock, 153
Kids First! Coalition, 176n83
King, Rodney, 156
Kirby, David, 73, 82
Kittredge, Clare, 165
Klaas, Polly, 130
Klee, Paul, 64
Knowledge, 183–184, 186, 235, 300;
    authority and, 111, 233; border
    pedagogy and, 60; collective, 293;
    commodity and, 267; construction of,
    114, 205; corporate time and, 265–266;
    critical agents and, 190; cultural forms
    of, 30, 53; everyday life and, 62; global
    capital and, 266; high-status/low-
    status, 24; objectivity of, 96; pedagogy
    and, 57, 185, 202–203; politics of, 305;
    postmodernism and, 47; power and,
    25–26, 51, 63, 64, 94, 95, 212, 301;
    production of, 112, 115, 273, 275;
    school, 9; social, 94, 109; technologies/
    forms of, 112; working-class, 14
Kopkind, Andrew, 120n42

Labor, 23, 230n25; academic, 263–264;
    division of, xxvi, 3, 9, 10, 33, 77–78, 90,
    203, 204, 299; manual/mental, 25, 26, 29;
    skills/rules of, 9
Laclau, on postmodernism, 54–55
LaCour, V. J., 136
Language, 182, 234; critical pedagogy and,
    192; experience and, 94; learning/dissent
    and, 193; politics of, 192
Lapham, Lewis, 162
Lather, Patti, 296n22
Leadership, 261, 268; civic, 115; corporate
    culture/corporate time and, 264;

educational, xiv, 264; moral, 20; politics/
    pedagogy and, 212
Learnfare programs, 98
Learning, xxi, 39, 40, 182, 186; body and, 16;
    critical, xix, 60, 162, 197, 228, 261, 266;
    democracy and, 262; dom:∗ ∴tion and, 15;
    experience and, 111; quest for, 90; radical,
    262
Lee, Spike, 74, 87n11, 105
Levitas, Ruth, 270
Lewis, Tamar, 165
Liberation theory, xx
Liberty, 55, 302
Life Magazine, 133
Linklater, Richard, 102, 104
Lipsitz, George, 171n11
Literacy, xxi, 126, 190–191, 205; border, 305;
    citizenship and, 126; critical, 12, 285, 305;
    politics of, 288
Literary theory, xiii, xiv, 118n18, 236, 301,
    306
Lloyd, David, 58, 63
Location: politics of, 285, 288; privilege/
    power and, 285
Loewy, Raymond, 76
Logos, 75, 76, 82, 83
Louima, Abner, 156, 246

Macedo, Donaldo, 289, 290
Mandatory sentencing, 157, 159, 163
Marable, Manning, 157, 162
Marcuse, Herbert, 36, 297–298, 305
Marcuse, Peter, 172n18
Maris, Roger, 221
Mark, Ellen, 134–135
Market: agendas, 263; education and, 298;
    forces, 257; principles, 212; social justice
    and, 160; strategies, 110
Marketing, 70, 73, 140
Marsden, Michael T., 144n45
Marx, Karl, 3, 40n2, 301
Marxist theories, 4, 19, 44n59, 45n85
Masculinity: black, 104, 105, 173n35; ideals
    of, 105; representations of, 105–106
Massad, Joseph, 298
Materialism, 18, 249n18, 262
McDonalds, 110, 265
McGwire, Mark, 221
McMahon, Debra, 128
McMartin preschool case, 127
McRobbie, Angela, 31–32
Meaning, 40, 48, 52

Media, x, xxiv, 21, 31, 89, 107, 190, 202, 205, 224, 259; advertising and, 80; commercialization of, 221; consolidation of, 186; corporate control of, 302; crime and, 120n29; cultural studies and, 197; culture, 120n29, 219, 220; democratization of, 228; education and, 220; JonBenet and, 129, 130, 131–132, 134; multinational corporations and, 219, 297; pageants and, 137, 145n49; politics and, 191; power of, 112; studies, xiv, 111; youth and, xxii, 96, 97, 99, 104, 127, 128, 254

Medicare, 151

Memories, 61; buried/abandoned, 62; communities of, 58; public, 186, 205, 206, 207, 223, 227, 297; social, 116, 287, 293; visual, 76. *See also* Counter-memory; Remembrance

Menace II Society (film), 107

Mercer Management Consulting, 128

Microsoft, corporate culture of, 264

Militarization, xxii, 154, 187, 190, 300; domestic, 156, 157, 159, 160, 166, 167, 170, 175n77, 256

Miller, Lois, 136

Miller, Toby, 195

Miller, Tyisha, 156

Mills, C. Wright, 257, 258

Minorities, assault on, 244

Minority youth: demonization of, 245, 247; opportunities for, 234

Misogyny, 108, 139, 145n49, 152, 153

Miss America pageant, 138, 145n47

Miyoshi, Masao, 259

Modernism, xiv, 110–111, 289; guardians of, 85; notion of, 47, 50; political culture of, 110; postmodernism and, 47–48, 49; problematic elements of, 288

Modernity, 52, 55, 64, 280n69; discourses of, 54; political closure of, 54; progress and, 253

Money, 136

Mooks, portrayal of, 152–153

Morality, xv, 40, 71, 112, 125, 152, 186

Moral panics, 127, 130, 160, 166, 245, 246; right-wing, 153; zero tolerance and, 164

Moral regulation, 23, 224, 225

Moral uplift, 98, 126

Morris, Meghan, 195, 230n22

Morrison, Toni, 154, 269

Moss, Kate, 135, 139

Mouffe, Chantal, 55

Mrysiades, Kostas, 117–118n16

MTV, 79, 99, 103

Multiculturalism, 78, 91, 111, 121n53, 244, 248nn2, 6, 249n16; academic, 233–235, 236, 241, 247; border crossing and, 249n12; critical, 235, 236, 237, 238, 240; cultural politics of, 239; culture and, 240; difference and, 238; higher education and, 233; pedagogy and, 233; politics and, 233, 237–238, 239, 247, 248n2; power and, 238; radical approach to, 237–238; segregation and, 240; textualization of, 236

Multinational corporations, 222; advertising and, 220–221; corporate time and, 265–266; media and, 219, 297

My Own Private Idaho (film), 100, 101, 102, 104

Narratives, xxi, 114, 234; coming-of-age, 105, 107, 109; cultural, rewriting, 60; historical, 206; master, 48, 60, 116; struggle, 58; youth, 104

National Association of Secondary School Principals, 166

National Center for Health Statistics, 96

National Criminal Justice Commission, 161

National identity, 93, 111, 138, 186, 235; dynamics of, 91; global conglomerates and, 229n11; shaping, 227

Nationalism, 48, 64, 104, 184, 248n2

National Opinion Research Center, 174n62

National Parenting Association, 151

Neoconservatism, xiv, 151, 167, 190, 300, 307–308; social/political costs of, 149; universities and, 299; youth and, 154, 168

Neoliberalism, xiv, xxiv, 151, 159, 160, 167, 190, 209, 210, 211; alternatives to, 272; consumer culture and, 168; corporate culture and, 259; corporate time and, 260; criticism of, 212, 213, 277n2; culture and, 155, 199; democracy and, 148, 168; dominance of, 148, 169, 174, 301; economic life and, 155; economics/social costs and, 169, 256; education and, 254; market forces and, 257; opposition to, 169, 213, 214; politics and, 149, 168; public goods and, 147; public sphere and, 258; public time and, 262; youth and, 154, 254

New Jack City (film), 105, 107

Newport Folk Festival, xvi, xxviiin11
New Right, xxii, 151, 307
New Sociology of Education, xix
Newsweek, Snoop Doggy Dogg in, 96
New World Order, xxii, 101
New York State Department of Corrections, 159
New York Times, 175n77, 302; on academic work/partisan activity, 301; on cultural landscape, 155; on homelessness, 255; on jailhouse chic, 159; on pageants, 132; on Reifenstahl, 303; on welfare mothers, 98
New York Times Sunday Magazine, 149, 152, 309–10n16
Ngugi Wa Thiong'O, 253
Nihilism, 64, 105, 107
Njeri, Itabari, 107
No Kidding!, 150
Nomura International/London, 74

Objectification, 15, 131, 137
Objectivity, 13, 36, 96, 174, 207, 289, 305
Obsession, advertisements for, 139
Offe, Claus, 22
"Old Mr. Rabbit's Thanksgiving Dinner," 98
Olin Foundation, 298
187 (film), 243, 246; cultural texts of, 247; depictions of, 244–245; pedagogy and, 240–241; popularity of, 247; public discourse and, 245
Oppression, 47, 210, 213, 304; social relations of, 174
Oregon Corrections Department, 160
Orientalism (Said), 249n18, 302
Other, 63, 86, 288; dominating, 293; humanity of, 59; identities of, 286–287; oppositional, 51; pathological, 246; plight of, xxiii, 183; politics of, 292; stories/social memories of, 293; voices/experiences of, 289; women as, 60
Out of Place (Said), 303
Ovitz, Michael, 223

Pageant Life, 133, 134, 136
Pageants: advertising and, 134, 138–139; analysis of, 138, 143n24, 144n28; child abuse and, 130, 138; consumer culture and, 137–138; criticism of, 134, 137, 145nn47, 49; gender roles and, 138; genealogy of, 132–139; innocence and, 131, 139; media and, 137, 145n49; popularity of, 132, 136–138;

rationalization of, 129–130, 135; shock of the real and, 130–132; support industries for, 133
"Painted Babies" (*Under the Sun*), 144n28
Parental Rights and Responsibilities Act (1995), 142n4
Parenti, Christian, 156
Parry, Benita, 289
Patriarchal society, 33, 47, 81, 135, 288
Pedagogy, xii, xvi, xvii, 32, 53, 70, 129, 149, 162, 163, 170, 259, 260, 266, 272; accessing, 243–247; authority, 96; border, 50–64, 181; challenge of, 110; cultural, 141, 303; democracy and, 89, 196; developing, 60, 69, 141, 185; education and, 50, 118n18, 189, 273, 275; function of, 52, 210–211; importance of, 92–95, 196; meaning of, 52, 92, 93, 110, 192; multicultural, 240; as object of analysis, 40, 197; politics and, xvii, 85, 86, 118n18, 174, 187, 189, 192, 199, 200, 206, 209–210, 225–229, 271, 273, 290, 306; postmodern, 84, 85, 86; power and, 116, 140, 197, 202, 227; practice, 57, 63, 262; public, xiv, xviii, xxiii–xxiv, 188, 190, 191, 193, 198, 209, 222, 228, 239, 244, 246, 271, 306; radical, 19, 35, 38–39, 40; self-reflective, 174, 276; strategies, 96; traditional, 93, 205. *See also* Critical pedagogy
Pedagogy in Process: The Letters to Guinea-Bissau, 288
Pedagogy of the Oppressed, 288
Pedophiles, 127, 128, 166
Performance, 99, 141, 207
Perlstein, Daniel, 167
Peters, Michael, 265–266
Picasso, Pablo, 308
Place, 51, 203
Pluralism, 61, 79; counter-memory and, 58; liberal, 55, 77; radical, 59; youth and, 99
Police: abuse, 157; school discipline by, 157; social functions and, 166
Political: politicizing education and, 115; problematizing/pluralizing, 216n8
Political agency, 149, 168, 170, 186, 189, 210, 262, 273, 288; devaluing, 270; freedom/justice and, 271–272; modes of, xxiii, 195, 272; notion of, 193, 212; rethinking, 169; undermining, 167; youth and, 99
Political economy, xiii, 7, 8
Political education, xvii, 197, 210; critical pedagogy and, 115; hegemony and, 44n54

Index

Political struggle, 18, 184, 300, 308;
collective, 38; legacy of, 77; replacement
of, 256–257
Politics, ix, 193, 202, 261, 294; aestheticization
of, 81; challenge to, 306; citizenship and,
141, 147, 168, 183, 258; conception of, 64,
260; crisis of, 155, 299; critical awareness
and, 305, 308; culture and, 226, 233, 237,
240, 291, 306; death of, 214, 308; definition
of, 50, 300; democracy and, 26, 168, 196;
of despair, 101–104; education and, xvii,
115, 210, 211–215, 274–275, 276; identity,
56, 91, 236, 237, 275, 307; multiculturalism
and, 237, 238, 248n2; pedagogy and, xvii,
85, 86, 118n18, 174, 187, 189, 192, 199,
200, 206, 209–210, 225–229, 271, 273, 290,
306; power and, 227, 275; public life and,
49, 202, 257, 301; public time and, 260;
representational, xxi, xxiv, 69, 70, 71, 78,
79, 81–82, 84, 234, 240, 287; reworking, 71,
213, 308; textualization of, 235–237. *See also*
Cultural politics
Popular culture, xx, 48, 52, 109, 110,
111, 112, 141, 186, 190, 197, 203; civic
discourse and, xxiv; commodification
of, 79, 100; cultural studies and, 92;
culture and, 126, 291; curriculum and,
53; discourse on, 85; dynamics of, 91;
education and, 219–220; moral decay
and, 152; pedagogy and, xxiv, 93, 121n52;
politics/analysis and, 51; youth and, 53,
96–98, 99, 153, 155
Pornography, 152, 153
Position: habitus and, 16; social, 53
Possibility, xxv, xxvi, 48, 307
Postcolonialism, 93, 292, 294, 295n22, 298
Post-Fordism, 76–80, 86
Postman, Neil, 125, 126
Postmodernism, xiv, xv, xx, xxi, 53, 64, 104,
109, 110, 111, 191, 234; collapse of, 69;
cultural, 47, 69; cultural studies and, 93;
depoliticized, 306; deterritorialization
and, 54; discourse of, 289, 294;
epistemology of, 201; modernism and,
47–48, 49; power/knowledge/space/
time and, 47; referents of, 48, 49; social
theorists and, 69
Poststructuralism, 234
Poulantzas, Nicos, 22, 25–26, 27
Poverty, 148, 237, 256; child abuse and, 129;
children and, 97, 126, 128, 171nn3, 16,
255; war on, 156

Powell, Colin, 308
Power, xx, 28, 91, 109, 192, 202, 225, 234,
239, 261, 293, 301, 302, 307; commercial,
211; corporate, xxiv, 110, 155, 222, 259,
266, 268, 299; cultural, 271; cultural
capital and, 14; cultural studies and, 92,
199; culture and, 95, 111, 112, 115, 116,
195, 234–241, 247, 304, 306; distribution
of, 198, 201, 275; dominant, 8, 62, 83,
115, 201; economic, xiii, 151, 183, 199,
207, 227; in higher education, 233–234;
inequality and, 238, 247; knowledge
and, 25–26, 51, 63, 64, 94, 95, 212, 301;
location and, 285; material relations of,
198, 206, 249n18; multiculturalism and,
238; pedagogy and, 40, 116, 140, 185, 197,
202, 227; political, 4, 38, 115, 140, 151,
200, 207, 227, 247; politics and, 227, 275;
postmodernism and, 47; production of,
198; relations, 5, 48, 56, 59, 109, 247, 285;
State and, 21; struggle against, 56, 306;
symbolic forms and, xiii, 207–208; using,
21, 210, 211, 287
Powerlessness, 128, 135
Prisoners, 173n38, 245; labor of, 158, 160,
174n53
Prison-industrial complex, 156, 162, 174,
256; growth of, 157, 158, 159, 161, 209,
239
Prisons, 160; construction of, 255; juvenile,
159; privatization of, 157–158, 173–
174n53; schools and, 167, 254; spending
on, 159, 246; zero tolerance in, 161–162
Prison style, market for, 159–160
Private, xxii, 212; public and, 149, 169, 193,
199
Privatization, 74, 78, 82, 151, 162, 186;
citizenship and, 148, 188, 228, 237;
culture and, 256–257; of education, 168;
public goods and, 148
Privilege, 18, 128, 293, 310n16; culture and,
14, 112; location and, 285
Production, xix, 195; capitalist, 3, 22;
cultural, xxiv, 17, 30, 48, 103, 112, 115,
141, 202, 207, 222; post-Fordist, 78; self-,
6, 273
Professionalism, 112, 174, 191, 204, 210,
305, 306
Proposition 21, 160
Public, 182, 189; private and, 149, 169, 193, 199
Public culture, xxiii, 70, 230n25, 238;
commercial culture and, 259;

Public culture *(continued)*
commodification of, 228; critical
pedagogy and, 84–86, 269; humanities
and, 187; intellectual work and, 113;
market values and, 97; pedagogy and,
84–86; reforming, xxii, 228
Public good, xiv, 188, 254, 258, 264
Public goods, 147, 148, 172n18, 186
Public institutions, 162, 269; assault on, 215
Public intellectuals, xxv–xxvi, 182, 215,
301–302; absence of, 299; corporate
largesse and, 264; higher education and,
211; political education and, 210; private
intellectuals and, 298; role of, 93, 211,
212, 303, 304; secular criticism and, 307;
teachers as, 111, 113, 184, 189
Public issues, 149, 158, 188; privatization of,
213
Public life, xxv, 50, 149, 212, 240, 263;
citizenship and, 276; counter-memory
and, 59; critique/crisis and, 307; demise
of, 167, 258, 259, 268; democratic, 56,
58, 63, 113, 163, 224, 235, 277; education
and, 198, 258; language of, 56; notion of,
131–132, 188; politics and, 49, 202, 257,
301; private economy and, 169; quality of,
141, 151, 254; remembrance and, 57–58;
schooling and, 168–170; social problems
and, 208; worldly space of, 185
Public memory, 186, 207, 297; editing, 223;
pedagogy of, 206; rewriting, 205; shaping,
223, 227
Public relations, 189, 298
Public service, 115, 213, 254; privatization
of, 186; social value of, 259
Public space, 111, 139, 147, 151, 155, 182,
204, 257, 260, 211, 297; assaults on, xxii,
148, 259, 272; corporations and, 138;
militarization of, xxii, 254; providing, 149,
154
Public spheres, 141, 154, 227, 254, 255;
activism in, 215; importance of, 222;
neoliberalism and, 258; noncommodified,
152; oppositional, 40; pedagogy and, 306
Public time, xxv, 182; civic education and,
262; corporate time and, 260–268, 272;
democracy and, 262; neoliberalism and,
262; politics and, 260
Punishment, 155–156, 159

Race, 4, 47, 92, 114, 128–130; child abuse
and, 129; class and, 109; configuration of,

84; democracy and, xxiii; dynamics of, 91,
233; gender and, 109; moral panic about,
245, 246; politics of, 91; resistance theory
and, 33; violence of, 104–111
Racism, 31, 60, 64, 84, 139, 155, 166, 167,
174, 238, 256, 292; children and, 128;
cultural politics and, 239; identifying,
118n16; problem of, 59, 86; reemergence
of, 239
Radical democracy, 91, 147, 149, 189, 262;
liberty/justice and, 55; notion of, 56, 57,
64; reality and, 148
Radical educators, 3, 27–28, 181, 285;
emancipatory interests and, 39; resistance
theory and, 39
Radical humanism, 184
Radical needs, theory of, 35
Radical pedagogy, 19, 35; framework of, 40;
language of, 35; resistance theory and, 38,
39, 40; schooling and, 38–39
Raheem, 105, 106
Ramsey, JonBenet, 128–130; media and, 129,
130, 131–132, 134, 136
Rangeview High School, suspension at, 164
Rap music, 96, 106, 128, 132, 152, 171n11;
popular culture and, 104; symbolism of,
153
Rather, Dan: on JonBenet tapes, 132
Rationality, 263, 289, 291; capitalist, 3, 4, 26
Ravitch, Diane, 206
Reading formation, 51, 83
Readings, Bill, 212
Reagan, Ronald, 102, 156, 254
Realism, 81, 82, 268
Reality, 103; image and, 48
Reconstruction, 30, 181, 289
Recontextualization, 81, 83
Reeves, Jimmie, 246
Reflexive thought, 17
Regime of the political, realm of politics
and, 168
Reifenstahl, Leni, 303
Relationships, xvii; cultural, xii, xviii;
economic, xii; faculty and, 263, 264–265;
mediating, 28–29; social practices and, 34
Remembrance: as counter-memory, 57,
58–59; public life and, 57–58; specificity/
struggle and, 57. *See also* Memories
*Report of the National Criminal Justice
Commission,* 158
Representation, xxii, 48, 86, 182, 195, 239;
agency and, 206, 273; colonialist, 289;

cultural politics and, 71; of masculinity, 105–106; pedagogy of, 70, 71, 100, 240; of politics, xxi, xxiv, 70; of resistance, 105–106; self-, 11, 60, 169, 190, 272, 293; social, 108; of youth and, 96–98

Reproduction, 29; cultural, xix, 6, 7, 12–19, 27, 200; political-economy model of, 7; process of, 9, 30; resistance and, 6; social, 27, 200; theory, 3, 4–5, 6, 7–27, 28, 32, 40n2

Reservoir Dogs (film), 107

Resistance, xix, xx, 11, 18, 62, 151, 256, 288, 302; collective, 212; concept of, xiii, 5, 28, 35–36, 36, 45n79; culture and, 27, 294, 300; dynamics of, 77; forms of, 33, 45n77, 145n47; ideology of, 29; individual, 214; legacy of, 307; neo-Marxist theories of, 7; pedagogy and, 40, 52, 215, 234; political, 215, 294; popular culture of, 79; postmodernism of, 49, 50, 54; representations of, 105–106; schooling and, 27–35; struggle and, 31

Resistance theory, 6–7, 27, 29, 30, 34; developing, 35–40; features of, 5–6, 31; gender/race and, 33; radical educators and, 39; radical pedagogy and, 38, 39; schools/domination and, 32

Responsibility, xvi, 174, 181, 223, 268, 269, 275; democratic institutions and, 270; ethical, 183, 267; fiscal, 264; intellectuals and, 188; moral, 85; pedagogy of, 182; personal, xxii; politics/agency and, 276; responsibility for, 300; social, xvii, xxiii, 74, 78, 80, 112, 154, 162, 185, 201, 210, 212, 215, 228, 238, 261, 262, 263, 266

Reynolds, Kevin, 241–242

Rhoades, Gary, 265

Rich, Frank, 132–133

Rich-poor gap, 255, 308

Ricoeur, Paul, 271

Riding, Alan, 303

River's Edge (film), 100, 101–102, 104

Roberts, David, 74

Rocky Mountain News, on zero tolerance, 164

Ronge, Volker, 22

Roper Organization, 110

Roseanne, 131

Rowan, Kelly, 243

Roy, Arunhdhati, 270

Ruling class, 22, 23

Safer, Morley, 136–137

Safety, 127, 165, 172n18

Said, Edward, 189, 249n18, 268; as border crosser, 305; on censorship, 308; colonial discourse analysis and, 301; criticism by, 306, 307–308; on cultural production/ reception, 227; on culture/pedagogy, 121n54; on democracy, 308; on home/ homelessness, 291; on human agency/ pedagogy, 307; on language, 193; on "Orientalist" scholarship, 292; Palestinian people and, 301, 305; on politics, 226, 301; postcolonial studies and, 301; on professionalism, 306; on public intellectuals, 301–302, 304, 306, 307; on Reifenstahl, 303

St. Pierre, Ray, 166

Scholasticism, 301, 306

Scholes, Robert, 51–52

Schooling, 84, 101, 116, 186, 190; concerns about, 36, 97; critical theories of, xix, 31, 38, 89, 192; democracy and, 163; domination and, 5, 18–19, 32; economy and, 8; ethnographic literature on, 28; ideology and, 17; liberal views of, 3; modernist version of, 110, 121n52; public, 26; public life and, 89, 168–170; radical theories of, xix, 7, 38–39, 40; reproduction theory and, 4, 6, 7–27; resistance and, 27–35; role of, 3, 50, 91; social control and, 16; socialist theories of, 3; State and, 20, 24, 25, 27; student responses to, 38–39

Schooling and the Struggle for Public Life: Critical Pedagogy in the Modern Age (Giroux), xxv

School policy, 26

Schools, xxiv, 22, 95; as black boxes, 28; citizenship and, 211; commercialization of, xi, xxii; corporate interest in, 219; crisis over, 154; cultural/political economy of, 203 democracy and, 163; discipline in, 157, 166; ecology of, 10; higher education and, 238; Hollywood and, 241–242; investment in, 159; militarization of, 246, 250n31; national standards for, 98; prisons and, 167, 254; privatization of, 167; reform of, 92, 246; regulation of, 167; ruling class, 17–18; society and, 40; zero tolerance and, 149, 156, 161–167

Security, 162, 253, 257; airport, 161; children and, 99, 127, 139; economic, 97; school, 166

Segregation, 239, 240, 247

Self: definitions of, 113; social order and, 262

Self-affirmation, 39, 49
Self-criticism, xviii, 91, 92, 208, 210; social
criticism and, 306
Self-definition, 268, 300
Self-determination, 90, 135, 168
Self-esteem, 134, 135
Self-formation, 29, 38
Self-government, 60, 257, 261, 266
Self-interest, 147, 151, 162, 263, 297;
celebrating, 269; politics and, xv–xvi, 260
Self-reflection, xii, 36, 135; action and, 49;
pedagogy and, 276
Self-representation, 11, 60, 190, 272, 293;
education and, 169
Sexism, 31, 32, 60, 64, 139; children
and, 128; opposition to, 59; social
representation of, 108
Sexuality, 91, 114, 130, 135, 233
Sexualization, xi, xxii, 130; children and,
131, 132, 134, 135, 139; dynamics of, 128;
innocence and, 129; self-esteem and, 135
Sexual predators, 127, 128, 130, 143n10
Shakur, Tupac, 105
Shampoo Planet (Coupland), 73
Sharp, Geoff, 266, 267
Shor, Ira, 289
Sieber, R. Timothy, 18
Signification, logics of, 235
Simon, Roger, 197, 261–262, 273
Singleton, John, 105
Sixty Minutes, on pageants, 136–137, 144n28
Slacker (film), 100, 102, 103, 104
Slacker culture, 120n42
Smith, Bruce James, 57
Smith, R. J., 152
Smith, Tom, 153, 154, 171n16, 174n62
Snoop Doggy Dogg, 96
Social: death of, 270; democratic notion
of, 267; higher education and, 257–259;
pedagogy and, 210, 273
Social agency, 30, 185, 192, 203, 212,
214, 234, 244, 271, 273, 299, 301, 309;
consumerism and, 260; educated hope
and, 272; spirited commitment to, 210;
taking back, 308
Social analysis, 139–140
Social change, 80, 83, 90, 185, 186, 189, 196,
197, 215, 294; cultural studies and, 94;
education and, 192; learning from, 306;
promoting, 214
Social citizenship, 147, 148, 169, 213;
democracy and, 189; war against, 170

Social conditions, 49, 98
Social contract, 182, 186, 190, 253, 254
Social control, 16, 22
Social costs, 159, 256, 262
Social criticism, 63, 77, 82, 264, 289, 291;
self-criticism and, 306
Social Darwinism, 148
Social determination, 38, 82, 83, 107
Social development, 140, 188
Social disenfranchisement, youth and, 97
Social engagement, 169, 247
Social formations, 23, 62, 63, 92, 169, 185,
188, 241, 261; home and, 287; importance
of, 268; working-class student, 11
Social forms, 22, 51, 54, 56; difference and,
55; pedagogy and, 61
Social functions, 166, 188
Social hierarchies, xiii, 211
Social identities, 45n77, 61, 92, 92,
234, 236; higher education and, 257;
transformation of, 96
Social indifference, 170, 177n100
Social issues, 84, 247, 300
Socialization, 15, 141
Social justice, 40, 70, 74, 78, 184, 214, 265,
267, 309; discourse about, 151; market
and, 160; pedagogy and, 109; struggle
for, 59
Social life: erosion of, 155, 259;
marketization of, 186; restructuring of,
270
Social movements, 55, 78, 111, 141, 230n25,
301
Social order, xiii, xix, 13, 154, 206, 225,
271, 301; child abuse and, 129; higher
education and, 267; racialization of, 238;
radicalization of, 116; self and, 262
Social policy, xxii, 159, 211, 239;
criminalization of, 156; global
conglomerates and, 229n11; stereotypes
and, 174n62
Social practices, 17, 28, 37, 42n21, 54, 196;
challenging, 140; dominant, 3; education
and, 186; regulating, 220; relationships
and, 34
Social problems, 80, 101, 141, 148, 185, 209,
214, 268; advertising, 81; cost of, 155–156;
criminalization of, 256, 257; public life
and, 208
Social provisions, 151, 213, 253
Social relations, 8, 14, 36, 40, 113, 174, 189,
197, 199–200, 202, 204, 210, 212, 214, 235,

240, 245, 254, 260, 292, 306; capitalist, 29; classroom, 6, 25, 26; contesting, xxvi; hidden curriculum and, 9; notion of, 19, 22; reality/promise of, xvii, 23
Social responsibility, xvii, xxiii, 74, 78, 112, 154, 162, 201, 215, 238, 261, 262, 263, 266; demands of, 228; encouraging, 80, 210; human agency and, 212; worldly space of, 185
Social security, 151, 213, 270
Social services, 147, 171n3, 174, 198
Social theory, xiii, 40n2, 51, 69
Social transformation, 64, 115, 168, 174, 210, 211, 240, 271; democratic, xxv, 189, 214; forms of, 29, 30, 49
Social vision, 152, 294
Society, ix, xiii, xv, 182; democratic, 184; higher education and, 300; schooling and, 8, 40
Sociology, xiii, xiv, 16, 35
Solidarity, 39, 39, 59, 69, 116; counter-memory and, 58; political, 212
Solomon, Deborah, 309–310n16
Space, 10; civil, 287; cultural, 199, 234, 287; domestic, 256; ethical, 189, 214; imagined, 291; institutional, 236; pedagogical, 201; political, 199, 287; postmodernism and, 47; private, 150; rhetorical, 201; school, 246, 250n31; social, 152; worldly, 185. See also Public space
Specialization, 201, 204, 210
"Spirit of Justice" statue, 308
Spivak, Gayatri, 93, 293
Star Talent Management, 136
State: capital and, 20; class rule and, 22; culture and, 21; defining features of, 22–23; domination and, 19; economy and, 23; education and, 20; Marxist formulations of, 21; power and, 21; schooling and, 20, 27
Stereotypes: behavior, 174n62; cultural, 96; racial, 84, 96, 161, 244, 246
Structure, 266; action and, 15; agency and, 7; lived effects and, 31; reform, 91; social, 7, 28, 35, 151
Struggle, 5, 36, 39, 57, 59, 109, 138, 151, 168, 273, 309; collective, 214, 215, 302, 308; democratic, 214; historical process of, 191; individual rights and, 26; narratives of, 58; political, 18, 38, 77, 256–257, 308; resistance and, 31; social, 77, 116, 212, 214

Subjectivity, 8, 36, 61, 100, 288; childhood, 224; collective, 288; identity and, 249n18; student, 9
Subordinate groups, 6, 23, 29, 59
Substitute I, The (film), 241, 246
Szeman, Imre, 201, 202

Talbot, Margaret, 174n63
Taxes, 150, 151, 255
Taylor, Mark, 258
TCI, 222, 229n5
Teachers, 50; behavior of, 90; border pedagogy and, 61; as cultural producers, 115; cultural studies and, 113; empowerment for, 184; knowledge production and, 273; and prison guards compared, 159; as public intellectuals, 111, 113; as transmitters of information, 115. See also Educators
Teachers as Intellectuals: Towards a Critical Pedagogy of Learning (Giroux), xxv
Technology, 111, 114, 182, 187; communications, xxiii; culture and, 220, 228; electronic, 77, 103, 186, 204, 205, 267; media, xxi, xxiii, 183, 196, 228; print, xxi, 205; scope/impact of, 220
Telecommunications Act (1996), 226
Television, 142n4, 229n8
Terrorism, 303; pedagogical, 115; war against, 257, 264, 302
TESOL, 192
Textuality, multiculturalism and, 235, 236
Theory, xii, 63, 118n16, 141, 191, 233; political/public responsibilities of, 185; public life and, 300
Theory and Resistance in Education: Towards a Pedagogy for the Opposition (Giroux), xiv, xxv
Thompson, E. P., 119n20
"Three strikes and you're out" policy, 157, 159, 163
Time, 10; postmodernism and, 47
Time Warner, 222, 229n5
Timmendequas, Jesse, 130
Tirozzi, Gerald, 165–166
Tompkins, Jane, 118n18
Toscani, Oliviero, 72, 74, 75, 76, 88n28
Transdisciplinarity, 203, 204
Transformation, xiii, xvi, 267; counter-memory and, 58; social, xxv, 29, 30, 49, 64, 115, 168, 174, 189, 210, 211, 214, 240, 271
Trebay, Guy, 159

Trend, David, 197
Trump, Ivanka, 139
Tupac, 153
Tyler, Liv, 139

Ulmer, Gregory, 118n18
Unconscious, 17, 42n21
Under the Sun, 144n28
Unemployment, 97, 148, 239, 244; increase
in, 237, 245
United Colors of Benetton, 72, 77, 82
United Colors of Benetton (book), 87n11
United Nations, *Guernica* and, 308
Universalism, 81, 99, 115; discourse of, xxv,
80, 286
University: changing forms of, 267;
civic freedoms and, 269; corporate
restructuring of, 266; corporate time and,
264–265, 268; devaluation of, 299; role of,
260, 299–300
USA Today, on expulsions/suspensions, 164,
165
Utopian thinking, 270, 271, 272

Values, 61, 188, 196; commercial, 148;
cultural, 152; family, 126, 139; market,
97; pedagogical, xxi, 300; political, 154;
public, 235; social, 148, 259
Vanguardism, xvii, 288, 292
Van Sant, Gus, 101
Village Voice, 132
Violence, 97, 139, 152, 153; black youth
and, 96, 104–111; children and, 128,
129; culture of, 96, 250n31; film/TV,
105; gangsta rap and, 119n28; inner
city, 120n29; pedagogical, 289; racially
coded, 97–98, 104–111; school, 247; self-
destruction and, 108; symbolic, 13, 18
Violent Crime Control and Law
Enforcement Act (1994), 157
Virilio, Paul, 99
Vogue, 134–135
Voice, 50, 60, 61, 289

Wackenhut Corrections, 174n53
Walker, Jim, 33
Walt Disney Company, 223, 224
War on drugs, 156, 157, 164, 245
War on Poverty, 156
War on Terror, 257, 264, 302
Weber, Samuel, 259
Weiner, Anthony, 298

Weiner, Eric, xiv
Welfare, 246, 270; children and, 126, 127;
public, 254, 256; social, xxi, 126
Welfare reform bill, 126, 170n3, 256
Welfare state, 128, 141, 174, 208, 302
West, Cornel, 107, 292
Western culture, 111; dominant models of,
53; Otherness and, 293
Westinghouse, 222, 229n5
*What's the Relationship between AIDS and Selling
a Sweater?* (Benetton), 87
White Heat (film), 106
White Hood (film), 105
Whiteness, xiv, 234, 248n7, 250n24
White supremacy, 84
White youth: arrests for, 161; culture of, 104;
films about, 105; politics of despair and,
101–104; popular culture and, 99, 153;
representations of, 97
Williams, Raymond, xiii, xxi, 189, 222; on
cultural studies, 94, 95, 119n21, 182,
195; on culture, 186, 199; education and,
95, 199; on pedagogy, 94, 200; work of,
119n20, 196
Willis, Ellen, 250n24
Willis, Paul, 4, 30
Willis, Susan, 75
Winfrey, Oprah, 131
Wolf, Naomi, 135
Wolin, Sheldon, 300
Women: deterritorialization of, 60; as Other,
60
Work ethic, 23
Workfare programs, 238
Work force, feminization of, 77
Working class, xi, 19, 29
Worldliness, xxvi, 301, 304–305, 307
World Pageants, Inc., 132–133
Worth, Fabienne, 109

Yagemann, Scott, 241–242
Young, Robert: on postcolonialism, 292
Youth: black, 96, 104–111, 119n28, 120n29,
153, 154, 161, 165; changing conditions
of, 97–98; class/racial anxieties and, 256;
commodification of, 104, 131, 132, 139,
141, 149–155, 224; crisis of, xxii, 257;
cultural studies and, 111–115; democracy
and, 253, 257, 268, 309; education
and, 254; framing, 98–100; future and,
253–257; mass culture and, 96–98; media
and, xxii, 96, 97, 99, 104, 127, 128, 254;

middle-class, 99, 101, 104; minority, 234, 245, 247; neoconservatism and, 154, 168; neoliberalism and, 154, 254; pedagogical representation of, 100; popular culture and, 53, 96–98, 99, 153, 155; postmodern culture and, 99; privatization of, 149–155; problems with, 89, 92; production/ regulation of, 130; public analysis and, 96; social contract and, 254; social identities of, 92; treatment of, 154, 190, 244–245, 254; white, 97, 99, 101–104, 105, 153, 161; war against, xxi–xxiii, xxv, 155, 171n12, 255, 256–257; working-class, 11, 101–102, 104

Youth films, 101–103; black, 105, 106–107, 108, 109

Zero tolerance, 149, 150; crime rate and, 157; democracy and, 168; domestic militarism and, 160, 170; harshness of, 161, 163–164, 167; minorities and, 165, 175n63; poor/people of color and, 155–156, 157; schools and, 161–162, 163–167

Zinn, Howard, 206

Credits

৩

Chapter 1: Henry A. Giroux, "Theories of Reproduction and Resistance in the New Sociology of Education: A Critical Analysis," *Harvard Educational Review* 53:3 (August 1983): 257–293. Copyright © 1983 by the President and Fellows of Harvard College. All rights reserved.

Chapter 2: Henry A. Giroux, "Border Pedagogy in the Age of Postmodernism," *Journal of Education* 170:3 (1988): 162–181. Copyright Trustees of Boston University. Used with permission.

Chapter 3: Henry A. Giroux, "Consuming Social Change: The 'United Colors of Benetton,'" *Cultural Critique* 26 (Winter 1993–1994): 5–32. Used with permission.

Chapter 4: Henry A. Giroux, "Doing Cultural Studies: Youth and the Challenge of Pedagogy," *Harvard Educational Review* 64:3 (Fall 19945): 247–277. Copyright © 1994 by the President and Fellows of Harvard College. All rights reserved.

Chapter 5: Henry A. Giroux, "Nymphet Fantasies: Child Beauty Pageants and the Politics of Innocence," *Social Text* 57 (Winter 1998): 31–53. Used with permission.

Chapter 6: originally published as Henry A. Giroux, "Mis/Education and Zero Tolerance: Disposable Youth and the Politics of Domestic Militarization," *boundary 2* 28:3 (Fall 2001): 61–94. Copyright © 2001, Duke University Press. Used with permission.

Chapter 7: Manuela Guilherme, "Is There a Role for Critical Pedagogy in Language/Cultural Studies? An Interview with Henry A. Giroux," *Language and Intercultural Communication* 6:2.

Chapter 8: originally published as Henry A. Giroux, "Cultural Studies, Public Pedagogy, and the Responsibility of Intellectuals," *Communication and Critical/Cultural Studies* 1:1 (March 2004): 59–79. Used with permission of the Taylor and Francis Group, http://www.tandf.co.uk.

Chapter 9: originally published as Henry A. Giroux, "Public Pedagogy and Rodent Politics: Cultural Studies and the Challenge of Disney." *Arizona Journal of Hispanic Cultural Studies* 2 (1999): 253–266. Reprinted with the permission of the *AJHCS*.

Chapter 10: Henry A. Giroux, "Racial Politics, Pedagogy, and the Crisis of Representation in Academic Multiculturalism," *Social Identities* 6:4 (2000): 493—510. Used with permission of the Taylor and Francis Group, http://www.tandf.co.uk.

Chapter 11: Henry A. Giroux, "Youth, Higher Education, and the Crisis of Public Time: Educated Hope and the Possibility of a Democratic Future," *Social Identities* 9:2 (2003): 141–168. Used with permission of the Taylor and Francis Group, http://www.tandf.co.uk.

Chapter 12: Henry A. Giroux, "Paulo Freire and the Politics of Postcolonialism," *Journal of Advanced Composition* 12 (1992): 15–26. Used with permission.

Chapter 13: Henry A. Giroux, "The Promise of Democracy and Edward Said's Politics of Worldliness: Implications for Academics as Public Intellectuals," unfinished paper.

About the Author and Editor

⚘

Henry A. Giroux holds the Global TV Network Chair in the English and Cultural Studies Department at McMaster University, Canada. He is the author most recently of *Stormy Weather: Katrina and the Politics of Disposability* (Paradigm 2006); *Beyond the Spectacle of Terrorism* (Paradigm 2006); *Schooling and the Struggle for Public Life,* 2nd ed. (Paradigm 2005); and *The Terror of Neoliberalism: Authoritarianism and the Eclipse of Democracy* (Paradigm 2004). He also edits a series for Paradigm Publishers called Cultural Politics and the Promise of Democracy.

Christopher G. Robbins was Henry Giroux's research assistant at Penn State University, and he is an assistant professor in Social Foundations of Education at Eastern Michigan University. His research interests include sociology of education and cultural studies with a focus on the interrelationships of social and educational policy, racism and racial inequality, and the processes of militarization and criminalization. He has published in *Radical Teacher, Thinking Classroom/Peremena,* the *Journal of Critical Education Policy Studies,* and the *Journal of Negro Education.*